GV
958.5
.I9
B47
2001

Bernstein, Mark F.

Football.

$29.95

DATE			

BAKER & TAYLOR

Football

Football

The Ivy League Origins of an American Obsession

Mark F. Bernstein

University of Pennsylvania Press
Philadelphia

10 9 8 7 6 5 4 3 2 1

Published by
University of Pennsylvania Press
Philadelphia, Pennsylvania 19104-4011

Library of Congress Cataloging-in-Publication Data
Bernstein, Mark F.
    Football : the Ivy League origins of an American
obsession / Mark F. Bernstein.
    Includes bibliographical references and index.
    p. cm.
    ISBN: 0-8122-3627-0 (cloth : alk. paper)
    1. Ivy League (Football conference). 2. Football —
United States — History. I. Title.
GV958.5.I9B47 2001
796.332/63/0974 21   2012345116

FOR REBECCA

CONTENTS

Mention the term "Ivy League" to a hundred people on the street and you are apt to conjure images of shady campuses and tweedy undergraduates; of academic excellence, certainly, but also an attitude, an outlook, and perhaps even a style of dress.

Mention the term "Ivy League football" and many will regard it as an oxymoron, a quaint collection of undersized history majors who cannot compete against the Nebraskas and Florida States of the modern age.

Yet the story of football is very much the story of the Ivy League, and the story of the Ivy League is very much the story of football. This book is the story of both, for one cannot be understood without the other.

There is, to be precise, no such thing as the Ivy League. The official name of the conference is the Council of Ivy Group Presidents, emphasizing that it is the presidents, and not the athletic directors or alumni boosters, who run the show. In alphabetical order, its members are Brown, Columbia, Cornell, Dartmouth, Harvard, Princeton, the University of Pennsylvania, and Yale, though as everyone knows, they are seldom thought of in that order.

Ivy League football games never appear on network television anymore, even though Penn effectively created the national broadcast contract and almost got expelled from the NCAA for doing so. It seems absurd to think of an Ivy team playing in anything as prestigious as the Rose Bowl, though half the members of the league have done so, or winning the Heisman Trophy, though three Ivy players have won it and the award itself is named for an Ivy League coach.

Although the Ivy League is less than fifty years old, it is no exaggeration to say that its members created American football and that almost every facet of the game bears their imprint. From the day Princeton played the first intercollegiate game in 1869, they were its first powers. They invented the All-America team and filled all the early ones, produced the first coaches, arranged the basic rules, conceived many of the strategies, devised much of the equipment, and even named the positions.

Much of the culture that surrounds American football also has its roots there. Ivy League football has occupied the attention of presidents and captured the imagination of writers such as Jack Kerouac, artists such as Frederic Remington, songwriters such as Cole Porter—even revolutionaries such as John Reed, who liked to cheer up strikers with Harvard fight songs. The college fight song itself is very much an Ivy League creation, as are the marching bands that play them.

To a surprising extent, the story of Ivy League football is also the story of scandal. Far from being an athletic ivory tower, the eight colleges have wrestled with all the problems of intercollegiate athletics, from payoffs to recruiting abuses, and from overpaid coaches to undermotivated players who left campus as soon as the season was over. Football was almost abolished at the turn of the twentieth century because of violence in Ivy games—at the same time those games were bringing in money on a scale that dwarfed the rest of the university's revenues. As former Ivy League director James Litvak bluntly puts it, "There is nothing wrong in this world [of intercollegiate athletics] that we didn't invent."

Ivy League football, however, is also the story of confronting those abuses, and in doing so developing our ideals about the proper role of athletics in college life. Although football was not the first intercollegiate sport, our notions of what it means to be an amateur or a professional, and why one is better than the other, were played out most publicly on the Ivy gridiron before the modern Olympic games were born. These eight colleges, in short, were chiefly responsible for creating intercollegiate athletics as we know them today. It is impossible to read the modern sports page (which was developed, in part, to provide news of Ivy football teams to a voracious national audience) without encountering their legacy.

The popular perception of the Ivy League, both romantic and snobbish, is something else that owes much to football. Fictional heroes such as Frank Merriwell and real ones such as Hobey Baker perpetuated the image of the ivory tower, while the popular press has also celebrated many of the worst Ivy excesses. Cornell's president once attributed his school's inclusion in the Ivy League—and the status that goes with it—to its longstanding athletic rivalries with Penn and Dartmouth.[1] And yet, as one sportswriter has observed, "Everybody hates the Ivy League."

Often regarded as monolithic, the eight colleges are quite different from one another in style and history, size and tradition, and these differences have caused bitter rivalries. Harvard and Princeton have twice severed relations over football, while lesser disputes have soured relations between Brown and

Dartmouth, Yale and Columbia. As John L. Powers, a Boston sportswriter, once coldly put it, "Yale feels inferior to both Harvard and Princeton, Dartmouth feels inferior to Harvard, Princeton, *and* Yale, and everyone entirely dislikes Pennsylvania."[2] The story of the Ivy League is thus also the story of the universities' own developing sense of being members of a group, a process that continued long after sportswriters gave them a common name.

The Ivy League consists of these eight colleges simply because it always has. Certainly, they shared certain characteristics: they were old, wealthy, and prominent; their academic standards were high; they began playing football early; they played each other; and they played well. Yet because an Ivy League existed for years only in the popular imagination, membership has hardly been static. Princeton played its first game against Rutgers, yet Rutgers was never considered one of the group. Dartmouth once belonged to a conference with Amherst and Williams, yet those two schools have always been football inferiors. Sportswriters once regarded Army and Navy as Ivy League colleges, while others omitted Brown or Cornell. In the past few decades, the Ivy presidents themselves have considered adding Northwestern, William and Mary, and others as members.

One question, though, has eluded an easy answer: Where did the term "Ivy League" originate?

From time immemorial, ivy was a symbol of vivacity, if not erudition, and was often hung on English tavern signs as a symbol of drink. How it came to be associated with higher education is unclear. Because it tended to grow on old buildings, those with a romantic bent may have associated it with classical learning. Not everyone has thought it an appropriate emblem. "We need a symbol of our own," Cornelius Howard Patton and Walter Taylor Field wrote in 1927, attempting to distinguish these colleges from ivy-clad Oxford and Cambridge, "something *sui generis*, a product of New England soil—robust rather than clinging." They proposed the elm, an idea that went nowhere.[3]

There have been several theories as to the source of the name. The most exotic holds that it refers to an 1898 alliance among Harvard, Princeton, Yale, and Penn, who were dubbed the "IV" league, denoting the Roman numeral four. No one, however, has ever been able to cite any instances of the term "IV League" being used in this way.

Shortly after the first Ivy League agreement in 1945, Al Laney, a columnist for the *Herald Tribune*, wrote a piece titled "How the Ivy League Got Its Name."[4] The term, Laney said, "was thought up and first used by Stanley Woodward, sports editor of the Herald Tribune and generally accepted as the nation's No. 1 football writer. Coach Woodward first used the term a dozen or so years ago, at a time when he was joyfully needling some of the group, especially Harvard, for their snootiness.... The name was so apt and was so eagerly adopted by all other football writers that in no time at all it became semiofficial and its source was forgotten. For the record, though, it was the Coach who started it."

Unfortunately, another New York sportswriter, Robert Harron, later embellished the tale. On October 14, 1937, Harron wrote, the editors at the *Tribune* were deciding who would cover that weekend's football games. Woodward took the marquee game, Fordham versus Pittsburgh at the Polo Grounds. Caswell Adams, the *Tribune*'s boxing correspondent, was assigned to cover Columbia and Penn at Baker Field, a distinctly second-tier match-up. According to Harron, Adams asked, "Whyinell do I have to watch the ivy grow every Saturday afternoon? How about letting me see some football away from the ivy-covered halls of learning for a change?" Woodward liked the term and began to work it into his columns. Harron ended by saying he had once asked Adams if he had ever received any "scholarly recognition" for his contribution to the American lexicon. Adams said he had not.[5]

This story gained such wide currency that Woodward himself adopted it in later years. It is the story the Ivy League itself still gives today. Unfortunately, it is wrong.[6]

The Ivy League was one of the last major athletic conferences to be formed, well after the Big Ten, the Southeast Conference, and even the Missouri Valley Conference. Although the Ivy colleges, or groups of them, had formed leagues in baseball, basketball, and several other sports by the early part of the twentieth century, these were known simply as the Eastern Intercollegiate League. While some referred colloquially to Harvard, Yale, and Princeton as the "Big Three," football simply brought in too much money, and engendered too many disputes, to permit a conference in that sport.

The Depression made some sort of gridiron alliance desirable, and so when Harvard and Princeton announced in January 1933 that they would play each other again after a seven-year break, sportswriters began to speculate about a league. It was generally assumed that the members of such a league would be the members of the Eastern Intercollegiate leagues, or some subset of them. Stanley Woodward, for example, predicted that financial necessity would soon force Harvard, Yale, and Princeton to add Dartmouth and constitute themselves a football Big Four, "whether they like it or not."[7]

By the fall Woodward had broadened membership and coined a nickname, writing on October 14, 1933, that "A proportion of our eastern ivy colleges are meeting little fellows another Saturday before plunging into the strife and the turmoil."[8] He then listed eight schools: Columbia, Yale, Harvard, Dartmouth, Brown, Princeton, Army, and Penn, later adding Cornell to the list. This was the first public use of the "ivy" appellation. (Caswell Adams, incidentally, spent that afternoon covering a prep school game between Kent and Hotchkiss.)

Woodward's term did not spring into general use overnight. Even he used it only intermittently for almost a year and a half, sometimes invoking them as a symbol of excellence—contrasting, for example, "the ivy colleges and the academic boilerplates"—while others dubbed this putative grouping the "Big Seven." Alan Gould, sports editor of the Associated Press, appears to have been the first to use the exact term "Ivy League," in an article dated February 8, 1935.[9]

Woodward's colleague, Jesse Abramson, was the first to give the mock Ivy standings, although he bumped the membership to ten colleges by adding Navy. "We take it for granted that you know of the Ivy Conference," Abramson told readers that fall. "Although none of the graduate managers will admit the existence of the Ivy Conference, since they have no actual organization, we can dispense with confirmation of the league in this instance. It does exist."[10]

Now Woodward began to use the term regularly as well, sometimes with playful variations—referring, for example, to the "division of the clinging vine circuit" or "the realm of Hedera Helix, Nepta Hederaiea, and Rhus Toxodinor."[11] A year later, the student editors at seven of the eight colleges published a joint editorial in which they called for the creation of an entity they called the "Ivy League." (Adams, in fact, wrote the story for the *Tribune* a year before Harron says he inspired the term.) By the time Macy's department store began running newspaper advertisements in 1938 hawking its fancy men's overcoat as "Champion of the Ivy League," the phrase, with all its connotations, had entered the lexicon.

1820-1910

CHAPTER ONE

The Big Three

As America is the daughter of Europe, President John F. Kennedy once joked to open a commencement address in New Haven, Connecticut, so he was pleased to be at Yale, the daughter of Harvard.

Kennedy, a member of the Harvard class of 1940 and a former scrub on the freshman football team, was on friendly territory and his wry remark was greeted with smiles by the Elis assembled. Yet it contained a kernel of truth. Not only Harvard and Yale, but indeed all eight colleges that comprise the Ivy League share a filial, or at least a fraternal, bond.

Harvard, of course, came first.

The oldest college in North America was founded in 1636 with a bequest by John Harvard, a Calvinist minister. Protective of their position even in infancy, the Harvard authorities tried to squelch the establishment of a rival college in Connecticut a few years later, arguing that "the whole population of New England was scarcely sufficient to support one institution of this nature, and the establishment of a second would, in the end, be a sacrifice of both."[1] Nevertheless, in 1701 a group of Harvard-trained Congregationalists founded a college in New Haven, which they soon renamed in honor of Elihu Yale, a prominent Welsh benefactor who never set foot on the campus.

Long before the Ivy schools battled over football, they squabbled over God, adding a dimension of competition to that of kinship. As leaders of the educational and religious establishment, Harvard and Yale resisted the Great Awakening, prompting many of their dissenting alumni to found new colleges that would restore orthodoxy. The College of New Jersey was founded by Yale and Harvard graduates in 1746 to train Presbyterian ministers and shortly thereafter moved to the town of Princeton. Alumni of the three colleges continued to spread their influence throughout the colonies. In 1770, Eleazer Wheelock, another Yale alumnus, relocated his Indian Charity School from Connecticut to the North Woods of New Hampshire and renamed it after the Earl of Dartmouth. Rhode Island College, founded by Baptists with a Princeton minister as its first president, was renamed Brown University in 1804 to honor Nicholas Brown, a wealthy alumnus.

Ivy schools outside the orbit of Calvinism also arose amid the intellectual tumult of the eighteenth century. King's College in New York City, which was named for King George II, was founded in 1754 and renamed Columbia after the Revolution. Benjamin Franklin founded the Charity School in Philadelphia in 1740, which went through several identities before becoming the University of Pennsylvania in 1779.

Cornell, the only member of the Ivy League not founded before the Revolution, was a private land-grant college chartered in 1865 and named in honor of Ezra Cornell, a prominent benefactor who had made his fortune in Western Union telegraph bonds. It is a peculiar hybrid, a private college that nonetheless has some departments subsidized by the State of New York.

Owing in part to this background, the first eastern colleges shared similar views on the proper role of physical training. They regarded it as decadent—to the extent, that is, that they regarded it at all. Their concern was with improving minds and souls, not bodies.

The situation at Princeton is illustrative. Professors, most of whom were clergymen, were strict taskmasters who frowned on the frivolity of games. Students took almost no exercise save walking or horseback riding and their diet was, by modern standards, terrible. What early games they did play were unorganized and certainly unsanctioned by the college administration—perhaps a quick footrace or a game of quoits. As late as 1846, one student could note that "The old puerility of playing marbles is again arrived on the campus." [2]

With a mixture of priggishness and quack science, the faculty denounced outdoor diversions as "low and unbecoming gentlemen and students" and "attended with great danger to the health by sudden and alternate heats and colds." [3] Even sleigh riding was forbidden. As might be expected, relations between professors and students, already strained thanks to the narrow, monotonous curriculum, occasionally spilled into outright rebellion. When the Princeton faculty disciplined several undergraduates in 1807, their classmates rioted, forcing the administration to suspend classes for several days. Bored and overworked, students of this era wasted their free time lounging around, smoking, and drinking. Brawls and even duels were not uncommon.

Athletics was one of several outlets students began to find for their energies in the first half of the nineteenth century. Perhaps because it provided a shared social experience combined with the familiar thrill of the brawl, football proved especially attractive. American football has its origins in soccer, a game that dates back to antiquity, when Greeks played a game called "harpaston" in which the object was to kick or carry a ball across the end line of a marked field. The Romans introduced soccer to England, where games became so raucous that in 1349 King Edward II banned it on pain of imprisonment. Henry VIII, Elizabeth I, and later Charles II issued similar bans, which proved equally ineffective. Shakespeare mentioned the game and its roughness in *A Comedy of Errors* and in *King Lear*.[4] The Pilgrims are thought to have brought soccer to the New World, and may have played it on the first Thanksgiving, thus anticipating one of the great American traditions.

By the 1820s, Princeton students are reported to have been playing a form of football game called "balldown" on a field next to Nassau Hall, dividing themselves into teams according to the first letter of a student's last name. All the Ivy colleges share some version of this story. Harvard students played an annual game that came to be known as "Bloody Monday," as early as 1827 (Winslow Homer captured it a generation later in one of his earliest drawings) and something of its style can be guessed from the name. Columbia claims football antecedents dating from 1824, while Penn students were playing local high school teams as far back as the 1840s. Yale also started an annual freshman-sophomore "rush" in the 1840s, a kind of mass hazing ritual that soon grew into an event of great formality, with exploits commemorated in songs and poetry:

> *There were yellings and shoutings and*
> *wiping of noses,*
> *Where the hue of the lily was changed to*
> *the rose's,*
> *There were tearing of shirts, and ripping*
> *of stitches,*
> *and breaches of peaces, and pieces*
> *of britches.*[5]

Yale students had to abandon the rushes in 1858, however, when the city of New Haven refused to let them use the town green. When they tried to move the game elsewhere, the faculty, which had long taken a dim view of all this foolishness, banned it outright. Harvard outlawed Bloody Monday in 1860, while the Brown faculty halted its annual freshman-sophomore game two years later, only to reinstate it in 1866.

Rowing, however, was the first intercollegiate sport, and many of the rivalries that today characterize the Ivy League, not to mention many of the ills that still plague intercollegiate athletics in general, had their origins on the water rather than the gridiron. In the 1840s, while football players were still slugging each other on campus greens, both Harvard and Yale organized their first crews. When the two met on New Hampshire's Lake Winnipesaukee in 1852, in the nation's first intercollegiate athletic contest, their expenses were paid as part of a railroad promotion to lure tourists to the White Mountains. Intercollegiate match races proved so popular with spectators (including gamblers) that they were moved to Saratoga, the fashionable New York summer resort and horse racing capital that was something like the Las Vegas of its day. Within a few years, Brown, Columbia, Dartmouth, and Princeton crews were also competing in what came to be known as the Rowing Association of American Colleges. Unable to dominate the sport any longer, Harvard and Yale withdrew from the association in 1875, vowing henceforth to row only against each other. Others tried unsuccessfully to continue the regattas, but learned an early lesson in how important affiliation with the Big Two could be.

It was with this background, then, and among the broadening associations among these colleges, that intercollegiate football followed.

Sports and entertainment of all sorts received a boost at the end of the Civil War when, as it would after both world wars in the next century, the nation indulged itself in the pursuit of money and recreation. College campuses swelled with returning veterans, many of whom brought with them a love of vigorous games and impatience with college prohibitions against them. In the fall of 1869, a group of Rutgers students issued an invitation to Princeton to meet them in a series of three football games—an attempt, so the story goes, to avenge Princeton's 40-2 routing of Rutgers in baseball three years earlier.[6]

Rutgers' challenge was received by William S. Gummere, captain of Princeton's baseball team, who is better known to history for his contributions on the diamond as the inventor of the hook-slide, and in the courtroom as chief justice of the New Jersey Supreme Court. Gummere corresponded with his counterpart to agree on a set of rules for the contest. The field was to be 360 feet long and 225 feet wide. The object was to drive the ball between two goal posts eight paces apart (with no crossbar) by kicking it or batting it in the air. Throwing the ball or running with it was forbidden, though players were allowed to catch it. There were to be twenty-five men to a side, as well as four judges and two referees. Tripping and holding were the only fouls.

Saturday, November 6, 1869, was fixed as the date for the contest, because there were no classes on Saturday afternoons and students would have been forbidden to play on the Sabbath. At nine o'clock on the morning of that first game, a "jerky little train … crowded to the aisles and platforms with a freight of eager students" chugged out of the Princeton depot for New Brunswick. The Rutgers students met them at the station and showed their guests the sights of the town (including the local billiards parlor) before lunch.

Admission was free to the more than one hundred spectators who seated themselves on the ground or perched atop a fence that partially enclosed the field. Although the game had few of the trappings of college football games even a few years later, one thing the Princeton partisans did bring with them was their famous "rocket" cheer, which hissed like an exploding rocket: "Hooray! Hooray! Hooray! Tiger sis-boom-ah, Princeton!" By the 1890s, the rocket cheer would develop into Princeton's famous "locomotive," the cadence of which imitates the sound of a train engine gathering speed and is still heard at football games today.[7]

None of the players in that first game wore uniforms, although the Rutgers students did sport scarlet "turbans," which one imagines resembled the modern "do-rag." The Princetonians simply stripped off their coats, vests, and hats, rolled up their sleeves, and prepared to play. For the most part they were not big men, even by the standards of their time; one historian has estimated that they averaged only about five-foot-eight in height and weighed perhaps 150 pounds.[8]

One tradition that was present from the very beginning was the pregame coin toss, but this time there were two of them; one to determine who would kick to whom and a second to determine who would defend which goal. Rutgers won the first toss and elected to receive. Shortly after three o'clock, Princeton kicked off from a tee made of piled up dirt, and intercollegiate football was under way.

Princeton had something to learn about tactics, for it chose to kick off into the wind and shanked the ball to one side. This enabled Rutgers to take over in excellent field position, from where it began dribbling toward Princeton's goal. Both teams appear to have played a crude zone defense, posting a few men to guard the goal and assigning everyone else to cover certain parts of the field rather than a specific man on the other team. By carefully shielding the man with the ball, Rutgers was able to score first, about five minutes into the game.

Finesse became intercollegiate football's first casualty. Gummere decided to change tactics and instructed one of his teammates, a behemoth named Jacob Michael, known as "Big Mike," to break up the Rutgers cocoon. This he did and "scattered the players like a bursting bundle of sticks."[9] Soon afterward, Princeton tied the score on a long kick. From there, the game turned into a siege. At one point Big Mike and a Rutgers player made for the ball at the same time and crashed through the fence, toppling spectators.

The game was to be played until someone scored six goals. Noticing that the taller Princeton men were able to bat down high kicks, the Rutgers captain ordered his men to keep their passes short and low to the ground. This was made difficult owing to the quality of the ball, which kept getting deflated. The adjustment to crisp passing worked, though, and Rutgers scored the last two goals to win, 6-4, in just over three hours.

A week later, Rutgers journeyed to Princeton for the second game of the series. This time Gummere tried a new strategy of short kicks and fair catches, which left Rutgers "wholly outclassed" and on the losing end of the sport's first shutout, 8-0. The rubber match, scheduled for Rutgers, was never played. Already faculty at both schools had become alarmed at the passionate attention the new game generated among the students, and ordered the match canceled.

Not two weeks after intercollegiate football was born, in other words, the faculty had concluded that it was drawing too much attention.

Nevertheless, games between colleges proved to be popular. The following year, 1870, Princeton won twice at home against Rutgers while Rutgers, in turn, introduced Columbia to the sport. Columbia's first captain was Stuyvesant Fish, son of President Ulysses S. Grant's Secretary of State. The Fishes were an old New York family, but it was soon apparent that there was no room for gentility on the football field. One Rutgers player, James Van Rensselaer Weston, later recalled, "While lying prostrate on the ground I saw Stuyvesant Fish, the Columbia giant, trying to jump over me. He landed with his No. 14's just grazing my cheek. As he was nearly as large and raw-boned as Abe Lincoln, I had a narrow escape." [10] No intercollegiate games were played in 1871, but when Columbia met Rutgers again the following year, the teams agreed to an experiment in which a score could be made by kicking the ball over, rather than under, the crossbar of the goal.

Yale's intercollegiate football debut was the highlight of the 1872 season and one of the important moments in the history of the sport. Credit for reviving the game in New Haven goes to a student, David S. Schaff, who had spent a year studying at the Rugby School in England. [11] Nevertheless, Yale played the soccer variety of football favored by other American colleges.

The Elis had hoped to arrange a game with Princeton, but faculty at both colleges refused to excuse their teams from classes long enough to travel to the other school. A compromise permitted games against closer rivals: Princeton again met Rutgers while Yale hosted Columbia. The Yale-Columbia game was played at New Haven's Hamilton Park, on a field both longer and wider than that used in the first Princeton-Rutgers game—400 by 250 feet—with a crossbar added to the goal, 15 feet off the ground. At least four hundred fans attended, paying twenty-five cents to get in, making it probably the first football game at which admission was charged. Clearly, the days of playing in vacant lots were over.

Several New York papers were curious enough to send reporters. The Columbia men, wrote the *New York World*, "entered upon their work lightly clad and distinguished by light wrappers and blue caps, while their rivals were dressed in all ways, and presented an appearance not unlike that with which Yale men are wont to seek the scene of the annual rush." [12] There was still an appealing informality to the affair. "As the excitement slacked," the reporter continued, "a youth might be seen retiring behind an adjoining fence to replace a dilapidated pair of pants." Such motley appearance notwithstanding, Yale scored all three goals before the match was called on account of darkness.

The Yale-Columbia rivalry never generated as much enthusiasm in New Haven as Yale's rivalry with Princeton, which began the following year when the faculty relaxed their ban on travel. Yale won a coin toss and so agreed to host that game, again at Hamilton Park. It was to be Princeton's only game of the season, and the team seems to have regarded the affair with appropriate seriousness. A week or so beforehand, one of their players, J. H. Vandeventer, proposed that the team run around the block each evening to improve their stamina. "But the idea," one historian notes, "was too revolutionary for serious consideration, and was summarily turned down." [13]

Wearing an orange badge with the word "Princeton" printed in black, Henry Moffat started the game by kicking off for the visitors, sending the "round, black rubber ball" into Yale territory. No one had scored after thirty minutes when a Yale and Princeton player both tried to kick the ball at the same time. It burst, leaving the teams unable to continue the game. A collection was taken up and play suspended for half an hour while someone was dispatched back to campus in a wagon to buy a new one. The November weather was cool and during the hiatus the Princeton players wisely kept warm by practicing while the Yale players relaxed on the grass. When play resumed, Yale was stiff and Princeton got two goals from Henry Beach in a 3-0 victory. But Yale refused to play Princeton again the following year because of a dispute over rules and the series did not resume until 1876.

Interest in the sport was stirring elsewhere in the East. Up in Ithaca, New York, a group of Cornell students, who had begun playing intraclass football games, petitioned President Andrew D. White for permission to travel to Cleveland for a game against Michigan. White famously refused, declaring, "I will not permit thirty men to travel 400 miles to agitate a bag of wind." [14]

Rule making and association forming also continued. Princeton had organized the first football committee in 1871 to set rules and support the team, and both Harvard and Yale soon followed. Because the codes they devised were unique to each school, several sets of rules existed. Harvard followed a variation of rugby popular in Boston that reduced the size of a team to between ten and fifteen men and permitted running with the ball under certain circumstances. Yale and Princeton stuck more strictly to soccer and did not permit running with the ball. Such divergences were fine if the games were going to be intramural, but unacceptable if the schools were going to play each other. Princeton took the lead in promoting coordination, calling a conference at the Fifth Avenue Hotel in New York for October 19, 1873, to hammer out a common set of rules. Princeton, Rutgers, and Yale sent representatives. Columbia chose delegates but did not send them.

Standoffish from the start, Harvard declined to participate on the grounds that its Boston rules were so different from those of the other colleges that they could not be reconciled. Its letter explaining this to the captain of the Yale team is an unintended masterpiece of patronization. "You perhaps wonder on your side at our rules; but I assure you that we consider the game here to admit of much more science, according to our rules. We cannot but recognize in your game much brute force, weight and especially 'shin' element. Our game depends upon running, dodging and position playing.... We even went so far as to practice and try the Yale game. We gave it up at once as hopeless.... I would send you a copy of our rules but we do not have a spare copy." [15]

Those students who did attend the conference formed the Intercollegiate Football Association, the sport's first governing body. The game they agreed upon still very much resembled soccer; no throwing or carrying the ball was permitted. Teams were to have twenty men to a side, although Yale argued for eleven on the theory that it might be easier to gain faculty approval for fewer men to travel to away games. These 1873 rules, which lasted only one season, were ultimately of little significance. Harvard eventually prevailed, but first Harvard's own game had to change.

The occasion was a pair of matches in May 1874 against a visiting team from McGill University of Montreal. The first of the two contests was played under Harvard rules, the second under the All-Canada Rugby Rule Code. Harvard won the opener, 3-0, in just twenty-two minutes, while wearing for the first time "magenta handkerchiefs bound round their heads." [16] Although the second game ended in a scoreless tie (in part because McGill had neglected to bring a Canadian rugby ball, assuming erroneously that they could buy one in Boston), Harvard students who had recently derided the Canadian rules as "wholly unscientific and unsuitable to colleges," so preferred the new game that they decided to adopt it.

With some justification, Harvard insists that its refusal to attend the 1873 rules conference saved modern football. For had Harvard attended, the argument goes, it would have been forced to adopt the association rules favored by the other schools. It would not have played McGill, and the American game would have remained soccer. [17]

Harvard still wanted to play Yale, which was already well established as its chief athletic rival, but that was impossible so long as each played a different game. In order to bridge their differences, representatives of the two schools met and agreed to what they called "concessionary rules." The concessions, however, were almost all made by the Elis. Although Harvard agreed to Yale's request on a few scoring rules, Yale, which again wanted to limit teams to eleven a side, acceded to Harvard's request to play with teams of fifteen. As the younger and still less prestigious college, Yale had little choice but to play Harvard's game if it wanted Harvard's rivalry. [18]

The first meeting in what became known simply as "The Game" took place at Hamilton Park, which had now become established as the Elis' home grounds. The game was called for 2:30 P.M. on a slightly cloudy day. More than two thousand people showed up (including about one hundred and fifty Harvard students), paying fifty cents apiece—twice as much as the fee for the Princeton-Yale game the year before. Each school would have taken home $500, more than enough to cover expenses in Harvard's case and a tidy profit, testifying to the enormous financial potential of college football as entertainment.

Yale's team wore dark pants, blue shirts, and yellow caps; Harvard sported crimson shirts and stockings. They used what was known as a "No. 6" ball, thirty inches in circumference and less rounded at the ends than a rugby ball, which is twenty-seven inches around. (By comparison, a modern football is only twenty-one and one-quarter inches around.) There were two types of No. 6 ball, the Association ball and the English match (rugby) ball. It is not clear which one was used. The former was made of heavy canvas "thoroughly saturated with rubber." The latter consisted of an inner rubber bladder in a leather outer shell, much like a modern football. [19]

The game was divided into three thirty-minute periods. As the Crimson's account noted, "The adopted rules were not fully understood by either team." But Harvard clearly had not conceded too much by playing under their preferred style and won easily, 4-0.

From the beginning, the Harvard-Yale weekend was an occasion. After the game, the Yale students hosted a dinner for their Cambridge guests and then invited them to join a sing-along on campus. However, the *New Haven Register* also reported that seven Harvard students were arrested that evening "for creating disturbances by hooting and singing in the public streets. They all gave fictitious names and deposited their watches and other articles of jewelry as security for a fine of $5.29 in each case." [20]

The new game under the new rules made a favorable impression on fans as well as participants, including W. Earle Dodge and Jothan Potter, two Princeton students who were watching from the stands. After Dodge and Potter persuaded their schoolmates to give up soccer for rugby (Princeton, likewise, had little choice if it hoped to play either Harvard or Yale), the two young men called another conference to "establish a system of rules by means of which the colleges shall be enabled to compete with one another at football upon a uniform and satisfactory basis." [21] The following November, representatives from Harvard, Yale, Princeton, and Columbia met at the Massasoit House in Springfield, Massachusetts, to form a second Intercollegiate Football Association.

The 1876 conference was considerably more successful than the 1873 conference. The students established sixty-one rules, twenty-two of which still govern college football games today, including those defining a tackle, a punt, a placekick, a kickoff, a fair catch, a lateral, and a dead ball. The dimensions of the playing field were set at 140 yards by 70 yards, the playing time was to be divided into two forty-five minute halves, teams were to consist of fifteen players on each side, and a goal counted as four touchdowns. Cleats were outlawed, as were tripping and "hacking." The participants further agreed that the two best teams from the previous year would play each other for the championship on Thanksgiving Day. They were not interested in expanding membership, however, as they also provided that no new members could be added to the association without unanimous consent. Yale again argued forcefully for eleven-man teams and against counting touchdowns in the scoring. Voted down, they withdrew from the fledgling association, though they continued to send representatives to its meetings and, more important, continued to play its members. By sweeping Harvard, Princeton, and

Columbia that fall (the latter in eight-degree weather), Yale won what was, in effect, the first college football national championship.

Other colleges, meanwhile, were also joining the intercollegiate ranks, though not yet the IFA. The University of Pennsylvania played its first game in 1876, hosting Princeton after promising the Tigers fifty dollars in expenses to induce them to make the trip, apparently the first financial guarantee offered to a visiting team. Although it had recently adopted red and blue as the school colors, Penn took the field wearing white flannel cricket suits. Princeton was bedecked in what has been called the first complete football uniform: black knee pants, black tights, and black woolen shirts trimmed in orange and an orange "P" on the breast, baseball shoes, and a small cap. Canvas pants would replace the tights beginning in 1878.

Still played with scarcely any protective equipment at all, early football was rough and players did not always behave like gentlemen. An account of the Columbia-Princeton game of 1876 notes that "Nicholl, of Princeton, was kicked in the abdomen and hurt, and Lindley, of Columbia, in another melee was kicked in the ribs and had to be carried from the ground, the game being stopped." [22] Broken noses were also not uncommon as players batted at the flying ball. As usual, the players seemed to take it all in stride, much as they had in campus pick-up games. Before the Harvard-Yale game in 1879, Frederic Remington, the noted painter and sculptor, dipped his jersey in blood from a local slaughterhouse "to make it look more businesslike." [23] According to Remington's biographer, one of his Yale professors "remarked that the often bruised Remington was the most unusual art student he ever had." [24]

Sitting in the stands at that 1879 Harvard-Yale contest was Theodore Roosevelt, then a Harvard student, who was too nearsighted to play the game but would later play an important role in saving it. He noted in a letter shortly afterward, "I am sorry to say we were beaten, principally because our opponents played very foul." Yet a fierce Crimson loyalty was already exhibiting itself. "I am very glad I am not a Yale freshman," Roosevelt added. "The hazing there is pretty bad. The fellows seem to be a much more scrubby set than ours." [25] They were, though, nattily dressed. Yale took the field wearing blue shirts with a large white "Y," white pants, and a blue cap and knee socks—more or less the uniform they wear today.

By this point, each of the "Big Three" schools (though the term would not come into use for a few more years) had made an important contribution to the development of football. Princeton had played the first intercollegiate game and initiated both early rules conferences. Harvard had pioneered the rugby style of game that turned American football away from soccer. And Yale quickly became the acknowledged leader in the development of rules and, for two generations thereafter, the sport's flagship program.

Credit for that achievement is owed largely to the work of one man. No one was more responsible for the development of football at Yale, or indeed in the country, than Walter Camp. John Heisman, who made many contributions of his own, once declared, "What Washington was to his country, Walter Camp was to football—the friend, the founder, and the father."[26] Camp also embodied Yale football for two generations, providing the personal link and institutional memory that transformed its great teams into a powerful program. The journalist Richard Harding Davis later joked, "There is only one man in New Haven of more importance than Walter Camp and I have forgotten his name. I think he is the president of the university."[27]

He was an Eli to the core. Born in New Britain, Connecticut, in 1859, Camp matriculated at Yale in 1876 at the age of seventeen, just in time for the second Harvard game. He played on the varsity for six years, the final two as a medical student (there were as yet no eligibility rules for either freshmen or graduate students) and was captain for the last three. Teams had no coaches as such in those days; instead the captain devised plays and supervised training. Camp became notorious for his attention to the fundamentals, for himself no less than for his teammates. One story has it that Camp found the watermelon-shaped rugby ball hard to handle and so carried it around with him wherever he went, including class.

His playing career must have been frustrating, as he continually performed well only to have it count for nothing because of the rules. In 1877, Camp made two long touchdown runs against Princeton but neither counted because Yale could not convert them into goals. In 1878, he made a thirty-five-yard drop kick that would have beaten Harvard, but it was disallowed because the final whistle was blown while the ball was in the air. In 1879, a forty-five-yard drop kick against Harvard was nullified on a penalty.

Of far greater importance than anything he achieved on the field, though, Camp became a member of the IFA's Rules Committee in 1878, and it was there that he exerted his lasting influence. Until the formation of the NCAA in 1906, the Rules Committee was the organization that most shaped college football and the place where the game evolved. Camp served on the committee until his death in 1925.

The list of techniques and tactics Camp pioneered reads like a football glossary. It was Camp who first thought to start each play with a snap from scrimmage, and he was the one who initiated the natural corollary of that reform, the offside penalty. Camp was the first to propose painting yard lines on the field, the first to popularize having the quarterback call out signals (and the first to call the position "quarterback"), the leading force behind reducing the size of the teams to eleven men and permitting tackling below the waist, the originator of the four downs to gain ten yards system of play, the neutral zone, and the long snap on punts, and the first to name an All-America team.

According to one biographer, "As a football legislator, Walter Camp did not have a particularly bold or imaginative mind. But he was keenly analytical, laboriously methodical, and crafty enough to keep his own counsel until others had their say."[28] When he thought the situation called for it, however, Camp was willing to force his opinions through, and sometimes threatened to quit unless his point of view prevailed. "He seldom failed to control the team completely," historian John McCallum has written. "He wasn't a prig. He just wanted to win."[29]

Nevertheless, Camp was also known for his scrupulous fairness. His opponents thought so highly of him that Princeton asked him to referee their game with Yale in 1885. He dogmatically opposed professionalism, a position consistent with keeping the noble aspects of sport above the grubbier aspects of commerce. "A gentleman never competes for money, directly or indirectly," Camp wrote in 1893. "Make no mistake about this. No matter how winding the road may be that eventually brings the sovereign into the pocket, it is the price of what should be dearer to you than anything else—your honor."[30]

Yet for all his achievements, football could never be more than a part-time job. He did not earn all his sovereigns from football. Throughout his career, Camp worked for the New Haven Clock Company, rising to become its president. The job often made him late for practice, so he had his wife, Alice, walk the sidelines and take notes that Camp would then review at night. As Yale's football fortunes sagged in the second decade of the century, though, Camp was forced out of his post as treasurer of the Yale Field Association, his only official connection to the university. However, he left the association with a large surplus, which was shortly thereafter used to build the Yale Bowl.

By 1877, newspaper accounts of college football games were beginning to get a little color. A good example is the *New York Times*' report of Princeton's victory over Yale, which also reveals how sophisticated fans were becoming. The styles may have changed, but the routine is immediately recognizable:

> *The hour set down for the game was 2 o'clock, and at that time the two rickety shanties provided for spectators were crowded with comely young woman and portly old gentlemen, who, together with innumerable young men with short hair and canes, and Scotch terriers, viewed the game from the beginning to the close, and expressed their interest in every new phase of the contest. Many of the young ladies had pencils and note-books in their hands, and jotted down the events of the game from time to time, and not a few of them jumped up and down excitedly, and added shrill treble notes to the general yell of approbation at some exceedingly interesting tussle.*[31]

Although Princeton won, the match was characteristically rough and the papers meticulously detailed the violence as well. At one point, Princeton's Hugh Stevenson "received a kick in the stomach which demoralized him badly for a few seconds." Later, the *Times* noted, "when one man was knocked down by six others and obliged to bear their combined weight for a minute or so, he maintained the utmost good humor, and, upon regaining his footing immediately helped to knock down another man and sit upon him." [32]

The significant innovation of 1877, however, was sartorial, and again the leader was Princeton. In a game against Harvard played in April (postponed from the previous fall to give Princeton more time to practice under the new rules), they unveiled laced canvas jackets designed by a student, Ledru P. Smock. The jackets were snug and thus difficult to grab, which made players harder to tackle (tackling was allowed only above the waist) and saved jerseys from being ripped. A few Princeton players made themselves still more difficult to tackle by greasing themselves with tallow, a practice later outlawed. These jackets, which became known as "smocks," were soon copied by other schools and remained a standard part of the football uniform until 1902. Underneath them, Princeton wore black jerseys with orange stripes on the sleeves, and matching striped socks. They looked like tigers and soon adopted the nickname—the first official college nickname in the country. The Princeton Tigers still wear similarly striped jerseys today. [33]

It was growing impossible to maintain a football association when the member teams still could not agree on all the rules. In 1878 and 1879, Harvard and Princeton were the only two members of the IFA to participate in its meetings. Harvard and Yale did not play each other in 1877 because they could not agree on the size of the teams; Harvard and Princeton played their 1877 game under compromise rules with fourteen men on a side and did not count touchdowns, only goals kicked from the field. When Yale could not persuade either Harvard or Princeton to play their eleven-man game in 1878, they conceded to play fifteen to a side. The Harvard-Yale match at Boston that year marked the first time the Yale faculty had ever let the team play away from home.

In 1878, Harvard and Princeton also met again in Hoboken, this time in a driving rainstorm. Princeton blamed the Crimson's 1-0 victory on a poorly maintained field and complained that the IFA had been forced to pay $300 for the "few wretchedly tended square feet of Jersey mud for two short hours." [34] The secretary of the Tigers' board of coaches that season was Woodrow Wilson, then a senior who still went by his given first name, "Tommy."

Brown made its intercollegiate football debut in 1878 with a 4-0 loss to Amherst. The Brunonians took the field wearing white canvas uniforms and brown stockings, which they had bought two days earlier "for a fifty-dollar down payment and Brown Football Association President George Malcom's watch as security for the balance." They attributed Amherst's goal kicks to luck and a favorable wind. [35]

A significant innovation in tactics—blocking by the offensive line—developed during the 1879 Harvard-Princeton game and was occasioned by Princeton's cheating. In rugby, any offensive blocking is illegal. Princeton ignored the rule and placed defenders on either side of the ball carrier to run interference for him. Although the referee, Walter Camp, warned Princeton that they were breaking the rules, he not only failed to call a penalty, but borrowed the tactic for Yale later that season.

That game also saw a second innovation, the onsides kick. It had been standard practice to kick off by booting the ball down the field, but the Princeton kicker, Bland Ballard, instead nubbed the ball forward a few feet, picked it up, and ran with it. The play was perfectly legal (kickoffs did not yet have to travel ten yards before they could be recovered) and for the next fifteen years, long kickoffs all but disappeared from the game.

Harvard would take greater exception in coming years to what it considered Princeton's bending of the rules, although squabbling and backbiting continued to taint its athletic relations with Yale, as well. In its account of the 1879 Princeton-Yale contest, the Harvard *Crimson* could not resist a gratuitous dig at its archrivals. Describing Camp's officiating as "highly satisfactory to both parties," it added that "the utmost good feeling was displayed on either side—an agreeable contrast to the treatment experienced by our teams at New Haven." [36]

Though it still trailed baseball and crew as the most popular sport on campus, by the end of the game's first full decade American football had already developed from a rowdy diversion to an increasingly formal and lucrative form of entertainment. The game itself, however, remained a hodgepodge, part soccer and part rugby, but not quite either. In the coming decade, football would assume a much more distinctive character, both for good and bad, that would establish it as a national institution and the Ivy teams that played it as national powerhouses.

CHAPTER TWO

Making the Rules As You Go Along

Two rule changes in 1880 at last gave shape to American football. Camp had proposed both a year earlier when the Elis were still boycotting the IFA and lacked a vote on its rules committee. Once Yale rejoined the association, he was able to put his reforms through.

First, Camp reduced the size of a team to eleven men. The need for such a change had become clear as larger teams simply clogged up the field, producing tedious, low scoring games. Often it was different for anyone to score. The 1879 Princeton-Yale game had ended in a 0-0 tie, giving Princeton the championship, but spectators had been disappointed. "Yale gained a foot and lost it," the *New York Times* reported. "Then Princeton did the same, and for 10 minutes a writhing mass of legs and arms turned and twisted 20 ways at once, while the ball was not moved three feet." [1] Those who favored reduction argued that smaller teams made the game more interesting by increasing action, and safer by reducing chaos. Eleven carried the added weight of consistency as it was the size of both rugby and soccer teams.

Arguing from their own considerably narrower self-interest, several Princeton students opposed reducing the size of the team for precisely the reason that it might boost scoring. They were confident that their defense could force an endless series of shutout ties even if they themselves could not score, which would enable the Tigers to retain their title. "Why, then, should we, merely for the gratification of the spectators, risk what has cost us so many hotly contested games to secure and keep up to the present time?" they asked. [2]

The year's second rule change was even more significant. Despite all the innovations of the previous decade, football in 1880 still resembled rugby. Whenever a man was tackled, the ball would be placed in the middle of a mass of players, arms locked around each other, known as a "scrum" or "scrummage," who would then push and shove until someone could kick the ball free to a teammate waiting around the fringes. The scrum penalized the team that had last held the ball because they could not be sure of keeping possession after their man was tackled.

Camp replaced the "scrummage" with a "scrimmage," which started a new play and enabled a team to keep possession of the ball. The full text of the rule adopted that winter deserves to be reprinted in full: "A scrimmage takes place when the holder of the ball, being in the field of play, puts it down on the ground in front of him and puts it in play while onside, first, by kicking the ball; second, by snapping it back with his foot. The man who first receives the ball from the snap-back shall be called the quarterback, and shall not then rush forward with the ball under penalty of foul." [3]

He had crammed quite a lot of innovation into just seventy-four words. Note that the ball was originally snapped with the foot to a kneeling quarterback, placing both the center (as the "snap-back" soon came to be called) and quarterback in very vulnerable positions to start the play. The lineman adjacent to center would help guard him from being knocked over by bracing his foot behind the center's nonkicking foot; thus the position first known as the "next-to-center" became known as guard. Centers soon learned to steady the ball with their hands and by 1890 the modern between-the-legs snap was legalized. [4] By prohibiting the quarterback from rushing with the ball, the rule also made both the quarterback sneak and the option play illegal. But more than any other innovation in the game's history, the line of scrimmage defined American football and turned it away from rugby.

A logical corollary of the rule that a play did not start until the ball was snapped was that anyone who crossed the line of scrimmage early was offside. The offsides penalty, then, was written into the rulebook the following year, the first "rules" penalty as distinguished from a roughness penalty such as tripping. And Camp made the penalty severe. The first time it happened, the play would be taken over. But if a team jumped three times on the same play, the ball would be turned over to the defense.

Camp had revolutionized football, but there was a large hole in his rules. By starting each play from scrimmage, the team with the ball could hold it indefinitely until it either scored or fumbled or the half ran out. A strategy of "six inches and a cloud of dust" was entirely practical without a requirement that the offense advance the ball within a certain number of plays. To make matters worse, there was no penalty for a safety; if a team was caught behind its own goal line, it not only kept possession of the ball but actually got better field position, restarting at the twenty-five-yard line.

The potential for abuse was obvious, and Princeton was the first to exploit it. In its game against Yale at New York's Polo Grounds in 1880, Captain Francis

Loney refused to kick when stymied by the Yale defense and instead took eleven safeties (to Yale's five) until the game was over and he had forced a 0-0 tie. The outcome must have been frustrating all around, particularly for the "unusual number of young collegians" whom the newspapers reported "swung handsful of greenbacks in the air, loudly calling for bets."[5] Loney then had the audacity to argue that Princeton should retain its 1879 championship because it had not been beaten. Fortunately, the IFA was not about to allow such manipulations and refused to award a championship to anyone.

The Rules Committee tried to address the problem by providing that if the score were tied at the end of regulation, the teams would play two additional "innings" (as they were still called) of fifteen minutes each—in other words, overtime. They also provided that in case of a tie, the team that had suffered fewer safeties would win.

Princeton's ingenuity managed to stay a step ahead of Camp's as they took advantage of yet another loophole. According to the rules, the goal line extended out indefinitely past the sideline. If the ball was downed behind a team's goal line but in-bounds, that was a safety. But if it was downed behind the goal line but out of bounds (outside what would now be called the end zone, in other words), that was called a "touch-in-goal." Harvard and Yale had tried to have a touch-in-goal counted as a safety, but Princeton refused, and as a result, the touch-in-goal did not count at all in the scoring. The team simply started another play at the twenty-five-yard line.

Unable to take unlimited safeties anymore, Princeton forced ties with both Harvard and Yale in 1881 by repeatedly taking touches-in-goal. In the Yale game, as soon as Princeton took possession near their own goal line following a Walter Camp punt, their halfback, Alfred Burt, tossed the ball out of bounds for a touch-in-goal. The ball was brought out to the twenty-five-yard line where Princeton ran play after play into the line. When they were eventually pushed back again toward their own goal, they simply threw the ball out of bounds again, took another touch-in-goal, and started the whole sorry process over. According to Henry Twombley, Yale's quarterback, Princeton managed to keep the ball for almost the entire forty-five-minute half without gaining ten yards.

Taking possession for the second half, Yale decided to do the same thing and held the ball for the rest of regulation and the first overtime. The second extra period had to be called on account of darkness, but everyone was so disgusted by that point that an end was welcome. The final score of what became known as the "block game" was yet another 0-0 whitewash, the third in a row for Princeton and Yale. Shamelessly, the Tigers again tried to argue that they retained the championship, but the IFA awarded it to Yale on the basis of its hardly sterling win over Harvard by the odd score of zero to four safeties.

The block game "so disgusted spectators that it was absolutely necessary to make a change," Camp later wrote.[6] They hissed and hooted and threw garbage on the field. It wasn't cheating, because the tactic was perfectly legal under the rules, but it was of very doubtful sportsmanship and deathly boring to watch. Camp called a special meeting of the Rules Committee in April 1882 to fix things, but they could not reach agreement. By the fall, though, they had agreed to a new rule that eliminated the touch-in-goal and required a team to advance the ball at least five yards in three plays or "downs" or else surrender it to the other side. Curiously, the original rule also gave the team a first down if it lost ten yards—a team could continue to hold the ball, in other words, by losing ground as well as by gaining it.

Camp allowed the referee to decide whether a team had made the requisite yardage for a first down. But if a team was required to make a certain number of yards, there had to be some way of measuring their progress. Here came Camp's next brainstorm—painted yard markers on the field.

"We shall have to rule off the field with horizontal chalked lines every five yards," Camp is reputed to have explained.

"Gracious!" exclaimed Ned Pearce, Princeton's representative at the meeting. "The field will look like a gridiron!"

"Precisely," Camp replied.[7]

Play-calling was another offshoot of the scrimmage system. Because the ball could now be put into play in an orderly way, teams could decide ahead of time what they wanted to do on a particular down. They had to communicate this choice to everyone on the team, though, and so Camp borrowed a trick he had seen Michigan use and had Yale's captain call signals before the snap.

There were only five signals at first and they were unsophisticated by modern standards. Twombley recalled many years later that in signal number one, the call of "Look out quick Deac," "Look out," "Quick" or "Deac" meant that Twombley (whose nickname was "Deacon") would pitch the ball to the halfback and lead the blocking. "Play up sharp Charlie," "Play up," "Sharp," or "Charlie" meant that the ball would be pitched to another back, Wyllys Terry.

"Cheese it" was the signal for the first trick play in football history. According to Twombley, that had been the signal in his childhood to look out for police. Twombley made it the call for a fake field goal. Against Princeton in 1882, with punter Gene Richards standing back to try a drop kick for goal, Twombley called "cheese it." He took the snap directly, and as the Tigers rushed in to block the kick, pitched the ball out to Charles "Doc" Beck, who walked in for a touchdown, the first Yale had scored against Princeton in five years.[8]

Yale also had physical signals, which soon became more popular than vocal signals because they did not require the players to be heard over a cheering crowd. One of these was the "hat signal." Players at the time still wore knit stocking caps. If the quarterback pulled his hat down on the left side, the ball was to be tossed to the left end. If he pulled it down on the right, the ball was to go to the right end. Still another gesture signaled a pitch back to the halfback. Sometimes the center could call the play; by holding the ball perpendicularly or "reproving Frank

Peters," he indicated that Louis Hull, another back, would run the ball. Princeton introduced the more familiar number signals in 1888 and made the quarterback, not the captain, responsible for calling them. Thus, the role of quarterback as field general was born.

In 1883 Camp pushed through a new scoring system. There were to be four ways of scoring: a safety was worth one point, a touchdown worth four points, a goal after a touchdown—the modern extra point—worth four points (reduced to two the following year), and a goal from the field (or field goal, as we would now call it) worth five points.

By making action on the field more predictable and orderly, the rule changes of the early 1880s enabled the game's first stars to emerge, players with specialized talents and defined roles. Quarterbacks were not yet as well known because the rules prohibited them from throwing or even running with the ball. The stars were the runners and, to a degree they would not enjoy again, the kickers.

The value placed on kicking was evidenced by the fact that booting the ball over the crossbar after a touchdown was worth as many points as the touchdown itself, and a field goal was worth more than either. In the 1882 Yale-Princeton game, which was won on Twombley's "cheese it" call, Princeton's J. Triplett "Jerry" Haxall, a 158-pound tackle, booted a sixty-five-yard field goal from placement, which remained a collegiate record until 1976 and is still longer than the professional record of sixty-three yards. Haxall and a teammate, Tommy Baker, had been practicing in their free time, kicking down the long corridor between Reunion Hall and the old Princeton gymnasium, moving gradually further back as their accuracy improved. Baker learned to spot the ball by tilting it back toward the kicker, while Haxall learned that by kicking the ball at its end, rather than in the middle as was commonly done, it would spin end over end and travel farther.

Punting was also valuable. Until the early 1920s, the "goal after touchdown," or extra point, had to be attempted from the spot where the goal line had been crossed. If it was crossed in the far corner of the field, the kicker had to line up at an extreme angle to the goal posts. The rules permitted a team to avoid this by granting them a free kick from the end zone back into the field of play. If they caught the punt, they could then attempt the extra point from that spot. If they muffed it, the ball went over to the other side.

One of the great early punters was Princeton's Alexander Moffat, younger brother of Henry Moffat who had kicked off to start the first Princeton-Yale game in 1875. The diminutive Moffat, who weighed less than 140 pounds and was nicknamed "Teeny-bits," is credited with perfecting both the drop kick and the spiral punt. In 1883, he kicked thirty-two field goals in fifteen games, including four in a single game against Harvard, two with his left foot and two with his right.

The eighties were also the last decade for thrilling, open-field running. At the end of the 1880 Harvard-Yale game, Yale's captain, Robert W. Watson, ran one hundred yards for a touchdown, which did not count in the final score (a 1-0 Yale victory) because time expired before Yale could kick a goal. Yale's Wyllys Terry ran 115 yards for a touchdown against Wesleyan, a record that would stand forever once the field was shortened.

One who could run as well as kick was Henry Ward Beecher, Yale's captain and grandson of the famous minister, who scored nineteen touchdowns in 1887 and kicked thirty-three extra points. The elder Beecher became an ardent Yale rooter, declaring from his pulpit following the 1883 Princeton game, "I always did hate Princeton, but I took notice there was not a coward on either side, although I thank God that Yale beat [them]."[9] It was said that he gave his grandson a dollar for each touchdown he scored, which induced Beecher's teammates to hand him the ball as often as possible. Beecher returned the favor by using the money to buy everyone champagne.

An even more famous run was Henry "Tillie" Lamar's scamper for Princeton against Yale in 1885, which has been called "one of the most celebrated plays of the nineteenth century."[10]

Princeton began the game with a running attack, while Yale punted frequently in hopes of gaining better field position, but midway through the first half the teams switched tactics. Shortly before halftime, Beecher fielded a punt for Yale at his own forty-five-yard line and ran it up the sideline for an apparent touchdown. Showing remarkable impartiality before a seething crowd, Camp, who was referee, nullified his own team's score because Beecher had stepped out of bounds. Yale kicked a field goal instead and led, 5-0.

There the score stood until almost the end of the game. With less than five minutes to go, Yale was stuck deep in its own end. Uncertain whether to kill time by running into the line or risk punting the ball away, captain Frank Peters went to the sideline to seek advice from Ray Tompkins, a former Yale player who now helped with the coaching. "Oh, kick it and have some fun," Tompkins advised.

G. A. Watkinson sent a long kick that caromed off the chest of a Princeton back, Henry "Kid" Toler. Lamar fielded it on a bounce at about his own twenty-yard line "and with a peculiar loping motion, darted through the oncoming group of Yale forwards." Reversing field, Lamar flashed along the sideline toward the end zone. He had three men to beat. The first two, Beecher and Watkinson, tried to squeeze him out of bounds, but Lamar dodged at the last second and sent them crashing into each other. As he neared the goal line, Peters, the last Yale defender, closed the gap. "Peters leaped, but Lamar with a reserve of speed leaped out of Peters' arms and crossed the line for a touchdown, having covered eighty yards in his flight."[11]

Yale argued that Lamar had stepped out of bounds, but Camp ruled against his own school again. Princeton still trailed, 5-4, but kicked the extra point to win, 6-5. Fans rushed onto the field and ripped Lamar's jersey off his back for souvenirs. It was to be the only game Yale would lose from 1881 until they played Princeton again in 1889.

Notwithstanding the dominance of the Big Three, as the triumvirate of Yale, Princeton, and Harvard were coming to be known, other Ivy colleges also played football during the 1880s.

"Like the tide," one historian has written, "Columbia continued to come and go" from the ranks of intercollegiate football.[12] Having dropped out of the IFA in 1877, it petitioned for readmission in 1880. It was accepted but was subject to dismissal by a simple majority vote. Columbia won only three games over the next four years and lost eleven before letting its membership in the association lapse and dropping the sport again. "The pleasures of the metropolis have far greater attractions than the exhilarating sport of the football field," claimed the student paper, thus making what has been Columbia's excuse for more than a century.[13]

Football had a hard time competing with baseball at Brown. "Is there any good reason why our men should not sit together and cheer together instead of dividing into four or five small groups, each keeping different time from the others?" asked the *Brunonian*.[14] After fielding a team in 1880 that lost the only game it played, they did not compete again until 1886 when they scored a rather embarrassing 70-0 win over Providence high school. Varsity football then lapsed again until 1889. In the meantime, John Heisman, who went on to become one of the greatest college coaches, grew bored with playing on Brown club teams and transferred to Penn. "I was irreparably crushed," he later wrote, "to learn that from a football standpoint I had chosen my college badly."[15]

As at other colleges, Dartmouth students had been playing their own ball game for decades, an idiosyncratic hybrid of soccer and rugby known as "Old Division" in which teams of seniors and sophomores took on the freshmen and juniors. The game grew so popular on the isolated campus that it retarded the development of football, which was viewed as an affectation imported by "those students who came from the cities and large preparatory schools."[16]

Inspired by the Harvard-Yale rivalry, however, a few students erected a set of goal posts in 1876, and four years later a freshman named Clarence Howland formed the Dartmouth Football Association, borrowing uniforms from Princeton. One imagines these first Dartmouth football players scrimmaging in orange and black, although students had claimed green as their color in 1867. Given the remoteness of the campus and the faculty's unwillingness to let the team out of class to travel, the problem from the start was finding someone to play. So it was not until a year later, in 1881, that Dartmouth competed in its first-ever game, a loss to Amherst. A rematch at Springfield (the faculty having relented on travel), which was scheduled for Thanksgiving Day, was postponed because of snow, though the teams played a brief exhibition for fans who had braved the elements to attend.

Fortified by a daily training table diet of roast beef and "two mugs of Bass's Ale," Dartmouth's team was thriving, but campus support for football continued to be uncertain. Their first victory came against McGill in 1882 in an odd, thirteen-men-a-side match, but a few weeks later Harvard demolished them, 53-0, the most lopsided score in intercollegiate history up to that time. "Rugby Is Dead!" shouted a campus editorial, which went on to recommend that "if there is any other game that Dartmouth can play better than football, it would be well to encourage it." [17]

Other students thought they could drum up support on campus by paying national powerhouses to come to Hanover. What interest Yale's 113-0 whipping of Dartmouth in 1884 might have generated cannot be said, for the sport was dropped altogether the following year. It returned in 1886 and shortly thereafter Dartmouth was invited to join Amherst, MIT, the Stevens Institute, Wesleyan, and Trinity in what was called the Northern Foot-ball League. The Green tied for the championship in their second season and won it outright in 1889.

Cornell became the last Ivy school to play an intercollegiate football game, making its debut in 1887 against Union College. Like almost everyone else, Cornell students had invented their own game, which they had demonstrated for a visiting British member of parliament in 1870. Two other things they had established were the college colors, carnelian (or cornelian) and white, which first appeared at President White's installation ceremonies in 1869, and the famous Cornell yell, "Cornell-i-ell-i-ell-i-ell, Fol-de-rol-de-roll-roll-roll!" which was first shouted at a crew race in 1875 to imitate a Yale cheer. [18]

Most athletes, however, received little encouragement from White, who liked to boast in later years that he had never even seen a game of baseball, football or basketball. It was hard to avoid football as the matches were played directly beneath his office window, but White drew the shade and stuck to his desk.

Nevertheless, by their third season, Cornell posted a 7-2 record, including a 20-0 shutout of Columbia. College officials, however, remained skeptical. One noted disapprovingly that, "The football team has been both weak in its play and strong in its tendency to noise and profanity during the games. It looks as if a movement may be made to quash them." [19]

Students were also ambitious at Penn. After six straight losing seasons, the Quakers' first breakthrough came in 1884 when they tripped Harvard at Cambridge, 4-0. In 1885 Penn and Wesleyan were admitted to the IFA, replacing Columbia and Harvard. The team got its first coach, Frank Doyle, a year later, and by 1888 Penn football players were required to live together in what was the first athletic dormitory.

Such emphasis on gridiron success rubbed the Big Three the wrong way, although it was easy for them to take such a position given their own status. Penn grew more aggressive in pursuing good players, scouring the high schools, and even finding sinecures for older players in its graduate schools. Certainly, Penn was eager for attention wherever it could get it. In 1889 they played an exhibition game inside Philadelphia's Academy of Music against a team comprised mostly of Princeton players, and another game a year later against Rutgers in Madison Square Garden. These were the first football games ever played indoors or at night, but they did not start a trend.

In the meantime, though, Penn and everyone else were just cannon fodder for the Big Three. Yale's cumulative record from 1883 to 1892 was 112-3-2, one hundred of those victories coming by shutout. During this same period, Princeton's combined record was 95-8-2 with 76 shutouts, and Harvard's was 92-14-0 with 72 shutouts. When Walter Camp named his first All-American team in 1889, five of the eleven players were from Yale, three were from Harvard, and three were from Princeton. He was not just being provincial.

Harvard, Princeton, and Yale played longer schedules than they had ever played before or would ever play again, often squeezing in minor games on Wednesday afternoons, and all games except those against their Big Three rivals were played at home. Harvard played fourteen games in 1886 and Yale played fifteen in 1889, including three against Wesleyan (wins of 38-0, 63-5, and 52-0), two against Williams (36-0 and 70-0) and even one against a noncollege team, the Crescent Athletic Club (a mere 18-0 victory). Princeton also fattened up on the weak. In 1885, for example, they won all nine games they played, seven of them by fifty-seven points or more. Some of the slaughters were embarrassing, such as a 115-0 win over the University of Virginia in 1890, a 108-0 win over Johns Hopkins in 1888, and the all-time record, 140-0 over Lafayette in 1884.

These were not just the three best teams in the country, they were really the only three good teams, and this simply highlighted the huge disparity in college football talent. Penn's 1886 record provides an example. Though regarded as a good team, one that finished with a respectable 9-7 record, in consecutive weeks the Quakers lost to Princeton, 28-6; beat Rutgers, 65-0; lost to Yale, 75-0; beat Vineland College, 96-0; lost to Lehigh, 28-0; and lost to Harvard, 28-0.

Already acknowledged as the country's academic elite, the Big Three were growing used to preeminence on the gridiron, as well. Feelings continued to run strongly between them. At Harvard's bicentennial celebration in 1886, Oliver Wendell Holmes, Sr., read one of his last poems, which included a dig at Princeton's rough play. Princeton President James McCosh took offense at Holmes's crack and caught an early train home. At the dedication of Harvard's new football field a few years later, H. L. Higginson, a prominent Crimson booster, tried to calm passions by declaring, "Princeton is not wicked; Yale is not base." [20] Some of his listeners must have needed reminding.

Although the Harvard-Yale game had not yet reached the significance of Princeton-Yale, there was much high feeling and a growing sense of tradition carried over from crew and baseball. One such tradition began at the 1884 game. On his way into the stadium that day, Harvard freshman Frederick Plummer bought a maroon pennant with a black "H" in the middle, which he waved to cheer on the team. Plummer attended fifty-nine consecutive Harvard-Yale games and waved the flag at each one. Upon his death, the flag was passed down to another rabid Harvard fan and has been ever since. Now in the hands of its seventh "curator," the Rev. Harold Sedgwick, the pennant, which has been worn away to the size of a pocket-handkerchief, is still waved (albeit very carefully) at Harvard-Yale games today.

But on the gridiron, at least, the Big Three were still really the Big Two. Princeton and Yale remained the Nebraska and Florida State of their age, and so under the IFA rules, their game in New York each November continued to decide the national championship. Throughout the decade, the Tigers' tiffs with the Elis were the sport's most important games, and often its most exciting, resulting in as much gamesmanship off the field as on it.

Things grew so contentious between the teams that again they could not break a deadlock. The 1884 game, another Thanksgiving affair at the Polo Grounds, ended in a state of limbo. Yale led, 6-4, in the second half when the teams got diverted by so many long disputes over fouls and rulings that the referee, Ralph M. Appleton of Harvard, finally threw up his hands, announced "I resign," and walked off the field. It took half an hour to coax him back, by which time it had grown too dark to finish the game. At a hurried meeting that night at the Fifth Avenue Hotel, traditional Yale headquarters, Appleton showed up wearing full evening dress and an overcoat trimmed in sealskin. He was on his way to the theater, but stopped long enough to declare the match a draw. No championship was awarded.

Matters were even worse in 1886. Despite the IFA bylaw requiring that the Yale-Princeton game be played at the Polo Grounds—neutral territory—Princeton insisted both that the Thanksgiving Day game be played at Princeton (claiming that the faculty would not permit a game in New York) and that a Princeton alumnus act as referee, threatening not to play unless they prevailed. "They've got to play with a Princeton referee," one undergraduate was quoted as saying. "We've had too many games stolen from us."[21]

Yale reluctantly accepted but found only one of the referees Princeton proposed, Tracy Harris, acceptable. When someone whispered to Harris a few hours before game time that Yale thought he was biased, Harris refused to serve. Princeton tried to prevail upon Yale to accept one of its other candidates, which included Alex Moffat, but the Elis smelled a setup. All was chaos and the kickoff was delayed an hour and a half as a packed house wondered if the title game would be played at all. Although Harris was rumored to be in the stands, Princeton failed to produce him, which Yale partisans said was a trick to force them to accept Moffat. Finally, Harris appeared and was persuaded to act.

Compounding the unpleasantness, conditions were terrible. By midafternoon there was a driving rainstorm and gusting winds that soaked the crowd of five thousand fans who had crammed a Princeton field that could not accommodate nearly that many. So keen was the interest in the contest that Harvard and Pennsylvania had played their own game in Philadelphia early in the morning in order that players and fans could catch the train to Princeton in time for the kickoff.

It was after three before the game finally got under way. "The Yale men were not in a pleasant humor, and the Princeton men were not feeling particularly amiable," wrote the *New York Times* correspondent. "The ground was like a dish of butter and that contributed to the general tumblefication."[22] No one could get any traction, so the game degenerated into a shoving match or worse. When one Yale runner was tackled, "his blue stockings described sulphurous circles in the air and he plunged headlong into the mud, plowing a big furrow in it with his nose, while the Princeton men jumped as high as they could and came down on him with all the weight of their avoirdupois and theology."

Even by the standards of the day, which were low, the game was brutal. The *Times* reporter noted chillingly that "a person standing two-thirds of the length of the ground away from the players could hear the spat, spat of fists on faces constantly. One Princeton man on the rush line threw down the man opposite him and deliberately tried to kick him in the head." There were two long delays when Princeton argued over fouls.

Thanks to those holdups on top of the late start, it was once again impossible to finish the game before darkness set in and so a wretched day was capped by a draw. Worse, the rain had gotten even heavier, sending everyone to the exits wet and disgusted. "Yale and Princeton played football on the grounds of the latter college yesterday," the *Times* reported, "and more was done to make the game unpopular than in all the previous history of football in this country. The utter folly of undertaking to play a championship match in such a place as Princeton was demonstrated to the satisfaction of everyone save the Faculty and undergraduates of the old Presbyterian institution."

Without a winner, without even an official game (the incomplete contest was declared a "no game"), another emergency meeting was called at the Fifth Avenue Hotel to determine the champion. Camp expressed the hope that Princeton would magnanimously offer Yale the title on the grounds that they had been winning when the game was called, but of course he hoped in vain. Once again, the association decided to award no one the title.

By the end of the decade, though, the two schools had assembled powerhouses and seemed willing at last to settle matters on the field. Yale's 1888 squad was the most dominant college team of all time. They won all thirteen games they played and outscored their opponents, 694-0. Only the Princeton and Harvard games were close at all, and the latter was won by forfeit. A story, perhaps apocryphal, is that their captain, William "Pa" Corbin, called the squad together at the Yale goal line after their final game and made the underclassmen swear they would never let their end zone be defiled.

This was the first real team of stars, and like all great teams their tempera-
ments and abilities complemented each other. Corbin, at center, was their quiet
leader. Rather vainly, he wore a handlebar mustache and bushy side burns, which
proved too tempting a target in skirmishes on the line. In the 1887 Harvard game,
Corbin several times complained to Walter Camp, "Mr. Referee—this Harvard
man is pulling my whiskers!"[23] He got his revenge, though. Twice in that game,
rather than snap the ball back to the quarterback, Corbin kicked it forward,
picked it up, and ran with it, the second time for a touchdown.

Kid Wallace, who played one end, was the team clown. He came from a
wealthy family, "but delighted in being a brawler of the Pier 6 type."[24] At the
opposite end was Amos Alonzo Stagg, a twenty-seven-year-old divinity student
and star of the baseball team who would become one of the great figures in collegiate football history. He was a stickler for discipline and clean living—sometimes too clean. As an undergraduate, Stagg tried subsisting on crackers and
water and developed beriberi. He was so much respected (or feared) that years
later, Fritz Crisler, Princeton's coach, stubbed out a cigarette in the palm of his
hand when he saw Stagg approaching. Yet on the gridiron, notwithstanding his
religious training, Stagg perfected a vicious head slap that was described as
"Stagg's Ministerial Uppercut."

Forced to give up the ministry because he stammered, Stagg became a coach,
and paced the sidelines for the next seventy years at several schools, finally ending
his run as kicking coach at Stockton Junior College in California when he was
ninety-eight. He is credited with inventing the tackling dummy, introducing the
huddle, and perfecting the T formation. Incredibly, in 1943 the Associated Press
named Stagg its Coach of the Year at the age of eighty-one. When he died at the
age of 102, the NCAA named the Division III championship game the Amos
Alonzo Stagg Bowl in his honor.

In the Yale backfield was a freshman halfback from Tennessee named Lee
"Bum" McClung, who later served as treasurer of the United States. McClung was
superstitious and against Princeton in 1889 wore the same knit cap Tillie Lamar
had worn against Yale when he made his famous touchdown run. Anchoring the
line at right guard was George Woodruff, a Phi Beta Kappa student who also
threw the hammer for the track team and was the strongest man on campus. As a
baby, he had been carried to Nebraska in a covered wagon and amused his college
classmates by arriving for his freshman year wearing a coonskin cap.

The greatest of them all, though, was Yale's left guard, William Walter
Heffelfinger. His teammates called him "Heff" but everyone else called him
"Pudge," the nickname he had acquired as a farmboy in Minnesota. Heffelfinger
is remembered as a mountain, and by contemporary standards, he was. He stood
six foot three and weighed 188 pounds as a freshman but by his senior year had
bulked up to about 200, at a time when the rest of the line averaged only 176
pounds.

By all accounts, he was a terrific lineman who anchored Elis squads that lost only two games during his four years. Heffelfinger is credited with pioneering the "pulling guard" play in which the guard leads interference for the ball carrier around the end. He preferred to await the snap standing upright on the line rather than hunched over with his fingers on the ground, a technique he said better enabled him to read the play's development. "I hit my man with a shoulder lunge on attack and used my hands to start his head in the direction I wanted to move him," he explained years later.[25] When Princeton tried to run their V wedge against Yale, Heffelfinger got a running start and vaulted the line, hitting the man at the apex of the wedge in the chest feet first. That, he said, took the steam right out of the play.

Camp named him to the first All-American squad in 1889 and he made almost every All-Time All-American team thereafter. In the 1930s, the Touchdown Club of New York voted him the greatest college football player of all time. Heffelfinger was also the original Old Grad, a raconteur and author of books and articles with glorified titles such as *This Was Football* and *Nobody Put Me on My Back*. For years after graduation, Heffelfinger went back to campus to coach the line and swap stories the week before the Harvard and Princeton games. In a 1916 scrimmage, at the age of forty-nine, he broke one Yale starter's ribs, and was still playing in charity games when he was sixty-five years old.

Yale and Princeton each entered their championship game in 1888 undefeated. Princeton, too, had won its first ten games by shutouts and had easily beaten Harvard the week before, 18-6. Neither side could score a touchdown, but the Elis won, 10-0, on two field goals by their kicker, Billy Bull, the second a thirty-seven-yarder at a sharp angle with only a minute left to play.

They got a rematch the following year. Yale rushed through its schedule, 15-0, and carried a thirty-eight-game winning streak into the showdown. Princeton entered the finale with a perfect 8-0 record.

In the days before helmets, Princeton players grew their hair long to protect their heads. Critics mocked their "chrysanthemum" hairdo, but other teams soon copied it as players around the country wore shoulder-length locks until Yale changed the fashion by winning the title in 1895 with short hair. The mop-headed Tigers of 1889 were led by a few legends of their own. Their captain was Hector Cowan, playing in his fourth year on the varsity. He had graduated the previous summer ranked fourth in his class but badly wanted another chance to beat Yale and enrolled in the Princeton Theological Seminary in order to remain in town. Cowan was solidly built, five feet, ten inches tall and 189 pounds, but could run the hundred-yard dash in eleven seconds. As was the case with many of the young men he played with and against, he had never played football when he entered college, yet still scored seventy-nine touchdowns in his career.

Like Stagg, Cowan played rough but his harshest profanity was "Oh, sugar!" or "By Dad!" Once when an opponent tried punching him on the line,

Cowan is said to have advised him, "Keep your hands for pounding the Bible, don't be sticking them in my face." [26] Cowan, too, was on that first All-American team, was later voted to the All-Time All-American team, and was a charter member of the College Football Hall of Fame.

Joining him was eighteen-year-old Edgar Allan Poe, grandnephew of the poet. Poe was a Phi Beta Kappa student, and though he stood only five-foot-four and weighed just 138 pounds, he was named quarterback on the first All-American team and led the Tigers to a 32-2-1 record during his three seasons. A young lady attending the Princeton-Yale game at around this time asked her escort, "It he related to the great Edgar Allan Poe?"

"He *is* the great Edgar Allan Poe," came the reply. [27]

The team had more than its share of reprobates, as well, most prominently running back Knowlton Ames, nicknamed "Snake" because of his shifty running style; Ben "Sport" Donnelly, whom Heffelfinger observed was the only man he had ever played against who "could slug you and at the same time keep his eye on the ball"; and Walter "Monte" Cash, who had played for Penn as a law student the previous year. Cash had dropped out at the end of football season, but returned east from his home in Wyoming at Princeton's invitation to play against Harvard, arriving on campus with a deck of monte cards—hence the nickname—and two pistols. When the faculty tried to explain to him that flunking out would be a disgrace, Cash is said to have replied, "It may be in the East, but we don't think much of a little thing like that out West." [28]

Harvard, however, did, and provoked an acrimonious and very public dispute over Cash's eligibility that marred the 1889 season. Yale and Wesleyan had called for a special meeting of the IFA's Graduate Advisory Committee to do something about tightening the eligibility rules. Walter Camp drew up a code that required all football players to be bona fide students who had never received payment for playing football and regularly went to class. To Princeton, this was nothing more than an attempt to wreck their team. They took a swipe at Yale, Harvard, and Penn by filing a counterproposal barring all postgraduates and students in professional schools. When Camp's proposal prevailed, Harvard immediately tried to exclude Cash, Ames, and thirteen other members of Princeton's team. The Tigers tried to retaliate, though they could only support challenges against four members of the Crimson.

There matters stood as the date for the Harvard-Princeton game approached until Wesleyan forged a compromise by moving to table Harvard's challenges. Princeton promptly withdrew its own challenges and the game went on.

Perhaps Ames' pride was wounded, for he played well. Harvard led Princeton 15-10 at halftime before the Snake took control, rushing for five touchdowns in a 41-15 thrashing. His exploits, and the recent controversy, were immortalized in a clever "dirge" written afterwards by an anonymous Harvard student, titled "The Ghost of Poe's Raven," which began:

> *Once upon a field momentous, while I faced a team portentous,*
> *Making many a slug and tackle followed by a flow of gore,*
> *While the prejudiced ascetic, jaundiced, glum and unpoetic,*
> *Damned all manly sports athletic; suddenly I heard a roar,*
> *And a ball went whizzing by me, whizzing as I'd seen before,*
> *Only* Ames, *and nothing more.* [29]

Whipped on the field and stymied in its attempts to tighten eligibility rules, Harvard again withdrew from the IFA and refused to play Princeton for the next five years.

The stage, though, was set for Princeton's showdown with Yale, which was played in New York on the swanky grounds of the Berkeley Athletic Club, situated at 155th Street on the banks of the Harlem River. A club brochure described it as "an opulent and eminently successful athletic club, with a membership of several hundred of the 'best people' of Gotham." [30] It claimed to be able to accommodate twenty thousand spectators for football and the field was described as "finely turfed and rolled, and presents a beautiful picture." More important, "beneath the ground are 12,000 feet of drainage, so that the path and the football field are dry a few minutes after a rain."

That was false advertising. Once again, the weather for the game was miserable and the field was a morass, with pools of water up to ten inches deep at midfield and at the goal lines. Carpenters, who had also not finished building the grandstands, tried to soak up the moisture by strewing the field with sawdust, but it was no use.

To make conditions even worse, the Thanksgiving Day contest was the second half of a double-header. Penn and Wesleyan battled on it first, tearing up the field even more. Police forced the crowd to exit and reenter for the second game, but the weather-depleted spectators had to stand on the muddy sidelines because the Club had not received permission from the city building inspectors to use the bleachers they had quickly thrown up. Hundreds were still filing in when the game began and many, men and women alike, shimmied over the fence or took perches in the surrounding trees.

Princeton deployed its new alignment, a dangerous trick called the V wedge. Nine Princeton players formed a blocking wedge in the shape of an arrowhead, with the ball carrier tucked in behind and a last man blocking behind him in order to ward off attack from that side. There was nothing subtle about it, just weight and brawn concentrated on breaking through a single point in the defense. It was effective but it was dangerous because once the V got its momentum going they rolled over everything in their path. On the muddy field, however, it bogged down (this was the play Heffelfinger stopped with his flying leap) and the game became a punting duel. Princeton's center, William George, was taken from the field with torn knee ligaments and Bum McClung was laid out by Poe. Ames made one long run but missed the thirty-five-yard field goal and the first half ended without a score.

In the second half, Yale's captain, Billy Rhodes, was tossed out of the game for slugging. Ames made a run deep into Yale territory only to fumble. Later, he tried to a field goal, but the waterlogged ball did not carry. Instead it rolled into the end zone, a live ball, where three Yale defenders dove desperately for it. Princeton's Ralph Warren pounced on it for the touchdown and a lead.

The game was still close, but late in the second half Princeton scored again. Although quarterbacks called out signals, they did not yet indicate the snap by yelling "hike," but instead nudged or even pinched the center. With less than a minute to play and Yale pushed back on its own five-yard line, quarterback Bill Wurtenberg settled under the center, Burt Hanson, then turned around to check that his backs were lined up correctly. According to legend, Princeton's guard, Joseph Thomas, who had been studying Wurtenberg, swiftly reached across the line. "He pinched where a pinch had special significance. Immediately the ball was put in play." [31] It bounced off Wurtenberg's leg and into a puddle. Cowan dove on it, then pulled himself across the goal line for a second touchdown, dragging several Yale men with him.

Yale could take some small consolation at the debut that season of Handsome Dan, an English bulldog. Dan had been purchased by a freshman, Andrew B. Graves, from a New Haven blacksmith for five dollars. Graves began taking the dog to watch practice and it was soon dubbed Yale's mascot. Others were not so charitable. "In personal appearance, he seemed like a cross between an alligator and a horned frog, and he was called handsome by the metaphysicians under the law of compensation," wrote the *Hartford Courant*. Some respected Dan's pedigree, though, for he won first prize at a New York City dog show in 1891.

One of Yale's favorite tricks was to ask Dan to "Speak to Harvard," whereupon the dog would dutifully go berserk barking. "He was always taken to games on a leash," wrote the *Philadelphia Press*, "and the Harvard football team for years owed its continued existence to the fact that the leash held." Upon his death in 1897, Handsome Dan's remains were stuffed, and can still be seen inside a display case in the Yale museum.

By the 1880s, football violence had come to concern more than just nannyish college officials. Newspaper reports about the audible "spat, spat of fists on faces constantly" were hardly isolated. The Harvard *Advocate* casually noted after the 1881 Yale game that, "Yale did not try to maim our men as much as she usually does…. Still, there can be no excuse for the use of teeth in football." [32] Five years later, Amos Alonzo Stagg related similar depredations by the Crimson: "Harvard was outclassed and roughed the Blue eleven up to offset the 29 to 4 score. George Woodruff brought home a broken nose from Cambridge; George Carter, guard, came out of the game with a cut over the eye needing eight stitches; and Burke, who had beaten me out for right tackle, was a campus curiosity for several days. Both his eyes were closed and his lips were mangled and hideously swollen. He had had the bad luck to play opposite Remington, the Harvard champion heavy-weight boxer." [33]

Some of the fouls bordered on the homicidal. During the Harvard-Yale game of 1880, played on a rain-soaked field in Boston, one Crimson player accused a Yale man of trying to drown him by holding his head underwater in a puddle after play had stopped. Even Camp, who was still a member of the team at the time, acknowledged later that the charge was "not without some ground." [34]

Student ball games had always been bloody, but this was different. For one thing, this was no longer a rollicking campus free-for-all, but an increasingly formal, organized affair in which brutality had become an established part of strategy. For another, teams were now playing a dozen or more games a year instead of only one or two. Moreover, thousands of screaming people were now paying money to come watch the mayhem.

This was not the image college officials wanted to present, and to be fair, not what they thought was in the best interests of the students in their charge. By the late nineteenth century, the modern American research university was beginning to emerge as places where, in Lord Bryce's words, "teaching that puts a man abreast of the fullest and most exact knowledge of the time is given in a range of subjects covering all the great departments of intellectual life." [35] College presidents such as Charles Eliot at Harvard, James McCosh at Princeton, and Seth Low at Columbia, along with other progressive educators around the country were trying to build a new empire of the mind, based on rational, scientific principles. Bear-baiting spectacles on autumn Saturdays had no place in their vision.

Yale's resistance to most football reforms owed much to Camp's influence, but much too to the influence of its president, Noah Porter, who, in stark contrast to Eliot, liked things the way they had been, both in and out of the recitation hall.

Although football came in for a lot of criticism in the press and from the pulpits and lecture halls, it is far from clear that sports fans minded at all. Public positions on the matter were nicely delineated in a flurry of letters to the *New York Times* following the violent Princeton-Yale game of 1886. On one hand someone wrote "it makes me blush for the colleges that would send out such a bunch of roughs to pommel each other in the mud on such a day for the pleasure of the thing." [36] On the other hand, observed another reader, "Is it such a terrible thing for Tom or Harry to come home with a 'black' eye or a broken nose? His fond mother says: 'Oh, those horrid Yale men. What brutes they are,' or 'What common roughs are those Princeton fellows;' and Tom's father says: 'You young rascal.' But all alone and by himself he smiles a grim smile and recalls his own fighting college days and gives Tom an extra hundred for Xmas." [37]

There were two matters at issue: violence promoted by the rules (such as the V wedge), and simple dirty play. Both could be legislated out of existence, but college football officials in the 1880s turned their attentions mostly toward the latter while permitting the former to grow even worse. The efforts of the Rules Committee of the late nineteenth century may stand, ultimately, as a monument to the futility of trying to outlaw something the participants do not entirely want to give up.

The scrimmage, which was supposed to redress some of the rugby violence, unintentionally made other kinds of violence worse by enabling players to ram each other head on rather than mosh around in a scrum. Camp had pushed unsuccessfully for a neutral zone between the opposing lines. Without one, defensive linemen awaiting the snap routinely tried to poke the ball away from the center— one of the reasons centers began to hold it with their hands. Sparring before the snap by both offense and defense (here was the "spat, spat" of fists on faces the reporter had heard) was so blatant that one referee looking down the line said it resembled seven pairs of windmills.

Another horrific wrinkle in the rules was something descriptively called a "maul-in-goal." Until 1889, a touchdown did not count until the ball was physically touched down on the ground beyond the goal line. If the ball carrier landed on his back, for example, or crossed the line standing, any opposing players who were in on the tackle could do anything they could to take the ball from him before he could touch it down. As Stagg recalled in his memoirs, "It was strictly a private fight between the man with the ball and the man or men who had their hands on him when he crossed the goal. No one else could join in." [38] It was a fight stemming from a maul-in-goal that led to the declaration of a "no-game" in the 1884 Harvard-Princeton contest.

Throughout the first half of the 1880s, new penalties were adopted directing the referee to eject a player who had been warned twice about rough or illegal play. As Harvard was quick to point out, though, the "three strikes" rule in effect permitted players two free punches. Following Princeton's loss to Yale in 1882, the *Princetonian* editorialized:

> *The match on Thanksgiving revealed still more clearly than ever before the methods of our sister college. You may call it rowdyism, or anything you choose. It is simply this: Play a rough game—so far we all agree—but secondly, and above all, make as many fouls as possible without being warned three times. In other words, Yale would have us to understand that it is fair to do what is prohibited by the rules, if, by any means, the referee can be deceived and the player escape the penalty of a foul.... Here then, is Yaleism—an underhanded and constant evasion of the rules.* [39]

In an attempt to put a stop to the constant and lengthy arguing over fouls, another penalty was introduced that provided for a forfeit if either side refused to resume play within five minutes of being ordered to do so by the referee.

Some had become concerned about the officiating itself. The first officiating "crews," as they would later be called, consisted of a referee, whose job was to enforce the rules, and four (later two) umpires, who were nothing more than representatives of the competing schools, whose job was to argue their case to the referee "like an opposing pair of football lawyers."[40] It was not unknown for umpires deliberately to try to distract the referee while their team was committing a foul. One reform was to require that all officials be alumni of one of the competing colleges, demonstrating a telling if perhaps misplaced reliance in the honor of gentlemen.

This became too much for Harvard, and after the 1884 season, the faculty abolished intercollegiate football and the school withdrew from the Football Association. As early as 1883, Harvard had become concerned, as its athletic committee put it, "that the game of foot ball, as then played in intercollegiate games, had become brutal and dangerous, and that it involved not only danger to life and limb, but what was much more serious, danger to the manly spirit and to the disposition for fair play on the part of the contestants."[41] In the spirit of scientific inquiry, a group of faculty made a point of observing all Harvard's games in 1884. The brutality disgusted them, including "fighting with closed fists" and cries from the crowd of "Slug him!" "Knock him down!" "Break his neck!" and "Kill him!"[42] They complained that the rules rewarded dirty play because "it is profitable when it succeeds and it is unlikely to be detected by the referee."[43] Furthermore, the faculty declared, providing for the expulsion of players appeared "to allow of no other inference than that the spirit of fair play is not expected to govern the players, but that on the contrary the spirit of sharpers and of roughs has to be guarded against."[44]

Crimson undergraduates, for their part, believed they knew what their team's problem was and it wasn't passivity, but size. An item in the *Lampoon* made the point with withering sarcasm: "There is the usual grumbling about our foot-ball prospects, but we wish it to be understood that Harvard will be represented by a team this year that would do credit to any kindergarten in the country. The men are light and portable, so that they can be packed in a bandbox and expressed to any quarter at a very trifling expense. After a good deal of hard training it may be possible to send the eleven by mail, provided permission can be obtained to send live bait through that channel."[45]

Harvard's withdrawal confronted the IFA with yet another crisis. Coupled with Columbia's withdrawal the year before, it left only Princeton and Yale as members of what was supposed to be the sport's governing body. Camp tried to coax Harvard back by jiggering some more with the rules. He reduced the number of warnings for unnecessary roughness to one and began to award points to the other team for slugging, delaying the game, or deliberately jumping offsides. Frederic Remington, Camp's old teammate, chided him about such changes saying, "You're not going to civilize the only real thing we have left, are you?"[46] By

1887, football captains at all IFA schools signed a pledge "to use all means in our power to coach our teams to stop holding in the rush line, slugging and all other objectionable features."

This proved enough to satisfy Harvard, which returned to the fold in 1886 after a year's absence. Ironically, the brutality problem only got worse after Harvard's return, and previous efforts to tame the sport undone, thanks to two more rules changes in 1888.

The first legalized tackling below the waist and above the knees; the second prohibited offensive linemen from blocking with their hands or extended arms. As any high school coach will attest, high tackling is ineffective; the way to bring a runner down is to hit him low. Prohibiting offensive linemen from blocking with their hands made it more effective for them to block with their bodies, and hence to bunch the line close together. The two changes had the unintended effect of ending the era of open field running that Camp had always favored. Five yards for a first down was not a lot to make and was more effectively gained by bulling through the line rather than dancing around it.

Mass offense had to be defended with mass defense, further increasing the number of injuries. At its most extreme, in the "turtle back" play of the 1890s, only the center remained on the line of scrimmage. The remaining nine men were set up in the backfield surrounding the ball carrier. Laterals disappeared from the playbook. If the runner did try a sweep around the line, he was now likely to do it with the guards pulling to run interference.

In May 1888, the Harvard Board of Overseers voted to curb some of the abuses in intercollegiate football by restricting all future games to Cambridge, New Haven, or "such other New England city of town as the Committee on Athletics shall from time to time designate."[47] (They pointedly did not include Princeton.) By keeping the games on campus, the overseers thought they could eliminate the rough element that attended them in the big cities, little appreciating the rough element on the field.

Attitudes toward physical training in general were changing, as the Overseers discovered when they appointed a committee to examine the broader state of athletics at the college. Using the then-novel sociological device of a questionnaire, the committee surveyed about one thousand undergraduates. Their report, issued just six weeks later, provides a remarkable insight into student opinion.

Many educators still believed that athletics, particularly football, were dangerous to participants and wasteful for those who watched. Typical in this respect was Brown's president, Ezekiel Robinson, who stated in 1884, "As matters now stand, only a small portion of our students receive any personal benefit from our athletic sports. Those who take part in them merely to fit themselves for the match games, too often run into hurtful extremes; others, engaging in them fitfully and unintelligently, fail of the good they might otherwise receive; while the majority, content with merely looking on and applauding, get no real benefit whatever from them." [48]

At Harvard at least, the situation was quite different. The university had extensive athletic facilities, though still not enough, the committee found, and students were taking advantage of them. Exercise had become a regular part of undergraduate life. Indeed, 80 percent of the respondents stated that they exercised between one and three hours a day, primarily by working out at the gymnasium, walking, rowing or playing tennis, baseball, and football. Students were healthier and more active than ever before. The report asserted that there were already about a hundred students on campus who were stronger than the strongest student had been just eight years earlier. [49]

Not only did athletics benefit participants, spectators benefited, too. "Many students who do not consider themselves especially interested in athletics," the committee wrote, "express the pleasure which they have in witnessing athletic sports; they find they are thus drawn away from their books when they need rest, and in many instances led to take exercise themselves. These and others believe that if athletic sports were done away with, the energy which is now expended on them would be expended in ways not at all beneficial to the students, and probably very disagreeable to the authorities of the College and the people of Cambridge." [50] As for taking students away from their work, the questionnaire showed that roughly three-quarters had not missed any classes to attend an intercollegiate athletic match. [51] These findings helped persuade the committee that athletics, including football, could be reformed and gave ammunition to those who would fight attempts to abolish the sport in coming years.

The debate over football violence, like the broader national debate over the character of American society in the decades after the Civil War, was centered around the Ivy colleges. That debate in turn shaped the philosophy of what came to be the Ivy League.

To many, extreme physical violence in football seemed increasingly anachronistic in a world ever more dominated by science and by the ordered routine of the industrial business world, but it was precisely that anachronistic quality that others found so valuable. The workplace was becoming bureaucratized while the home, like the church, was teaching the wrong values. "American Protestantism was becoming feminized... stressing feminine values like humility and meekness, and was unable to reach out to young men." [52] Many among the upper class feared that their sons, often the first generation of the family to attend college, were coming to adulthood with more money, more temptations, and more idle time than was good for them.

Athletics, then, came to be seen as a tonic to Gilded Age lives of idle dissipation. In an 1890 magazine article titled "Professionalism in Sports," Theodore Roosevelt declared, "There is a certain tendency to underestimate or overlook the need of the virile, masterful qualities of the heart and mind...

There is no better way of counteracting this tendency than by encouraging bod-
ily exercise and especially sports which develop such qualities as courage, resolution and endurance."

Oliver Wendell Holmes, Jr., also expressed this creed in an address delivered at Harvard in 1895. "Out of heroism," he told the graduating class, "grows
faith in the worth of heroism…. Therefore I rejoice at every dangerous sport
which I see pursued…. If once in a while in our rough riding a neck is broken, I
regard it not as a waste, but as a price well paid for the breeding of a race fit for
headship and command."[53] This was Social Darwinism, the survival of the fittest,
a concept that was well-received as well at Yale, considering that Professor
William Graham Sumner, one of the doctrine's most articulate proponents, was
also Walter Camp's brother-in-law.

The doctrine also resonated with many students, who had grown up on their
father's stories of the Civil War, and who sought ways to prove themselves and
earn honors of their own. Beating Yale was a poor substitute for beating the rebels,
but it was something and the college generations of the 1880s and 1890s
embraced it with all the fervor and hoopla that an earlier generation had done
marching into battle. And with many of the trappings, too, in the colors, the songs,
and the cheering that had defined football from the beginning.

Yet seldom acknowledged by men like Roosevelt, who championed football
for the archaic values it fostered, was the fact the game had become a perfect
embodiment of the modern industrial age.

Just as in an efficiently run factory, football broke a complicated activity into
simple and discrete parts—each player on the line doing his assigned part to produce the desired end under the supervision of a manager. Production could be
measured, by yards gained or tackles made, and in fact *was* measured by coaches
whose job was to promote those who played well and replace those who did not.
Unlike baseball, where each player got his turn at bat, football required almost
everyone on the offense to "find their fulfillment in the collective, orderly func-
tioning of the system."[54] Camp's reforms and rules changes were responsible for
rationalizing a chaotic system.

Training became scientific, which is to say, bureaucratic. Probably because
football was less well-organized than rowing, training had lagged behind. Harvard,
for example, had installed rowing weights in its gymnasium as early as 1864, upon
which the crew would row a thousand practice strokes a day. But in the 1870s,
football teams at least did not train; it was up to the individual to get himself into
shape if he thought it necessary.

During the 1880s, teams began to spend increasing numbers of hours practicing, learning plays and perfecting them—a fact that did not go unnoticed by
their professors. Harvard introduced the first spring practice, but almost all the
successful teams were now also returning to campus early in the fall, as well, to get
back to work. One newspaper account of football training methods declared,

"The laborious work of the men who made up the teams of Princeton, Yale, and Harvard last fall is not equaled in athletic training even by the work of men preparing for a championship prize fight." [55]

The training table, which had been used to oversee the nourishment of college crews since the 1860s, was adapted to football. According to a description of the Princeton training table, "Not a single delicacy was placed before them.... scarcely any variety of food was given to them, they were many times thirsty and were not allowed to drink, and, in fact, they were deprived of every enjoyment." [56] Again imitating crews, teams such as Penn began hiring paid, full-time coaches, as well as medical and training staff. Those coaches made daily practice schedules, concentrating on different aspects of the game on different days. No longer knights girding themselves for battle, players were becoming agents of a larger corporate entity.

It was no coincidence that football was the first sport in which time played a role. Baseball and rowing had no clock, but those sports had become popular a quarter-century earlier or more. Indeed, the first intercollegiate football games were played until a certain number of goals were scored. Not until 1873 were periods in a football game timed, but by 1883 (the year the United States first adopted uniform time zones) referees were directed to take time off the clock for excessive delays, and by 1889 they were given stopwatches. This could hardly have been accidental, given that Walter Camp spent his life working for a clock manufacturer. Camp broke the game into its elemental pieces and polished each, customizing them, just as Frederick Winslow Taylor was doing in the industrial world.

Although it hardly seemed possible, the pace of change responsible for creating that different rhythm only accelerated. In sync with the times, football seemed to be on a course of ever-faster acceleration. In fact, within five years it was in a state of utter chaos.

CHAPTER THREE

Wonderful to Behold and Terrible to Stop

The first trains began arriving at Grand Central Station shortly after daybreak on Thanksgiving morning, November 30, 1893. Those coming into New York from the south bore Princeton partisans bedecked in black and orange, who crossed paths in the cavernous main terminal with blue-draped Yale rooters down from Connecticut. All had come to watch their colleges decide the national football championship.

The streets were unusually quiet because of the holiday, which gave the pregame festivities added prominence. "In the good old days when boys went to college to study and a grand old thick-bound piety was the ruling spirit of the home, Thanksgiving Day was a fireside festival," wrote the *New York Herald*. "In these times,...[it] is no longer a solemn festival to God for mercies given. It is a holiday granted by the State and the nation to see a football game."[1] By the 1890s, it is estimated that some five thousand games, involving 110,000 participants, were being played on Thanksgiving Day around the country. Harvard and Penn enjoyed a spirited rivalry on that day for a number of years, as did Penn and Cornell later.

But the Thanksgiving centerpiece, the big game in all of college football at the end of the nineteenth century, was Yale versus Princeton. Many New York churches had been forced to change the hour for services that day in order to enable worshipers to make it up to Manhattan Field in Harlem in time for the kickoff. An 1880 editorial in the *Princetonian* asked that the time of the Thanksgiving game be changed to enable students to dine with their families. A decade later, it was usually dinner that was rescheduled.

Fans had begun arriving in New York as early as Monday, and by Thursday morning there were thousands of them. Thousands more who would not attend the game nonetheless sported the colors of the opposing teams. Shopkeepers all along Broadway decked their windows in blue or orange, adding perhaps a stuffed bulldog or tiger doll, capitalizing on the arrival of the students and football fans to kick off their own Christmas selling season. "From Ninety-fourth Street in Harlem to lower Broadway, where the battle of business is thickest, and from the east side to the North River" wrote Richard Harding Davis in *Harper's Weekly*, "the same colors in every form and texture hang on the outer walls, and the cry is that 'they come.'" [2] Florists sold out of violets and chrysanthemums. Souvenir salesmen lined the sidewalks, hawking everything from pennants to streamers to little replica footballs, all done up in the contrasting team colors. A particular novelty was the program and scorecard, printed in the shape of a football complete with leather cover and laces.

Along Fifth Avenue, a big Yale flag flew outside the Vanderbilt mansion; although the Commodore himself had been a high school dropout, his great-grandson was an undergraduate. The flag offered the one thing many of the nouveau riche lacked: a pedigree, tying the new world of business to the old world of learning. Their neighbors, the Sloanes and Scribners, matched the Vanderbilts with Princeton regalia. The Yale-Princeton game was now the start of the winter social season and everyone wanted to be a part of it. As one paper remarked, "Nearly every man in New York who had ever been within hailing distance of a college diploma" turned out for the game. [3]

Princeton men made their headquarters at the Murray Hill Hotel, the "crowning glory of the elegant 1890s," and located fashionably uptown on Park Avenue at Fortieth Street. Yale supporters still stayed at the Fifth Avenue Hotel near Madison Square, the "center of the city's social and political life in the Gilded Age." The following year, though, Yale would also follow the pull north and relocate to the Plaza at Fifty-Ninth Street.

Trainers woke the teams at around eight, fed them a breakfast the content of which was kept secret from the press, and sent them out for a brisk walk. Walter Camp described the anticipation among the Yale players:

> *They eat but little, as, in spite of their assumed coolness, there is no player who is not more or less nervous over the result. Hurriedly leaving the table, they go to their rooms and put on their uniforms. One after another they assemble in the Captain's room, and, if one might judge from the appearances of their canvas jackets and begrimed trousers, they are not a set of men to fear a few tumbles.... The Captain then says a few words of caution or encouragement to them, as he thinks best.... Then they drive to the grounds.... Hardly a word is spoken after the first few moments, and one fairly feels the atmosphere of determination settling down upon them as they bowl along through the Park.* [4]

The team hotels were more than a hundred blocks south of where the game was to be played, so diehards gathered there first to cheer the players as they boarded their bunting-decked omnibuses for the long procession uptown. Among the students, such attention was not reserved for game days; hundreds of them now watched practice daily, a custom that had developed a certain amount of social coercion. Standing outside the Fifth Avenue Hotel on Thanksgiving morning, 1891, was fifteen-year-old Bill Edwards, destined to star for Princeton later in the decade, who recalled the send-off scene vividly for the rest of his life:

> *The air was charged with enthusiasm, and I soon caught the infec-*
> *tion—although it was all new to me then—of the vital power of*
> *college spirit.... Men were standing in groups, and all eyes were*
> *centered upon the heroes of the team.... The whole scene was*
> *intensely thrilling to me, and I did not leave until the last player*
> *had entered the "bus" and it drove off. Crowds of Yale men and*
> *spectators gave the players cheer after cheer as they rolled away.*
> *The flags with which the "bus" were decorated waved in the*
> *breeze, and I watched them with indescribable fascination until*
> *they were out of sight.* [5]

Students and alumni followed the buses up Fifth Avenue in coaches, broughams, and tallyhoes that were rented for as much as $125 for the day and had to be booked a full year in advance. "Everything on four wheels ... in the city of New York goes up Fifth Avenue Thursday morning," wrote Davis. "Every coach carries twenty shouting men and excited young women covered in furs; and the flags, as they jerk them about, fill the air with color."

Those of lesser means rode the elevated trains, which were also jammed. Incoming trains were backed up for twenty blocks south of the field because earlier arrivals could not be unloaded fast enough. Between noon and three P.M., eighty-two trains carrying an estimated forty-two thousand people arrived at the One Hundred and Fifty-Fifth Street station just outside the gates, an average of one every other minute.

The sixteen thousand tickets made available to the schools had been snatched up in a matter of days. Such crushes had come to be expected; for big games, it was not unusual for students to camp out overnight in order to be first in line. Nevertheless, the Yale and Princeton papers were full of ads from students seeking tickets.

Demand had been so heavy in previous years that the schools arranged to auction off tickets for the general public. In 1891, the Manhattan Athletic Club, which handled financial arrangements for the game, netted more than $11,000 this way. Reserved field boxes that listed for $30 sold for more than three times that amount. A year later, for the first time at a football game, tickets were printed with two parts; one piece to be taken by the ticket collector and a stub to be retained by the seat-holder.[6]

Scalping had become such a problem that the treasurer of the University Athletic Club, which handled arrangements in 1893, thought it best to work with the speculators openly, allotting them up to 750 tickets on the condition that they not charge more than a fifty-cent markup. Still, detectives remained on the lookout for others, particularly undergraduates, who bought up all the extra tickets allotted to the two colleges and sold them at a huge premium. Yale students coordinating the effort were expected to clear $1,200 selling grandstand seats and boxes for five times their listed price. Those who could not buy tickets made their own. By 1895, it was estimated that at least 1,700 forged tickets had been sold.

The big game had also become a gambler's paradise. Alumni of the two schools, and many others who were not, had been making book on the floor of the New York Stock Exchange all week. The action was entirely open and the press reported some of the larger wagers. In 1890, there were reports that $4,000 had been sent to Princeton with orders to bet it on Yale at odds of 5-1 or better. Former Yale star Henry Ward Beecher was seen wandering around before the 1891 game offering $2,000 that Princeton would not kick a field goal and $1,000 that the Elis would win by more than twenty points.

Fans began arriving at the field as early as nine o'clock—five hours before kickoff. Peddlers outside had a brisk trade selling hot dogs and fruit, including some oranges dyed a revolting blue to appeal to the Yale crowd. Carriages were parked three deep for more than five blocks and on all the side streets. The papers estimated as many as three thousand vehicles in and around Manhattan Field during the game.

When the gates opened at eleven, thousands holding unreserved tickets poured in, piling at least six deep against a four and a half-foot high wooden fence that kept them off the playing field. One inspired entrepreneur cleaned up selling soap boxes to stand on for a dollar apiece.

Crowd control had become a matter of safety as well as order. In 1890, when the game was played at Eastern Park in Brooklyn, the police had been overwhelmed by spectators rushing the field and had beaten them back with clubs. A few moments later, a section of the bleachers collapsed under the weight of the crowd, injuring fifty. A member of the Eastern Park management attributed the accident to "a crowd of Princeton enthusiasts who persisted in dancing and stomping on the seats to keep time with their unearthly yells."[7]

Seating arrangements carefully preserved social distinctions. That was one of the attractions of Manhattan Field, where the game had been played since 1891, and one of the reasons it had been moved there. While students and many younger alumni crowded around the fence, the older and well-to-do sat in private boxes, the clubhouse, or the covered grandstand. Many of the wealthy rode their carriages right into the stadium, parking in a special section along one sideline and blocking the view of those unfortunate enough to have seats in the lower rows of the grandstands behind them. Up on the roofs of their vehicles, they opened elaborate tailgate lunches.

Among the notables who attended the 1893 game were the Whitneys, the Vanderbilts, Chauncey Depew of the New York Central Railroad, New York City mayor Thomas Francis Gilroy; Richard Croker, boss of Tammany Hall; theater impresario Colonel Jacob Ruppert; Theodore Roosevelt; House Speaker Thomas B. Reed; at least two U.S. senators; and (it was rumored) former president Benjamin Harrison.

Cheaper views could be had up on the surrounding escarpment known as Coogan's Bluff or "Deadhead Hill," as it was known, where those who didn't mind passing around field glasses could take in the game for fifty cents. Another five hundred people crowded onto the Washington viaduct and the elevated railroad tracks overlooking to the field. A few even climbed Fordham Heights across the Harlem River, almost a mile away.

The size of the crowd, and the amount of consumption, was all the more remarkable considering financial conditions in the country that fall. The Panic of 1893, which saw American banks fail throughout the summer, was being keenly felt. By January 1894, just weeks after the game, surveys estimated that there were more than one hundred thousand unemployed in New York and Brooklyn.

As they awaited the kickoff, the rival crowds bombarded each other with cheers and taunted anyone who happened to venture onto the field. Not only Princeton and Yale students, but also delegations from Dartmouth, Brown, Cornell, Penn, and Williams were also in attendance. Although the UAC had banned the sale of alcohol, "The tilting of black bottles and the flash of up-raised sleeve buttons was seen in all directions."[8] Students made a popular sport of throwing their empties at policemen. Others croaked the standard Yale cheer, lifted from Aristophanes' *Frogs*: "Brek-ek-ek-ex-ko-ax-ko-ax, Oh-op, Oh-op, Parabalou!"[9]

When the teams finally took the field, the noise reached a crescendo. During warm-ups, the players acted "precisely as would a lot of puppies to whom there has been given unexpected freedom." Princeton's men limbered up vigorously. "Balliet turned hand springs. Lea, Ward, and Wheeler did little punt scrimmage acts and buried their noses in the dirt as if they loved the odor.... The Yale men, as became veterans with the flush of victory on them, were much more sedate."[10] The players were still small by modern standards; the average height of the teams in 1892, for example, was five-foot-ten, and their average weight was 168 pounds. They ranged in age from eighteen to twenty-five. Behind them stood "a score or so of rubbers and spongers and joint setters and wound binders and water-carriers and blanket-bearers" carrying enough medical supplies for an army.

The sheer size of the spectacle was itself remarkable. Attendance at the 1880 Princeton-Yale game had been about 5,000, but had leapt to almost

15,000 by 1884, to 25,000 by 1890, and to as high as 40,000 in 1893. Also present that afternoon were 600 policemen and stadium employees; 150 members of the press sitting in the first press box ever erected at a football game (including telegraph operators who were reporting the game live); 100 coaches, substitutes, and trainers; 250 persons in the clubhouse; and perhaps 500 souvenir salesmen and others.

During breaks in the action, scrubs for both teams, who doubled as cheerleaders, ran out onto the field and waved their warm-up blankets to whip up the crowd. They might have enjoyed another innovation, the first football scoreboard, which was unveiled in Cambridge for the Harvard-Penn game that afternoon.

Following Princeton's upset victory in 1889, Yale had gone back on one of its customary tears, defeating the Tigers the next three years by shutouts and winning the national title in 1891 and 1892. Sparking interest even higher, though, both schools entered the 1893 game with perfect records. Just five days earlier, Yale had defeated previously unbeaten Harvard, ensuring that the Thanksgiving showdown at Manhattan Field would decide the championship.

This time, the Tigers prevailed. Princeton pulled a 6-0 upset to claim their first title in four years. When quarterback Phil King, adored for his golden locks, scored midway through the first half, "the Princeton rooters deafen[ed] heaven and themselves." Up in New Haven, hundreds of Yale partisans followed the game, watching blue and orange puppets dance along a painted board according to reports coming in by telephone.

The victorious Princeton locker room was raucous. "The players and coaches jumped over seats, clasped one another in their arms, hugged and kissed each other and yelled for full twenty minutes." [11] Then, perhaps remembering that they did attend a Presbyterian school, they formed a circle, and the coaches removed their hats. "And standing as they were, naked and covered with mud and blood and perspiration," Davis wrote, "the eleven men who had won the championship sang the doxology from beginning to end as solemnly and as seriously, and, I am sure, as sincerely, as they ever did in their lives, while outside the no less thankful fellow-students yelled and cheered, and beat at the doors and windows, and howled for them to come out and show themselves."

It took forever to get everyone home, amid much stamping and cursing. Elevated trains left at one-minute intervals for more than two hours. Several women fainted in the crush, and the *World* reported scornfully that "many persons bearing the appearance of gentlemen acted as brutally as could be expected of the lowest ruffian. It was everybody for himself to get on a train and the devil take the hindmost." [12] Some crawled in through the car windows.

Like the Super Bowl, the game was a financial windfall not only for the host city, but also for the participating teams. The 1879 Princeton-Yale game, played in Hoboken, had netted the schools exactly $238.76 apiece. By 1889, playing now in Manhattan, they made almost $5,500 apiece from the

Thanksgiving game, and in 1893 split gate receipts of more than $30,000, making it a most lucrative payday.[13]

Faculty who abhorred the excesses the big game had come to generate, and the misplaced priorities it displayed to the world, could only have quaked when they read about what their charges did that night, under the banners of Princeton and Yale.

Ignoring newspaper warnings from the police commissioner to behave themselves, students who had suffocated in bucolic Princeton or sleepy New Haven cut loose on a holiday to the big, sinful city, joined by alumni who happy to help them have a good time. Princeton tried to curb this by requiring students to report back to campus by midnight, but many persuaded friends to sign in for them and remained in New York.

Some made dinner reservations at Delmonico's, the most celebrated restaurant in the country. Others took their dinner in liquid form and set out on the town. One popular destination was Koster and Bial's Music Hall. According to Richard Harding Davis, Koster's got so crowded on game night "that after nine o'clock a man who wished to leave it had to be passed out over the heads of the crowd."

Flush with victory, the Princeton students sang, wolf-whistled, and drowned out everyone on stage. As one reporter described the scene after an earlier Thanksgiving game, "The appearance of every young woman in the procession was hailed with a complimentary uproar proportioned to the degree with which her attire receded from her ankles and her ears."[14] When the high-kicking chorus girls came on stage, the boys heckled them with drunken witticisms like, "My! How she can punt!" and "Say, dear, try for a goal."[15] At the Imperial Music Hall, fans went crazy for Mlle. Valeca, "the trapeze marvel" who wore "long flesh colored tights and a very short salmon-colored silk jacket,"[16] while those at the Academy of Music hooted for La Sirene, Eglantine, Serpantine, and Dynamite, the four "French quadrille dancers."[17]

Turned back onto the streets, students resumed barhopping, eventually making their way to the Hoffman House, the notorious Tammany hangout that was acknowledged to have the most popular bar on Broadway thanks to "an inspiring display of mythological nudities" painted on the wall.[18] "It was like getting into the Vatican to get to the counter at the Hoffman House art room," wrote one reporter.[19] The din was overwhelming and the air blue with cigarette smoke. In a dark corner, "Billy" Edwards, an ex-boxer turned bouncer, universally acknowledged as the Thanksgiving game's semi-official bookmaker, settled up on bets. He had been carrying around more than $5,000 in cash since the previous night.

This was the sort of education students would not get in class. As a reporter for the *Journal* remarked in 1896, "It would have greatly surprised the fathers of the young gentlemen, who so ably represent the highest learning of American universities, to have seen how much at ease they were against a bar or over a table; at ease whether their vis-à-vis was a blonde in furs or a bartender in an apron."[20]

Edwards, or men like him, most likely directed at least some of the visiting football fans around the corner to one of the seven adjacent brothels on Twenty-Fifth Street known as the "Seven Sisters," which often sent engraved invitations to groups they knew were arriving in town. Some of the students probably found what they wanted with less trouble. According to an account in the *Journal* following the 1896 game, "Scores of women who might pass for forty two with the broadway lights behind them were on the streets last night. They congratulated Princeton, even if their congratulations were unsolicited—is that the word? They sympathized with Yale, even if their sympathies were unsought. The streets were full of these women.... It was a great pity. The girls whom these young men will marry went home. Then out came the women who look best with the electric lights behind them." [21]

Late into the night students danced around with hotel lampshades on their heads, stole a hat rack, hijacked a handsome cab, and pulled other stunts more or less destructive. Police were quick to crack down on singing and cheering, yet every year, it seemed, there was an item in the Friday morning papers about a young man wearing Princeton colors found stripped of all identification and passed out at the corner of Thirty-Sixth and Broadway at nine o'clock at night. [22] Or another taken in at Thirtieth and Sixth Avenue, "insensible from drink." [23]

More than a dozen students woke up the next morning in the West Thirtieth Street police station. According to the papers, most had been taken in for drunkenness and disorderly conduct. In many cases accompanied by their fathers, the students were each fined $5 and discharged by a lenient magistrate, though not before making the front page of the newspapers. "Heads were aching," one reported, "chrysanthemums drooped, and badges of orange and black were crumpled and dirty. Moppy locks were tangled, hats were battered, and baggy coats were streaked and wrinkled." [24]

As these accounts of the day illustrate, Ivy football also shaped, and was shaped by, the development of the popular sporting press in the late nineteenth century. The modern sports page owes much to the exploits of Harvard, Princeton, Yale, and later Pennsylvania, which in turn helped fuel a circulation war between two of New York's biggest daily papers.

The earliest college football games received scant attention in the New York press, and barely any at all in other cities. At most, accounts involving the bigger schools would receive a few paragraphs. Only the most important games received more than a column. The 1878 Princeton-Yale game at Hoboken was the first to make the front page.

Things began to change in 1883 when Joseph Pulitzer bought the *New York World*. Having already established himself as a newspaper magnate in St. Louis, Pulitzer decided to take on New York, buying the moribund *World* from financier Jay Gould for $346,000, payable in installments. Like heavily leveraged media moguls throughout history, Pulitzer's most pressing need was to service his debt, and the way to do that was to sell more papers. The way to sell more papers was to make them more entertaining, more sensational, to give the people, in other words, what they wanted.

Pulitzer soon introduced the first newspaper sports page, as well as the first women's page, children's page, Sunday magazine, and color comic strips. He also added a society page that enabled the strap hangers to look into the world of the privileged. Within months, the *World* was the biggest selling paper in New York. By 1892, it claimed two million readers, many of them among the city's shop clerks and sales girls. Soon almost every major daily in the country had a sports page.

Competition grew even more heated in 1895 when William Randolph Hearst bought the *New York Journal* and made it into the ideal of the yellow press. Hearst went Pulitzer one better, splashing sensational news—including football—in banner headlines across the entire front page, running even more illustrations and cartoons, and hiring prominent writers such as Davis and Stephen Crane to cover important games, and insiders such as Walter Camp, Pudge Heffelfinger, and the captain of the Yale team to provide expert commentary. Even the relatively staid *New York Times* (which adopted the motto "All the news that's fit to print" in 1897) felt compelled to start playing the Princeton-Yale game as the lead story on its front page and to devote two full pages to coverage.

All those papers needed something to write about, and college football fit nicely. For one thing, it filled a lull in the yearly sports cycle, coming after the baseball and horse racing seasons had ended. It also filled a hole in the weekly cycle, generating news on Saturdays, traditionally the slowest day of the week, and providing material for the rapidly growing Sunday editions. Even more, college football—meaning at the time Ivy football—provided a cultural text that meshed perfectly with the changing attitudes of the time. Rather than just stating facts, modern journalism sought to provide an instantly accessible narrative. And football certainly told a story.

American sport at the end of the Civil War was heavily stratified by class. The wealthy followed horse racing and cricket, while boxing and later baseball appealed more to a working-class audience. Pulitzer had initially scorned football as a game for rich college boys, but by the early 1890s had come to appreciate its broader appeal. Football, especially at the prominent Ivy colleges, played to both highbrow and lowbrow audiences, and was covered accordingly.

Attention was given to their excesses as well as their glories. At Harvard, Yale, and Princeton one found the princes of the nation, young men of wealth and breeding, who could nevertheless trade sucker punches on the line when conditions permitted. Such coverage appealed to the love-hate feelings the working class harbored for the wealthy. Thus while the press lionized the players as heroes, they also played up the Thanksgiving carousing with morning-after headlines such as "Dungeon Cells for College Boys." [25]

More generally, though, in illustrations as well as in text they presented the Ivy colleges, particularly Princeton and Yale, as the ideal—socially, athletically, and morally. By presenting college football, especially Ivy football, to its readership, many of whom had only the faintest idea of college life, the press helped perpetuate the ideal of the Ivy colleges as something grand. Such attention connected not only football, but football fans, with the social elite. These schools became not just fine academic institutions, but someplace special, thus feeding the schools' own conceptions of themselves as such. The Ivy League reputation we know today was burnished on the pages of the New York press.

While the press may have recorded youthful excesses with amusement, college officials certainly did not. If the 1893 Thanksgiving game highlighted the glories of college football—the spectacle, the thrill, and the pageantry—it also illuminated its darker side: the excess, the overemphasis, the debauchery, and the loss of institutional control.

Faculty were particularly unhappy at having their games made entertainment for the masses, little appreciating the benefits that coverage was also producing. President Charles Eliot of Harvard used just these examples to summarize the evils of overemphasis on football. "The disadvantages of athletic sports in colleges,' he wrote in his annual report, was that "they induce in masses of spectators at interesting games an hysterical excitement which too many Americans enjoy, but which is evidence, not of physical strength and depth of passion, but of feebleness and shallowness." [26]

The 1893 contest was the last Thanksgiving game the Big Three played in New York. Beginning the following year, the game was moved to a Saturday, and in 1897 the games returned to campus. [27]

Whatever Harvard's claims to academic preeminence, their inability to beat Yale had become embarrassing. The Crimson had begun to take the game more seriously, instituting the first spring practice in 1889 and appointing their first head coach and team physician. The physician could only have been alarmed at captain Arthur J. Cumnock's training techniques, which included work on a hundred-pound tackling dummy hung from a rope in the gymnasium. The dummy, a five-foot wooden cylinder with a wooden shelf protruding at about waist height, was supposed to force players to tackle low. Unfortunately, the apparatus had so little padding that more than one man broke his collarbone on it.

Nevertheless, in 1890, Cumnock, quarterback Dudley Dean, and tackle Marshall "Ma" Newell (so-called because he mothered freshman players) broke an eleven-year losing streak against Yale on their way to Harvard's first national title. Here training did make a difference. At halftime, while the Yale players shivered on the field, Harvard retreated to a nearby shed where they relaxed, got rubdowns, and tended to their wounds, which many said contributed to their victory.

Harvard's withdrawal from the IFA in 1889 over Princeton's use of "tramp" athletes not only cost them the big Thanksgiving game in New York, but also pushed the IFA to the brink of collapse. There were rumors that Yale would withdraw and join Harvard in forming a dual league. Princeton dropped hints that it ought to be included, too, but the New England schools were cool, considering the Tigers too sharp for their tastes. "I do not think it necessary to say that Yale will not play Princeton," Yale professor E. L. Richardson told the press. "It might be a very healthy thing, however, for Princeton if she were left out a year." [28]

Although many excesses also haunted football during the Gay Nineties, two in particular brought about the IFA's demise. One was eligibility and the other was brutality. At the intersection of both sat the University of Pennsylvania, which by the middle of the decade realized its ambition of gridiron parity with the Big Three.

More than any other issue, eligibility epitomized the ongoing struggle of Ivy football, and football as a whole, to define its place in college life. In 1882, the IFA had limited players to five years in games between IFA schools but had said nothing about other games, a considerable loophole considering the regular fluctuations in that body's membership. Camp had pushed them a step further in 1889 by making it illegal to use men who had been compensated for playing sports.

Princeton had defended Monte Cash by arguing that it was "a novel position . . . that it is a very serious matter for a man to enter college to play football. This has been going on in English and American colleges since the time athletic sports were first introduced." [29] Snake Ames had tried to lure a Crimson player, H. O. Stickney, to transfer by promising that, "I can get your board, tuition, etc., free. The athletic men at Princeton get by all odds the best treatment in any of the colleges." [30] Although Stickney declined, he did offer his services to Yale, prompting Pa Corbin to ask Camp what they could offer.

The notion that it was wrong to pay athletes for playing sports, or even for them to associate with professionals, was a new one. No one had criticized Dartmouth in the 1870s when it awarded silver inkstands as trophies at track meets. Charles Eliot himself had rowed for large purses as a Harvard student, and Ivy baseball squads in the mid-nineteenth century routinely scheduled professional teams. [31] Even when this practice declined, many college football players accepted money for playing baseball during the summer, often under an assumed name.

Concerns about student integrity, though, were not confined to athletics. Harvard undergraduates could scan the pages of the *Crimson* almost daily and find advertisements for canned term papers or lecture notes. Princeton responded to its growing problem of classroom dishonesty by instituting an Honor Code in 1893. The size of the student body was growing at a much faster rate than the faculty, and many of the new matriculants were thought to have been raised on the wrong values. "The students," one professor complained, "come from homes saturated with the worship of material success." [32]

The creation of an amateur ideal was one way in which the Ivy colleges fought back against this trend. Not playing for money, being above things material, became a sign that distinguished the wealthy not just from the working class (many of them immigrants), but from the entrepreneurial middle class, as well. American apostles of amateurism, such as Walter Camp, invoked the British ideal of Oxford and Cambridge—hardly democratic institutions—at which the line between amateur and professional was plainly based on class. Gentlemen did not have to earn their living by playing for money, and shunned those who did. There was an obvious tension in the distinction, for if the athletes themselves were amateurs the teams for which they played were anything but, employing professional coaches, charging admission, and selling game programs filled with advertisements.

Still, the Ivy colleges, especially the Big Three, pushed the new amateur ethos with particular fervor in football. One of the first to remark on this was Thorstein Veblen, a graduate of Yale and Cornell, who addressed football's social underpinnings in *The Theory of the Leisure Class*, published in 1899. Almost everything about college football advertised conspicuous leisure, Veblen observed. The elaborate uniforms, the martial emphasis, the ritual, the playacting all demonstrated that players did not engage in productive work.

Another aspect of the eligibility question was the more mundane one of whether graduate or professional school students should be permitted to play. Some men stayed on into their mid- or even late twenties, often lining up against freshmen ten years their junior. For those schools that had them—primarily Harvard and Penn—it was an easy thing to ensconce someone in a professional school and so keep him around for a few extra seasons, a tactic that became a source of controversy in rowing, as well, and even in as cloistered an activity as intercollegiate debating.

Yale, which at the time did not have many professional schools, took the lead in trying to ban graduate students in 1893. Only Penn opposed the measure, and when it passed, the Quakers resigned from the IFA, leaving it with only two members, Princeton and Yale. The Quakers' charge that the other colleges were ganging up on them gained credence when Yale and Harvard turned around and agreed that they would not apply the so-called "undergraduate rule" to their own game, but would let each school set its own eligibility rules.

That was far from the end of the matter, but before exploring its consequences it is necessary to backtrack and revisit the issue of brutality.

Harvard may have routinely decried football violence, but they were as guilty as anyone in perpetuating it. The flying wedge, unveiled in 1892, was the brainchild of Loren F. Deland, a construction engineer who had no ties to Harvard and had never even seen a game of football until 1890. But Deland, who loved military strategy, took to heart Napoleon's dictum about the concentration of forces and persuaded Harvard captain Bernie Trafford to try a new play that adapted the idea to the football field. It may be the only fan-suggested play that has ever worked.

Trafford practiced the flying wedge all summer, but waited until the end of the season to spring it on Yale. The Elis suspected something was afoot. Cambridge buzzed with rumors the week before the game that spies from New Haven were observing practice from the tower of Mount Auburn cemetery, prompting Harvard officials to raise the fence.

There was no score when Harvard lined up to kick off the second half. Trafford stood by the ball at midfield with freshman Charlie Brewer behind him. The other nine men lined up on either side, the four heavier players angling off on Trafford's right about fifteen yards back, the lighter men in a diamond to his left about five yards back. Trafford first tried to lure Yale offside by making a false start (legal at the time), but the Elis did not bite. "Boys," Yale captain Vance McCormick warned his men, "this is something new, but play the game as you have been taught it." [33]

When the captain finally gave the signal, the heavy line started racing diagonally across the field toward the Yale defenders. Just as they were about to pass Trafford, he nudged the ball forward, then pitched it to Brewer as the two fell in behind the lighter line, now part of a huge, rapidly moving arrowhead. Harvard's phalanx hit the stationary Yale men at a dead run and threw them back, gaining thirty yards on the play. It was, John Heisman later wrote, "something wonderful to behold, and terrible to stop." [34] But because the play was only designed for kickoffs, Harvard had no further opportunity to use it as Yale went on to score the game's lone touchdown for a 6-0 victory. The only casualty that afternoon, in fact, was Pudge Heffelfinger, in the stands now as an alumnus, who became so excited that he leaped over a fence surrounding the field and had to be removed by three policemen.

Among the Harvard rushers that afternoon was William Henry Lewis, a law student and former star at Amherst, who thus became the first African-American ever to play for an Ivy League school. Lewis also became the first black football captain (for a single game against Penn) and the first black All-American. Some considered him the best center in the history of the game until that point. [35] The son of slaves, Lewis went on to become assistant attorney general of the United States under President William Howard Taft.

Success of the flying wedge brought imitations, such as Yale's "turtle back" play, which it used against Harvard the following year. Here, the players formed a large oval surrounding the ball carrier. Everyone hunched over double, exposing what looked like turtle backs, and the oval slowly revolved toward one end of the line. Defenders who pushed forward at the far end of the line only helped the oval rotate, until the ball carrier spun out and ran downfield.

Football injuries increased as gangs of running men crashed into opponents who could not themselves move without being offsides, and all of whom were wearing minimal protection. In 1891, Edgar Allan Poe donned the first nose guard, a ridiculous-looking metal plate strapped to his forehead, but even the leather helmet would not become popular for another decade (and would not be required until 1920). Two years later, Princeton's Phil King tried wearing a steel plate over bruised ribs, a precursor of the flack jacket.

One of the roughest, and in the opinion of many dirtiest players of the age was Yale's Frank Hinkey. He stood only five-foot-nine and weighed perhaps 150 pounds, yet he became one of only four men Walter Camp named All-American four times and led Yale to a career record of 52-1. Hinkey was a lonely man; small, nervous, a brooder and a chain smoker, which was either foolish or tough or both, as he also suffered from a precursor to tuberculosis which would kill him at the age of fifty-four. Pudge Heffelfinger described him as "a scrawny, sunken-eyed, deathly pale little hellcat"—and this was from someone who liked him. [36]

Hinkey kept to himself, seldom spoke, and had few friends, though some had the temerity to call him by his nickname, "Gussie." But anchoring the line at end, he was fast and he was fearless. Camp claimed Hinkey slipped into opposing backfields like a "disembodied spirit" and tackled like "an exploding bomb." His teammate George Foster Sanford once remarked, "Hinkey in action was a raving maniac who frothed at the mouth." [37] On another occasion, Sanford intervened in one of Hinkey's not infrequent off-field brawls, pulled him off his victim, and threw him into a corner. Dazed, Hinkey looked up. "Sanford," he said, "that was the greatest sensation I've ever experienced—try it again." [38]

Whether he played tough or dirty depended very much upon whom you asked. Opponents hated Hinkey, called him a cheap shot artist who kicked men when they were down. "No father or mother worthy of the name would permit a son to associate with the set of Yale brutes on Hinkey's football team," is how one paper put it. [39] Yale partisans, on the other hand, staunchly defended him. Certainly, he feared no one. Once, when a Harvard player slugged him in the jaw, Hinkey just stared at him like Clint Eastwood. "My friend," he finally replied, "if you hit me that hard again you will break your hand." [40]

Hinkey was also smart. In 1893, Penn tried a "flying interference" play against Yale in which the end, tackle, fullback, and halfback joined hands to form a human chain as they rolled around the end ahead of the ball carrier. The first time the Quakers ran it, they cut down the Yale defenders in their path and scored a touchdown. The second time they tried it, Hinkey dropped to the ground as the sweep passed over him, then leapt up and nailed the ball carrier for a loss.

After graduation, Hinkey bounced around, selling real estate, running a zinc smelter, and working as a stockbroker before returning to Yale as an assistant coach in 1913. He was made head coach the following year, compiled a 7-2 record, but was forced out because his smoking, foul language, and heavy drinking offended Camp. The day he died in a North Carolina sanitarium, he sent a message to his old teammates. It read: "Charon is at the crossing." [41]

By the end of the 1893 season, the IFA had dwindled to just Yale and Princeton, which were powerless to act as a rulemaking body for an increasingly far-flung sport. In February 1894, the University Athletic Club of New York stepped in, inviting representatives of Harvard and Penn to join the two in forming a new body, called the Intercollegiate Rules Committee. The IRC made several changes in hopes of reducing brutality—restricting mass momentum plays, ending the flying wedge by requiring kickoffs to travel at least ten yards, and shortening the game to seventy minutes.

Amid all this confusion, enter Pennsylvania. Always insecure about its status, Penn had been aiming for parity with Harvard, Princeton, and Yale both on and off the field. Academically, the school had made great strides following its move to West Philadelphia in 1872, yet it continued to live hand-to-mouth. Lacking a large endowment, Penn was forced to rely on tuition payments from a large student body, one of the reasons it expanded its professional and vocational schools so rapidly. Some of those vocational schools, however, were notoriously lax—a student could be admitted to Penn's dental school, for example, without taking an entrance examination—which made them ideal places to stash tramp football players but hurt Penn's academic reputation.

The Quakers decided to improve their football fortunes by hiring away someone who knew the game well. In 1892, they lured George Woodruff, who had starred with Heffelfinger and Stagg on the great Yale teams of the late 1880s, with a promise of $1,300 a year and free tuition at the law school. A graduate student himself, Woodruff freely made use of others. In 1894, only six of the eleven Penn starters were undergraduates and the average age of the team was twenty-four. Yale alleged that the Penn players were "mature married men, age twenty-two to thirty, one with a child eight years old." [42]

Woodruff brought a firm organization and a shrewd strategic mind. He taught his teams reverses and double reverses, as well as a trick called the "quarterback kick," in which the quarterback would boot the ball up the field, where a teammate would fall on it. When the IRC outlawed the flying wedge, Woodruff came up with a play called the "guards back." At the signal "guards back," both Penn guards would retreat into the backfield while the remaining linemen shifted over. When the ball was snapped, these guards provided extra blocking protection, an armed escort as it were, for the ball carrier. The play, Stagg later wrote, "raised havoc with all teams Penn played" and marked the beginning of their renaissance. [43]

Tactics are nothing without players to execute them, and Woodruff attracted talent, too. A power offense demanded bulk, which Woodruff got from two huge guards: Charles "Buck" Wharton, six-foot-two and 212 pounds, and Wiley Woodruff (no relation to the coach), six-foot and 205 pounds. He also added three future All-Americans: halfback Arthur Knipe, who later became famous writing children's books; fullback George Brooke (who, as a punter, is credited with coining the term "coffin corner kick"); and end Charles Gelbert. Carrying the ball was Winchester Osgood, a Cornell transfer student, whom one sportswriter described as "a picture of rhythmic motion, a smooth, effortless runner, always in balance." [44] Harry A. Mackey, later mayor of Philadelphia, and Henry W. Thornton, who was eventually knighted after making a fortune in Canadian railroads, rounded out this first Penn powerhouse.

Woodruff's team began to draw notice. Like everyone else, they had been padding their record against smaller schools such as Swarthmore and Tioga. An 11-2 record, like the one they compiled in 1890, may have looked impressive, but everyone knew it meant nothing if they were still getting thumped in the big games. And except for its lone victory over Harvard in 1884, eight years earlier, the Quakers had not beaten one of the eastern elite, nor even come close.

That changed in Woodruff's first season, when Penn nipped Princeton, 6-4. The Tigers were humiliated. Woodrow Wilson's wife, Ellen, wrote to a friend shortly afterward that only Grover Cleveland's election to the presidency a few days later had helped her husband overcome it. "We needed something as great as this victory to enable people here to endure the overwhelming football calamity, and defeat by the U. of Pa. . . . Really, I think Woodrow would have had some sort of collapse if we had lost in politics too!" [45]

Woodruff's men suffered a setback in 1893, losing all their matches against the Big Three, although the Princeton and Yale games had been close. When Penn withdrew from the IFA over attempts to restrict its use of graduate students, there was a sense that its newly won and desperately craved prestige was slipping away. "The public began to wonder," the *Philadelphia Press* wrote, "whether the Quakers' spurt had not been only spasmodic and to doubt whether Pennsylvania was really anything but a leader in the second brigade." [46] If Penn had a button to push, this was the one.

Anxiety increased when Yale also dropped the Quakers from its schedule. Harvard, which had unexpectedly found itself supporting Penn over the eligibility of graduate students and the free use of mass-momentum plays, agreed to resume games with them, provisionally. The Quakers dearly wanted to be made a permanent addition to the Crimson schedule, but Harvard, which knew the hazards of wedding outside its class, kept the dalliance at arm's length. As one Philadelphia paper put it, "Harvard, in self-defense, could not go hand in hand with one below her level, no matter how charitable her intentions." [47]

When the Crimson trounced Penn in 1893, they began to sound noncommittal about continuing the series. They would be only too happy to torment Princeton for a while by substituting Penn on the schedule, but wanted to keep their options open. Worse, Princeton now balked at scheduling a home-and-home series with the Quakers, casting doubt on whether it too had any intention of playing them beyond 1894. It was becoming all too clear that whatever their differences with each other, the Big Three were not going to admit interlopers.

Penn saw its only hope on the field. If it could defeat either Princeton or Harvard, the loser could not honorably refuse a rematch and Penn would be established as a worthy foe. Tremendous importance was thus attached to the Princeton game, which fell first on the 1894 schedule.

Certainly it was the biggest game in Penn's history up to that point. Omens were not auspicious, as Princeton had won twenty-nine of the thirty previous meetings between the schools. Bookmakers made the Tigers a 2-1 favorite, and a confident pair of Princeton students set up shop on the Penn campus the week before the game, "armed with a gigantic roll of bills," to take bets on behalf of more than a thousand of their classmates.[48]

For a change, the weather for a big game was favorable as more than twelve thousand people ringed the field at the New Jersey State Fairgrounds in Trenton, preferring to stay close to the action rather than sit in the grandstands. Penn partisans had the better of the singing, including the following sung to the tune of "John Brown's Body":

> *Break the Princeton rush-line,*
> *Let your aim be true!*
> *Crush the Black and Orange!*
> *Raise the Red and Blue!*
> *Play for love and honor,*
> *Drive the leather in,*
> *We will yell for good old Penn,*
> *Pennsylvania win!*[49]

Early in the game, Woodruff's mighty line stopped Princeton six inches short of a touchdown. The first half ended without any score, although feeling among the spectators ran so high that when a black dog ran out with a Princeton ribbon tied around its neck, someone hit the poor creature with a brick wrapped in a red and blue flag.

Woodruff's ingenuity paid off in the second half. Wiley Woodruff blocked a Princeton punt, which Carl Williams ran in for a score. Princeton had been outplayed all afternoon and was now getting desperate. Near the end of the game, Williams, who was also Penn's quarterback, tried a quick kick which M. G. Rosengarten (whose brother was on the Princeton squad) recovered inside the five-yard line. Two plays later, Win Osgood broke in for the second score. Penn had recorded a 12-0 victory. Princeton refused to play them again for forty-one years.

If Penn's status as a football power was now assured, another game two weeks later between Harvard and Yale upset the already weakened intercollegiate athletic structure. A 12-4 Yale victory at Springfield's Hampden Park, which gave the Elis yet another intercollegiate championship, was nonetheless shockingly brutal. "It seemed to be Hinkey's main object to disable the best players of Harvard," the *New York Times* observed, although he was by no means the only one guilty.[50]

Some of it was allegedly dirty play, but much appears to have been simply run-of-the-mill roughness. One man suffered a broken leg, another had a broken collarbone, several more had broken noses or other head injuries. There were even reports that Yale tackle Fred Murphy had died in a New Haven hospital, although it turned out he had suffered only a "contusion of the brain" and had been in a coma for several hours. At least a third of the players that afternoon suffered some sort of injury—a casualty rate, the *Nation* pointed out, considerably higher than that of Napoleon's army at Waterloo.[51] When Yale played Princeton the following weekend, policemen ringed the field and the commissioner announced that he would to stop the game at the first sign of slugging.

Those who supported football found themselves increasingly vulnerable. Princeton president Francis Patton, for one, had defended the sport on the rather specious grounds that it attracted men to college who might otherwise not attend, but officials at several colleges were now considering abandoning football.[52] In an attempt to calm them, Walter Camp had cochaired a blue ribbon committee in 1893 to investigate charges of brutality. One former Princeton player, Luther Price, wrote that he had been forced to leave the 1887 Harvard game "due to sheer weakness and loss of blood." Camp suppressed the letter, as well as a finding that fully 20 percent of ex-players reported having suffered some permanent injury. His final report, *Football Facts and Figures*, was something of a whitewash, emphasizing football's redeeming qualities. Nevertheless, events such as the "Bloodbath at Hampden Park," as the 1894 Harvard-Yale game came to be known, produced still louder calls for reform.

The IRC was having no more success than the IFA in getting control over the game. Harvard, which had already severed relations with Princeton over eligibility, now cut off Yale over violence, and in 1895, amid a decade of simmering bad feeling over eligibility, rough play, and miscellaneous other forms of cheating by its members, the IRC fell apart. Camp and Moffat invited representatives from Harvard and Penn to resurrect the moribund IFA, but negotiations stalled over whether to ban mass play. As Amos Alonzo Stagg observed, the proposal put Penn, which owed its success to the guards back formation, "in the position of being asked to vote itself back into the minor leagues."[53]

In the East that fall, two sets of rules were followed; Princeton and Yale outlawed mass play while Cornell, Harvard, and Penn permitted it. Harvard refused to play either Yale or Princeton, while Yale and Princeton refused to play Penn. Cornell's faculty voted to restrict all further games to campus. Columbia had dropped football altogether in 1891 and there were persistent rumors that Harvard might do the same. Although Princeton hoped to create a new alliance among the Big Three, Harvard held aloof.

Centrifugal forces were also tearing college football apart. Schools in other parts of the country were reluctant to submit to an organization located so far away, particularly one in a more or less perpetual state of chaos. In 1895, six mid-western universities formed their own conference to make rules and coordinate schedules, which eventually became the Big Ten. This and other organizations soon took the lead from the eastern colleges in pursuing reforms such as limiting freshman eligibility and instituting faculty oversight. The center of football innovation and reform was moving west, never fully to return.

Harvard, Princeton, Penn, and Yale eventually went back to the IFA, recognizing that even an imperfect governing body was better than nothing. A stricter rule finally curbed mass play by requiring that at least five men be on the offensive line of scrimmage. A second prohibited a player in the offensive backfield from taking more than one step forward before the snap without coming to a complete stop. Both rules are still in force today. The running back who goes in motion by running parallel to the line of scrimmage is executing an ancient attempt to end the flying wedge.

Penn's second victory over Princeton was the takeoff point for Quaker football. Under Woodruff's direction, the team won thirty-four consecutive games between 1894 and 1896, and when that streak ended with an upset loss to Lafayette, the Quakers ran off thirty-one more wins, claiming the de facto national championship in 1895 and 1897. In all, Woodruff compiled a record of 124-15, the best in school history. He also made good use of his legal training. After leaving the Quakers in 1901, Woodruff became assistant attorney general of the United States, acting secretary of the interior, a federal judge in Hawaii, and the attorney general of Pennsylvania.

Two other Penn players from the late nineties went on to the College Football Hall of Fame. The first was John Outland, a medical student who was versatile enough to be named All-American in consecutive years at two different positions, guard and back. For years after his graduation, he championed the often-ignored men in the trenches. In 1946, when the Football Writers Association of America decided to create an award for the best lineman in the country, they named it the Outland Trophy in his honor.

Had the award existed in the 1890s, a certain winner would have been another massive Quaker guard, Thomas Truxton Hare. A huge man at six-foot-two and 208 pounds, Hare made Camp's All-America team four years in a row (one of only four players ever to be so honored) and later was chosen along with Pudge Heffelfinger on the All-Time All-American team. A workhorse in the guards back formation, Hare played every minute of every game for all four years and was so strong (he was also an Olympic hammer-thrower) that he often carried as many as five tacklers. He later wrote a series of thinly autobiographical novels set at fictional Warrington University, "one of the larger of the eastern colleges," with titles such as *A Junior in the Line* (1925), *A Senior Quarterback* (1910), and *A Graduate Coach* (1911).

The other Ivy schools playing football during the decade—Cornell, Brown, and Dartmouth—continued to make their own way. Although Cornell posted very successful records in 1892 and 1898, their progress against the Big Three was slow. Ithaca toasted a 6-0 loss to Princeton in 1891 as if they had won the championship. "One Solitary Touchdown!" boasted the *Cornell Daily Sun*. In 1895, quarterback Clint Wykoff became the first Big Red All-American.[54]

Of considerably greater importance to the game, though, was Glenn Warner, who joined the Cornell team as a twenty-one-year-old law student in 1892 and earned the nickname "Pop." He returned as coach in 1897 and 1898 and again in 1906, amassing 319 career victories in forty-four seasons at several colleges, a record until Bear Bryant broke it in 1982. Warner invented the huddle, the spiral pass, the screen pass, and the rolling block, among other innovations. Like all good coaches, he was a passionate teacher, who went so far as to give coaching courses by correspondence.

In Providence, Brown was getting the hang of the game, hiring their first coach. They were courted to join a league with Tufts, Bowdoin, the Stevens Institute, and MIT. A year later they posted their first winning season and in 1894 captured the league title. By 1895, Brown managed to tie mighty Yale, 6-6, the first points they had ever scored against the Elis and an event of such importance as to be memorialized on a bronze plaque. In 1896, Dave Fultz became their first All-American.

Brown's manager that season was John D. Rockefeller, Jr., a devout and insecure young man who knew so little about football when he started that he called the center the "middle." Junior certainly had his father's parsimony, refusing to hand out a new pair of shoelaces until the player could account for his last pair. Still, there were benefits to having a Rockefeller around. When Brown played Carlisle at the Polo Grounds in 1898, his parents attended. John Senior, who had never before seen a football game, "started out in the stands, calmly surveying the spectacle, then grew so excited that he rushed down to the field in his tall silk hat and began to race up and down the sidelines with the coaches."[55]

While many other colleges were considering dropping football, Columbia finally returned to the sport in 1899 with high ambitions. They hired George Foster Sanford as their coach at $1,500 a year and boldly scheduled Yale, Cornell, Army, Dartmouth, Princeton, Navy, and Carlisle. Surprisingly, the Lions more than held its own, finishing 8-3, the highlight being a 5-0 shocker over Yale on Harold Weekes' long touchdown run. Weekes was also the centerpiece of the "hurdle play," one of the most bizarre configurations in the game's history. The 210-pound fullback would climb up on the shoulders of two teammates, who would then catapult him over the line, where he would try to land on his feet and keep running. When defenses checked this by heaving their own men at the airborne Weekes (one cringes at the thought), the play was abandoned.

Dartmouth fared well in the Triangular League with Amherst and

Williams, but some thought they should set their sights higher. If the football team could only find a way to attract the athletes already on campus, the *Springfield Union* wrote, "the New Hampshire College would stand close up to the big four and make Cornell hustle for her laurels." [56]

Underlying the debates over professionalism, of brutality, and overemphasis was the much larger issue of who should control football. Should college games be run by the students, by the faculty, by the alumni, or by some combination of the three? These questions, unresolved in some senses even today, lay at the heart of what became the Ivy League.

Football—as was the case with baseball, crew, and other early campus sports—began as an independent fiefdom, run at first by the team captain, and later by the student football association, a booster club. Though conferring considerably less social standing, football managerships were almost as much political plums as captaincies. Tryouts at Cornell in the first decades of the twentieth century consumed almost the candidates' entire junior year. Managers did everything now done by the athletic department: they scheduled games, arranged transportation, purchased equipment and supplies, corresponded with their counterparts at other schools, and haggled over guarantees, money paid to induce a rival to make the road trip or to compensate the team for costs it would incur by traveling.

The correspondence of Harvard's football managers provides a fascinating example of the way this system operated. Owing to faculty restrictions and its own prominence, Harvard almost always played at home. Its manager was thus required to wave enough money under the nose of smaller rivals to induce them to make the trip to Cambridge. Typical was the following letter to Tufts in 1893:

> *Dear Sir,*
>
> *I am sorry you do not see fit to accept my terms for a game on Oct, 18th. I do not see how I can give you a larger guarantee than I mentioned [$25], as the game is to be played on a Wednesday. This means a small attendance. Then we take the risk of a rainy day, in which case there would be no gate receipts.*
>
> *You say that we give larger guarantees to other college teams and that you can give us as good a game as they can. That may be true, but you must bear in mind the fact that other college teams travel farther, hence they have big expenses. They make scarcely anything out of their games here. The guarantee is eaten up by their traveling expenses.*
>
> *You had better think over the terms. Meanwhile I will keep the date open for you.* [57]

Gate receipts accounted for most of the team's revenue, but the football associations also raised money from dues or by levying taxes on fellow undergraduates, appealing to their school pride or exerting social pressure.[58] At Dartmouth in 1899, for example, class participation ranged from 75 percent among the sophomore class to 87 percent among the seniors—perhaps not always cheerfully.[59]

By the end of the nineteenth century, football had become not just the biggest moneymaking activity on campus, but often the *only* moneymaker. The Yale Football Association took in more than $31,000 in 1893, an amount greater than the annual receipts of the Yale's medical, art, or music departments.[60] Within a decade, Yale's annual football receipts had soared to more than $100,000, more than one-eighth of the total income for the entire university.

The faculty's decision to wash their hands of what students did during their free time had come to look foolish, not to say irresponsible. For not only were football and other sports growing, so were nonathletic extracurricular activities. Many educators began to view with alarm a growing source of student energies, which was beginning to dwarf the rest of the university financially yet lay entirely outside their control.

Although college authorities had neither the inclination nor the ability to run the teams, they could try to control abuses such as excessive absences from class and, if matters continued to get out of hand, threaten to abolish an activity altogether. In 1881, Princeton formed the Committee on Athletics and Music Clubs, which in one move placed an official hand not only over the football and baseball teams, but also the glee club, which had caused a stir by planning a long tour during the school year. Harvard created a similar committee the following year, confined solely to athletics, and others followed.

In the face of faculty attempts to regulate athletics, the students found a new and more powerful ally—the alumni. Graduates had been providing coaching assistance for years and were always among the first ones students turned to for help when the football associations could not pay their bills. In exchange for financial support, the graduates demanded greater control and tighter bookkeeping. Thus, at many colleges the individual booster clubs came to be consolidated into campuswide athletic organizations to coordinate fundraising for all the major sports.

Faced with mounting deficits from its football program, Princeton organized an alumni advisory committee in 1885, the first of its kind, which five years later had sufficiently established its authority that it could issue bonds to pay for improvements to University Field. When the Tiger football team tried to ignore the committee's recommendations, the graduates had the team formally placed under their supervision. Dartmouth also placed its struggling football program in the hands of an alumni athletic committee, which built a new field and operated the gymnasium. Harvard and Penn reorganized their faculty oversight committees to include graduates, and later students, as full members. At Columbia, on the other hand, the inability to find a workable system for financing athletics was a principal reason for dropping football during most of the 1890s. Only at Yale, thanks to the enormous influence of Walter Camp, did football escape faculty, or even alumni, oversight.

By the end of the century, control of college football, at least on the financial side, had passed almost entirely to the graduates. The alumni took a greater role in many affairs of the colleges, which had ambitious expansion plans of their own and a similar inability to pay for them. At almost every Ivy college, alumni magazines began to appear at around this time, in large part to pass along news about the football team. Early subscribers to the *Yale Alumni Magazine*, in fact, were lured with the offer of a prized pair of football tickets.

Alumni influence often outweighed that of the faculty. In 1895 the Harvard faculty voted by a two-to-one margin to abolish football following the Hampden Park Bloodbath. The student- and alumni-dominated athletic committee, however, voted unanimously to keep it. Faced with a standoff, the committee asked the Harvard Corporation, the university's ultimate governing body, to decide: "Does the continuation or abolition of intercollegiate football rest with the Committee or with the Faculty?" The Corporation sent an unmistakable message by siding with the athletic committee.

So long as colleges were still hashing out internal control over football, any formal coordination between them to set standards was impossible. Furthermore, eligibility and academic standards were too different, and the disputes between colleges too frequent and acrimonious for any formal intercollegiate oversight organization to flourish.

Harvard, with Princeton's support, tried to bring the northeastern colleges together throughout the 1880s to adopt common standards of eligibility and amateurism, but were stymied because Yale refused to participate. A conference at Brown in 1898 (which Yale boycotted) produced a report containing a number of far-sighted, but in the short term futile, proposals for reform. Only bona fide students would be permitted to participate in intercollegiate sports, freshmen would be excluded, professional athletes would be barred, eligibility would be limited to four years, fall practice would be curtailed, games would be restricted to campus, training tables would be eliminated, and a faculty-dominated committee would be established at each school to regulate schedules and approve the hiring of all team personnel. Yet not a single college adopted the Brown proposals. In most places, alumni control continued.

Not even the flying wedge could keep the Crimson from reverting to their old ways of losing to Yale. At the start of the 1894 season, after three consecutive shutout losses in the only game that mattered, even the aloof Henry Adams was moved to complain. "Are you going to get another licking at foot-ball this year?" he chided a friend in Cambridge. "You must have put real genius into discovering how not to win." [61]

Charles Eliot's efforts to abolish football met with fierce opposition from students and the school's very prominent alumni. "I would a hundred fold rather keep the game as it is, with the brutality, than give it up," Theodore Roosevelt wrote to Walter Camp.[62] Henry Cabot Lodge and Charles Francis Adams also weighed in for reform rather than abolition, Adams arguing that football "educated boys in those characteristics that had made the Anglo-Saxon race pre-eminent in history."[63]

Even someone as stubborn as Eliot could not withstand that much pressure. His timing was also bad, as the Crimson were finally getting good again. Under the leadership of coaches Cameron Forbes and Benjamin Dibblee, they went thirty-two games without a loss and won two more national championships, in 1898 and 1899. Harvard and Yale also agreed to resume athletic relations in 1897 for a five-year trial period.

Eliot belittled those who insisted that football developed warriors, noting that in modern warfare combatants rarely even saw each other and so would have little occasion to attempt the guards back formation on the battlefield. Yet when war did come in the summer of 1898, Ivy football players were well represented in the armed forces. Roosevelt was proud of how many enlisted in the Rough Riders, including Dudley Dean of Harvard, John Greenaway of Yale, and Roscoe Channing of Princeton. Hamilton Fish, whose cousin by the same name later starred for Harvard, was killed on San Juan Hill. Two years earlier, Win Osgood, the Penn running back, joined the Cuban insurrection and was shot dead while loading his artillery piece. His death was immortalized in the popular ballad, *Just Break the News to Mother*.

The Poe family gave the nation both soldiers and football heroes. Edgar Allan was the first but by no means either the most colorful or illustrious of the six brothers who played for Princeton. John Prentiss Poe, Jr., or "Johnny" as he was known, was elected freshman class president the day after he arrived on campus and starred at halfback on the football team (although he was only five-foot-five and 143 pounds), but was kicked out of school that spring for poor grades. The morning Poe left for home, his entire class escorted him to the train station to say good-bye. He returned the following fall and did even better on the football field, scoring two touchdowns in a game against a Chicago Athletic Club team that included Pudge Heffelfinger and Snake Ames. A perfectionist in things he cared about, Poe would go back to his room after practice and spend hours pitching a football into a pile of sofa pillows until he got it right. Unfortunately, such dedication to his schoolwork remained lacking and he was expelled again, this time permanently.

In between stints as a gold miner and soldier of fortune, he stuck around Princeton, helped with the football team and served as an assistant on the 1903 championship squad. As a motivator, he is best remembered for remarks he made at half-time of the Harvard game in 1896—"If you won't be beat, you can't be beat"—words which would be recalled to inspire the Tigers in a celebrated upset of the University of Chicago in 1922. The John Prentiss Poe Football Cup, given to the university by his mother, is awarded annually to the member of the team who best exemplifies courage, modesty, perseverance, and good sportsmanship. It is Princeton's highest football honor.

If Johnny Poe was not as good a football player as his brother Edgar, their younger brother, Arthur, was more famous than either. The family's second All-American, he almost single-handedly beat Yale two years in a row, the first time the Tigers had ever done that. In the 1899 game, he pulled off what is still recalled as one of the greatest plays of the nineteenth century.

Arthur started as a quarterback before knee injuries forced him to move to end. In 1898, he was a sensation, leading the team to an 11-0-1 record. He broke an eighty-yard touchdown run against Navy and a forty-yard run against Brown, but was most famous for his performance against Yale, when he returned a fumble ninety-five yards for the only score of the game.[64] Even the Elis called it "a nice piece of football."[65] It could have been even better; Poe's ninety-yard touchdown run from scrimmage was nullified by a penalty.

In 1899, the Tigers raced through another good year, with only a 5-0 upset loss to Cornell going into the finale against Yale. The ground at New Haven was frozen and a fierce wind was blowing. Princeton scored first for a 6-0 lead, but Yale got back into it when they recovered a blocked punt for a touchdown. A drop-kick field goal made it 10-6 Yale, and there the score stayed until late in the game.

Then Princeton got a break. With four minutes left to play, Bill Roper (who later coached the Tigers) fell on a fumble at the Yale forty-yard line. Coach Biffy Lea had replaced both Princeton kickers earlier in the game, and under the rules at the time a player once removed could not return. With only thirty-two seconds to go, Princeton had not advanced beyond Yale's twenty-five-yard line. Poe asked to try a field goal. Although he had never tried one before in a game, he had challenged Alex Moffat to a kicking contest earlier in the week and beaten him, and was kicking with a strong wind at his back.

Poe dropped back to the thirty-seven-yard line. Because he didn't have square-toed kicking shoes, he was forced to kick with his instep, a soccer-style drop kick. Yale thought he was going to try a fake. Big Bill Edwards, Princeton's right guard, remembered the next few moments vividly. "To be frank, I was afraid I would block it—that Poe couldn't clear me, that he would kick the ball into me," he wrote. "I crouched as low as I could, and the more I worried the larger I seemed to be.... But finally, as I realized that the ball had gone over me and was on its way to the goal, I breathed a sigh of relief and said, 'Thank God, it cleared!'"[66]

Few men ever get to bask in the kind of adulation Poe enjoyed because of that kick for the rest of his life. His celebrity was immense. As Poe's class yearbook noted the following spring, "He gave Lady Burr complete control of his correspondence and Carl was kept busy making photographs and composing replies, most of which began like this: 'Mr. Poe directs me to thank you for the lock of hair. He prizes it highly and regrets that another engagement will prevent his presence at Cadwalader Park, Friday evening.'" [67]

Somehow, football managed to increase its grip on the popular imagination despite the efforts of its most ardent Ivy supporters, both on the field and off, to kill it.

CHAPTER FOUR

More Work for the Undertaker

Things looked bleak for the Bulldogs:

The gray of November twilights, the haze that settles over the struggles of the gridiron like the smoke of a battle-field, began to close in. And then a sudden fumble, a blocked kick, and by the swift turn of luck it was Yale's ball for the first time in Princeton's territory. One or two subs came rushing in eagerly from the side lines. Every one was talking at once:

"What's the time?"

"Five minutes more."

"Get together, Yale!"

"Show 'em how!"

"Ram it through them!"

"Here's our chance!"

Stover, beside himself, ran up to DeSoto and flung his arms about his neck, whispering in his ear:

"Give me a chance—you must give me a chance! Send me through Regan!"

He got his signal, and went into the breach with every nerve set, fighting his way behind the great bulk of Regan for a good eight yards. A second time he was called on, and broke the line for another first down.

Regan was transformed. All his calm had gone. He loomed in the line like a Colossus, flinging out his arms, shouting:

> *"We're rotten, are we? Carry it right down the field, boys!"*
> *Every one caught the infection. DeSoto, with his hand to his*
> *mouth, was shouting hoarsely, through the bedlam of cheers, his*
> *gleeful slogan:*
> *"We don't want to live forever, boys! What do we care? We've got*
> *to face Yale after this. Never mind your necks. We've got the doc-*
> *tors! A little more murder, now! Shove that ball down the field,*
> *Yale! Send them back on stretchers! Nineteen—eight—six—*
> *four—Ha-a-ard!"* [1]

Alas, Dink Stover and his teammates lost to Princeton, 18-0, that fictional afternoon, but when Owen Johnson's novel *Stover at Yale* was serialized in *McClure's* magazine in 1911, it added to an already rich vein of football literature. The plot possibilities of the game were obvious, particularly when set in a glamorous location such as an elite university. Stories about football almost always recount the triumph of good over vice, of hard work over sloth.

A generation of American youth grew up on these novels, inculcated in the values of fair play and conditioned to associate it with the Big Three, or thinly disguised copies. Amid the chaos of a changing society at the turn of the century, writes literary critic Michael Oriard, depictions of football at places like Yale "implied a rule-governed contest in which the better man won through superior merit, affirming a meritocracy that exalted the winners without altogether diminishing the losers." [2]

The first short story to mention football was "Richard Carr's Baby," which Richard Harding Davis published in *St. Nicholas* magazine in 1886. [3] Carr, captain of the Princeton football team, accidentally knocks down a crippled boy standing along the sidelines. Concerned for the boy's welfare despite the many other demands on his time, Carr visits him, hires a doctor to treat his crooked spine, decks the lad out in the colors of Old Nassau, and brings him to practice, where he is treated like a kid brother. The boy gets well and enters Princeton himself. Although Davis's story predated the Spanish-American War and the advent of American imperialism, it is not hard to catch the geopolitical message.

Most famous of all athlete-heroes in American literature was Frank Merriwell, the Yale icon and hero of more than 850 Gilbert Patten dime novels beginning in 1896. Merriwell was the embodiment of all that was virtuous: a gentleman, an aristocrat, and a Yale man, through and through (Patten, who had not gone to college, modeled him after Davis). He was handsome, physically big but not freakish, a good student but not an intellectual, democratic, "industrious, persistent, honest, brave, steady, generous, self-sacrificing, and serious to the point of humorlessness." [4] Yale and to a lesser extent Princeton men were almost always portrayed in fiction as heroes, while Harvard men were prigs or worse. "'You are a cheap cad,' Frank told the overdressed Harvard bully," is a typical line. [5] In the sixteen years the stories appeared, Frank Merriwell (and later his brother Dick) never lost an important game. And they always got the girl.[6]

There was more than enough actual glory to go around. Yale began and ended the 1890s with teams that compete for the honor of being their greatest ever. But the era in which even the big eastern powers could dominate national intercollegiate football for the nation was ending and new schools, including Dartmouth, began to achieve prominence. Eventually Harvard, traditionally the weakest of the Big Three, took Yale's place atop the football totem. That is, when Harvard was not trying to tear the totem down altogether.

The Elis of 1900 were Yale's twelfth undefeated team. Although Walter Camp had not adopted the flying wedge, he had found considerable success with the turtle back play, putting nine men in the offensive backfield to run interference for the ball carrier. When that play and Penn's "guards back" were rendered illegal thanks to a rule that required at least five men on the line of scrimmage, Yale had been forced to look for something else.

The solution was the "tackles back" play, in which one of the tackles was placed in the offensive backfield, usually behind the other tackle, leaving the required five-man front while also providing more muscle to guard the ball carrier. Although Camp is credited with popularizing the play, authorship rightfully belongs to Dr. Harry Williams, a Yale alumnus, who perfected it at the William Penn Charter School in Philadelphia before passing the information along to New Haven. Camp was not interested at first, but changed his mind in 1900 when Williams persuaded Army to try it in a victory over Navy.

Before the first practice, Camp called coach Malcolm McBride and captain Gordon Brown into his office, explained that the new system would take a while to learn, and asked for patience. Although the Elis won all their early games, they looked disorganized and drew criticism from the legions of critics who followed their every move. When reporters questioned McBride about the ragged new offensive scheme, he replied with a certain strained loyalty, "If Walter says it is all right, it probably is all right."[7]

Their toughest game turned out to be against Columbia, but play calling had little to do with it. Yale had arrived in New York expecting to play on a dry field, but Columbia coach George Foster Sanford, borrowing one of the oldest tricks in the book, had Manhattan firefighters soak the field for hours with hoses, turning it into a muddy mess. He then handed out wooden cleats to his own squad. The Lions took a 5-0 lead over the sliding Bulldogs before McBride could find a carpenter willing to nail wooden cleats onto his own team's shoes. They arrived at halftime, and Yale rallied for a 12-5 victory.

Just as predicted, the Elis hit their peak for the big November games, crushing Carlisle (35-0), Princeton (29-5), and Harvard (28-0) in consecutive weeks. All eleven Yale starters made All-American that year (Camp, after all, was doing the selecting), seven on the first team.

Even more than the team's sterling record or the terrific individual perform-ance of Gordon Brown, Yale fans remember the 1900 season for its musical side. Three songs made their debut that year, and are still sung by Yale rooters today. The first was "Bright College Years," written by H. S. Durand, Class of 1881, the final line of which ("For God, for Country, and for Yale") has been derided as the great-est anticlimax in literature. Although it has stood the test of years, some at the time decried it as "absolutely unsingable except by a very few well trained voices."[8]

Against Harvard a week later, Bulldogs first sang the "Undertaker," Yale's ultimate morale-snuffer of the olden days:

> *Ohhhhhhhhhhhhhh,*
> *More work for the undertaker,*
> *Another little job for the casket maker,*
> *In the local cemetery they are very very busy*
> *On a brand new grave—*
> *No hope for Harvard.*

They also sang "Boola Boola," which was composed by a senior, Allan M. Hirsch, catcher on the baseball team, who also led the singing at football games using a bat as a baton. No one knows just what "Boola" means or where it comes from. Some say Hirsch borrowed it from a popular show tune, "La Hoola Boola." Others say it was the Polynesian word for "kill."[9] Nevertheless, the *Yale Alumni Weekly*, while conceding that "as poetic literature they are considered something short of immortal," nevertheless countered that it was the opinion of even "the most conservative of the English and Musical Faculty that the defiance and fight and accelerating speed of football were never better expressed."

This was the golden age of college fight songs and as Yale's new president, Arthur Twining Hadley, observed, there were rules for a successful one. "The fit [between tune and subject] is the most important thing, the tune probably next, the words last of all. The best college song in the country is [Princeton's] *Old Nassau*. The words by themselves are abominable; the tune can hardly be said to rise far above mediocrity; but the fit is something absolutely extraordinary."[10]

Harvard had never been particularly fertile ground for football tunes. "Fair Harvard," which has nothing to do with football, was adapted in 1831 from the maudlin English ballad, "My Lodging Is on the Cold Ground." The opening of the new stadium in 1903 seems to have provoked a trickle, including "Soldiers Field," "Harvardiana," and "The Gridiron King."[11] Dartmouth men at the time were lustily singing the gloriously un-P.C. tune, "Eleazer Wheelock," which was written around 1894 for $50. Penn introduced two of its standards, "The Red and Blue" and "Hail, Pennsylvania" (the latter set to the tune of the imperial Russian national anthem). Cornell cheerleaders offered a $25 prize for a "football song indigenous in words and music," but not "boastful, bumptious or vainglorious because the prospects looked pretty punk for the team." Romeyn Berry, a recent graduate, dashed off some words and had them set to music. His entry, "The Big Red Team," won first prize and gave Cornell a nickname.

Brown students began singing, "I'm a Brown man born/I'm a Brown man bred/And when I die/I'm a Brown man dead." Meanwhile, Theodore Francis Green, later a U.S. senator from Rhode Island, persuaded the school to adopt the bear as its mascot. He thought it a perfect fit; the bear was brave, indigenous, intelligent, and "capable of being educated (if caught young enough!)."[12] A live brown bear named Dinks was rented to make his athletic debut in 1905, but when Dinks refused to cooperate, students pressed his cagemate, Helen, into service instead.

Even Columbia showed itself well. In 1904, the school's first band appeared at a game against Cornell, a 12-6 victory. Most likely they played "Sans Souci," a new hit on campus, although they would have missed another Columbia classic, "Stand Up and Cheer," by a few years. Rather like the team, no sooner had the band appeared than it disappeared, not to be revived until the teens.

Though Charles Eliot continued to rail against the evils of football, Harvard's athletic authorities had grown tired of losing at it to Yale. In twenty-one meetings between the schools through 1900, the Crimson's record was a dismal 3-14-4. Imitation may be the sincerest form of flattery, but Harvard at last decided to adopt some of Yale's techniques.

One was the tackles back play. Another was coaching. In 1901, they brought back William Reid, who had starred on the 1898 team. Coaches were hampered by a rule that forbade them from sending in plays during a game. Nevertheless, Eliot professed himself shocked when he learned that coaches routinely ignored the prohibition. "It is not a thing done in hot blood, but prepared coolly beforehand. Can there be a meaner training for young men?" he wrote Hadley.[13]

Reid improved upon the techniques he had learned from Cameron Forbes and led Harvard back to an undefeated national championship. They smashed Yale, 22-0, the last time they beat the Elis at home until 1913 and the last time they scored a touchdown against them until 1915. Harvard's Crawford Blagden suffered an attack of appendicitis the Thursday before the game but vowed, "I'll play if it kills me," and managed to see action with braces strapped around his abdomen (he was operated on the following day). Others were also taking precautions; players by this time were already wearing leather helmets. Reid left after just one season, a victim of overwork, but returned a few years later for a more eventful, if less successful, tenure.

More than a quarter of the class tried out for Harvard's freshman team in the fall of 1901, among them Franklin D. Roosevelt, who had given up cigarettes in order to improve his conditioning. Too light to be much of a prospect, he was cut and assigned to the "Missing Links," lowliest of the eight intramural teams, though he was elected captain. "It is the only [team] composed wholly of

Freshmen and I am the *only* Freshman Captain," he proudly wrote his parents.[14] FDR did more for the service of Harvard athletics as editor of the *Crimson*, and as an usher and cheerleader.

An unmistakable sign of brighter things in Cambridge was the dedication of Harvard Stadium in 1903. A gift of the Class of 1879 (Eliot had refused to contribute a nickel of the university's money), it seated forty thousand, cost $325,000, and sat on the site of Soldiers Field, which had served as Harvard's home grounds for many years. The horseshoe-shaped stadium incorporated elements from both Greek and Roman architecture. One observer wrote that he expected to see "an arched gateway swing upon and pour forth a flood of Gauls and Thracians, of Samnites and retarii, all crying 'Ave Caesar.'"[15]

Much to their embarrassment, the Crimson opened their new home with an 11-0 loss to Dartmouth. Cheering for Harvard that afternoon, though, were two hundred Italian construction workers who were still putting the finishing touches on the structure they had completed in just four and a half months. Omens were not good; Harvard lost to Yale there the following week, and did not record their first victory in the stadium until the following year.

As their victory proved, Dartmouth had at last arrived. "In the past we have taken what she [Harvard] has been willing to give us, but today we have taken something that she was very reluctant to part with," one student wrote. After several successful seasons in the Triangular League with smaller schools, Dartmouth made its breakthrough in 1901 with a 22-0 pasting of Brown. They were ranked as high as seventh in the country in 1902, putting up a gallant fight before losing to Harvard in a game so dark by the end that the referee had to light a match to spot the ball. The 1903 team that spoiled the Crimson's opening was led by coach Fred Folsom, Ralph Glaze, and Leigh Turner. All but one of Dartmouth's linemen that season stood over six feet tall, and their average weight was almost 220 pounds, a monstrous line for the time. They finished the year again ranked second; only a loss to Princeton kept them from the national championship. When Dartmouth went undefeated in 1904, they replaced Penn on Harvard's schedule.

Two men who should have met in that upset at the new stadium were Dartmouth's Matthew Washington Bullock and Harvard's William Clarence Matthews. Bullock was born in North Carolina; later his parents, both former slaves, moved to Massachusetts with seven children and ten dollars. Bullock earned enough money singing at New England summer resorts to afford tuition at Dartmouth, where he played end on the football team for four years (winning honorable mention All-American in 1903), ran track, and sang in the glee club. When the team traveled to Princeton in 1903, they were refused lodging at the Princeton Inn, and Bullock's career was ended in that game on what some alleged was a deliberate foul.

He went on to attend Harvard Law School, supporting himself by coaching football on the side. At what is now the University of Massachusetts, Bullock became the first African-American head coach at a predominantly white school. He practiced law in Atlanta and Boston, ran unsuccessfully for the Massachusetts legislature, was cited for bravery on a humanitarian mission to Europe during World War I, and served on the state parole board.

William Matthews had attended Tuskegee Institute but pursued further education at Andover and at Harvard. As a shortstop, he was considered the best player on a Crimson team many believed was the best in the country, hitting over .300 in each of his three years on the varsity and stealing more than forty-two bases. In an expose of college athletic abuses, *McClure's* magazine singled him out as "the best there is in a college athlete." [16]

Matthews resisted the temptation to play professional baseball during the summer, even though several of his white teammates did, but while a player in the outlaw Northern League of Vermont in 1905, Fred Tenney, manager of the Boston Braves, was reported to be considering defying the unofficial color bar and signing Matthews for the pennant drive. When the league office squelched that idea, Matthews spoke with wounded pride. "As a Harvard man, I shall devote my life to bettering the condition of the black man, and especially to secure his admittance into organized baseball." [17]

He had faced such prejudice at Harvard, too—President Eliot remarked that blacks at Harvard made their mark, not academically, but "on account of their remarkable athletic merit"—though he appears to have suffered no such hazing as a football player. [18] One incident, however, suggested that he did. Against Yale in 1904, Matthews was knocked out of the game on a hard, and some said deliberately rough, hit while covering a punt. The *New York Sun* suggested that Yale had targeted Matthews because he was black, but he publicly repudiated the idea, saying the tackle had been clean, and noting that he and several of the Yale players had prepped together at Andover. "I do not believe any Yale man tried to use me unfairly," he announced in an interview. [19]

The ethnic composition of Ivy football teams was changing considerably faster than their racial makeup. The colleges had traditionally drawn only Anglo-Saxon stock, with a growing number of Germans mixed in during the latter part of the nineteenth century. As they expanded in size, and changed their educational mission from the training of clergy to the cultivation of the nation's business elite, the colleges also began to draw a more diverse student body.

First to come were the Irish. In 1902, Yale featured what was called its "Irish line" including Jim Hogan, Tom Shevlin, Chuck Rafferty, and Ralph Kinney, as well as Ned Glass, George Goss, and Henry Holt. Dan Hurley captained Harvard's eleven in 1904 while James L. Cooney starred at Princeton.

Except for their ancestry, Hogan and Shevlin could not have been more different. Hogan was born in County Tipperary and grew up poor; his father was a stonemason and his mother took in laundry. He worked for the Union Hardware Company until he could save enough money to enter Phillips Exeter. Because he had to work his way through college, he did not graduate until he was twenty-eight, making him older than the Yale football coach. But Hogan made the most of his chance. He was a three-time All-American tackle, was tapped for Skull and Bones, and managed the Yale Dramatic Association. His classmates mentioned him by name in the classic Yale fight song, "Down the Field," which contains the lines: "We'll give a long cheer for Hogan's men/We're here to win again/Harvard's team can fight to the end/But Yale will win!"

Shevlin, on the other hand, was a sport. The son of a Minnesota lumber magnate, he sailed through college on an allowance, buying cars and forty-cent cigars. He was a star end and made first-team All-American as a freshman. Unlike Hogan, though, one senses that Shevlin was not well-liked by his classmates, who may have resented his nouveau riche airs whereas they were drawn to Hogan's earnestness; none of the senior societies tapped him.

Like many old grads, Hogan was later pressed to fill in as a coach at Yale where, decked out in "a big fur coat and derby and a diamond-studded cane, [he] inspired players with his energy, enthusiasm, resourcefulness, and courage." While pacing the sidelines in 1915, Shevlin contracted pneumonia, and died at the age of thirty-two. At halftime of the Harvard game the following year, coach Tad Jones tried to inspire his troops by invoking Shevlin's name. "If any of you boys believe in the hereafter," he said, "you will know that Tom Shevlin is pacing up and down across the river, smoking that big black cigar, and asking the boys to go out there and do it once again for papa." Perhaps sensing that this was not enough, it was only then that Jones added his immortal peroration: "You are about to play a game of football against Harvard. Never again will you do anything so important."[20]

Together, Yale's Irish line won another national championship in 1902 with an 11-0-1 record, their only blemish a tie against Army. Featured in the Eli backfield was Harold Metcalf, a star rusher uncharitably nicknamed the "Human Wreck" by his teammates because of his pasty appearance caused by a bout with typhoid.

In 1903, it was Princeton's turn on top. They were not a high-octane offensive squad, but yielded only six points in winning all eleven games they played. Leading them was John DeWitt, a lineman who was also the Tigers' star kicker. DeWitt broke an eighty-yard touchdown run against Dartmouth, then kicked a fifty-yard field goal the following week against Cornell. In a showdown against also-unbeaten Yale, he combined his talents, returning a blocked punt eighty-five yards for a touchdown, adding the extra point, then kicking a forty-eight-yard field goal from a sharp angle to score all Princeton's points in an 11-6 victory.

DeWitt also inaugurated created another Princeton tradition. At season's end, he and his teammates visited a local photographer to have their team portrait taken. DeWitt brought along his tattered jersey, which was pronounced unacceptable. The photographer scrounged up a white sweater with a black "P" on the front, the wearing of which has since become a prerogative of all captains of Princeton championship teams. [21]

Pennsylvania returned to glory the following year. Shunned by Princeton and Yale, the Quakers decided to look elsewhere for opponents. They began playing a longer schedule than any of the Ivy schools (fifteen games in 1902), fattening up on smaller local colleges in October, but moving on to Carlisle, North Carolina, Chicago, Army, and Navy in what became known as the "championship season" in November.

George Woodruff had left in 1901, succeeded by Dr. Carl Williams, an eye specialist who had starred on the great Quaker teams of the mid-nineties. (Williams resigned in 1907 when coaching began to take too much time from his medical practice.) He introduced an aggressive, swarming defense, a departure from the more flexible style then popular. In 1904 and 1905, Penn's defense surrendered just thirty-seven points in twenty-five games. The Quaker stars included end Wharton Sinkler, center Bob Torrey, and guards Frank Piekarski (the "Terrible Pole") and Gus Ziegler (the "German Oak"), whose nicknames testified to the team's ethnic diversity.

Quarterback Vince Stevenson, a pivoting, hurdling runner, was the principal beneficiary of a rule change that permitted a quarterback to run with the ball so long as he crossed the line of scrimmage at least five yards from the spot at which it had been put into play. In order to enforce the five-yard rule, it became necessary to paint longitudinal lines on the field in addition to the yard stripes, making the field look like a checkerboard for several years until the rule was repealed.

In 1904, the Quakers went 12-0, scoring 222 points while giving up only four. Given the strength of their schedule, several writers, including George Trevor of the *New York Sun*, have called this team the greatest Quaker squad of all time. They could not claim the national championship in the eyes of many, though, because they had not played Yale or Princeton. The following season, only an unexpected tie with Lafayette spoiled another perfect record.

The Elis, who lost only to Army, capped their 1904 season with a pair of shutouts over Princeton and Harvard. The New York, New Haven, and Hartford Railroad ran six special trains to New Haven for the game against the Crimson. In attendance that afternoon were Alice Roosevelt, the president's daughter, Vice President Charles Fairbanks, and financier J. P. Morgan, who had ridden up in his private Pullman car. Certainly, little had been lost by playing on campus; at around this time, the Yale alumni magazine estimated that The Game added $150,000 to the local economy. [22]

During these years, Columbia was led by a pair of "Wild Bills." Quarterback "Wild Bill" Donovan (a nickname he earned later, as a soldier) went on to greater fame during World War II as director of the Office of Strategic Services, forerunner of the CIA. Coach "Wild Bill" Morley (so called because he came from New Mexico territory) led the team to a 26-11-3 record from 1902 to 1905, giving him the highest winning percentage of any coach in school history. He thought the state of the game was fine, touting the death rate in football as "wonderfully small."

Yet Morley was the last coach to lead Columbia for some time, as the college abolished football midway through the 1905 season. The various ills of college football—rough play, eligibility, and general overemphasis—had been patched over by the sport's governing bodies but never solved. In the first years of the new century, the muckrakers, who had been exposing corruption in many areas of American life from oil refining to meat-packing turned their attention to football, another adjunct of growing American corporatism.

They found no shortage of material. Despite attempts to set rudimentary eligibility standards, colleges were still cheating, and if anything, given the increasing revenue and competition as more schools fielded competitive teams, getting more blatant about it. In the fall of 1900, the *New York Sun* alleged that the Tigers had recruited two players—former Cornell quarterback Charles Young and Howard Reiter, a Princeton alumnus—out of the stands at halftime of their game against Columbia, slipping them into the second half in disguise.[23] Penn and Cornell engaged in more than one angry dispute over the issue of eligibility and threatened to sever athletic relations, though as the Quakers were Cornell's only big game, they were forced to back down. Brown, too, had earned a reputation for using professionals, though mostly on the baseball diamond.

The day before the 1901 Harvard-Yale game, Yale alleged that Oliver Cutts, a twenty-eight-year-old former railroad brakeman and star in the Crimson backfield (who was already a graduate of Bates College), was ineligible because he had taught athletics for money at the Haverford School outside Philadelphia. Harvard fired back that Ned Glass, part of the Irish line, was also ineligible because he had played the previous year for Syracuse. Yale agreed to hold Glass out, but Harvard played Cutts, on the strength of affidavits from both Cutts and the Haverford headmaster swearing that he had not been paid for his services and thus remained an amateur. Only after the game did Cutts concede that he had given private boxing and fencing lessons for money. Harvard apologized but did not offer to forfeit the victory.

Columbia was a particularly bad case. Only three players on its 1900 team were undergraduates. Newspapers reported that the student manager had paid the tuition of five members of the 1899 team out of football receipts, made phony bookkeeping entries to hide the payments, then lied about them when questioned. Readers of the *New York Sun* on March 24, 1900, read the following remarkable letter:

> *We wish to emphatically deny the current rumors that we received any pecuniary or educational benefit from playing Football with Columbia last season. Eighty-seven dollars were paid by the*

> *Football management to the university in order that our names*
> *would appear on the rolls, and thus make us eligible to play on the*
> *team.*
>
> *We did not receive tuition for playing football, as has been*
> *stated, as it is a well-known fact that we did not attend lectures*
> *and never had any intention of so doing. We played as a favor to*
> *Columbia and at a great sacrifice to our business.*

R.E. Larendon
G.H. Miller [24]

In 1902, it was discovered that a Columbia freshman, Thomas J. Thorp, had been playing for Manhattan College under an assumed name while still in high school. Although Columbia eventually disqualified Thorp for the rest of the season, they had to fight the alumni-dominated football committee in order to do so and he was later reinstated, granted an extra year of eligibility, and made captain of the team.

In order to field a competitive team quickly, the Columbia football association had run up huge debts. The rent on Manhattan Field alone was $15,000, and they could not bring in enough to pay it. Team officials were also forced to borrow money to pay Coach Sanford's $5,000 a year salary (which they soon raised to $8,500 in order to keep him, before turning to Morley who, as an alumnus, could be expected to work more cheaply). Because the anticipated football surplus was needed to pay the debts of Columbia's other money-losing teams, there was a threat that the entire athletic structure would collapse. The football association tried to schedule even more big games to generate more revenue, which instead only led to more blowouts, depressing attendance. A tougher schedule also meant longer practices, forcing many players enrolled in the colleges of Mines and Law to skip classes, which team officials then asked the faculty to overlook.

The lid blew off in 1905 with a two-part expose in *McClure's* written by Henry Beech Needham. The magazine's publisher, Samuel McClure, believed that the greatest threats facing the country were corruption and big business, and college football lay at their confluence. Needham detailed an appalling list of abuses at the supposedly noble Ivy colleges and elsewhere that touched many of the greatest players of the age. [25]

Recruiting, which was frowned upon although not outlawed, was rampant. There was much competition among the Big Three to develop "pipelines" from the top prep schools, and Needham reported that Penn had tried to keep up its end by wining and dining a group of Exeter stars over Thanksgiving break. Alums at other Ivy colleges promised cushy jobs to help pay tuition or were strategically placed on the prep school coaching staffs to steer boys toward their alma maters. In 1902, Charles Patterson, a wealthy Princeton alumnus, persuaded thirty-one

Andover students to sit for the Princeton entrance examination; seventeen were caught cheating on it. [26]

Most explosive were Needham's accusations against prominent Ivy players. James Hogan, the earnest Yale lineman who worked his way through school, turned out to have received quite a lot of help from the football association. He was given a room in the poshest dorm, took all his meals at the exclusive University Club, and was sent on a ten-day vacation to Cuba after the season that was hidden on the books as "miscellaneous expenses." Needham also alleged that Yale football authorities had arranged spending money for Hogan by letting him keep all proceeds from the sale of scorecards at Yale baseball games in addition to granting him the exclusive franchise to sell cigarettes on campus for the American Tobacco Company. [27]

Penn was singled out for special criticism. Several of its top players had been recruited away from other colleges, accepted after failing the entrance examination elsewhere or placed into professional programs such as the dental school which did not require an examination. Andy Smith was a rare case even by these low standards. He played so well for Penn State in a game against the Quakers in 1902 that he was recruited away over the weekend and showed up at *Penn's* practice the following Monday. During the next month, while working out with the Quaker scrubs, Smith still managed to play three more games for Penn State, claiming that he was "not in college" at the time. He jumped back to Penn in 1904 and helped them defeat Harvard.

Needham even slammed the Crimson for their "unmistakable air of self-satisfaction or smug self-righteousness—a 'holier than thou' contentment." Although Needham did not substantiate these accusations, we know that the gist of them were accurate thanks to the diary kept by Bill Reid when he returned to coach Harvard in 1905. In addition to providing a fascinating insight into the coaching methods and strategies of a bygone age, it is also a revealing look at the extent to which coaches would go to win.

Much as some football coaches must do today, Reid spent a lot of his time, especially in the off season, trying to keep his players academically eligible and out of trouble. He called on professors about giving men passing grades, bailed players out of jail, and considered "red shirting" injured freshmen. "No man of even ordinary ability can possibly fail to get through Harvard if he attends his lectures regularly and does a little work with some thinking," he noted once in exasperation. [28]

Reid tried to persuade 225-pound tackle Preston Upham to adhere to the straight and narrow, making him sign a pledge that Upham would not "cut [class] for any reason for a period of two weeks, and that I will also prepare every lesson in that time, giving to each study not less than one hour of real preparation." When, despite these efforts, Upham got into a brawl in which he knocked out three policemen, Reid huddled with the dean to try to keep him in school. "[Upham] seemed to lack all idea of responsibility or sense of decency," Reid wrote, "and all interest in things except loud women. I consulted some doctors to see if he could not be relieved in some way from this, but found it was impossible."

The coach showed particular diligence in pursuing Harry LeMoyne, whom he called "one of the greatest natural athletes Harvard has ever had." But LeMoyne had already failed out of Harvard and, so far as anyone knew, had gone out to Idaho to work on a sheep ranch. Reid was determined to bring him back, wooing his parents, consulting his old professors, and procuring a tutor to help him bring up his grades. He also secured a free railroad pass to bring LeMoyne back to Cambridge and lined up several easy jobs to give him spending money. When Reid tried to contact LeMoyne to tell him all this, he received no response. Letters and telegrams went unanswered as the season began to slip away. Reid even went so far as to arrange for a storekeeper in Idaho to deliver a letter to LeMoyne's ranch on horseback. Nothing. Eventually, Reid was forced to give up.

Some of these abuses were no doubt attributable to what muckrakers liked to call "the money power" in intercollegiate athletics. Clarence Deming, a Yale alumnus, published an article in 1905 in which he revealed that the Eli football association, under Camp's supervision, maintained a $100,000 slush fund.[29] In 1903-1904, the program took in more than $106,000, an amount that could have paid the salaries of thirty full professors. Such finances, which included an $8 per student "subscription" or athletic dues, enabled the football heroes to live in style. Among the team's expenses for the previous year were almost $10,000 for hotels and meals, $7,200 for equipment, and $6,500 for travel. President Hadley appointed a committee to look into the matter as a way of deflecting public criticism, but its confidential report did not recommend substantial changes.

Brutality also continued despite the IRC's efforts over almost two decades to do something about it. "I saw a Yale man throttle—literally throttle—Kernan, so that he dropped the ball," wrote Caspar Whitney of the 1902 Harvard-Yale game; "the two hands reached up in plain view of every one—and all saw but the umpire—and choked and choked; such a man would cheat at your cardtable.[30]" Pressure for reform began to build again in different parts of the country. Even supporters such as the *New York Times* began to have second thoughts.

In early October 1905, when a Wesleyan player jumped on a downed Columbia runner, the game degenerated into a brawl. Players and fans rushed onto the field in a melee during which coach Morley attacked the Wesleyan player and had to be restrained by police. A few weeks earlier, Groton's headmaster, Endicott Peabody, had written to Theodore Roosevelt, now president, proposing that Roosevelt call together officials from Harvard, Princeton, and Yale to agree on a plan to curb excessive violence. Roosevelt, who had also read Needham's articles and met with him privately, took Peabody up on the offer. When word leaked, Columbia tried to secure an invitation, too, but the president demurred lest he then have to invite Penn and everyone else. If the Big Three could agree on reforms, Roosevelt believed, other colleges would follow.

Roosevelt convened his conference at the White House on October 9, 1905.[31] Attending were Reid and team physician Dr. Edward Nichols from Harvard, Walter Camp and coach John Owsley from Yale, and coach Arthur Hildebrand and Professor John B. Fine from Princeton, as well as Secretary of State Elihu Root, a Hamilton College man. The president began by expressing his support for football, but pointing out instances in which each of the Big Three had been accused of foul play. According to Reid, Camp was evasive while both Yale and Princeton piously denied having done anything of the sort. Roosevelt left for a while to attend to other business, and when he returned sent them home with a request that the draw up a joint statement on the train. That statement, issued three days later, read as follows: "At a meeting with the president of the United States, it was agreed that we consider an honorable obligation exists to carry out in letter and in spirit the rules of the game of foot-ball, relating to roughness, holding, and foul play, and the active coaches of our universities being present with us, pledged themselves to so regard it and to do their utmost to carry out that obligation."[32]

The conference was a public relations triumph but even a superficial reading of the communiqué reveals its shortcomings. No one acknowledged that there were any problems with the game that a stricter application of the existing rules would not fix. In this sense, the statement was little different than the 1887 pledge captains had signed to train their teams in the rules against brutality. Although Roosevelt wanted something done, he did not have anything specific in mind. That might have been the end of that.

Instead, things got worse. The conference had been held at the beginning of the season. Nineteen-five turned out to be the worst—or at least the best-documented—year ever for football violence. At the end of the season, the *Chicago Tribune* reported that eighteen young men had been killed and 159 seriously injured in football games around the country. Harvard's Dr. Nichols published a study in the *Boston Medical and Surgical Journal* that Crimson football players collectively had missed 175 days of class due to injury and 1,057 days of incapacitation.[33]

In Cambridge, President Eliot had long since reached the conclusion that the game was past saving. No cloistered academic, he had in fact captained one of Harvard's first crews and took credit for selecting crimson as the university's color. At his inauguration in 1869, Eliot had lauded athletics—but athletics had changed and so had his conception of a university.

Nor was he one to shrink from a clash with Harvard's most famous alumnus. Although relations between the two presidents were outwardly polite, in private Eliot decried Roosevelt's "lawless mind" while Roosevelt called Eliot a "mollycoddle," one of his favorite epithets. "If we ever come to nothing as a nation," he wrote to Henry Cabot Lodge at around this time, "it will be because of the teachings of Carl Schurz, President Eliot, the *Evening Post* and futile sentimentalists of the international arbitration type."[34]

Eliot had greater influence than Roosevelt over the Harvard Corporation, however, and pushed them to abolish the game outright. Herbert White, a former Crimson football manager, tipped Reid off that a decision was pending. Recognizing the impact such a vote would have, Reid secretly met with other Harvard football supporters, including William Henry Lewis, to undercut Eliot. They carefully drafted a public letter to the Harvard Graduate's Athletic Association in which they cribbed Eliot's complaints almost verbatim but called for reform rather than abolition. The effect of the letter was twofold—to stall the Corporation's vote, and also to take the lead from Yale in proposing its own football reforms. Reid and Harvard's football proponents were now fighting a two-front war, against Eliot on one side, and Yale on the other.

Events continued to outpace them. Within days of Reid's letter, the Harvard-Penn game turned into another melee. Not only had the Quakers tried the old trick of soaking the field (which caused Harvard to break off relations with them), but a Penn player was accused of kicking Harvard's center in the groin, upon which Harvard's man struck the Penn player in the face and was ejected from of the game.[35] When Roosevelt summoned Reid to Washington for an explanation (a meeting held with the visiting German ambassador in attendance), Reid laid out the facts and asked the president what he would have done in such a situation. His face flushing red, the ex-Rough Rider hissed, "It wouldn't be good policy for me to state."[36]

An even more infamous incident occurred two weeks later at the Harvard-Yale game. Yale's James Quill laid out Harvard's Francis Burr after Burr had signaled for a fair catch, a flagrant foul that went uncalled by the referee, Paul Dashiell, who also happened to be president of the IRC.[37] Henry Higginson, a prominent Harvard booster, sent a note from the stands directing Reid to pull his team off the field, though Reid declined to do it. Although Quill later claimed that he was mad because Burr had bit him, this was, as one football historian has put it, "the wrong play at the wrong time with the wrong official."[38]

Harvard fans were beside themselves with anger. TR, who had not attended the game, was nonetheless sufficiently upset when he read about it to write Dashiell demanding an explanation. Dashiell was at the time an assistant instructor in chemistry at the Naval Academy, and in Reid's words coveted a promotion to full professor as "the ambition of his life." All faculty appointments to Annapolis had to be approved by the secretary of the navy, who of course reported directly to the president. Roosevelt let it be known that he was now unsure "whether that kind of man was fit to teach the boys at Annapolis." At about the time he received Roosevelt's angry letter, Dashiell must have realized that he had just made a *very* bad career move.

"I am deeply sorry, Sir," Dashiell groveled in reply, "from every personal feeling, that the matter should have been brought to you in so unfavorable a light…. I regret the injury that it has done the game, now in so critical a condition."[39]

Nevertheless, Roosevelt sat on his appointment papers for six months before signing them. Needless to say, Dashiell never again refereed a Harvard-Yale game.

This and events like it were enough to push Nicholas Murray Butler to act.
Butler was a curious mixture—a philosophy professor, future Republican vice presidential candidate, and Nobel Peace Prize recipient—who ran Columbia for forty-
four years. Roosevelt called him "Nicholas Miraculous Butler," yet one observer
said he presided over the university "with the nonchalance and efficiency of the
head of a railroad system or a department store, combined with the ideals of a
philosopher."[40] Early in December, Butler announced that Columbia was abolish-
ing football. "We ourselves cannot reform this game," he informed alumni over
howls of protest, "and the experience of years has shown that the Rules Committee
do not desire to reform it."[41] He was, however, careful to time the announcement
for Thanksgiving break, when most students would be away from campus.

The dominoes were beginning to fall. MIT, Northwestern, Trinity, Duke, and
others also abolished football that fall and winter. Stanford and California
announced that they were switching to rugby. The *Harvard Bulletin* came out for
ending football, though not just because of the violence. "Something is the matter
with a game which grows more and more uninteresting every year," they wrote.[42]
The Crimson's Karl Brill announced that he was quitting. "I came to Harvard to
get a degree as a mining engineer," he said. "For the last two years Varsity football has played havoc with my studies."[43]

On the same afternoon as the Harvard-Yale game, a Union College player
was killed in a game against New York University. NYU President Herbert
McCracken urged Eliot to put Harvard's imprimatur behind a call for a national conference to discuss the football situation. When Eliot declined, no doubt
recalling is own unsuccessful efforts to do just that years earlier, McCracken went
ahead anyway.

Although the rest of the Ivy colleges refused to participate, Butler sent a representative with instructions to press the case for abolition. At the conference's first
meeting on December 8, 1905, the question was put: "Ought the present game of
football be abolished?" Five of the thirteen colleges attending, including
Columbia, voted in favor; eight voted against. Had only two more switched, intercollegiate football might have suffered a fatal blow.

When the Intercollegiate Athletic Association of the United States, as they
began to call themselves, met again, sixty-eight colleges were in attendance. They
voted to create their own rules committee, outlaw mass play, set strict eligibility
rules, and end brutality. They agreed to seek to affiliate with the IRC, but if
rebuffed were prepared to go their own way.

The IRC, meanwhile, had been dragging its feet, notwithstanding its members' promise to President Roosevelt. Public criticism had been turning on Camp,
who as overlord of college football could not have been ignorant of its many abuses. For all Camp had done to build the sport, he and the IRC were viewed as arro-

gantly out of touch with the rest of the football-playing world. Membership in the IRC remained principally the elite eastern colleges (its lone midwestern representative was Amos Alonzo Stagg), and as an alumni-dominated organization, its interests ran counter to the faculty-dominated ICAA. Francis Bangs, Columbia's athletic director, had warned Butler about the "self-perpetuating, non-representative, pig-headed, oblivious to public opinion and obstinate" IRC, by which he meant Camp.[44] As frequently happens, the revolutionary had become the reactionary.

Under pressure, the IRC proposed a series of mild reforms. Roosevelt, who had also come to blame Camp for many of the game's problems, surprised everyone by declining to endorse them. He further assured Reid privately that he would support a joint committee including members of both groups. No clearer signal was needed that Camp no longer ran the show.

The rival rules committees eyed each other warily during an informal meeting at Philadelphia's Bellevue-Stratford Hotel just before New Year's. Harry Williams, now coach at Minnesota, asked Camp on behalf of the IRC to merge the two groups and rewrite the rules. Stalling for time, Camp said he would have to seek instructions back home.

Two weeks later, the committees met on the same day in nearby New York City hotels. During the interval, with Roosevelt's encouragement, Reid and members of Harvard's Graduate's Athletic Association had devised a set of nineteen new rules that opened up the game. They limited sparring on the line by separating the teams with a neutral zone, reduced the use of mass plays by requiring six men on the line of scrimmage, forced more imaginative play-calling by increasing the distance needed for a first down to ten yards (still in three downs, however), and spread the defense by legalizing the forward pass. They also shortened the game from seventy minutes to sixty.

Eliot persuaded the Harvard Overseers to kill football unless the rules were adopted. Reid used this to his advantage. When the IRC met, he threw Harvard's considerable weight around and explained the new facts of life to Camp and the others. Either the new "rules go through or there will be no football at Harvard," Reid told them; "and if Harvard throws out the game, many other colleges will follow Harvard's lead, and an important blow will be dealt to the game."[45]

Having first warned Camp, Reid then made a dramatic, if grandstanding, gesture. He walked out of the IRC meeting and walked over to the ICAA, backed by Dashiell. (Roosevelt, who did not want Harvard to bolt alone, had seen to that as part of Dashiell's penance.) For four hours, intermediaries negotiated between the two groups before the IRC agreed to form a joint rules committee. L. M. Dennis of Cornell, a representative of the ICAA, was chosen as president of the joint group while the IRC's James Babbitt of Haverford was voted secretary. To Yale's dismay, Babbitt immediately resigned in favor of Reid, placing a Harvard man in control and shutting Camp out completely.

The IRC did not formally go out of existence, however, and continued to meet as an independent if neutered body until 1916 when its last remaining member, Navy, switched. Four years after its creation, the ICAA renamed itself the National Collegiate Athletic Association or NCAA.

Even so, it took the new rules committee months to hammer out a new code (at meetings subsidized by the Spalding sporting goods company—so much for amateurism). Agreeing to do something was not the same as agreeing on what to do. Camp, who still possessed considerable prestige and influence, continued to drag his feet, but could not afford to be seen publicly as opposing change.

In particular, Camp hated the forward pass, thought it a bastardization of the running game he loved, much as present-day purists decry the designated hitter in baseball or the three-point shot in basketball. When it became clear that support for the pass was building, he proposed instead to open up the game by making the field forty feet wider. Initially, this met with some support, until someone in Cambridge measured and discovered that a wider field would not fit inside the new $325,000 Harvard Stadium. The Crimson immediately jumped off that bandwagon, and the forward pass carried easily in the next vote.

After much difficulty, the joint committee agreed to several rules changes based on the reforms Harvard had proposed. In May 1906, the Harvard Corporation voted 15-9 to keep playing football for another year, while the Overseers concurred, 17-6. Eliot voted no on both occasions. "It is childish," he wrote, "to suppose that the athletic authorities which have permitted football to become a brutal, cheating, demoralizing game can be trusted to reform it." [46]

The NCAA was slow to gain acceptance. Of all the Ivy schools, only Penn and Dartmouth joined; the major Midwestern and West Coast colleges stayed out at first. Penn's case was particularly instructive. When Harvard broke relations after 1905, the Quakers lost their last tie to the Big Three. Still, Penn continued to field good teams. Behind All-Americans Bill Hollenback (whom Jim Thorpe called the toughest man he had ever faced) and Hunter Scarlett, they went undefeated in 1908, the last time that would happen until 1947. But they could not claim national prominence without having played any of the Big Three. Penn joined the NCAA at the first opportunity because they needed opponents.

Even colleges that had called for reform were reluctant to relinquish control, and so the NCAA was forced for decades to rely on moral persuasion rather than rules. In order to boost its reputation, the NCAA actively courted the old members of the IRC. Columbia and Harvard joined in 1909, followed by Princeton in 1913, Yale in 1915, Cornell in 1920, and Brown not until 1929.

The greatest innovation of the "Revolution of 1906," as it has been called, was the adoption of the forward pass. Ever since the pass was legalized, there has been a debate over whose idea it was. The candidates include some of the brightest lights in college football history. Various sources attribute the pass to John Heisman, John Bell of Penn, Harry Williams, and Paul Dashiell, among others.

Whoever deserves authorship, it is clear that the Ivy colleges did not embrace the pass. For one thing, Camp had exerted his influence by making the first passing rules draconian. Passes could only be attempted from five yards behind the line of scrimmage and then had to be thrown at least five yards to either side of the center. An incomplete pass on first or second down resulted in a fifteen-yard penalty. An incomplete pass on third down was a turnover, as was any pass that hit the ground without being touched or crossed the goal line. A pass that went out of bounds belonged to whichever team could get to it first. Interference by the defense was perfectly legal.

Wesleyan may have attempted the first forward pass in football history, in a game against Yale, for an eighteen-yard gain.[47] Allie Camp, still her husband's chief scout, had seen the play coming and was so excited it was almost as if she had thrown it.[48] Still, Camp was not entirely unwilling to experiment. That November, the Elis connected on a thirty-yard strike from Paul Veeder to Clarence Alcott that led to a touchdown in a 6-0 victory over Harvard.

Despite all he had done to save football, Bill Reid could not save his own job. The loss to Yale was Harvard's fifth in a row, all by shutouts, and that was the only game on Reid's schedule that mattered. The pressures on him were enormous—his $7,000 salary package was higher than any tenured Harvard professor's and almost as much as President Eliot's. Burdened by a compulsive and brittle personality anyway, Reid was worn out by the stresses of coaching; he had lost weight and was getting sedatives from the trainer to help him sleep. Such were the perils of a professional coach. As former Yale star Frank Butterworth remarked, "Players like to win, but head coaches and especially paid coaches had to win."[49]

One reform Reid did not want was the one that did him in. He had planned a blockbuster team for 1906, drawing heavily from Harvard's graduate schools—"a man's team," he wrote, "not one of college boys"—but the athletic committee undercut him when it entered into a triple agreement with Yale and Princeton that finally barred graduate students, as well as freshmen, from intercollegiate football.

Theodore Roosevelt had stewed during a cabinet meeting in 1907 when his Secretary of the Interior, a Williams graduate, celebrated his alma mater's victory over the Crimson by suggesting that Harvard try scheduling Vassar instead.[50] But in 1908, he and fellow Harvard alumni finally found what they were looking for when they hired Percy Haughton, who had played for the Crimson and coached at Cornell for two moderately successful seasons. Over the next nine years, Haughton's teams went 71-7-5 and won two national championships. With some justification, Haughton's hiring has been called "the most important event in Harvard football history.[51]

Haughton was something of a cross between Vince Lombardi and Tom Landry; "an aristocrat, stern of mien, brusque of speech, curt at best to sports reporters on the field and an iron disciplinarian whose men feared, even hated him, in some instances before they got to know him." Strategically, he liked fakes and misdirections, used an unbalanced line and often had his teams quick-kick on first or second down to get better field position. Because of this, he often had his quarterbacks line up in kick formation. He was the first to employ defensive signals, given both by number and by gesture so the backs would not miss them. Deception and secrecy were important parts of Haughton's strategy—not even Harvard's president was permitted to attend practices.

Where others shied away from the forward pass, Haughton did not, and is credited with being the first to have his quarterback lead receivers, throwing to a spot ahead of them rather than to a man, which also helped confuse defenses.[52] His teams never huddled; he preferred his quarterback to look over the defense before deciding which play to run. He also required his men to wear helmets during practice as well as during games.

In 1922, Haughton wrote a book, titled *Football and How to Watch It*, a revealing look into his philosophy of the game.[53] He did not like players to train too hard during the summer; coming into camp at playing weight was a sign of impending burnout. Players who exhibited signs of "overtraining" during the season would be given a few days off and encouraged to relax with a bottle of beer. Haughton also wanted players to stay out of the weight room, lest they become muscle-bound.

Under their new leadership, the Crimson rolled through the 1908 season, tying Navy but winning everything else, including a 17-0 win over Jim Thorpe and the Carlisle Indians. They relied on defense, scoring just 132 points in ten games, but giving up only eight.

Their captain and only real star was Hamilton Fish, latest in a long line from the prominent New York family who had played Ivy football since its earliest days. He was brilliant, graduated cum laude in only three years, and was reported to be the strongest man on campus. But he was also irascible and apparently not well liked. During his senior year, Fish stood for one of the three class marshal posts, running on what was called the "Gold Coast" ticket, a reference to Harvard's ritziest dorms and final clubs along Mount Auburn Street, the wealthy residents of which traditionally controlled class offices. Social prominence notwithstanding, it was a position the captain of the football team should have been able to claim by right. Fish finished fourth, the victim of an insurrection by the "unclubbables" who lived in Harvard Yard. (T. S. Eliot was, however, elected class "odist.") Humiliated, he left school, vowing never to return. President Lowell personally counseled him to come back to Cambridge.

After graduation, Fish coached offensive linemen at Army (including cadet Dwight D. Eisenhower) and followed the family tradition by entering politics, but resigned his seat in the New York legislature when the United States entered World War I. Much like Robert Gould Shaw, a Harvard man from an earlier generation,

Fish led an all-black regiment, the Fifteenth New York Volunteers known as "Harlem's Hellfighters," at a time when President Woodrow Wilson was actively discriminating against African-Americans in the service. In all, the regiment spent 191 days at the front, longer than any other American force. Fish himself was awarded both the Croix de Guerre and the Silver Star.

Elected to Congress after the war, Fish was one of the leading advocates of civil rights for blacks, yet it was one of the contradictions of his character that he is better known for his rabid isolationism prior to World War II. He had known all the young bohemians (and late in life appeared in the movie *Reds*), but where they had dabbled in radical politics, Fish became a virulent anti-Communist and so found Hitler less distasteful than Stalin. His neighbor, FDR, whom he loathed, lampooned him, yet when war came, Fish unhesitatingly supported American victory. He remained cantankerous to the end, outliving most of his critics, divorcing his third wife at the age of ninety-five, and marrying his fourth at the age of ninety-nine. He died at 102, the last surviving member of Walter Camp's All-Time All-America team, closing more than one chapter in American life.

Yale, of course, was the showdown for Haughton's 1908 squad. The modern age was poking its way into The Game—more than a thousand automobiles were seen around Yale Field that year. Haughton disdained the field goal, calling it a "chicken way to score," but willingly accepted Vic Kenard's fifteen-yard drop kick for a 4-0 victory that ended Yale's winning streak. Kenard, who had practiced a quick snap over the summer, so fooled the Elis that many did not realize he had gotten the kick away until it sailed over their heads.

That game also produced what may have been the first halftime show. A group called the "Hearst Club" had been organized two years earlier, performing spoofs of William Randolph Hearst, who at the time was running for governor of New York. In 1908, the same group formed the "Bryan Club" to lampoon an equally broad target, William Jennings Bryan, the Democratic presidential nominee. For their big performance at the Harvard game, the group did a skit about the questionable methods of registering voters in New Haven.

Yale's 1909 team must be regarded as one of the best ever. Undefeated, untied, and unscored upon, they so dominated their games that no opponent crossed their twenty-yard line all season. Their coach was Howard Jones, an alumnus from the 1906 and 1907 teams, whose brother, Thomas Albert Dwight (known simply as Tad), would later coach the Elis himself. Their fullback, Ted Coy, holds a seat close to the center of Yale's athletic pantheon. George Trevor, the great writer for the *New York Sun*, once described Coy as "a leonine figure, with a pug nose and a shock of yellow hair like a Gloucester fisher girl." [54] He was an Eli through and through; a Whiffenpoof and nephew of former Yale president Timothy Dwight. Amory Blaine, protagonist in F. Scott Fitzgerald's novel *This Side of Paradise*, counts Coy as one of his high school heroes (that is, before Blaine goes on to Princeton). A two-time All-American, Coy lost only one game in the three years he played on the varsity.

In 1907, Coy and Tad Jones had rallied the Bulldogs from a 10-0 deficit to beat Princeton, 12-10 (the Tigers' Edwin Harlan missed six field goals). He scored two more touchdowns in a 12-0 win over Harvard, in a game which saw the Crimson bring the ball to the Yale six-inch line yet fail for the sixth year in a row to score a point. Coy missed the first four games of the 1909 season after his appendix was removed, but returned well before the match with Harvard.

Both teams entered that contest undefeated, the last time that happened until 1968. European fans of the two universities gathered at the Heidelberger restaurant in Berlin to listen to play-by-play reports being dictated from a special telegraph line. Playing in his final game, Coy kicked a pair of field goals to give his team an 8-0 victory. While one of them was still in the air, Coy reportedly turned to referee Bill Langford and remarked, "Mr. Langford, did you ever see a prettier kick than that one? Don't tell me you aren't going to give me a goal?" [55] Earlier in the week, Hamilton Fish had vowed that, despite an injury, he would play that Saturday "unless he was killed." This prompted one Bulldog to quip, "He won't be killed unless he commits suicide when he hears the final score." [56]

On the sidelines, armed with a megaphone, was Fish's classmate, John Reed, who became better known as chronicler of the Russian Revolution, confidant of Lenin, and author of *Ten Days That Shook the World*. Yet long before he was a cheerleader for Bolshevism, Reed was a cheerleader for Harvard. It must have been the red uniforms.

Always more of a romantic than a revolutionary, Reed shunned the Socialist Club founded by his classmate Walter Lippmann and instead ran for class office—and lost to the reformers—on the same Gold Coast ticket as Fish, who liked Reed in spite of his politics. Reed wrote bad fight songs ("twist the bull-dog's tail... call up the hearse for Eli Yale") and mordant sports commentary for the *Lampoon*: "It is true the backfield is very slow, but this is made up by their exceeding lightness. The line is ... awkward, but this is offset by the grit with which they lie down in front of our plays." [57]

For his senior year, Reed was elected to lead the cheers at football games, some of which he later taught to striking silk workers in Paterson, New Jersey. Lippmann recalled, "At first there was nothing to recommend him but his cheek. That was supreme. He would stand up alone before a few thousand undergraduates and demonstrate without a quiver of self-consciousness how a cheer should be given. If he didn't like the way his instructions were followed he cursed at the crowd, he bullied it, sneered at it. But he always captured it." [58] As Reed himself wrote, he was intoxicated by "the supreme blissful sensation of swaying two thousand voices in great crashing choruses," an experience of which he got plenty in the heady days with Lenin and Zinoviev a decade later. [59]

Although no one suspected it at the time, the 1909 season was to be a pinnacle of Yale football for a generation, and marked the beginning of the end of Walter Camp's long tenure.

In late October, Army captain Edward "Icy" Byrne collapsed and died on the field in a game against Harvard. Although some erroneously blamed Fish (who had made some hard tackles earlier but was not playing against Byrne at the time he collapsed), the accident drew national attention and reminded many that the reforms of a few years earlier had not worked perfectly.

Nor was Byrne the only football fatality that fall. After declining for a few years following the rules changes of 1906, the number of injuries began to rise again. Thirty players were killed on the gridiron that season (eight in college games) and 216 injured. Despite the requirement of a six-man front, vestiges of mass play continued, combined with wilder styles of offense such as hurdling. Most teams used the forward pass only to set up the run by forcing defenses to play further off the line.

Both the New York City and Washington, D.C., high schools responded by banning football, amid reports that more colleges, including Cornell, were considering doing the same. Opponents liked to point to Columbia, which appeared to be getting along quite well without football. Admissions were up and there were reports "that the autumn weeks have now, for the first time, become quiet, orderly and abundant in academic work." [60] Words to make a faculty's heart sing.

"We certainly have got to do something, Walter," Amos Alonzo Stagg wrote to his old mentor. [61] Camp's solution, however, which he claimed to have worked out in a series of "field trials," was to curb passing even further by restricting it to the area behind the line of scrimmage. This proposal passed the joint rules committee in February 1910 but a three-member subcommittee was appointed to add the finishing touches. One of the three, E. K. Hall of Dartmouth, adamantly opposed the forward pass, but the other two, Crawford Blagden of Harvard and Carl Williams of Penn, did not. They rallied those who supported the pass—and opposed Camp—and returned to the joint committee two weeks later with a radical proposal that rescinded most of the restrictive passing rules and penalties, required seven men on the line of scrimmage, and divided the game into four, fifteen-minute quarters. This proposal prevailed by a single vote. Camp, who had missed the meeting, refused to add his signature to the new rules. [62]

A year later, in 1911, Camp pushed one last motion to ban the forward pass, which the joint rules committee, after almost two days of debate, approved at two in the morning by a single vote. Delegates from southern and western colleges immediately threatened to bolt and write their own rules, a return to the chaos of the mid-nineties. Despite his long-standing hostility to the pass, Hall, who chaired the committee, recognized the damage Camp's proposal would do. He quickly reconvened the group and switched his vote, reversing the outcome.

There were, though, two crises in the winter of 1909-10. The second occurred among the Big Three, which fought a last, losing battle to retain control of football and its rules. Cooperative action was not something the proud, independent universities did well. But they also recognized that the growing numbers of the ICAA had given it the ability to promulgate its own set of rules, which the Big Three could take or leave, or have to take if they wanted to play other schools. If they were going to retain their influence, they had to work together.

The presidents also decided to act because their membership had changed. After forty years in office, Charles Eliot retired in 1909, devoting his last annual message to a denunciation of all the evils the game had produced, from violence to gambling. He was succeeded by Abbott Lawrence Lowell, a colder personality but one more amenable to football. Those searching for Lowell's philosophy could find it neatly summarized in his declaration that "The elite should be, if possible, both intellectually and physically superior. That among them some should be in mind and others in physique above the ordinary is not enough."[63] Yale's president, Arthur Twining Hadley, a high-strung expert on railroad regulation, had been selected a decade earlier by a committee of which Walter Camp had been a prominent member. Hadley and Lowell had reached a gentleman's understanding that each would invite the other to attend the Harvard-Yale game at the other's campus only when he thought the visitors were likely to win.[64]

In other sports, the Ivy schools had increasingly begun to see the wisdom of formal leagues notwithstanding Brown's decision in 1907 to break off all athletic relations with its chief rival, Dartmouth, over a disputed call in a baseball game. Harvard, Yale, and Princeton had been members of a lacrosse league since the early 1880s. Columbia, Cornell, Harvard, Yale, and Princeton formed the Eastern Intercollegiate Basketball League in 1901, soon to be joined by Dartmouth, Penn, and Brown. Leagues involving these colleges had also been formed in ice hockey, soccer, and even debating, when the Big Three began a triangular competition.

On November 28, 1909, days after the Harvard-Yale game, Hadley wrote to Lowell proposing a meeting to discuss the problems with football. When they met two weeks later, they agreed to promote a broader conference of eastern colleges to seek a solution to the problem. That such a conference might tend to undercut the broader-based ICAA did not bother Hadley or Lowell in the slightest.

The press, at least, seemed to be on to this from the beginning. "The 'big' colleges have no idea of permitting domination of football to pass from their hands if they can prevent it," the *New York Times* wrote of the Hadley-Lowell meeting. "They have no feeling of letting the 'little fellows' in except under their terms."[65]

As they had anticipated, the smaller eastern colleges were happy to defer to their betters and authorized Harvard and Yale to conduct their own investigation and make recommendations. By serendipity, Hadley received a letter the following day from Woodrow Wilson, who had reached a similar conclusion about the need for reform. Princeton had not been invited to the New England college summit but

Wilson must have heard about it. Wilson may also have been reflecting Princeton's longstanding insecurity about its status as junior member in the Big Three firm.

"I have entertained for a good many years," he wrote to Hadley and Lowell, "the feeling… that the Presidents of Yale, Harvard and Princeton could, if they were to agree upon a principle of action and insist upon it, very largely and perhaps completely control the methods of the game of football."[66] Might Princeton join the others in a meeting?

Hadley and Lowell were glad to have Princeton's prestige added to their effort, but when Hadley ventured down to New Jersey, he came away alarmed at what he perceived as Wilson's softness on the issues. More than his counterparts, Wilson took an alarmist view, promoting radical reforms and going so far as to suggest that Princeton might switch to rugby (the intelligentsia's preferred "manly sport") if it were not accommodated. Moreover, Princeton added another anti-Yale voice to the chorus. Harvard and Princeton, having lost to Camp's teams often enough, resented the blatant conflict of interest under which the man who ran the sport's most successful program also wrote the rules. They attributed much of Yale's success to those rules, overlooking its superior coaching system and huge budget. Still, at Harvard and Princeton it was hard to get past the fact that over the preceding thirty years, Yale's cumulative football record was 303-15-15.

Camp had even begun to come under fire at home from those who resented the way football hoarded all the money for athletics. As historian Robert Caro writes, "Camp had been squirreling away the annual surplus of the [Yale Athletic] Union with such enthusiasm that it had already reached $120,000, and he was not about to turn any of it over to sports he derided."[67] In 1909, Robert Moses, a member of the swimming team and future New York parks commissioner, went over Camp's head by appealing directly to the alumni for support, raising enough money to establish the Yale Minor Sports Association.

To the surprise of almost everyone, just before Christmas 1909, Harvard abruptly announced that it was joining the ICAA after all. Lowell insisted to Hadley that the Corporation had made the decision without his knowledge, which seems unlikely. That still left Yale and Princeton as prominent members outside the fold, but the cause of opposition was weakened by this defection. The *New York Times*, which wrote that Harvard's announcement came "like a bolt out of the clear sky," had no illusions that the growing strength of the ICAA was the real reason for it. "Coupled with which," the paper concluded, "was a fear lest the institutions composing this body refuse to meet the four outsiders on the gridiron unless the football rules were changed to suit the fifty-seven collegiate members of the [ICAA]."[68]

In the end, differing interests among their colleges doomed the Big Three presidential alliance before it got started, but it did continue the precedent of joint action and, as Yale found itself increasingly isolated among even its sister Ivies, made such an alliance more desirable. Henceforward, the Big Three would be less interested in shaping the national trends in football than in insulating themselves from them.

Camp's own long run came to an end less then a year later when he abruptly resigned as treasurer of the Yale Field Association, his only official tie to the university. The reasons for Camp's withdrawal were never made clear. Harford Powel, Jr., in his authorized biography of Camp—which we may take as reflecting Camp's own views—argues that he was done in by envy; his love of football spectacle, which permitted the wrong element to give the game a bad name; his determination to speak his mind; and the immaturity of players and graduates who thought they knew more than the old man.[69]

Those factors must have played a part, but it also seems likely that Camp succumbed to the same thing that fells many coaches: his teams stopped winning and suddenly his inflexibility came to look much more like a liability than an asset. Certainly, Yale fans had much to endure in Camp's last season. Brown finally ended its jinx with a 21-0 victory behind All-American Bill Sprackling, who passed for 180 yards. Even Vanderbilt held the Bulldogs to a 0-0 tie.

Horrifying as it must have been in New Haven, many Old Blues had concluded that it was time to emulate Harvard and hire a professional coach of their own, especially after the Crimson embarrassed them, 20-0, in 1912. Howard Jones was brought back at an annual salary of $2,500 despite Camp's efforts to orchestrate a letter-writing campaign to stop it. "We defeated Harvard year after year with monotonous regularity," he complained, "then because ... we play two ties and then get a beating, all the past is at once forgotten. We must imitate our rivals!"[70] In what must have been another bitter blow, Yale also placed football and all other sports under faculty jurisdiction for the first time.

Such changes may have brought Yale athletics into the modern age, but they were slow to translate into success on the field. In 1911, Yale lost to Princeton in all four major sports (football, baseball, track, and crew) for the first time ever and lost to Harvard in three. Camp's supporters believed they knew the reason. Although the father of football was periodically called upon for counsel in the decade that followed, "the old system disappeared with him, and the amazing series of Yale's victories disappeared too."[71]

1911-
1954

The Sign We Hail

The reforms of 1906 and 1910 did not cure the ills facing college football, but they did bring peace for the first time in almost thirty years. Football was safer, but boring. The seven-man front put an end to mass momentum plays, but conservative eastern coaches remained reluctant to add the forward pass to their offenses. As a consequence, games became battles of field position in which a team might punt as many as forty times, often on first or second down.

In many ways, the teens were a decade of Ivy prominence. Both presidential elections were all-Ivy affairs: Theodore Roosevelt defeated Woodrow Wilson and William Howard Taft in 1912, and Wilson beat Charles Evans Hughes in 1916. The national influence of Ivy football, however, continued to slip. In 1913, for the first time ever, the eight colleges failed to constitute a majority of the All-America team. Acknowledging the growth of football elsewhere, Ivy schedules began to change, as colleges such as the University of Virginia, the University of North Carolina, Notre Dame, and Penn State became regular opponents for Harvard, Yale, Princeton, and others. When teams opened bigger stadiums, it became more important to fill them regularly and not just for the one or two climactic games at season's end.

If Yale tried to emulate Harvard's Percy Haughton by hiring a professional coach, it could not have picked a more different man. Howard Jones was notoriously forgetful, often misplacing his keys or missing appointments. The team went 5-2-3 in his only season.

One reserve on Jones' 1913 team was Archibald MacLeish, future poet, winner of the Pulitzer Prize, head of the Library of Congress, and assistant secretary of state. "I have only one glorious memory of those four years," MacLeish later wrote, "and its setting is not Soldiers Field in Cambridge but the bar of the long-vanished Tremont Hotel in Boston. We—we being that Yale freshman team of the fall of 1911—had just held the best Harvard team in a generation to a 0-0 tie in a downpour of helpful rain, and we were relaxing, not without noise, when the coach of the famous Harvard freshman team approached us, looked us over, focused (he had had a drink or two himself) on me and announced in the voice of an indignant beagle sighting a fox that I was, without question, the dirtiest little sonofabitch of a center ever to visit Cambridge, Massachusetts. It was heady praise." [1]

Jones was succeeded by a more famous alumnus, Frank Hinkey, who became a pioneer in the use of game films to scout opponents. Hinkey's innovative, rugby-style offense, which made use of lots of lateral passes, confused Notre Dame in 1914 and left a lasting impression on their assistant coach, Knute Rockne, who wrote in his autobiography, "Modern football at Notre Dame can be dated from that game, as we made vital use of every lesson we learned." [2] Although Hinkey led the Bulldogs to a 7-2 record, Yale failed to have a single player named first-team All-American for the first time ever.

In 1915, Hinkey and the Bulldogs slumped to 4-5 as Yale was outscored by its opponents for the first time. Fans grown accustomed to greatness had to suffer through losses to Washington and Jefferson, Colgate, and Brown. By the time the climactic final games approached Hinkey was coach in name only as frantic Old Blues called back Tom Shevlin to pitch in as an assistant. Shevlin could not prevent a 41-0 humiliation at the hands of Harvard, the worst defeat in Yale history to that point. When fans asked why the team played so badly after upsetting Princeton the week before, Shevlin smiled grimly and replied, "You can't make two lemonades out of one lemon." [3]

Disappointing seasons were made easier to endure thanks to two new songs written by Cole Porter, a Yale undergraduate. The *Yale Daily News* held competitions for new songs each year, and in 1910 Porter won with "Bingo, Eli Yale":

> *Bingo! Bingo!*
> *Bingo! Bingo! Bingo!*
> *That's the lingo,*
> *Eli is bound to win!*
> *There's to be a victory,*
> *So watch the team begin.*

The song was a hit and was distributed nationally by a New York sheet music publisher. A year later, Porter won the contest again with an entry that would have a longer-lasting place in the hearts of Elis, one of the most famous of all college fight songs:

Bulldog! Bulldog!
Bow, wow, wow!
Eli Yale!

Bulldog! Bulldog!
Bow, wow, wow!
Our team can never fail!

When a son of Eli breaks through the line,
That is the sign we hail!

Bulldog! Bulldog!
Bow, wow, wow!
Eli Yale!

Porter, who was also a Yale cheerleader, penned more than three hundred songs during his undergraduate years, including more football numbers such as "A Football King" and "Beware of Yale." His work, though, was in a class above most other fight songs. Some objected to their martial, syncopated rhythm. Wrote one unhappy Dartmouth alumnus at around this time: "Dartmouth songs of late have been pretty feeble productions, football yawps for the most part, with 'green' and 'team' forced into unwilling matrimony of rhyme, obliged eternally to consort with 'might,' 'fight,' 'cheer,' and 'dear'—bumpily bounding to the clash of cymbals and the booming of an ardent drum."[4] As the writer suggested, the great age of fight songs was drawing to a close. Competitions continued but did not survive changing tastes or the disruption of World War I, which brought back to campus mature veterans less interested in musical trifles. By the late 1920s, new songs had all but ceased to appear—a loss to future generations of fans.

At long last, Harvard had supplanted Yale atop the collegiate football world. In 1911, the Crimson began a thirty-three-game unbeaten streak that spanned parts of five seasons before ending at Cornell's hands in 1915. The team was so successful that in 1916 the Athletic Association installed arc lighting at Harvard Stadium to enable the team to practice after dark.

Haughton had amassed a team that included some of the brightest names in Crimson history. Their captain, Percy Wendell, was a grinding runner whom George Trevor wrote was "fashioned like a steel bullet."[5] Eddie Mahan, a triple threat as passer, kicker, and runner, was so quick that he often eschewed blockers. "I simply give [onrushing tacklers] the foot, left or right, and then take it away," he explained.[6] Tack Hardwick, a Brahmin who later helped build Boston Garden, was reputedly the strongest man on campus and liked to wear leather wraps around his forearms, which he would use to smack opponents. Leverett Saltonstall, a reserve on the team, later became governor of Massachusetts.

Outstanding even among these luminaries was Charlie Brickley, a four-way star who was unanimously chosen All-American at a halfback. In the age of florid sportswriting, Harry Cross of the *New York Times* described him as "a short, chunky youngster of twenty-one summers. His black hair is curly, and there is always a smile on his boyish face. He has a nerve of chilled steel and is so cool that he could face the jaws of destruction without a quiver."[7] The summer before his sophomore year he competed in the Olympics (failing to win a medal in the hop, step, and jump), then returned to Cambridge where he single-handedly accounted for four Harvard victories that fall. He dropkicked a field goal to defeat Dartmouth, 3-0, scored the Crimson's only touchdown in a 7-0 victory over Maine, kicked three field goals and rushed for 106 yards (12 less than the entire Princeton team) in a 16-0 win over the Tigers, and capped the season by returning a fumble for a touchdown and kicking two field goals in a 20-0 victory over Yale. Bob Storer's touchdown earlier in that game had been Harvard's first against the Elis in eleven years. The undefeated Crimson were proposed for a postseason game against undefeated Wisconsin to decide the national championship, but the match never occurred because the Wisconsin faculty rejected it.

Brickley, though, was just getting started. As a junior, he scored six touchdowns and kicked three more field goals in early season victories over Penn State, Cornell, and Brown. In the big games, he dropkicked a nineteen-yard field goal to give Harvard its first-ever victory at Princeton. Against Yale, Brickley tied a record by kicking five field goals—the last three with blurred vision after being scratched in the eye—to account for all of Harvard's points in a 15-5 victory, its first over Yale in Harvard Stadium and first back-to-back triumphs over the Elis since 1875. "Most of Harvard's offense was Brickley," the *New York Times* wrote. "It was Brickley this and Brickley that, and Brickley the other thing."[8]

He missed most of his senior year with appendicitis but it made little difference as the Crimson went undefeated again.[9] After graduation, Brickley played for a year with the Massilon Tigers of the fledgling American Professional Football Association, forerunner of the National Football League. He remains Harvard's all-time leading scorer, with 215 points and twenty-three career touchdowns.

Haughton's men recovered from Brickley's loss because they had Eddie Mahan, an All-America running back in his own right, who took over the kicking when Brickley fell ill. As a senior in 1915, the year called "the zenith of the Haughton star in the blue sky of the ancient [Harvard-Yale] rivalry," Mahan scored four touchdowns in the 41-0 whipping of Yale.[10] More than a thousand people celebrated the victory at the Harvard Club in Manhattan, accompanied by a band.

Princeton claimed the national championship in 1911 before slipping into mediocrity. The Tigers owed their title to several lucky breaks. Against Harvard, in the first game the two schools had played against each other since 1896, Sanford White picked up a fumble and ran ninety yards for a touchdown. F. Scott

Fitzgerald, then a student at St. Paul's, was in the stands and saved his ticket stub, along with a note that read: "Sam White decides me for Princeton." [11]

Later in the game, White tackled Harvard quarterback Henry Gardner fielding a punt at the one-yard line and drove him back into the end zone for a safety, which gave Princeton an 8-6 victory. That winter, rulemakers had to clarify that in such situations the ball was dead at the spot it was caught. None of this mattered to delirious Princeton fans. "A very tornado seemed to break loose on Osborne Field," one reporter wrote. "The crowd surged and swarmed down on the field for the snake dance. In columns ten or six abreast they pranced about the field, chanting incoherently, beside themselves with happiness, and over the bars of the goal posts they tossed their hats, felts, caps, and derbies in accordance with ancient custom." [12]

In the waning minutes of a scoreless tie with Dartmouth the following week, Wally DeWitt attempted a forty-five-yard field goal that hit the ground and bounced over the crossbar to give Princeton a 3-0 victory—another fluke play that called for a change in the rules. A week later, White returned another fumble seventy yards to beat Yale, 6-3, even though Princeton's offense did not make a single first down.

Although the Tigers did not win another title during the decade, there was on that 1911 team one of the great figures in college athletic history. Hobart Amory Hare Baker—"Hobey," as he was universally known—was a genuine two-sport star. He scored ninety-two points in 1912 as a rusher, kicker, and punt returner, a Princeton record that stood until 1974, and was elected posthumously to the College Football Hall of Fame. As a hockey player, he was even better, the first American to be elected to that sport's hall of fame. The Hobey Baker prize is given annually to the best collegiate player in the country.

More than that, Hobey Baker was a romantic figure for a romantic age, perhaps the last and perhaps the greatest. Although he stood only five-foot-nine and weighed just 165 pounds, he had the blonde good looks of a demigod and was vain enough to know it, eschewing a helmet on the field. Men idealized him without embarrassment, worshiped him in a way that was almost sensual. Fitzgerald (who used one of Hobey's middle names, Amory, for the protagonist in *This Side of Paradise*) called Hobey "an ideal worthy of everything in my enthusiastic imagination, yet consummated and expressed in a human being who stood within ten feet of me." [13]

There was always a hint of tragedy just beneath the surface of Hobey Baker's life. He was born into Philadelphia society in 1892 but grew up in Princeton, where his father, Bobby, had played for the Tigers in the 1880s. By the time his parents divorced when Hobey was fifteen, he had been sent off to prep school, where he starred in football and hockey. But Bobby Baker had lost most of his fortune in the Panic of 1907 and could afford to send only one of his two sons to college. Hobey's older brother, Thornton, gallantly insisted that Hobey go in his place.

From the beginning, he was a sensation. Playing on the freshman football team, he scored Princeton's only touchdown in a 6-0 victory over Yale on a fake field goal. A year later, playing on the varsity, he returned a punt eighty-eight yards for another touchdown against the Elis. Rather than run under a punt and wait for it, Hobey judged the flight of the ball and timed his approach so as to receive it on the run, in full stride, all his momentum going forward.

His feats off the field were also legendary. Hobey once won a bet that he could walk the sixty-five miles from Princeton to New York in under ten hours. He could chin himself with one hand, juggle five balls at once, and liked to show off at parties by walking down the stairs on his hands, circle around, and then walk back upstairs the same way. True to the ethos of the Edwardian gentleman, he was modest, intelligent without being bookish, friendly without being challenging, the embodiment of effortless grace.

He became a flying ace during the war, and his untimely death in a plane crash sealed his reputation in myth forever. As George Frazier later wrote, Baker "haunts a whole school, and from generation unto generation, you say, 'Hobey Baker,' and all of a sudden you see the gallantry of a world long since gone—a world of all the sad young men, a world in which handsome young officers spent their lives tea-dancing at the Plaza to the strains of the season; a world in which poets sang of their rendezvous with death when spring came round with rusting shade and apple blossoms filled the air." [14] The self-perpetuating Princeton ideal of breezy aristocracy flows from Hobey Baker, much as Yale's reputation for earnest achievement comes from the fictional Frank Merriwell.

Columbia took up football again in 1915. Almost since the day Nicholas Murray Butler banned the sport in 1905 the student paper had daily carried a Cato-esque banner across its front page declaring: "INTERCOLLEGIATE FOOTBALL MUST BE REINSTATED AT COLUMBIA." [15] At first, Butler refused even student requests to play interclass games. "To revive the game at Columbia would be a step back into the Middle Ages," he declared. [16] But by 1914, when Butler permitted the freshman and sophomores to play on South Field in front of the Low Library, the Columbia *Alumni News* could write, "Football! The forbidden word has again been whispered on Morningside Heights." [17] At a mass meeting that December, students were asked to show their support by pledging to try out for football if a team were organized and subscribing two dollars toward its support.

The following February, the Columbia administration reinstated football, but with severe limitations. During a five-year probationary period, the team would be prohibited from playing any of the big schools—Harvard, Yale, Princeton, Penn, and Cornell were specified by name—all games would be restricted to campus, and freshmen would be barred (as they already were at the Big Three). The faculty committee that approved reinstatement seems to have been naïve about the changes a decade had brought. "A game of football radically different from the old has been developed," it reported, "a game which requires a less highly specialized, elaborate and prolonged training, which is less absorbing to the attention and less exhaustive of vitality, and which can be used with profit in the education of young men." [18]

Nevertheless, rumors abounded that Columbia was wooing Jim Thorpe and Hamilton Fish to be its coach, while another proposed Tom Thorp, the ex-Columbia star whose questionable eligibility had been one of the game's scandals a decade earlier. Instead, they chose T. Nelson Metcalf, who led the team to an undefeated season against an easy schedule in its first year back. They now carried the nickname "Lions," which had been adopted for all Columbia sports teams in 1910. Commercialism seeped back quickly and within a few years Columbia game programs featured advertisements for Perrier ("The Champagne of Table Waters") and Rolls-Royce.

In the fall of 1914, the Yale Bowl was opened, one of only three football stadiums in the country (Harvard Stadium and the Rose Bowl are the others) to be designated a National Historic Landmark. It had been on the drawing board for several years, postponed because Yale officials feared that poor teams could not draw sufficient crowds to fill it. Eventually, they grew tired of waiting for the glory days to return and built the structure anyway.

The Bowl was considerably larger than Harvard Stadium, seating half again as many people and spanning almost a sixth of a mile from rim to rim. "We suppose the Yale Bowl … can be seen through a telescope from Mars," the *New York Times* wrote upon its dedication. [19] At $507,000, it was also half again as expensive as Harvard Stadium, financed in large part by money Camp had been squirreling away as treasurer of the Field Association. Subscriptions were quickened by an offer guaranteeing heavy contributors good seats for the next twenty years.

Where Harvard had chosen a Greek U-shaped design, the elliptical Bowl was modeled after the Roman Coliseum, and like the Coliseum its playing surface was below ground level. Workers simply dug a huge hole and piled up the 300,000 cubic yards of dirt they excavated to form an oval, with enough left over to fill in twelve acres of swampland around the site, on which they later built a baseball stadium and a memorial arch to Walter Camp. Like Harvard a decade earlier, the Bulldogs opened their new home with a loss, this time a disastrous 36-0 shellacking by the Crimson. "Yale supplied the Bowl," one wag wrote, "but Harvard had the punch." [20]

There was a boom in stadium construction throughout the sporting world. Fenway Park, Wrigley Field, and many of the grand baseball parks were built during the teens, as were many of the great football arenas. Princeton opened Palmer Stadium in 1914. The following season, Cornell opened Schoellkopf Stadium, although its distinctive crescent seating on the home side of the field was not added until 1924. The seating capacity of the new college stadiums was many times larger than their undergraduate enrollment, undercutting all future claims that the games were intended first for the benefit of students. Colleges were now in the entertainment business.

Not even sumptuous seating capacity could quell griping about the allocation of tickets, which if anything became even more of a problem. Typical was a letter from one Yale alumnus who wrote, "a man who has been out of college for some years ought to get seats better than those directly behind the goal-posts." [21] Both Yale and Harvard tried to curb speculators by requiring everyone ordering tickets to sign a pledge that they would not transfer them to anyone else, though Harvard went a step further and stamped the purchaser's name on the ticket itself.

The demand for seats, even in venues located far from the big cities, testified to the enormous popularity football enjoyed in the years before the War, as well as to its money-making potential. Attendance at Harvard-Yale games played at Yale Field in Orange, Connecticut, had drawn an average crowd of thirty-four thousand during the first decade of the century, a figure that more than doubled when the Elis moved into the Bowl. The two schools split game receipts of almost $132,000 from the first game at the Bowl, and almost $156,000 from the second, including $2,700 from automobile parking fees. [22]

Detailed income and expense figures for Harvard's athletic program show the extent to which football now supported the rest of the growing athletic program. In 1914, only three of twenty-seven varsity, freshman, and club sports made a profit: varsity football, varsity baseball, and varsity track, but football profits were almost six times as large as the other two combined. Football income accounted for more than two-thirds of the Athletic Association's total revenue and enabled it to finish in the black. Receipts soared from just over $96,000 in 1911 to $194,000 just two years later and to almost $420,000 by 1922. [23]

A look at football expenses for the 1916 season also gives insights into the organization of a team. The Crimson incurred $101,000 in expenses (while taking in $208,000), ten times as much as any other team. Half that amount was paid to visiting teams in gate guarantees. The next largest item were game expenses such as operation of the scoreboard and payment of the referees, followed by $6,500 for travel, $4,300 for equipment, and $2,800 for doctors (the baseball team, by comparison, spent $343.34 for doctors). [24] "The cost of organized athletics is almost scandalous," wrote Dean LaBaron Briggs. "Captains, managers, and coaches ... tend to encourage an exaggerated fastidiousness in hotel accommodations, in food, and in clothing; they too often require for themselves and their men such luxuries of the table and of transportation as none but the rich can afford." [25]

Football was becoming more corporate in many respects and as it did so it became even more important to arrange the schedule to maximize the number of victories, and through them, revenue. A fascinating and unusually detailed early treatise on schedule building was written by H. J. Ludington, a Cornell student and candidate for team manager in 1915.[26] The first consideration, he wrote, was to start the season with a few easy games to give the coach time to evaluate his players. Ludington advocated putting Colgate on the Cornell schedule because it was located nearby and thus would not demand a large guarantee. Williams College was another good mid-season addition; a winnable game against a well-known team. "Consequently," Ludington wrote, "we would be assured of a large crowd to make the game a financial success. Moreover, this game would tend to bring Cornell into the minds of the sub-freshmen. Thus advertising for the University."

While the Big Three could afford to play almost all their games at home, Cornell did not have that luxury, so Ludington embraced the commercial possibilities of road trips. Playing Harvard in Cambridge, he argued, had the triple advantage of generating large gate receipts, bringing Cornell favorable publicity, and appealing to alumni in Boston and New York. Even though it might be possible to persuade Michigan and Penn to visit Ithaca, he favored playing those colleges on the road as well because of their larger stadiums and the opportunity to show off before alumni in different parts of the country.

As it turned out, Ludington's instincts were good. In 1916, Cornell played a shorter schedule than he had advocated, but one structured in the same manner. A schedule can only do so much, of course, and the Big Red finished with a 6-2 record, disappointing compared with what they had accomplished the year before—an undefeated, untied record and their first national championship. Football had been slow to develop in Ithaca, but had begun to take off in 1912 when Cornell hired Al Sharpe, another former Yale star, as its coach. Like other Walter Camp disciples, Sharpe brought rigorous organization and a love of secrecy, closing practice and posting guards to make sure students took the long route around the field. He turned a 3-7 record his first season into a 5-4-1 record in his second, including a victory at Penn that was celebrated, one Cornellian put it in retrospect, "like the Bolshevik Revolution."[27]

Cornell leapt again in 1914 to 8-2, winning its last seven games in a row and yielding not a single touchdown. Although no one on the team weighed more than 200 pounds, they boasted two first-team All-Americans, quarterback Charlie Barrett and fullback and punter Fritz Shevrick. Barrett in particular was so highly esteemed that after his death during World War I, a memorial tablet was erected at Schoellkopf Field with subscriptions from Penn's football team.[28]

Sharpe and his men picked up where they had left off in 1915, enjoying their new home field. For the opening of Schoellkopf Stadium, students dissatisfied with the team nickname brought a live bear cub mascot, which they dubbed "Touchdown I." The little bear would climb the goal posts to the roar of the spectators, but as the team's manager later recalled, "It was not cute and cuddly as it matured; it became perpetually hungry, mean, ill-bred, and dangerous. When allowed to climb the goalposts it was hell trying to get him down and a menace to try and recage him."[29]

During the team's trip to Michigan that season, Touchdown broke loose from his restraints and terrorized guests in the lobby of the Detroit hotel where the team was staying. A few weeks later, during a stopover in Atlantic City on the way to play Penn, Touchdown got loose again in a salt water taffy shop on the boardwalk, turning the place upside down before the manager could lure it into the ocean where it was subdued. That was enough to persuade even the most rabid partisan that the bear had to go, and it was donated to a New York zoo.

Meanwhile, back on the field, the Big Red stormed through a second season in 1915 without surrendering a touchdown. In late October, they traveled to Cambridge to take on Percy Haughton's Harvard team that was riding a thirty-three-game winning streak of its own. It was certainly the most important game in Cornell history up to that point. The press made much of the showdown between Barrett and Eddie Mahan. Barrett scored Cornell's first touchdown, and had broken loose for a second on a run around the end. He had only one man to beat—Mahan—when the two collided head-on. Barrett was knocked unconscious and Mahan may as well have been. Woozy, suffering what must have been a concussion, he was allowed to remain in the game but fumbled three times and dropped two punts. Shevrick took over for Barrett and kicked a field goal to seal a 10-0 Cornell victory.

When the Tournament of Roses Committee began to look for an eastern team to play in their newly resurrected football game that winter, Cornell was the likely choice. But the Big Red declined, citing its long-standing policy against playing in postseason games. So did Dartmouth, Harvard, Princeton, and even Columbia, which had just finished its first season in ten years. At last, the committee turned to Brown, which despite losses to Harvard, Amherst, and Syracuse, accepted.

The Tournament of Roses was a civic publicity stunt with Ivy ties and a motley history. The idea for a tournament had originated sometime in the late nineteenth century with the Valley Hunt Club, which liked to ride to hounds on New Year's Day and encouraged its members to boast to their eastern friends about balmy southern California. In 1890, a professor at Throop College of Technology (now Cal Tech), proposed that residents display roses as another way of advertising. This soon evolved into a parade, with the tournament part added as riders tried to spear a wreath of roses with a lance while riding at full gallop.[30]

By the turn of the century, the pageant had become a successful tourist attraction, which organizers decided to promote even further by staging a football game between top eastern and western college teams. Michigan so badly embarrassed Stanford in 1902, however, that the football game was discontinued. Tournament organizers played on the popularity of the novel *Ben Hur* and entertained the crowds with chariot races instead.

People eventually grew tired of watching rigged chariot races and so in 1915, speaking at a dinner organized by the Pasadena Chamber of Commerce,

Southern California coach Ralph Glaze, the former Dartmouth star, proposed reviving the east-west football game. Sitting in the audience that night was A. Manton Chase, a Brown alumnus, who along with another Brunonian, Ralph Elrod, immediately set out to secure an invitation for their alma mater. Chase was crestfallen to learn that the tournament committee had never heard of Brown.[31]

The Bears had only begun to make a name for themselves following the return of Eddie Robinson in 1910 for a stint as coach. That season, they upset Yale, 21-0, the worst defeat in the Elis' history until that point. The *New York Times* ranked Brown second in the country at the end of the season, behind only Harvard, while the *Sun*, the *Providence Journal*, and the *Boston Post* placed them third, behind Harvard and Penn.

Robinson's teams slumped the next few seasons, leading the alumni to search for an explanation. Many blamed the lack of faculty support or the lack of an identifiable rival toward which to build a season.[32] Others, probably more accurately, identified the lack of talent, a deficiency caused in part by Brown's failure to develop a pipeline from the top prep schools. Much was made of a survey done in 1913 by the *Yale Daily News* in which it found that top athletes from fourteen leading prep schools went to just four colleges: Harvard, Yale, Princeton, and Dartmouth.

Brown had to look for talent elsewhere. The turning point was the arrival of Frederick Douglass Pollard, known as "Fritz," one of the most prominent black athletes of his day and later the first African-American coach in the National Football League.

Pollard arrived in Providence by a very circuitous route. Growing up poor in Chicago, he received little encouragement to go to college at all. The prominent black newspapers in town, interested in more substantive advances for African-Americans, gave scant coverage to college athletes. Pollard simply showed up one morning for freshman practice at Northwestern, without even having applied for admission, and was politely asked to leave by the dean. He spent the rest of the 1912 season playing on semi-pro teams in and around Chicago.

The following fall, Pollard's family raised enough money to send him east. Dartmouth sounded appealing because he had heard of Matt Bullock, but his mother preferred Brown, a good Baptist college. On his way to Hanover, Pollard decided to make a side trip to Providence, where he secured an interview with President William H. P. Faunce. "Well, Pollard," Faunce said, "you're too far from home for us to let you go back. If you really have decided that you want to come to Brown, I guess we'll have to let you stay as a special student." Pollard, who had come only on a whim, stayed and tried to earn the necessary credits to enroll as a regular student the following fall.

When the fall came, Pollard learned that he still did not qualify for admission. He remained in Providence, got married, and worked at various jobs, including doing dry cleaning from Brown students. He had done nothing further academically when in the fall of 1914 he decided to finish his journey to Dartmouth. Coach Frank Cavanaugh let him practice with the team, but the administration wanted no part of college-jumping athletes and suggested that Pollard leave Hanover.

Pollard went next to Boston, where he called on William Henry Lewis, the former Harvard star who was now a prominent lawyer. Seeing a recruiting opportunity, Lewis invited Pollard to watch the Crimson's game against Bates that Saturday from the team bench. Pollard accepted, but somehow ended up on the train back to Maine with the Bates team that evening without even saying goodbye. Bates, needless to say, was not the answer either, and Pollard straggled back to Boston, having borrowed train fare from the president of the college. After two seasons, he still had not played a down of college football.

Ashamed, he went back to see Lewis, who called in another former black Ivy star, William Clarence Matthews, to set the young man straight. The two persuaded him to enroll in a Springfield high school, where he could earn enough credits to start a college career on the right foot. After doing so, Pollard applied to Brown that spring and was accepted.

Racism was no less a fact of life in the north than in the south around the time of World War I and Providence, as Pollard's biographer notes, with its heavy immigrant population, was particularly inhospitable. There were few black college students anywhere—fewer than two thousand in the entire country in 1915 and fewer than fifty in predominantly white colleges. The Ivy colleges dealt with black students in different ways, as Dartmouth President Ernest Martin Hopkins described:

> There are three attitudes among northern colleges which may be taken, one being that of Princeton, in which the color line is drawn with the utmost rigidity and the man is not even given access to the curriculum, even if he can pass all the examinations and even though every other conceivable color or race is granted admission upon the presentation of proper credentials. This is, of course, a straight result of the fact that Princeton has always made an appeal to and won a considerable number from the south. The second attitude is that of Yale, which gives colored men admission but where it is definitely understood that the man shall be denied all the privileges of membership in the college except that of attending classes and receiving a diploma. The third attitude is that of Harvard, Dartmouth, Brown, Cornell, and Pennsylvania, where the number of negroes who can qualify for admission to the college is an insignificant number of the total enrollment, and where the man who is enough an exception to the general standards of his race so that he can qualify for college

> *membership and then qualify in the stiff competition for*
> *membership on the athletic teams is neither given less nor more*
> *consideration than he would have under other circumstances.* [33]

Yet black athletes were not unknown at these colleges, even at the turn of the century. Harvard may have had the best record, but blacks had run track for Penn and played basketball for Columbia. Football, however, as the most prominent sport, was different.

Admirable as their attitude may have been in an age of increasing discrimination, the key, as Hopkins alluded, was numbers. Blacks, like Jews, were admitted so long as there were not too many of them. As Charles Eliot had assured alumni in 1907, "while Harvard will do its duty by the Negro, should his numbers swell to such a point 'as to impeded the progress of the College,' limitations would be imposed." [34]

On campus, Pollard endured the usual racial indignities, the social exclusion and whispered slurs. Robinson assigned him an oversized uniform and sent Pollard off to practice punting to himself. Midweek practices were known as "Bloody Wednesday" because Robinson allowed the scrubs to compete directly against the first team for starting jobs. At one of these practices, Pollard embarrassed John Butner, the first string end from Atlanta, faking him out two or three times for long gains. After a while, Butner went over to Robinson. "Say, we better let that nigger join us," he conceded. [35]

It was several more weeks, though, before Robinson let Pollard into a game. In his debut against Williams, Pollard ran for three touchdowns and had another called back on a penalty. When the father of one of Pollard's white teammates traveled from Tennessee to threaten that he would pull his son off the team if Pollard continued to play, Robinson faced him down. Led by Pollard, as well as quarterback J. C. Purdy, tackle Mark Farnum, and center Ken Sprague, the Bears began to win. When they played Yale, a group of black Yale students took seats on the Brown side of the field to cheer for Pollard, who was forced to enter the field by a separate gate to avoid abuse from other fans. Behind Pollard's running and punt returns, the Bears scored a 3-0 victory, only their second ever against Yale.

Brown had a good team, but not a great one. They lost to Harvard, 16-7, though Percy Haughton was criticized for playing his second team in order to send his starters off to scout Yale. At least some Brown alumni, however, took it philosophically. "The only way to compel Harvard to play all her stars against us is to put up a better fight against her." [36]

Brown had not expected the Rose Bowl invitation, but welcomed the chance for some rare national attention. No eastern team had ever played on the West Coast, so the trip received extensive coverage in the press. As Pollard's biographer has written, Brown officials prepared as if they were setting off into the wilderness, taking out insurance for each member of the team and packing drinking water for the train trip west. Pollard traveled with his teammates, a fact that had to be explained repeatedly to disconcerted black Pullman porters, who refused to serve him. Although the papers wrote that the team studied on the way west, in fact they spend most of the time playing cards in their underwear. Upon their arrival in Pasadena, the owner of the hotel where they were staying, a Harvard man, greeted them in full football regalia. Robinson held a few light practices, but allowed his team to go as a group to watch the Tournament of Roses parade.

Their opponent, Washington State, approached the trip as a business proposition. Coach William H. "Lone Star" Dietz, a Sioux Indian, made arrangements ahead of time for his squad to arrive early and work as extras during the filming of football scenes in the movie *Tom Brown of Harvard*. For two weeks, the players donned uniforms and tried not to tackle the film's star.

Ticket sales were brisk for a game between schools few in southern California would have known anything about, but by New Year's Day only seven thousand or so braved a steady rain, the first rainy New Year's in Pasadena in twenty-five years. The sloppy field bogged down Brown's running game. Pollard, who had left his long cleats at home, hardly imagining bad weather in California, was pulled in the third quarter and spent much of the rest of the afternoon imploring his coach to put him back in. According to Pollard, Walt Disney (then a young artist) was in the stands that afternoon and the sight of Pollard jumping up and down around Robinson stuck in his memory. One of Disney's earliest animated cartoons featured a football game in which Mickey Mouse begs to be sent in to face a group of lions, pleading, "Put me in, please, Coach, put me in!" [37]

Washington State won an easy 14-0 victory, enriching the Cougar players, who had bet heavily on themselves. They were the only ones who fared well financially. Game organizers, who had promised each school a $5,000 guarantee, lost more than $11,000. Brown had a leisurely train trip home, refilling their empty water barrels with California wine.

As he readily would have admitted, Pollard was at Brown to play football, not to study. That year he earned eight D's and two E's (a failing grade), yet somehow remained in school and eligible for athletics, starring that spring for the track team. The following year, 1916, Brown was even better, beating both Harvard and Yale in the same season for the first time ever, the only school other than Princeton ever to have achieved that feat. Pollard was named first team All-American. At a rally following the victory over Harvard, Brown's President Faunce boasted, "There is no bigger white man on the team than Fritz Pollard." [38]

A devastating late season loss to Colgate soured the Bears' season, but despite their record there was to be no return invitation to Pasadena. Stung by the financial debacle of the previous year, the chairman of the Tournament football committee journeyed east that fall to lure a bigger eastern name to the Rose Bowl. Yale turned him down, but Penn accepted—in mid-October, barely halfway into the season.

From a competitive standpoint, the committee could have done better. The Quakers finished 7-2-1, including an embarrassing 6-0 loss to Swarthmore. They were, though, an interesting team, one that included tackle Lou Little, future coach of Columbia's only Rose Bowl team; end Heinie Miller, future president of the National Boxing Association; and quarterback Bert Bell, future president of the National Football League. When someone asked Bell's father, John, the attorney general of Pennsylvania, where his son would attend college, he replied, "Bert will go to Penn or he'll go to hell." [39]

The best game of the 1916 season, though, did not involve the Quakers. It was Yale's 6-3 upset of Harvard, breaking a seven-year drought. The Elis were fired by Coach Tad Jones's famous declaration that they would never again in their lives do anything so important, and although no one knew it at the time, it was also to be Percy Haughton's last game as Harvard's coach. More than seventy-seven people filled the Yale Bowl, a crowd the newspapers pointed out was equal to the population of Kansas City or the state of Nevada. Officials estimated that seven thousand automobiles jammed New Haven streets. Ten of Yale's eleven starters played all sixty minutes, led by Captain Clinton "Cupie" Black, so nicknamed because of his resemblance to the Kewpie dolls then popular. Harvard might have won had not Eddie Casey's seventy-yard touchdown run been called back on a penalty, while Yale scored all its points on a plunge by Joe Neville, the only touchdown the Bulldogs ever scored against Haughton's Crimson. To make matters still more bitter in Cambridge, it was reported later that the game might have been five minutes short, owing to the field judge's balky watch. [40]

But Harvard would not play in a postseason game, so the Rose Bowl invitation went to the Quakers. After their perfect 1910 season, chaos had reigned at Penn. In 1912, they capped an otherwise mediocre season with a sensational 27-21 win at Michigan after trailing 21-0 at halftime, then upset Jim Thorpe's undefeated Carlisle team the following week. When they slipped to 6-3-1 in 1913 and 4-4-1 in 1914, nineteen of the twenty-one members of the varsity voted against keeping George Brooke as coach. Members of the freshman team immediately voted to keep Brooke (as did the out-going varsity captain, Al Journeay) and embarrassed the upperclassmen by telling the press that they routinely pushed the varsity around in practice. [41] Brooke was kept on for another dismal season, although Ollie Moffett, a reserve halfback, decided he had had enough and left Penn for a career in the movies.

In 1916, the Quakers hired Robert Folwell who energized the Quaker offense, shrewdly mixing in short "baseball" passes over the line, the only kind that could be thrown accurately with a fat ball. The team improved to 7-3-1, culminating in their trip to Pasadena. Penn rode west on a special train provided by the Reading Railroad, more than two hundred of their classmates tagging along as far as Chicago on their way home for Christmas break.

Their opponent was the University of Oregon, a team Tournament organizers had selected over the University of Washington because it was located 250 miles closer to Pasadena.[42] Nevertheless, Folwell questioned published odds of 5 to 3 in favor of the Quakers.

"Make it 3 to 1 and I'll take the short end that Oregon will win," he told the press.

Some of the Quakers objected when Folwell held open practice, and Bell later complained that Oregon scored its first touchdown on a reverse pass play Folwell had asked him to demonstrate in public.

The game was played in good weather, sparing relieved officials who had taken out rain insurance in case of a repeat of the previous year's downpour. Although Penn kept the ball in Oregon's territory for most of the afternoon, they could not score. One Quaker drive stalled at the Oregon three-yard line, whereupon Bill Quigley, who was playing in place of injured fullback Howard Berry, missed the easy field goal.

As Folwell would later admit, Penn had not taken the game very seriously, and by the second half Oregon began to wear them down, scoring two late touchdowns for a 14-0 victory. "The Pennsylvanians were decidedly of the city-bred type," sniffed one western writer, while another added that upon looking at the Quakers, "one immediately thought of yachts and automobiles."[43] Financially, though, the game was a huge success, in marked contrast to the year before, and tournament organizers began to plan a permanent stadium for the contest, which would thereafter be called the Rose Bowl.

Folwell did not accompany the team back to Philadelphia, staying west to go hunting. Within a few weeks, though, he unexpectedly found himself in the target of Penn's Faculty Committee on Athletics, which voted not to rehire him. The committee refused to state its reasons publicly, but hinted darkly that his conduct on the trip had been unacceptably "lax." It was later revealed that Penn officials had sent someone along on the train to spy on Folwell.[44] Demonstrating clearly, though, where power lay at the University of Pennsylvania, within a day of the announcement that Folwell would not be rehired, a gang of angry students and alumni, led by twenty-one members of the Pennsylvania legislature, had the decision reversed. Provost Edgar Smith promised to strip the faculty committee of its powers.[45]

Folwell recognized his bargaining position and promptly held out for more money. The committee agreed to pay him, but insisted on one concession. Folwell's contract would be voided in the event that the United States entered World War I and the upcoming football season were cancelled.[46]

The clause was well placed. Six weeks later, the United States went to war and intercollegiate athletics disappeared from popular attention. The Ivies were split. After canceling most of their spring sports in the excitement immediately after the declaration of war, Brown, Cornell, Columbia, Dartmouth, and Penn played more or less complete football schedules in 1917. Folwell, his hard-won contract in hand, was Penn's only paid athletic coach that fall as the Quakers, who returned most of their Rose Bowl squad, cleaned up.

Harvard, Yale, and Princeton, on the other hand, fielded only informal teams and did not play each other. They also curtailed most other sports (which had been unprofitable, anyway), a move which saved the Harvard Athletic Association $50,000.[47] The Big Three did organize freshman teams, membership in which was limited to those engaged in military training. Autumn afternoons were now given over to drilling and crash military courses for prospective officers. By the war's end, 121 of 138 Yale lettermen from the period 1910-1919 had either joined the armed forces or served in civilian war-related posts. At Harvard, Percy Haughton resigned along with his entire coaching staff and joined the service.

In 1918, Cornell and Yale did not field teams at all (despite Walter Camp's encouragement that the games go on), while Princeton and Dartmouth fielded informal teams and Harvard played a rump, three-game schedule against nearby colleges. Only Brown, Columbia, and Penn played regular schedules, with a few games substituted against military camps to fill the holes. The Quakers managed to go 5-3 even though Philadelphia health officials closed Franklin Field for the entire month of October because of the influenza epidemic.

How much ill will these schools generated by continuing to play is unclear. The country as a whole seems to have responded in different ways; professional baseball, for example, went on as before, although with a shortened schedule. The precarious financial health of Penn's athletic program suggests that the Big Three may have been the only ones who could afford to give up football for patriotism.

One hint that the old debate over football's role in college life remained unsettled was an obscure controversy over whether to sew numbers on players' uniforms. Today the whole matter seems silly, but it was taken with the utmost seriousness at the time. Dartmouth was the first Ivy team to number its players, in a game against Carlisle in 1913, seizing the honor from Princeton, which proposed doing so for its game with Harvard before backing out.[48] In 1916, the NCAA recommended numbering (though it would not require it until 1937), and the matter exploded.

The argument in favor of numbering players was straightforward; by making them easier to identify, it made the game more enjoyable for spectators. But this very rationale touched a hidden nerve about the nature of football and for whose benefit the games were being played. In the opinion of many, games were for the benefit of students only (who would recognize their classmates without a program), and anything that appealed to spectators smacked of creeping commercialism—an interesting attitude for a sport that was drawing fifty thousand people to big games and generating hundreds of thousands of dollars in annual revenue. Typical in this respect was Yale's captain, who declared, "if the spectators of a football game are not interested enough to learn who the players are without their being numbered, they will not be interested enough to learn who the players are when they are numbered."[49]

Most colleges followed the NCAA's recommendation but the Big Three remained holdouts. Yale announced before the 1916 season that it would number its players, thus ending what the *New York Times* called "the longest and most strenuous controversy in the history of Yale football," but changed its mind after one game.[50] Princeton said it would follow suit in 1919, prompting Yale to say it would go along too if the others would. Yet a year later the issue was still being bandied about, until Yale announced that it would wear numbers in the Princeton and Harvard games. Not until 1921 did all three agree.

Having lost much of their influence over the direction of football nationally, and facing increasingly stiff opposition on the gridiron from other eastern colleges that would eventually become members of the Ivy League, the Big Three continued to set themselves apart by establishing higher standards of amateurism. Princeton and Harvard adopted what came to be known as the "two-sport rule," limiting the number of seasons in which a student could engage in intercollegiate athletics. Although the rule was unpopular on campus and was later repealed, administrators defended their responsibility for regulating student life. "The number of sports a student engages in is very much the business of the Faculty," declared Dean Howard McClenahan of Princeton in an address to the NCAA in 1915, "for the mere passing of all examinations, with whatever grade, is not by any means the largest part of a college training."[51]

Breaches of the amateur creed that had been common even a decade earlier were no longer tolerated. Yale's Harry LeGore was disqualified for the entire 1915 season after it was discovered that he, like many before him, had played baseball professionally during the summer. Largely because of the unfavorable publicity the LeGore case generated, the Big Three presidents adopted their first joint eligibility code, which came to be known as the "Triple Agreement." Shortly after the war ended, they entered into another joint agreement reigning in athletic recruiting, declaring that "athletic proselyting in any form is injurious to college athletics." The three urged all alumni, undergraduates, and friends not to offer prep students any monetary inducement to enter their college, including offering "artificial hospitality of any sort, such as trips to the university, automobile rides, theater parties, etc."[52]

The effort to curb prep school recruiting can be seen as a kind of Big Three arms control, an effort not only to rationalize their dealings with each other but to set themselves apart from schools such as Brown or Penn, which were doing more to improve their teams. Nevertheless, it was vitally important to preserve those prep school connections—the "life line of empire" in James Bryant Conant's phrase. Harvard and Yale had monopolized them for a time but Princeton began to horn in, making competition even tougher.[53]

Not surprisingly, other eastern colleges viewed the Triple Agreement with misgivings, suspicious that they were being cut out. These fears were heightened when the Big Three announced in 1919 that they would hold a triangular track meet among themselves, to which the other eastern colleges would not be invited. Talk began to be heard about creating a rival organization consisting of Cornell, Dartmouth, Penn, Columbia, and Syracuse.[54] Finally, in March 1919, William McClellan, chairman of Penn's University Council on Athletics, called for a formal football league comprised of the seven leading eastern colleges "which, because of their student enrollment, traditions and other resources, are natural competitors."[55] McClellan identified the seven as Columbia, Cornell, Dartmouth, Harvard, Princeton, Penn, and Yale, leaving off Brown, which fit the group just as well as many of the others and had a less checkered gridiron history than Columbia. His proposal attracted little attention, although the *Cornell Sun* denounced any affiliation among the colleges as "athletic aristocracy."[56] For their part, the Big Three were not yet willing to concede parity to the others.

Given their emphasis on athletic purity, it was surprising to say the least when Harvard in 1920 became the third Ivy team in six years to play in the Rose Bowl.

In the opinion of some, Dartmouth, not Harvard, was the best team in the East. Clarence Spears, who had starred for the Green in 1915, replaced Frank Cavanaugh as coach in Hanover after Cavanaugh was gravely wounded at Verdun. Spears was one of those rare men who could stand up to two nicknames: "Doc," because of his medical degree, and "Fat," because of his five-foot-seven, 236-pound profile. Jolly off the field, he had a rough temper and as an undergraduate liked to toss furniture out his fourth-floor dorm window just to hear it crash in the courtyard below.

Spears assembled a squad of returning servicemen, led by "Dynamite Gus" Sonenberg, who liked to rip hotel radiators off the floor and later held the world professional heavyweight wrestling title. Dartmouth rolled over Penn State, preseason favorites for the national championship, and took on Colgate at tiny Alumni Oval in Hanover in a battle of undefeated teams. As so often seems to happen, the big game was played on a rain-soaked field. Colgate scored first when one of their backs stormed into the end zone so ferociously that he crashed into the goal post and was knocked unconscious when the crossbar fell on his head.

That crossbar was to figure prominently again. Dartmouth hung on, muffing several opportunities to tie the game. Guard Swede Youngstrom blocked three Colgate punts, only to see the Red Raiders recover each time and advance the ball for a gain. With less than a minute to play, Youngstrom again burst through the line, snuffing a fourth Colgate punt which he this time fell on in the end zone for a touchdown. Dartmouth still had to attempt the extra point. Lining up at a sharp angle, Jim Robertson's kick hit the upright and caromed over the bar for a 7-7 tie. In a rough game against Penn in the Polo Grounds the following week, Robertson and Youngstrom had to be carried off the field, but captain Jack Cannell helped the team hold on to a 20-19 victory.

Harvard also made a strong claim. Under new coach Robert T. Fisher and returning halfback Eddie Casey, the Crimson went unscored-upon through the first six games of the season until Princeton tied them, then pushed their way past Yale, 10-3, despite making only two first downs. The Elis, who had suffered an embarrassing loss to Boston College earlier in the year, might have won had not a missed signal on the Harvard one-yard line cost them the game. Some faulted the Elis for not throwing a single pass until the fourth quarter (Harvard had scored on a thirty-five-yard strike from Winslow "Babe" Felton to Casey). Yale emerged, as Grantland Rice put it, "from the stone age of football just exactly twelve minutes too late." [57] Although one of Harvard's all-time best teams, the Crimson were selected for the Rose Bowl on their reputation, as football commentators freely noted that they were not the top team in the east, let alone the nation.

Harvard received its invitation shortly after the end of the season, but it presented them with a dilemma. On the one hand was Harvard's refusal to play in postseason games. On the other was pent-up jealousy at seeing other eastern teams get national attention, as well as the recognition that an appearance would boost the university's ongoing $15 million endowment campaign.

President Lowell, while stating that he supported the trip personally, pulled the plug on it with the excuse that a cross-country trip would be unpatriotic given the national shortage of coal. So great was the outrage from Harvard alumni, coupled with a quick disavowal by national coal officials, that Lowell retreated and the trip went forward again. "Inconceivable though it be to some men," wrote Harvard's dean, "there are staid, middle-aged and even distinguished graduates of Harvard College in the West to whom the sight of a crimson jersey in…California is not unlike the sight of their country's flag in a distant land; and though anti-athletic people may regard them as fools, such feeling as theirs has a value that baffles words." [58]

As was by now routine for Rose Bowl trips, the Harvard train—a rolling card game, apparently—made its way leisurely west, stopping in Chicago to be feted by local alumni, jumping out for fifteen minute signal drills during stopovers in North Platte, Nebraska, and Green River, Wyoming, and engaging in at least one reported pillow fight. In Omaha, former Yale star Mac Baldridge let them know that someone had offered another Yale player $150 and expenses to give their opponents a scouting report—an offer, he said, that no self-respecting Old Blue would ever accept. [59]

Like almost all forms of American entertainment, the Rose Bowl game had grown bigger since the war. All twenty-eight thousand tickets were sold for the contest against Oregon. Demonstrating how seriously he took the game, Coach Fisher held the first Sunday practice in Harvard athletic history and even consented to have the Crimson wear numbers on their jerseys, the first time they had ever done so. Eddie Casey, issued unlucky number 13, refused to wear it.

They arrived in California early enough to mix heavy practice with a little sightseeing, meeting heavyweight boxing champion Jack Dempsey on a movie set and getting a studio tour from Douglas Fairbanks, who had previously declared his preference for Oregon. Overlooking this, the Crimson invited Fairbanks and Charlie Chaplin to watch the game from their bench. While riding around in a chauffeur-driven car, Casey and quarterback Bill Murray were stopped for exceeding the twenty-mile-per-hour speed limit, a jam Casey got out of by offering the policeman two tickets to the game. Governor Calvin Coolidge sent a telegram from home reminding the men that "Massachusetts knows you are game, believes you are superior, and hopes you will win." [60]

Among the thirty thousand fans on New Year's Day, 1920, were twenty-five hundred Harvard rooters, some of whom may have paid the twenty-five dollars scalpers were demanding for five-dollar seats. Shortly after two o'clock, a biplane buzzed the field as the pilot, a movie comedian, dropped a football decorated with the competing teams' colors, which was used to start the game.

Meanwhile, almost five hundred alumni, including Theodore Roosevelt, Jr., and Percy Haughton, crowded into the Harvard Club on Forty-Second Street in New York to listen to narrated telegraph reports while figures moved on a large magnetic gridiron. The throng cheered the good news and groaned at the bad, responding to Oregon drives with calls such as "Hey, stop that ball!" "That's far enough, quite!" and "Have a heart!" When the announcer reported that many of the fans in California were objecting to Harvard's rough play, Haughton clapped his hands and smiled. "Oh, they were all for gore at the Harvard Club," a reporter wrote. [61]

Harvard prevailed, 7-6, a tight defensive struggle sandwiching the second quarter, in which all the game's points were scored. Little-used substitute Freddie Church became a Harvard legend that afternoon filling in for Ralph Horween, who was injured trying to recover his own blocked field goal attempt. After taking an Oregon punt at the forty-yard line, the Crimson mixed passes from Murray with runs by Arnold Horween (Ralph's brother) until Church broke a fifteen-yard run for Harvard's only touchdown.

They still needed the extra point to win, however, and here Church made a smart play. The rule at the time was that a conversion had to be attempted directly opposite the spot at which the ball had been downed in the end zone, an archaic remnant of nineteenth-century play. Church alertly zigged across the end zone and placed the ball down directly behind the uprights, setting up an easy kick that proved to be the game winner.

The Ducks came close to winning in the waning minutes of the game on a twenty-four yard field goal—so close, in fact, that the scoreboard operator made the score 9-7, Oregon. But the referee immediately signaled that the kick had sailed wide of the upright, the score reverted to 7-6, and the game ended a few minutes later with Harvard having marched to the Oregon one-yard line.

The boys wound their way back home in time for the start of the second semester, buoyed by the $33,000 profit the athletic association had made on the trip. Harvard appears to have made as much of an impression on Hollywood as Hollywood did on Harvard. Actress Violet Dana, for one, told the newspapers that she had won the game for the Crimson with mental telepathy. It had all been grand fun, but Fred Moore, the graduate athletics manager, insisted that Harvard would not violate its tradition against postseason play again. "Once," he said, "will have to do." [63]

As the decade ended, so did Columbia's five-year experiment in small-time football. It was pronounced a success and plans went forward to build a stadium on the banks of the Hudson River so games would no longer have to be played in front of the library. President Butler recommended that the interim restrictions be lifted, clearing the way for the team to schedule bigger opponents. The consensus among Columbia alumni was that the Lions were still too weak to take on Harvard, Yale, or Princeton. But they might try Cornell or Penn. [64]

CHAPTER SIX

Team of Destiny

In the fall of 1924, Irving Harris, a Brown freshman, was disappointed to learn that his new college did not have a band to play at football games. He decided to organize one. Practicing with borrowed sheet music and instruments, a group of twenty-five aspiring musicians soon received their first invitation, a sendoff rally for the team as it embarked for a game at the University of Chicago.

The ragtag band knew only one tune and did not have a drum major's baton. Harris's roommate solved the latter problem by wrapping a broom handle with the belt from his bathrobe, and thus armed the musicians set off at the head of a student parade. Police cleared a path, which was fortunate as Harris had been in Providence less than a month and had no idea how to get to the train station. With rousing spirit, though, the band played their one selection over and over again, only to learn the next day that it was in fact a Harvard football song.[1]

Which Ivy marching band was the first to play at a football game is a matter of some debate. A Yale band was in the stands as early as 1899, but Dartmouth, Princeton, and Cornell all claim that that their bands are in fact the oldest in the Ivy League and thus the country. Whoever came first, martial music proved an easy fit for a martial game. Ivy football bands quickly drew attention, not least of all for spectacles such as Harvard's enormous bass drum, which was so large that it took the skin of an entire cow to cover the drumhead. John Philip Sousa led Penn's band at several concerts in the 1920s, while Yale, in a more modern spirit, boasted Rudy Vallee, the famous crooner and movie star, who sang through his trademark megaphone.

Hardly had marching bands gotten started when there were complaints about their shows. Harvard alumni criticized their band for slighting the visiting

Holy Cross team by playing only Harvard-Yale songs. "Cannot we use general phrases in our football songs, instead of just singing about Yale when we are actually playing some one else?" one asked.[2]

On the field, Harvard followed its undefeated Rose Bowl season with another undefeated mark in 1920, which eventually ran to twenty-five games. Yet the story of how the Crimson's winning streak ended is more interesting than the streak itself. That loss, to tiny Centre College of Danville, Kentucky, was later voted by the Associated Press as the greatest sports upset of the first half-century. And yet, memories cloud. Harvard should have seen it coming.

With an enrollment of only three hundred, a school such as Centre had little budget for football. Each player was assigned one uniform, which was expected to last him all season. Nevertheless, the Colonels, as they were called, went undefeated in 1919, including a victory over West Virginia, which had shut out Princeton a few weeks earlier. At halftime of that game, trailing 6-0, their coach, Charley Moran, assembled the team at midfield and led them in prayer, sparking their comeback in the minds of many and earning them the nickname "Praying Colonels." Walter Camp was sufficiently impressed with their season that he named three Centre players first-team All-Americans.

It also impressed Howard G. Reynolds, sports editor for the *Boston Post*, who decided the Praying Colonels might make an interesting opponent for Harvard: a bunch of pious country boys against the eastern aristocrats. Reynolds persuaded Eddie Mahan to go with him to scout Centre's final game against Georgetown College of Kentucky, which Centre won, 77-0. This convinced Mahan, who in turn persuaded Harvard's manager to put the Praying Colonels on the 1920 schedule.

Only three of the twenty-seven Centre players had ever been to a big city before they arrived at Boston's Back Bay station the following autumn. Crimson fans seem to have regarded their opponents, dressed in ragged yellow uniforms, as a curiosity, as well. More than forty thousand fans came out, an unusually large crowd for a minor opponent.

Harvard had not been scored upon in its first four games and a blowout seemed to be taking shape when the Crimson drove for a touchdown early. The Colonels soon changed that with a series of dashing runs. Later in the second quarter, "Bo" McMillan shocked the Crimson by faking a punt at his own five-yard line, then launching a perfect forty-yard strike that caught his receiver in stride for a touchdown. The supposedly iron Harvard defense had been torched for 170 yards in less than thirty minutes, and all of a sudden Centre led, 14-7.

At halftime, as was by now their custom, the Praying Colonels stayed on the field for prayer and a lecture from Moran. In the second half, the heavier Harvard line began to tell as they ground out a hard-fought 31-14 victory. Arnold Horween, Harvard's captain and later its coach, offered McMillan the game ball, which he declined. "We'll be back next year to take it home with us," he promised.[3]

Centre's good showing and the strong gate had assured them a rematch in 1921. Both teams were again undefeated, although Harvard had been made to fight for a 21-21 tie against Penn State. If anything, the Colonels were even more of a curiosity the second time around, and an even bigger crowd packed Harvard Stadium, led by a large contingent of MIT students who kept up the cheers for the visitors. In the locker room before the kickoff, future senator and baseball commissioner A. B. "Happy" Chandler, a Harvard law student by day but a Kentuckian by the grace of God, led the Centre squad in singing "Dear Old Southland."

After their experience the year before, Harvard should have been ready. Perhaps they were looking ahead to the Princeton game the following week, but whatever the excuse, they came out flat. Twice they marched near the Centre goal line only to miss easy field goals. At the half, the game was a scoreless tie.

Early in the third quarter, Centre took a Harvard punt in good field position, made even better thanks to a Crimson penalty. On the next play, McMillan sprang a reverse, taking off down the sideline for a touchdown. Harvard had its hopes dashed late in the fourth quarter when a bomb from Charlie Buell (who had missed the two field goals) was called back on a penalty. The Praying Colonels had won, 6-0. In Danville, delirious students painted the score on walls all over town, some of which are still visible today.

If the Harvard-Centre game of 1921 was the decade's most startling upset, Princeton's 21-18 victory over Amos Alonzo Stagg's University of Chicago team the following year may have been its most stirring triumph. Thanks to Princeton's publicity apparatus, that Tiger squad has been known ever since as the "Team of Destiny."

Their coach was Bill Roper, whose timely fumble recovery in the 1899 Yale game set the stage for Arthur Poe's winning field goal. During the off-season, Roper ran an insurance brokerage and served on the Philadelphia City Council where he loudly opposed Prohibition and the city's Blue Laws. Upon his death, the *New York Times* called him "the last of the romantic coaches," but in many ways Roper was a contrarian. He did not carp on diet, as other coaches did. He disliked spring practice. Many of his contemporaries, such as Brown's Eddie Robinson, believed in toughening their squads with long, hard scrimmages, but Roper would often send his team home early in order to conserve their energy. Except for shoulder pads and leather helmets, his Tigers wore practically no padding, which might slow them down.

Roper was, however, self-delusional in at least one respect. Although he piously insisted that players profited best from quiet, businesslike halftime talks, he was, in fact, he was one of the all-time great ranters, delivering fire and brimstone speeches to his teams that one historian has called "histrionic masterpieces."[4]

The University of Chicago surprised the Tigers at Princeton in 1921, winning 9-0. "Romantically it might be said that the invading eleven came out of the West like Lochinvar," wrote Heywood Broun, "or more realistically that it slaughtered Princeton like a steer."[5] That made the following year's rematch in Chicago even more important, the first time one of the Big Three had ever played in that part of the country. Princeton's season was disrupted before practice even began when their captain and two other players were declared ineligible for accepting money from a booster slush fund. Remembering back to his own playing days, Roper tried to regroup his team by hanging placards in the field house with an inspirational motto he had learned from Johnny Poe: "A team that won't be beat can't be beat." It became the 1922 Tigers' war cry.

Chicago officials received more than 100,000 requests for tickets to fill the 32,000 seats in Stagg Stadium. Fans who could not get tickets were not entirely out of luck, though. The game was the first ever to be broadcast over the radio.

For a while it looked like a repeat of the previous year. Chicago held an 18-7 lead going into the fourth quarter, which would have been larger had the Maroons not missed all three extra point attempts. With only a few minutes to go, the Tigers got a break when Chicago fumbled. Howard "Howdy" Gray, scooped up the loose ball and raced forty yards for a touchdown. The score was now 18-14. Momentum had swung to Princeton, and when they got the ball back they used their own offense and ill-timed Chicago penalties to move down to the Maroon seven-yard line. Burly Crumm, nicknamed "Maud," took it in with two minutes left, giving Princeton a 21-18 lead.

There was still time left, as Princeton knew. Suddenly, the Maroons started passing, driving down to the Princeton six-yard line with thirty seconds to play. Chicago could have attempted a tying field goal, but no doubt mindful of the three missed extra points, decided to play for the win. On first down, they picked up two yards. On second down, another two. On third down, Chicago bulled for one more yard. Fourth and goal, inside the Princeton one-yard line, with time almost gone. Thousands in the stands and thousands more listening held their breath.

Along the Princeton sideline, a man bounded out of the stands and cheerfully whacked quarterback Johnny Gorman (who was out with an injury) on his bad right shoulder. Gorman winced and reserve Brad Dinsmore grabbed the interloper, shouting, "Don't you see he's hurt? Get back in the stands where you belong!"

"O.K., I'm so sorry," the white haired man apologized. Only as he retreated did Dinsmore realize that the man was Princeton president John Grier Hibben.[6]

For their final chance, John Thomas, the Maroon quarterback called a triple shift, a foolishly complicated maneuver in such a tight spot, and one difficult to convey to his teammates over the raucous crowd. Someone missed a block and the Tigers' Harland "Pink" Baker blasted through the line to nail Thomas for a three-yard loss, the only play on which he had lost yardage all afternoon.

The Princeton-Chicago series created a great deal of excitement in the east for more intersectional games, yet the success of Ivy teams against Midwestern opponents was spotty at best, which only underscored how far the balance had swung. Henceforward, it would be the exception rather than the rule for an Ivy team to be considered among the best in the country. Several encounters were simply embarrassing. In 1923, Knute Rockne brought Notre Dame east to play Princeton. He made the game the focal point of the season, structuring Irish practices around how to stop the Tigers in particular situations. The result was an easy 25-2 Notre Dame victory that ended a ten-game Princeton winning streak. A year later, Notre Dame returned to Palmer Stadium, its backfield having been dubbed the "Four Horsemen" a week earlier after their victory over Army. One of the horsemen, Jimmy Crowley, scored two touchdowns while his teammate, Don Miller, had another called back, in a 12-0 Notre Dame victory.

Charlie Caldwell, a Princeton wingback and later a successful Tiger coach, remembered the game for the rest of his career. "I felt as if we were being toyed with," he wrote many years later. "I had been sold—hook, line, and sinker—on Rockne football. I wanted to coach, and more important, I wanted to learn everything I could about coaching a sport in which there were apparently a hundred and one opportunities to advance new thoughts, to develop partially explored theories and to blend the traditional with the unorthodox." [7]

Illinois' Red Grange, the "Galloping Ghost," turned in an even greater performance against Penn in 1925. The Quakers had managed to lure John Heisman back to lead them in 1920, but he could work no magic for his alma mater. The old coach was a great believer in rules, though, including the following:

1. *Don't fumble—you might better have died when a little boy.*
2. *Don't go on the field without your brains.*
3. *Don't get that "tired feeling."*
4. *Don't forget that a football player can still be a gentleman.* [8]

Heisman departed after three seasons with a disappointing record, largely padded against the weak sisters on the schedule. In 1922, Penn suffered an embarrassing defeat at home against the lightly regarded Alabama Crimson Tide.

Lou Young succeeded him and the Quakers improved dramatically to 9-1-1 by 1924, playing a non-Rose Bowl game at the University of California on New Year's Day, and claiming the national championship in the eyes of some sportswriters. In 1925, they owned a perfect record including a win over Yale, which was back on the schedule for the first time in thirty-two years. Then Illinois came to town.

Sixty-five thousand people turned out to see Grange's only collegiate appearance in the East. The Galloping Ghost remained underrated by eastern sportswriters who had never seen him play. Illinois did not have a strong team, but their coach, Bob Zuppke, had discovered that Penn always overshifted on defense, lining up with too many men on one side of the line, leaving the other end unprotected. He directed Grange to mix in plays to the weak side. The first time he tried it, Grange sprang loose for a fifty-five-yard touchdown. He later rushed for two more and helped run up the score by calling a flea flicker on a fake field goal with his team up by sixteen points. It was the best afternoon of Grange's collegiate career. In all, he rushed for 363 yards on a field so deep in mud that jersey numbers became unreadable. The Quakers were stunned, 24-2.

Cornell during these years enjoyed one of its greatest periods of success under a new coach, Gilmour Dobie. Success, but not levity. Dobie was a sour, sharp-tongued cynic—qualities that endeared him to the press, who saddled him with nicknames, including "Gloomy Gil" and "The Dour Scotsman." They even made an adjective of it. To be morose was to be "gildobian." [9]

He used the pass just often enough to keep defenses honest, but liked to grind out yards on the ground and drilled his teams until they ran their off-tackle plays to perfection. Not that he would ever have acknowledged perfection. "A football coach can only wind up two ways, dead or a failure," he liked to say. He never gave compliments and frequently at least feigned forgetting his players' names. Sometimes that was better than the alternative. "Gil always knew my name," halfback Andy Pierce insisted years later. "He unerringly referred to me as Fat Ass Pierce." [10]

The age of the alumni coach was ending, and Dobie was an example of the new breed who were hired for their won-loss records rather than for their ties to the university and its traditions. He had bounced from North Dakota State to the University of Washington to the Naval Academy before Cornell hired him with an unheard-of ten-year contract.

The Big Red had slumped since their undefeated season in 1915, but Dobie revived them with a winning record in 1920, followed by three consecutive years without a defeat, including the national championship in 1922. They were defensive powerhouses, outscoring their opponents over that twenty-four-game span by 1,022-81.

Linemen were of prime importance in Dobie's ground-based offense, and tackle Sunny Sunstrom became an All-American and team captain in 1923. But Cornell's attack centered around two of the great players of the decade. Teammates considered halfback Eddie Kaw a loafer, but his fifteen touchdowns led the nation in 1921. The highlight was the season-ending game against Penn at Franklin Field, a 41-0 Cornell victory in which Kaw rushed for five touchdowns on a muddy field. Rose Bowl officials invited the Big Red, but the Cornell faculty declined on their behalf.

Kaw also threw the ball and was the team's kicker. As a safety, he was adept at breaking up passes in the man-to-man defense Dobie insisted on using (over criticism that he switch to a zone). He later became the first Cornellian to be inducted into the College Football Hall of Fame.

George Pfann, the Big Red's other star, wanted to go to Yale but did not meet the entrance requirements and matriculated at Cornell instead, intending to transfer after his freshman year. He decided to stay in Ithaca and did not lose a game in three years on the Big Red varsity. Although listed as a quarterback, Pfann ran the single wing offense in which on a given play he might also act as a tailback or receiver. In 1923, Pfann led Cornell to their third consecutive Thanksgiving Day victory over Penn, at Franklin Field.

Pfann's career after college was no less sterling. He went on to study law at Oxford as a Rhodes Scholar, became assistant United States Attorney for the Southern District of New York during the thirties, and was highly decorated during World War II as a lieutenant under General George S. Patton.

Lost amid better teams at other schools in the early years of the decade was Yale. From 1919 through 1922, the Bulldogs lost seven of eight games against their Big Three rivals. They called back Tad Jones, who had last coached the team in 1916, but Jones had his work cut out for him. In 1920, Yale was shut out by both Princeton and Harvard, the first time that had ever happened. At times, they seemed not to be paying attention. Princeton pulled a fake punt for a fifty-one-yard gain, while a year later the Elis were caught napping when Harvard's Charley Buell (who had been signaling for fair catches all day) zipped a long punt return to set up the winning touchdown.

Harvard beat them again at New Haven in 1922 before seventy-eight thousand, including French premier, Georges Clemenceau, who said he found the game "sporting." [11] Clemenceau diplomatically moved from the Harvard to the Yale side of the Bowl at halftime (serenaded by the combined Harvard and Yale bands playing the "Marseillaise"), just as his countryman, Marshal Foch, had done at the Princeton-Yale game a year earlier.

Everything came together gloriously in 1923 as Yale produced another candidate for its best team of all time. Certainly, it would be its last undefeated team until 1960. It was an unusually colorful team, and by contemporary Big Three standards, an unusually blue-collar one. Four of the team's stars were transfer students, all of whom had complied with the Triple Agreement by sitting out a year before playing for Yale.

Century Milstead had gotten his name from his father because he was born on January 1, 1900 (and over the objections of his mother, who argued that the new century did not begin until 1901). Unusually large for the time (six-foot-four and 220 pounds), Milstead was a product of western Pennsylvania coal country and had to earn his way through college by stoking furnaces. Yale officials suspended him in 1924 when he got married while still in school, and refused to let him graduate with his class. [12]

Like Milstead, fullback Marvin Allen (Mal) Stevens had also starred for Wabash College before transferring to Yale, where he earned his tuition working for a local undertaker. Stevens, who would later coach the Bulldogs, also became a famous gynecologist, certainly the only Ivy League coach to hold those dual distinctions. Lyle Richeson had quarterbacked Tulane for three years. When he decided to leave, his father wired both Harvard and Yale, expressing interest. Harvard declined; Yale did not. Widdy Neale (whose more famous brother, Greasy, went on to a professional baseball career and coached the Philadelphia Eagles to an NFL title) had played both for West Virginia and Marietta College.

These four joined Tennessee-born fullback "Memphis Bill" Mallory and center Win Lovejoy in forming a balanced team that scored 230 points while surrendering only 38 on its way to a perfect season. The Elis were scarcely challenged, crushing North Carolina, 53-0; Georgia, 40-0; Army, 31-10 (before eighty thousand fans, still the largest crowd ever to watch a Yale game at the Bowl); and Princeton, 27-0, as they came to the finale at Harvard. Coach Bob Fisher's Crimson team, in contrast, was in a downward spiral, one that had seen it fight for a tie with Middlebury.

Whatever innate superiority Yale might have brought to the finale was obscured, as was everything else in Cambridge that afternoon, by a sea of mud churned up in an all-day downpour. The two teams combined for fourteen fumbles and were forced to punt a total of fifty-four times. (A year later, playing in another rainstorm, the Elis painted their arms with pitch in order to hold on to the ball). Early in the second quarter, Neale popped a soggy punt from deep in his own end, which Mallory jarred loose with a hard tackle. Raymond Pond, whose nickname, "Ducky," was certainly apt that day, scooped it up and ran sixty-seven yards for Yale's first touchdown at Harvard Stadium since 1907. Mallory somehow managed to kick two field goals in the morass to give Yale a 13-0 victory and an undefeated season.

"By winning today Yale clinches the Big Three football title and takes a long stride toward the swimming and water polo titles," the *New York Times* cracked.[13] Babe Ruth, a loyal Crimson rooter, appeared at the game as a news commentator. Suggestions of Harvard "snobbery," the Babe said, made him "sore."[14]

Dartmouth also had been disappointing since their sterling season in 1915. Doc Spears had rallied them to a 7-2 record in 1920, his final season, but a 59-7 thrashing at the hands of Dobie's Big Red the following year ensured that Jackson Cannell's tenure as his successor would be brief. Ernest Martin Hopkins received angry letters, including one that griped that a team comprised of "Phi Beta Kappa sissies with no red corpuscles in their bodies" was being outdone only by "a student body made up of perfect ladies."[15] Dartmouth was, however, becoming a better national draw, journeying to Seattle in 1920 to dedicate the University of Washington's new stadium (a 28-7 victory), then to Athens the following year to dedicate the University of Georgia's, a 7-0 victory on a fifty-yard pass from Jim Roberton to Ed Lynch.

The Dartmouth Indians, as they were now known, brought back Jesse Hawley, a former star on their 1909 team, as coach in 1923. Hawley was another member of the Gil Dobie all-business school of coaching, but he built a positive atmosphere and began to achieve success. In his first year, Hawley led Dartmouth to an 8-1 record, their only defeat at the hands of Dobie's Cornell juggernaut at the game dedicating Dartmouth's new $275,000 Memorial Stadium. A year later, they did not lose a game.

The only blemish on their 1924 record, a 14-14 tie against Yale, a team they still had never beaten, could be blamed on an overconfident quarterback. Eddie Dooley had driven his men to the Eli one-yard line, but it was fourth down and time was slipping away. In the huddle, Dooley called for a handoff to halfback Red Hall. At the snap, the line blocked perfectly. A great hole opened up, but when Hall rushed forward there was no ball. On an instant, Dooley had decided to take it in himself, and as Hall stormed into the end zone, Dooley was tackled by Win Lovejoy and the victory was lost.

Although Dooley injured his back over the winter and left school, Dartmouth's 1925 squad finished undefeated and was proclaimed national champions by the *Football Annual*. It remains Dartmouth's only national title.

As good as Dartmouth was on the football field, they matched it academically. Four starters on the 1925 team graduated Phi Beta Kappa—showing the unnamed alumnus who had written President Hopkins that they did indeed have red corpuscles. It was an unusually distinguished assemblage. Running back Myles Lane, nicknamed "The Big Green Train," scored forty-eight touchdowns and 307 points in his career, both still Dartmouth records. He was also a star hockey player, and along with Hobey Baker is the only man to be inducted into both the college football and hockey halls of fame. Lane later became a U.S. Attorney and prosecuted Julius and Ethel Rosenberg for espionage. George Champion, the left guard, became chairman of the board of the Chase Manhattan Bank. Captain Nate Parker, a future Rhodes Scholar, was so modest that one Boston sportswriter wrote, "He takes his hat off in a telephone booth before dialing central." [16] Charles Starrett, a reserve fullback, went on to fame in the movies as the "Durango Kid."

The Indians lined up in the T formation but frequently shifted into the single wing. Much of their success, however, can be attributed to Hawley's liberal use of the forward pass. That sort of offense required a strong-armed quarterback, which Hawley got in Andrew "Swede" Oberlander. Swede could throw the ball fifty yards in the air and was known for a deft touch which he attributed to rhyme. After the snap, Oberlander once explained, he would chant to himself, "Ten thousand Swedes jumped out of the weeds at the Battle of Copenhagen," then heave the ball, by which point his receivers would have had time to get downfield. [17] He went on to earn his medical degree at Yale while simultaneously serving as head coach at Wesleyan.

Dartmouth proved their strength by crushing Harvard, 32-9. That was just a prelude, however, to their game against Cornell, in which the Indians administered one of the worst intra-Ivy whippings ever. Although the Big Red's unbeaten streak had ended in 1924, Dobie had regrouped and led Cornell into Hanover with a perfect record, having given up only fourteen points in their first five games. But the showdown exposed all the shortcomings of Dobie's pig-headed approach.

Hawley attacked Cornell through the air, overmatching their defenders who were stuck in man-to-man coverage. Oberlander enjoyed one of the greatest afternoons any collegiate quarterback has ever had, passing for six touchdowns and rushing fifty yards for another as Dartmouth annihilated the Big Red, 62-13, and racked up seven hundred yards in total offense. His team a smoking ruin, Dobie grumped to reporters, "We won, 13-0. Passing isn't football." [18]

Fans in Hanover followed all the action thanks to something called a Grid-Graph, one of the developing wonders of communications technology, circa 1925. Purchased for a thousand dollars and set up on a handball court, the Grid-Graph was a fifteen- by twelve-foot, football-shaped board marked with a gridiron. As accounts of a game were received by telegraph, hidden operators would cue light bulbs next to the type of play—a punt, a plunge, an end run—the name of the man making it, and the name of the man making the tackle. Another hidden operator would move a lightbulb up or down the field to indicate the position of the ball. Broadcasts became festive events at which members of the college painting crew led cheers while vendors roamed the temporary wooden bleachers selling hot dogs and soda. [19]

Going into the last week of the 1925 season, Dartmouth was one of only three undefeated teams in the country. The Indians traveled to Chicago to face Stagg's Maroons, with $5,000 in cash for expenses sewn into the lining of the manager's pants. [20] Oberlander threw for four more touchdowns in a surprisingly easy 33-7 victory that sealed the national title in the minds of most reporters. There was the inevitable Rose Bowl invitation, but Dartmouth stuck to policy and declined.

They slumped badly to 4-4 the following year, but the most crushing loss came at Cornell, which exacted its revenge in the last game of the season. A 23-7 Indian lead at the start of the fourth quarter became a 23-21 lead with less than a minute to play. Cornell quarterback Vic Butterfield and fullback Ignacio Molinet had scored two touchdowns and the Big Red stood on the Dartmouth twelve-yard line with time ticking away. Captain Emerson Carey's easy field goal gave Cornell a 24-23 victory.

Even Columbia was now determined to rejoin the big-time. The Lions had played surprisingly well in the first few years after their return from exile, but once the war ended and the team was permitted again to play larger schools, their program returned to its expected level and collapsed. Fans in 1922, though, were treated to watch a handsome lineman and running back named Lou Gehrig, who scored two touchdowns in his first game, against Ursinus.

With construction of what would become Baker Field underway, it became all the more important to have a team that could fill those seats. A team takes time to build but a big name coach can be had overnight. So, at the end of the 1922 season, a group of Columbia boosters wooed Percy Haughton out of retirement with what was reported to be a $15,000 salary and a long-term contract. Harvard fans were apoplectic at the thought of their old coach turning traitor.

Haughton found Morningside Heights much more rocky soil in which to grow a winning team. The Lions actually slipped in his first full season, with lopsided losses to Penn, Cornell, and Dartmouth, the only three Ivy rivals they faced. Yet there were signs of progress, most notably Walter Koppisch, Columbia's first All-American since 1903. Five weeks into the 1924 season, however, Haughton took ill one afternoon before practice and died. "Tell the squad I'm proud of them," was his last message to the team.[21] Cornell graciously decided to postpone ceremonies opening the new crescent stands at Schoellkopf Field before their game with the Lions the following Saturday, as Haughton's widow asked that Columbia's season go on.

The following year, Columbia boosters set their sights on the biggest coaching name of all: Knute Rockne. According to Rockne, the pursuit had begun the previous January, when James R. Knapp, a prominent Columbia alumnus and chairman of the football committee, traveled to South Bend to offer Rockne the job. Rockne declined, pointing out that he was under contract. This was a tease Rockne liked to play. He would frequently speculate out loud about how nice it would be to coach somewhere else, then retreat behind his Notre Dame contract if the bidding got serious. At various times in his career, Rockne was reported going to half a dozen schools, including Princeton and Columbia.

Knapp renewed the offer as soon as the 1925 season ended and this time got the coach to sign an acceptance. Rockne was to receive the extraordinary salary of $25,000 a year, including $7,500 to teach chemistry. A week later, just as the deal was being announced publicly, Rockne tried to back out, claiming that it had all been contingent on his obtaining a release from Notre Dame which, as it turned out, he had not asked for. All well and good, Columbia insisted, but there was the small matter of the signed agreement they insisted was a binding contract. Rockne tried to pass himself off as the victim of shifty dealings by the New Yorkers, but the Rev. Matthew J. Walsh, president of Notre Dame, turned up the heat on the coach by issuing a statement that the Irish would certainly not stand in Rockne's way "if he wishes to better himself." Recognizing the impossibility of the situation, Columbia then backed off, claiming that they would never have entered into negotiations with a man they knew to be under contract to another school.[22]

After a series of disappointing seasons, Brown stepped forward in 1926 with a team that came to be known as the "Iron Men."

Eddie Robinson, who had taken Brown to the Rose Bowl in 1916, lasted in Providence through the 1925 season, the first at new Brown Stadium. Before he left, the Bears tried a radical innovation. In a game against Boston University, on November 7, 1925, the two teams agreed to dispense with the time clock and play under a system of forty plays per quarter. The system had been devised by Harry R. Coffin, a Harvard alumnus. A play was any recorded down, and there was no requirement that the teams divide the allotted plays evenly, although they could agree to play quarters with fewer plays. That they did, shortening the third and fourth quarters to thirty-five plays each because of impending bad weather. It would not have made any difference, as Brown won, 42-6.

Robinson's successor, DeOrmond "Tuss" McLaughry, came to Brown after several successful seasons at Amherst and immediately jolted the Bears to life. After four-loss seasons in each of the previous three years, Brown did not lose a game in 1926, outscoring their opponents, 233-36, though it was not until midway through the year that they got a reputation. McLaughry had substituted freely in the first four games, using all twenty-six men without settling on a definite group of starters. Against Yale, though, the Bears jumped to an early lead on a run by fullback Al Cornsweet. McLaughry decided to leave them in. "No one has been injured," he later recalled, "the team is hot, winning, and apparently fresh. Why break up a winning combination?" Those eleven men played the entire game, preserving Brown's victory.

Although all college players at the time played both offense and defense, there was something unusual about going a whole game without a substitution. Under the rules at the time, a player removed in the first half could not return until the second, and a player removed in the second half was done for the day. Nevertheless, teams routinely played twenty or so men a game. Records for the Harvard-Yale games of the first half of the decade, for example, show each school using anywhere from six to as many as thirteen substitutes.

The following week, McLaughry left his starters in again as they beat Dartmouth. Back in Providence, their classmates welcomed them with a parade as President Faunce presented them with imitation honorary degrees. This was now sufficiently heroic that the papers began to write about the "Iron Men" of Brown. McLaughry kept their string intact by playing only the second team in an easy 27-0 win over Norwich the following week, but the Iron Men went right back in when the Bears traveled to Cambridge.

Harvard Stadium was sold out, the biggest crowd Brown had ever played before. Movies of the game were shipped back to four Providence theaters to enable those who couldn't get tickets see the game. This time, though, McLaughry left the Iron Men in for only fifty-eight minutes before inserting the scrubs (who had become known as the "Wooden Men") so they could earn their varsity letters. Anxious to show what they could do, the reserves scored another touchdown, capping a 21-0 Brown victory. Captain Hal Broda credited the Bears' success to "moxie," a polite way of saying opponents found them obnoxious, for the Iron Men were accomplished trash-talkers who on more than one occasion incurred penalties for unsportsmanlike conduct.

Still, only Colgate stood between Brown and a perfect season. By now their fame was international. McLaughry and Broda both received good-luck telegrams the morning of the game from Gertrude Ederle, who had just become the first

woman to swim the English Channel. Though the Bears had a chance to break a
10-10 tie late in the game (having used only one substitute), kicker Dave Mischel
bounced a fifteen-yard dropkick off the goal post.

Three of the Iron Men were invited to play in the East-West Shrine Game,
but declined when advised that "they would be lowering to a commercial basis the
great college football game which they had done so much to exalt." Which is not
to say that all commercial possibilities were overlooked. A New York dairy pub-
lication ran an ad that winter lauding the Brown team and pointing out that "in
the great football game of life, you can have no finer friend than a cow." [23]

Even with the new stadiums (including a renovated Franklin Field in Philadelphia, the
only Ivy football stadium with an upper deck), colleges could not keep up with the
demand for tickets. In 1924, for example, Harvard drew an average of more than
forty-one thousand fans a game. Their game with Yale drew seventy-five thousand
fans, even though it was played in a terrific rainstorm.

Few perceived much of a threat from the new National Football League,
which superseded the old American Professional Football League in 1922.
"Professional sport is not the type of thing that we would suppose American college athletes would turn to naturally in any great numbers," the *Yale Alumni
Weekly* assured its readers, although it did demand that pro teams refrain from
recruiting college athletes until they had graduated. [24]

Demand increased ticket speculation, a problem that had plagued the big
games for decades. Fans complained that the Yale rooting section included "bootleggers, prize-fighters, and prosperous waiters," while fist fights broke out in
Harvard Stadium over ticket assignments, which college officials, as always, attributed to a rowdy element from outside. [25]

The Big Three devised elaborate distribution schemes and took pains to
thwart scalpers, inserting personal use clauses in their tickets, demanding that they
not be transferred. At the 1921 Yale game, teams of officials swooped through the
stands and took signatures from everyone sitting on the Harvard side, noting their
exact seat locations. They then compared these signatures against those of the persons who had ordered those tickets, with the result that more than fifteen hundred
who were not in their assigned seats were prohibited from buying tickets the following year. [26] By 1925, 135 Yale alumni had been permanently blacklisted.

More people simply wanted to see the games than there were seats to accommodate them, even in the big new arenas. "I have been away for two weeks" went
one typical request. "I forgot, like all the other men who have been away, to send
in a Dartmouth application. I hope … that I may be able to come out Saturday
afternoon—instead of raking leaves in Hingham—my second favorite fall
sport." [27] Another Harvard ticket seeker tried to explain how important it was that
his application be filled. "I expect to have a Senator as my guest."

Alumni magazines tried to create sympathy for the harried ticket departments with articles such as "The Human Side of Ticket Allotment." Princeton devised a mind-numbing allocation system blending class year and alphabetical order. Yale delineated a pecking order for tickets: those who gave money to the Yale Bowl Fund first, president of the university second, upperclassmen eighth— just ahead of the faculty, who were in turn just ahead of the freshmen.[28]

The money, meanwhile, continued to pour in. Football, like most forms of entertainment, soared during the twenties. Yale's football income rose from just over $400,000 in 1922 to $1.03 million in 1928.[29] Harvard's receipts almost tripled between 1920 and 1928.[30]

Revenue on such a scale could scarcely be imagined. In 1928, Yale's football team took in $100,000 more than the rest of the university had received in gifts and grants over the first 150 years of the university's existence combined. Yale's annual football receipts were larger than the endowments of all but a handful of private colleges and universities in the United States.[31]

As had been true for some time, such massive football receipts were necessary to support the rest of the expanded athletic department. At every Ivy college, football was almost the only athletic sport that paid, and the only one that paid handsomely. For example, Yale's football team, with a profit of $543,084, and its rifle team, with a profit of $13.11, were the only two sports to show a positive balance in 1928, the height of the boom.[32] This held true even at smaller schools, regardless of how well their teams played. That same year, Cornell's football team, with a 3-3-2 record, nevertheless produced a profit of more than $116,000, which mopped up losses from every other team and enabled the athletic organization to post a modest profit.[33]

Those profits made it possible to field teams in sports that lost money year after year, a fact often lost on those who complained about football's excesses. "If there were no football gate receipts," the *Literary Digest* explained, "Harvard might have fifteen tennis-courts instead of 105 tennis-courts, four squash courts instead of forty squash courts, no adequate field for the holding of intercollegiate track and field championships and Olympic tryouts and no fleet of 104 gigs, barges, and shells for the students who take part in Harvard's rowing program year after year."[34]

Football's economic importance had been understood for years, but the illusion that it remained part of the separate world of student games had persisted. Now even the students willingly spoke of their extracurricular activity in the language of business. Dartmouth quarterback H. T. Marshall took this to extreme but revealing lengths in an essay titled "What the 1925 Football Season Taught Us About Business Administration."[35]

Football helped strengthen alumni loyalty, which manifested itself in more generous donations to the university, swelling their endowments. That money was needed to accommodate a growing student body. Yale's undergraduate enrollment more than doubled between 1920 and 1950. A larger student body was drawn from an applicant pool that was both broader geographically and deeper socially, which in turn, from an athletic standpoint, influenced the composition of the athletic teams. Far from being limited to rich men's sons, by mid-decade almost half the members of the Yale varsity were working their way through college, several in such off-beat jobs as selling brushes door-to-door, shoveling coal, and answering the telephone at a mortuary.[36]

"All things considered," however, writes Marcia Synnott in her study of Ivy admissions policies, "Big Three football probably contributed to white Anglo-Saxon Protestant 'tribalism' during the 1920s and 1930s, while doing little to democratize collegiate life."[37] Football, in other words, being for the most part a conservative institution, became a vehicle for preserving social distinctions.

For one thing, prep school students continued to outnumber public school students at the Big Three until the 1950s, and the prep schools were even more socially exclusive than the universities (the Big Three, in fact, depended on this as a passive way of winnowing their applicant pool). More than two-thirds of all Harvard and Yale letter winners in football, baseball, and crew in the half-century from 1911 to 1960 were private school graduates. Because they dominated the most visible, and desirable, student activity, Synnott writes, "they exercised an influence on campus life far out of proportion to either their numbers or their academic attainments."[38]

At least among the Big Three, almost all football players were of northern European ancestry. Catholics were accepted, especially at Yale and Princeton, but only if they were Irish, not if they were Italian or Slavic or Hispanic. Crimson teams, on the other hand, boasted players named Zarakov, Guarnaccia, and Horween, whom one could not imagine seeing on, say, a Princeton roster. Although Princeton did have its first Jewish football player in 1925, every one of the forty-four members of the 1927 squad had come from private school.[39]

The other five Ivy colleges were more receptive to young men from newer immigrant families, especially Cornell, which also drew many foreign students to its engineering program. According to one visitor, who called Penn "the most cosmopolitan of American universities," Penn by 1910 had half again as many foreign students as New Englanders.[40] But Yale and Princeton (and to a lesser extent, Harvard) disdained their rivals for this. As one college ditty of the day ran:

> *Oh, Harvard's run by millionaires,*
> *And Yale is run by booze,*
> *Cornell is run by farmers' sons,*
> *Columbia's run by Jews.*[41]

Eligibility problems emerged again, but of a different sort than those of a few decades earlier. Rather than tramp athletes, the problem now was increasingly with students who could not maintain passing grades in a demanding curriculum while also trying to play big-time football. Yale lost one football captain, Shep Bingham, to academic difficulties before the 1925 season, and then almost lost his replacement, Johnny Joss, for cutting classes.[42]

Bill Roper declared that his Princeton teams had been "literally shot to pieces by failure of the men to meet scholastic requirements." He urged that better students volunteer to tutor the slower members of the team in a spirit of undergraduate brotherhood. The *Daily Princetonian* immediately took up the cause, urging that "all Phi Beta Kappa men and others of high standing ask the football management to assign them for supervision and assistance members of the first squad that are back in their studies."[43] "Whatever else may be said about this proposal," the *New York Times* editorialized, "there's no denying that its naivete is charming."[44]

Increasingly, criticism about football violence was directed, not at the players on the field, but at the students in the stands. Dartmouth's E. K. Hall, now head of the NCAA Rules Committee, complained about fans pelting officials with debris after Ivy games. The ritual of tearing down the goalposts after a victory began during the decade, but behavior was often much worse. Yale fans not only sacked the goal posts at Harvard Stadium in 1923, but also tore down a Crimson flag flying over the Harvard Union, an act the *Yale Daily News* decried as "excessively bad manners."[45] Fans singing "Bulldog" and "Down the Field" bore the posts through the streets before delivering them to the Yale Club in Boston where they were made into flagpoles. Eli officials thought they could prevent retaliation by embedding the goals at the Yale Bowl in concrete, but Harvard fans got them anyway.

Damon Runyon captured the mayhem in the stands in a short story titled, "Hold 'Em, Yale!" A group of scalpers working the Harvard game escort a dateless young woman into the bowl with one of their unused tickets. The Crimson win and students storm the goal posts, which the young woman tries to save by climbing up them. "Afterwards she explains that the idea is the Harvards will not be ungentlemanly enough to pull down the goal posts with a lady roosting on them," one of Runyon's wiseguys says, "but it seems these Harvards are no gentlemen, and keep on pulling, and the posts commence to teeter, and our little doll is teetering with them, although of course she is in no danger if she falls because they is sure to fall on one of the Harvards' noggins, and the way I look at it, the noggin of anybody who will be found giving any time to pulling down goal posts is apt to be soft enough to break a very long fall."[46]

Columbia students seem to have been the rowdiest of all. Incensed by an editorial in the student paper lambasting undergraduates for their apathy ("the sham of unemotionalism"), a group turned a pep rally on South Field into a riot in 1927, tearing down grandstands for firewood and hurling eggs and epithets ("Irish loafers" was one) at police who tried to assist firemen in putting out the blaze. Thirteen students arrested for disorderly conduct were released by an indulgent magistrate who blamed the incident on "too much youthful exuberance."[47] A year later, though, they were at it again, commandeering a New York City subway car after a pep rally, stripping it of lightbulbs, pulling the emergency cord, and ripping up seats and throwing them through the windows before fleeing at Times Square.

Problems such as these were what critics were referring to when they decried football's "overemphasis." The game was too far removed from the students, contained too many incentives to cheat, to overreach. "Nobody cares about the players having 'fun,'" wrote Harvard football historian Walter Prince. "What we want is that they play for our fun." [48] Despite the perennial glories of the game itself, football had always carried an ugly side, especially off the field, and reformers in the 1920s took another crack at addressing it.

The Big Three presidents—A. Lawrence Lowell of Harvard, James Angell of Yale, and John Grier Hibben of Princeton—took the initiative. There was precedent for their working together in the Triple Agreement of 1916. In 1922, a committee of alumni and faculty appointed to update the agreement issued a report that made several changes to the way the game would be conducted at Harvard, Yale, and Princeton. In some respects, it reiterated policies that had been in effect for years, barring, for example, anyone who had ever played for money, prohibiting postseason games, and discouraging recruiting in preparatory schools.

In other respects, though, the new agreement went much further. In order to curb under-the-table payments from alumni, each player was required to issue what was in effect a financial disclosure statement before each Big Three game listing all sources of income. All loans or scholarships had to be approved by an officer of the university, making it more difficult for freelancing boosters to operate. A player who received any money from "others than those on whom he is naturally depend-ent" would be barred from playing. Transfer students who had ever played inter-collegiate athletics were also barred from playing sports at their new college.

Three years later, they revised the Triple Agreement again, this time limit-ing the coaching budget to a total of $22,500. Harvard and Yale made a further agreement limiting the head coach's salary to $8,000 a year.

An even more radical proposal came from Dartmouth President Ernest Martin Hopkins. Unlike many of his fellow Ivy presidents, Hopkins liked foot-ball, liked it big and popular, and set out to fix it. "No agency of undergraduate life so powerfully binds the college community together, nor, on the whole, so advantageously permeates the ideals as do the undergraduate sports," he told an NCAA convention. [49]

In 1927, Hopkins unveiled a three-pronged reform plan, which was no less significant for being slightly daft. First, he proposed to limit athletic eligibility to sophomores and juniors, to give freshmen a chance to get their feet wet and seniors a chance to complete their studies. Second, he proposed that major games be played at home and away simultaneously, and that colleges thus field two varsity squads. This, he said, would double both the number of games and students playing them, and thus reduce the importance of any particular game. Third, Hopkins wanted to eliminate professional coaches and return the job to the undergraduates. [50]

The press loved Hopkins's proposals, while the colleges did not. (Michigan, the only school to try Hopkins's plan, it abandoned it after a year). "Well, it doesn't sound sensible to me," said Dean Henry B. Fine, acting chairman of Princeton's board of athletic control. "You know, we never did believe too much in that overemphasis business down here." [51] Romeyn Berry, Cornell's athletics manager, suggested a conference to do away with overemphasis on overemphasis. [52]

Coaches themselves sometimes initiated reforms. One was to outlaw the scouting of opponents, an expensive and time-consuming practice that to many also smacked of cheating. Tad Jones and Bill Roper had agreed not to scout each other's team in 1925, a gridiron arms control plan neither of them could have adopted unilaterally. By 1926, Yale persuaded all eight of its opponents to join a scouting ban, and the following year Princeton did the same. When Harvard tried it, on the other hand, only three of its eight opponents agreed, so the Crimson made a separate agreement with Dartmouth to permit scouting and in 1927 abandoned the idea altogether.

By the late twenties, most of the eight colleges that would come to comprise the Ivy League had been playing football for half a century. They had developed long-standing ties culturally, academically, and socially, as well as athletically, yet their football programs would remain autonomous for another generation. Why did it take so long to create an Ivy League?

Economics was largely responsible. Football had long since become a cash cow, one the wealthier colleges—principally the Big Three—were loath to share with their poorer fellows. Money, however, was also a surrogate for the deep differences that remained, not only between the Big Three and the other Ivy colleges, but among the Big Three themselves.

The prestige of the Big Three only increased during the teens and twenties, spurred in large part by the new popularity of boarding schools among the well to do. E. Digby Baltzell, chronicler of eastern WASP culture, wrote that by the 1920s, more upper class Philadelphians sent their sons to Princeton than to Penn, which was "considered to be socially inferior" to the Big Three, fostering a jealousy that tinges the rivalry between those two schools even today. [53]

Harvard, Yale, and Princeton were proud of their status as the three oldest and most prominent colleges in the country and certain of their influence. "What we make of collegiate athletics becomes the ideal for school athletics," a Harvard athletics committee wrote of the Triple Agreement, "where our mistakes and our sins are copied, and where their evil consequences are multiplied by the enthusiasm of imitation." [54] The Big Three were unwilling to qualify their social and academic position by recognizing even other top eastern colleges as equals.

Dartmouth, for example, was convinced that Yale looked down its nose at it.[55] Despite its insistence on remaining a college, Dartmouth was growing in size and prominence. Athletically, it found itself caught, too big for its old local rivals, too far removed from the rest of the Ivies. "It is not an altogether enviable relationship which Dartmouth has at the present time with her sister colleges," Hopkins wrote. "The athletic relationships of the colleges which draw from a like numerical strength have their own traditional and long-time athletic relationships which they are naturally not inclined to alter for one upon whom they look as something of an interloper."[56] Hopkins frequently compared Dartmouth to "the gentleman of affluence who has reached middle age without marriage and found himself with no source of amusement except to play with his friends' wives."[57]

Brown received an even balder put-down from Harvard when, after playing thirty-one consecutive games in Cambridge, it summoned the temerity to ask the Crimson to play a game at Providence. LeBaron Briggs, Dean of the College, urged the proposal on President Lowell, saying it would be "ungenerous" of Harvard not to make a short trip to help a sister university—one against which the Crimson had played more football games, in fact, than any other school.

But Briggs made the mistake of also mentioning that Brown hoped the Harvard game would help it raise money for a new football stadium. This raised the president's eyebrows. A football game raising money? Lowell, who had consented to let the Crimson play in the Rose Bowl only five years earlier in part to help Harvard's capital campaign, and whose football team was taking in several hundred thousands dollars a year, now climbed upon his high horse. "The proposition that appeals to me in regard to a football game at Brown," he wrote to Briggs, "is that we ought never to use any athletic team as gladiators performing to earn money, either as regards the game or the place where it takes place."

Briggs, who was now in the embarrassing position of having to spurn Brown's offer, brushed aside the president's argument. "I do feel a difficulty in saying no to a request which seems to me perfectly decent and the refusal of which may naturally,—and, I am afraid, not unreasonably,—increase our reputation for a rather superior attitude toward other colleges."[58] Nevertheless, the Harvard Corporation unanimously rejected Brown's invitation.

A few days later, however, Briggs returned with new information. Brown asked that Harvard come, not in 1924, but a year later, after the stadium was finished. President Faunce added his own fawning letter to Lowell, but even this proved barely enough, as a motion to spurn the amended invitation failed by only three votes. The Crimson did make the trip (a 3-0 victory), but gave the Bears cause to regret it when Harvard students poured onto the field afterward and tore down Brown's brand new goal posts.

Cornell students, meanwhile, fulminated that "The Big Three idea is a bit undemocratic and against the spirit of the times.... There is no university or group of universities possessing either the prestige or power to control the athletic affairs of American colleges. And it so happens that the Big Three idea is only taken seriously sans salt at Cambridge, Princeton, and New Haven." [59]

That is was, yet even relations among the Big Three were far from settled. Despite the popular perception from outside, they were hardly monolithic in spirit or in outlook. People had been writing about "Harvard indifference" since the 1880s. Yale, by contrast, was more lively. "A Harvard man," wrote Yale professor William Lyon Phelps, "would not be able to understand the Yale fondness for pure noise." [60] If Harvard prized intellectual aloofness and Yale favored ambition, it was the essence of a Princeton man "that he be neither a strong individualist... nor a conformist whose conformity was molded by an openly confessed ambition. He was, above all, 'smooth'—that is, socially adroit and graceful." [61]

In 1926, Princeton and Harvard went to war with one another, creating one of the great opera bouffes in the history of intercollegiate athletics, a rollicking story were it not for the fact that it may have delayed the creation of the Ivy League by a decade.

Athletic relations between the two colleges had never been easy, owing in part to their differences in style. In the nineteenth century, Harvard resented being shut out of Princeton's big end of the season rivalry with Yale while Princeton smarted under its perceived status as junior member of the Big Three. The two schools had broken athletic relations in 1889 over Harvard's allegations that Princeton used ineligible players.

Relations were more harmonious after the series resumed, in part because Harvard fielded better teams, but began to deteriorate after World War I when the Tigers beat Harvard two years in a row—games the Crimson claimed were marred by rough play. There were also frequent squabbles because of Harvard's insistence that the game always be played in Cambridge (Brown was not alone in this treatment). A war of words escalated before the 1922 game when Bill Roper warned a Princeton pep rally that "it has been intimated that Princeton must watch her back this Saturday or she may find herself off the Harvard schedule." Commenting on the game after the fact (a 10-3 Princeton victory), the *Crimson* noted "No one who was in the stadium doubts that bad feelings exist." [62] President Lowell noted to President Angell of Yale that "Our football men are not anxious to make an agreement that binds them to play with Princeton for any length of time." [63]

Harvard snapped its losing streak in 1923 and matters quieted down, only to flare again the following two years when Princeton recorded consecutive lopsided shutouts. It made no difference that these were some of the worst teams in Harvard football history, Crimson officials once again made much of Princeton's allegedly dirty play.

Rather than drop Princeton openly, Harvard decided to snub them. In the spring of 1926, Harvard athletic director William J. Bingham quietly made an agreement to replace Princeton on the Harvard schedule with Michigan in 1927 and 1928—a school the Crimson had beaten every time they had ever played.

Harvard could cite legitimate reasons for wanting to play the Wolverines—a series would appeal to western alumni and Michigan's president was a Harvard man—but that that was all pretext. When news of the agreement leaked, Hibben wrote an appealing letter to Lowell in which he pointed out that a series with Michigan would violate the Three Presidents, Agreement, which not only barred intersectional contests but implicitly contemplated that the three signatories play each other.[64]

Lowell's reply only made matters worse. While conceding Hibben's point about the legality of the Michigan series, he went on to explain that Harvard still would not play the Tigers. Many Princeton alumni, Lowell wrote, seemed to believe that Harvard had a "moral obligation" to play the Tigers every year, an obligation Lowell did not see. "If any college with which we have been in the habit of playing should announce that as part of its athletic policy it would play us only in alternate years, we might be extremely sorry, but we should have no right to consider it unfriendly or a cause of offense. Must we not, therefore, make this point clear?"[65]

Although Lowell did not acknowledge it, he was contradicting his own Committee on the Regulation of Athletic Sports, which in a report issued in May 1925 suggested shortening the season but urged "that this number should not be reduced unless by suitable agreement with our chief competitors, Yale and Princeton."[66]

In Princeton's opinion, it was a mortal insult to lump it as just one of the many colleges "with whom we have been in the habit of playing." And Old Nassau was not about to play poor sister to anyone. It would not do, though, to storm off in a huff. The Tigers were forced to wait for an opportunity to retaliate, which their game with Harvard that October provided.

Yale, which stood to be the innocent victim if a fight undermined the Three Presidents Agreement, tried to mediate. Although President Angell agreed that Princeton played dirty, he wrote privately to Hibben that he considered Harvard's agreement with Michigan "a blunder of the first magnitude and as inconsiderate as it is stupid."[67] George Nettleton, Yale's athletics chairman, called his counterparts to a summit in New Haven in an effort to resolve the growing breach. It appeared to work, as Harvard agreed to schedule a game with Princeton for 1927.

Whether miscommunication or perfidy is to be blamed, though, days later Lowell wrote to Hibben stating that the schedule between the schools in future years should be considered "open." In mid-October, Harvard voted to make only its final game with Yale sacrosanct. Henceforward, it would play all other colleges—including Princeton—only at "suitable intervals."

Princeton, however, did not know this. Although Lowell and Bingham were drafting a statement announcing the new policy, Coach Arnold Horween prevailed upon them to withhold it until after the Princeton game, lest the slight provide the

Tigers with added motivation. In effect, Horween proposed to give the policy extra sting: beat the Tigers and *then* drop them from the schedule.

Harvard officials might try to keep the change secret, but as the game approached everyone sensed an explosion was coming. The spark that lit the fuse came from a most unlikely source, the *Harvard Lampoon*, the campus humor magazine, which in its football issue, published on the day of the game, directed several volleys of insults, most of them funny but none too subtle, at its New Jersey guests.

One item, titled "A College Anthology," had this to say about Princeton students: "Give this lad his due. Don't expect brains—he wouldn't have gone to Princeton if he'd had any. But if you need a dependable quart, or a fifth-row seat at the last minute, or a good chorine, or a golf lesson—he's *there*." [68] Somewhat blunter was the satire about the prissy cheer leader exhorting students to give a yell for dear "Old Nausea" and a cartoon showing two pigs wallowing in a trough under the caption, "Come, brother, let us root for dear old Princeton!" A poem even disparaged the Princeton men's dates.

Relatively speaking, all this was just beating around the bush. The *Lampoon*'s lead editorial, on the other hand, went right for the throat. They saw no reason, the editors wrote, "to disguise the fact that the brotherly love and friendly rivalry existing between Harvard and Princeton are purely imaginary.... This is no fitful burst of feeling; it has been growing up steadily through the years and it culminated this summer in the proposal to drop Princeton from the Harvard schedule. That it was not carried out was due to no change of heart on the part of the Harvard undergraduates. They would still like to see Princeton dropped, but they would like even more to see her licked. No doubt Princeton's feelings are the same.... In the meantime, let us whoop it up. The Princeton brawl comes but once a year; it may never come again."

Copies of the *Lampoon* made their way quickly around the stands at Harvard Stadium, as well as into the Princeton locker room. Roper, who was in the middle of his pregame pep talk, paused to read a few excerpts to the team. Laying the issue aside, he said simply, "Now go out there and give them your answer." [69]

As bad luck would have it the game itself—a 12-0 Princeton victory, their third shutout in a row—was an ugly affair, reminiscent of games played thirty years earlier. The Tigers' field goal came on what even Princeton acknowledged afterward had been fifth down. Furthermore, three Crimson starters were forced from the game with injuries, two of them lost for the season. Under the eyes of fuming Crimson alumni, raucous Princeton students then sacked the goal posts. Fans leaving the stadium picked up copies of a joke issue of the *Crimson* (in fact put out by the *Lampoon*) which, under the headline "Princeton Wins," stated that Roper had dropped dead on the field.

The following Monday both sides tried to take a step back, perhaps recognizing that bounds had been crossed that should not have been. Princeton students made ostentatious show of paying no attention to Harvard's slights, but could not resist rubbing it in about the goal posts. More seriously, a campus editorial questioned whether the alliance was worth maintaining. "Princeton by no means feels that it is necessary, at further cost to its dignity, to preserve the Big Three." [70]

Harvard did its own part to deepen the rift. While acknowledging that Harvard often patronized Princeton, the *Crimson* dished out another dose in trying to explain the source of their rival's grievance. "Princeton for some time has felt it eminently necessary to remain a part of the Big Three. Even colleges must retain prestige. And Princeton has derived no little part of hers from the fact that she has long been included in the Big Three." [71]

In all, it was a very bad time for Bingham to deliver Harvard's mothballed resolution announcing that it would play Princeton only at "suitable intervals." This certainly undercut the letters of apology sent the previous day by Lowell and Dean Chester N. Greenough to their Princeton counterparts, and can only be explained by the odd compartmentalization taking place along the Charles. The *Lampoon* had considerably less to do with the breakup than the decision to drop Princeton from the schedule, for which apology was not made. From Princeton's standpoint, to be snubbed was one thing; to be snubbed and then insulted was intolerable.

Several hours after it received Bingham's notice, the Princeton Board of Athletic Control, meeting in New York, voted unanimously to sever all athletic ties with Harvard, including games already scheduled in other sports for the rest of the year.

"Excellent, it should have been done sooner," one Harvard undergraduate declared. Otherwise, though, the break stirred little excitement on either campus. [72] Harvard's student council proposed a summit with Princeton, but it fell apart. Both schools had upcoming games with Yale and turned their attention to those. Ironically, Princeton replaced Harvard on its 1927 schedule with Ohio State, an intersectional game that ought to have been prohibited under the Triple Agreement, while Harvard replaced Princeton with Penn, where as it would turn out, corruption was much worse than anything going on at Old Nassau.

Still, there were parting shots. With Princeton out of the way, Bingham announced that "so long as I have any part of directing athletics at Harvard, the Yale contests shall stand pre-eminent.... We do not feel that a Princeton-Harvard game ever could occupy the same position as our game with Yale." [73] As evidence that the breach was neither irreparable nor uncontainable, though, Lowell a few months later invited Hibben to deliver the prestigious Godkin lectures at Harvard. The Triple Agreement lived on in spirit if not in fact, as Harvard and Princeton simply made their own separate dual agreements with Yale.

Any chance of an immediate reconciliation, though, was sunk by an article titled "Dirty Football," which was published in *Liberty* magazine that winter (over Lowell's objection) by Wyant Davis Hubbard, a recent Harvard graduate. [74]

Hubbard made a long series of allegations that Princeton had engaged in dirty play going back as far as 1922. One of the most vivid was that Harvard fullback Al Miller had been punched in the face during the 1925 game and, as proof, bore the lasting scar of a Princeton signet ring on his nose. "No Harvard man wants to wear a tiger on the tip of his 'ruby,'" laughed the *Harvard Alumni Bulletin*; "for such a mark makes him easily liable to be mistaken for a Princeton man, and a worse fate at this time apparently does not exist, from the Harvard viewpoint." [75]

The story was not cleared up for almost sixty years. Joe Pendergast, contributing a page for a privately published history of Princeton football during the interwar years, explained that the Princeton team did not wear signet rings, but that he, Pendergast, did wear a family ring. Shortly after reading the *Liberty* article, Pendergast said, he sent a letter to Miller. "I don't believe your story," he wrote, "but if it is true, then I want you to know that the 'P' on your nose stands for Pendergast and not Princeton." [76]

Although the Big Three was broken, Harvard and Yale still managed to play some brilliant games. Fans were treated to two of the greatest players in Ivy League history: Yale's Albie Booth and Harvard's Barry Wood.

Booth seemed made for nicknames. A New Haven townie whose father was a foreman at the Winchester rifle factory, he stood only five-foot-six and weighed 144 pounds, prompting sportswriters to dub him "The Mighty Atom" or, more enduringly, "Little Boy Blue." He played tailback in coach Mal Stevens's single-wing offense, which meant that he also called the plays and occasionally threw passes, as well, in addition to being the team's kicker. Some compared him to Frank Hinckey, another diminutive Bulldog back, but Booth was Hinckey's temperamental opposite—shy and good natured.

In 1929, his sophomore year, Booth almost immediately became a Yale sensation. He scored every one of Yale's points in a 14-6 victory over Brown. A week later, against Army, Booth earned national headlines for one of the great games of the decade. Despite his performance the previous week, Booth had not started against the Cadets, perhaps because he was still a sophomore. Heavily favored Army jumped to a 13-0 lead in the second quarter and seemed well on its way to fulfilling expectations of a blowout when Booth entered the game.

The Yale crowd, which included Winston Churchill and Mr. and Mrs. John D. Rockefeller, Jr., began to buzz. "The line lost its sluggishness, the attack developed a co-ordination that had been lacking. The machine had gained a spark plug, and away it went in high." [77] On its first possession, the Booth-led Bulldogs marched thirty-two yards for a touchdown. In their first possession of the third quarter, Booth broke a thirty-five-yard run for his second touchdown, then kicked the extra point that gave Yale a 14-13 lead.

When Army was forced to punt, Booth received the kick and headed straight for the mass of gold jerseys. At the last moment, he sidestepped and outran his pursuers sixty-five yards for his third touchdown of the game. Captain Waldo Greene, nicknamed "Firpo" because of his resemblance to heavyweight boxing champion Luis Firpo, was the first to reach Booth as his teammates mobbed him, and "towering over him like a Great Dane over a terrier, almost picked him off the ground to pound him on the back." In all, Booth gained 233 yards on thirty-three carries in just over thirty minutes of play, prompting newsreel makers to caption their highlight films, "Booth 21, Army 13."

A week later, Yale met Dartmouth in a much-anticipated match-up between Booth, the new sensation, and the Indians' captain, Al Marsters, nicknamed the "Special Delivery Kid."

It began as a mismatch when Yale's Alpheus Beane returned a Marsters fumble for a touchdown, contributing to a 10-0 Eli lead. In the third quarter, though, Marsters put on what one reporter called "the greatest five minutes any individual star will ever know."[78] Dartmouth took the ball at its own seventeen-yard line. With everyone anticipating a run off tackle, he instead dropped back and threw a fifty-three yard bomb to Harold Booma, who had clear sailing ahead of him but slipped and fell. On the next play, Marsters hit Bill McCall to the Yale seventeen. After a plunge into the line, Marsters found McCall again for a Dartmouth touchdown. With three passes, Marsters had scorched the Yale defense for eighty-three yards.

The reeling Bulldogs fumbled the kickoff. Three plays later, Marsters dashed around the end all the way to the Yale three-yard line. On the next play, he scored again, to give the Indians a 12-10 lead. For the afternoon, Marsters passed for 112 yards and rushed for ninety-four more, much of it concentrated into that one brief span. But it was not enough, and in the fourth quarter, Marsters suffered a neck injury that ended his playing career.

Booth, meanwhile, gained 268 yards of his own, and had another 43-yard run called back on a penalty. His booming punts kept Dartmouth pinned deep in their own territory for most of the game, with the exception of Marsters's fireworks. That was enough for a 16-12 Yale victory.

Booth's rival, William Barry Wood of Harvard, can lay claim to the title of greatest Ivy League scholar-athlete of all time. Wood won ten varsity letters, something no Harvard athlete has done before or since. He was three-year starter on the football team, captain and quarterback, an All-American, and later an inductee into the College Football Hall of Fame. He was center on the ice hockey team for three years, and played first base for the baseball team, hitting .400 as a freshman. When the Harvard tennis team needed a replacement, Wood (who was the top-ranked player in New England) stepped in and led a Harvard-Yale squad to the Prentice Cup against a combined team from Oxford and Cambridge.

While doing all this, Wood also managed to graduate summa cum laude, number one in his class, and Phi Beta Kappa. His classmates voted him class president his freshman year and student council president his senior year. In what little free time he had, Wood did research in the biochemistry laboratory, analyzing blood samples he collected from his teammates. Wood went on to medical school at Johns Hopkins, became a renowned molecular biologist, and was named dean of the Washington University medical school at the age of thirty-two.

Even in an era when academic standards were allegedly higher than they are today, this attracted attention—perhaps suggesting just how unusual a young man Wood really was. Westbrook Pegler called him "close to the ideal conception of the American student, athlete, leader and sportsman." Added to it was the regal air of mastery Wood seemed to possess, the very epitome of a field general. "Wood makes you watch him," Damon Runyon wrote. "He makes you feel that he is the star performer of the drama from the moment he walks on the field. You at once get the idea that this chap is in command of the situation. That he is calm, imperturbable, and confident. The gods have been very good, indeed, to William Barry Wood, Jr." [79]

He appeared at just the right time for the Crimson, who had suffered through a string of bad years. In 1926, Harvard recorded its first losing season ever, a dismal 3-5 campaign in which they lost to tiny Geneva College in the opener. They closed with consecutive losses to Princeton (the last before the break), Brown, and Yale by a cumulative score of 45-7.

A portent of better things to come was Harvard's 17-0 victory over Yale to close the 1928 season. Writers now were calling Harvard a "Football Phoenix." [80] Booth and Wood had faced each other for the first time on the freshman team, Booth getting the upper hand in a 7-6 Yale victory.

Horween was slow to work Wood into his offense, which was led by All-American center Ben Ticknor. But against Army, Wood lofted a fifty-yard touchdown pass late in the game and added the extra point to forge a 20-20 tie. Several weeks later, he and Booth faced each other for the first time on the varsity stage—a game for which Yale had inaugurated airplane shuttle service between New York and New Haven ($20 roundtrip). Booth had two kicks blocked in the second quarter, one of them on a field goal attempt, while Wood made his field goal and added an extra point in a 10-6 Harvard triumph.

Booth might have been the hero that afternoon, instead of the goat. He took the second-half kickoff and burst up the middle, seemingly into the clear before Ticknor dragged him down from behind by his "billowy blue sweater." "If he had been arrayed in the garb of a South Sea Island swimmer," Grantland Rice noted, "he would have run ninety-six yards for a touchdown and would also have won the most dramatic game of football ever played."

Round 1, then, to Barry Wood. But the game was played just twenty-six days after the stock market crash, many in the stands no doubt blithely assuming that their portfolios would soon rebound as high as had Harvard's football fortunes. Wood and Booth faced each other twice more in the depths of the Depression, providing entertainment for a crowd that sorely needed it.

CHAPTER SEVEN

Red Ink

On October 24, 1929—"Black Thursday," as it came to be known—the New York Stock Exchange lost almost $4 billion in the worst trading session in its history. In terms of the immediate impact on the football programs at six of the eight Ivy colleges, however, the panic on Wall Street was not the worst event of the day. Further uptown that morning, the Carnegie Foundation for the Advancement of Teaching issued its final report on the state of intercollegiate athletics after a three-and-a-half-year investigation. It found widespread evidence of abuse at most of the larger colleges in the country, as well as Harvard, Princeton, Columbia, Brown, Dartmouth, and Penn. The results had hit the schools involved like a bomb.

In 1916, the NCAA called for a comprehensive study of college football, having had its own investigation stymied by Yale, which resented anyone snooping around its program. At first the Carnegie Foundation would have nothing to do with the request, calling football abuse "too hot a topic for concerted handling ex tempore." Calls kept coming, however, and in 1925 the foundation agreed to undertake a limited study of twenty colleges. Several months later, the Carnegie board broadened this into a full-scale investigation, naming Howard J. Savage, a former Bryn Mawr professor, to conduct it.[1]

Savage, who was joined by professors from Cornell and Columbia as well as a New York attorney, set out to make his study more comprehensive than anything that had been done previously, surveying conditions at 130 colleges and universities in every part of the country and in Canada. Rather than send questionnaires that let the subjects evaluate themselves, Savage and his team visited them in person, reading files and interviewing administrators and students. Their 347-page final report bore the innocuous institutional title "Bulletin Number Twenty-

Three," but was known by its subtitle, *American College Athletics*. Its contents were considered so explosive that the president of the Carnegie Foundation withheld advance copies from his own board of directors.

Savage, in fact, struck an evangelical if not particularly original note, blaming the evils of intercollegiate football on commercialization. Yet what distinguished his report from countless other diatribes against big-time football was that Savage named names. Harvard, for example, was tainted because its athletic department let athletes control the concession sales at football games (a practice Needham had found at Yale and Princeton almost a quarter-century earlier). Several schools subsidized athletes by finding them jobs selling insurance (Columbia), peddling sporting goods (Dartmouth), soliciting advertisements (Penn), or babysitting (Harvard). Members of the football coaching staff at Brown, and to a lesser extent at Columbia and Dartmouth, "had little to do but recruit and subsidize athletes." Brown, Dartmouth, and Princeton were accused of paying prep school stars under the table while Columbia maintained special scholarships for which only athletes were eligible. In all, the report found some form of subsidization at eighty-one colleges and universities. Among the Ivies, only Cornell and Yale were pronounced entirely clean.

For the most part, the colleges themselves denounced the Carnegie findings. "I cannot understand such bungling of a report," said Norman S. Tabor, chairman of Brown's board of athletic control, although a few days later the university was forced to concede that the charges against it were true. Harvard and Princeton complained that most of the objectionable practices identified at their schools had already been done away with. President Hopkins conceded that under Dartmouth's selective admissions process "it might easily be true that we should have increased the number of men of athletic ability. I confess to a hope that this may come to be true." [2] Bert Bell declared that "Pennsylvania is as clean in athletics as any institution in the world."

That last statement was a lie, and Bell should have known it. In fact, the Penn football program was plagued by abuses, the details of which had apparently eluded Savage and his investigators. It was a case study of an unaccountable and overextended program run amok.

Penn's athletic program had developed along a familiar pattern. Students, who founded the school's first athletic organization in 1873 (to support the track team), turned to the alumni for help when they could not pay their bills. The alumni-run Athletic Association, created in 1882, succeeded in bringing order to athletic chaos at Penn but fared little better financially. By 1894, it was more than $6,600 in debt and was forced to turn to the university for a loan to finish construction of the first Franklin Field. The university paid the Athletic Association's bills without exercising control over its activities except for the creation, in 1895, of a University Athletic Committee, a toothless watchdog that was unable even to enforce the university's own eligibility policies.

Unaccountable to anyone, the Athletic Association saw its budget swell from $95,000 in 1895 to more than $141,000 in 1906, yet found itself dependent on gate receipts to pay the bills. Thus, it became increasingly important to field good teams that would draw paying customers, whatever the cost to Penn's academic reputation. In 1917, Penn tried to curb the association by creating a new oversight board, the University Council on Athletics, composed of students, alumni, and faculty, which immediately revealed its true colors by electing the Athletic Association's president to lead it.

The UCA soon found itself in the same financial bind. Penn's Rose Bowl trip had convinced football authorities of a big stadium's potential as a revenue producer, so in 1922 they tore down the old, twenty-thousand-seat Franklin Field and started work on a stadium seating 54,500 to take its place. Even that soon proved too small, so in 1926, Penn decided to add an upper deck, floating $4 million in bonds through Drexel & Company to pay for the expansion, as well as the construction of a new basketball arena.[3]

In doing so, Penn had put itself on an even faster treadmill. Now, in order to make payments on their debt, the athletic program needed to clear a quarter of a million dollars a year, and because football was usually Penn's only paying sport, the football team had to produce almost all of that amount. Winning teams and sellout crowds now became a matter of economic urgency. "Obviously," wrote R. Tait McKenzie, chairman of Penn's Department of Physical Education and a rare voice of opposition, "nothing must interfere with the extraction of the last ounce of gold from this mine."[4]

Penn set out to field the best team it could, by whatever means necessary. In 1921, Sydney Hutchinson, a USC board member, founded the Pennsylvania Educational Aid Society, which recruited top high school athletes and paid their way if they came to Penn—all on top of the athletic scholarships the university was already awarding. From 1921 to 1930, the society subsidized 581 athletes to the tune of more than $200,000. In 1924, the university waived its prohibition against postseason games so that the team might travel to California, in hopes it would help spark interest in Penn's $10 million capital campaign.

Quaker athletes who still found they needed a little extra cash could always turn to Uncle Otto. That was the name given to Otto Schwegler, a Penn alumnus and football booster who funneled money to players by finding them easy jobs. One player received a new pair of football shoes every week during the season, while his father was given free railroad passes to attend Quaker home games. Uncle Otto also courted the parents of recruits to assure them that their boys would be taken care of.[5]

From a standpoint of wins and losses, the plan succeeded. From 1924 through 1929, Penn's cumulative record was 44-11-2. Not only were the Quakers holding their own against a schedule that included Kansas, Wisconsin, Georgia Tech, and Notre Dame, they were a good enough draw that they were also back in the good graces of the other Ivies, who proved little more than cannon fodder. During that same six-season stretch, the Quakers went 15-0-1 against Columbia, Cornell, Harvard, and Yale, outscoring them 302-50. Penn's football receipts also soared, so that by 1930 it was one of only four colleges in the country to take in more than $1 million.[6] But the pressure to keep up the pace was unrelenting.

Coach Lou Young's successor, J. R. Ludlow "Lud" Wray, came from a prominent Philadelphia family but tried to compensate for his background by affecting tough-guy habits such as chewing tobacco and teaching his linemen how to injure opponents without getting caught. Following a loss to Wisconsin in 1930, the Quakers came to the training table for lunch and found that he had ordered creampuffs set at each man's place, the only item on the menu. When the ill-nourished team took the field for practice that afternoon, Wray ordered the Franklin Field gates locked. "The last eleven men on their feet will start Saturday's game!" he barked, then ran a full-contact scrimmage for three hours.[7]

It didn't work. Later that season, in a reprise of the Red Grange game from five years earlier, Penn learned how far they still were from the big-time when they hosted Notre Dame. Eighty thousand spectators, including New York City Mayor Jimmy Walker, packed Franklin Field to see the Fighting Irish wallop the Quakers, 60-20, in what would be the last big victory of Rockne's career. Penn, wrote Allison Danzig, "was swept off its feet like chaff before a hurricane."[8]

After the season, the players revolted against Wray's abusive style. Halfback Warren Gette quit the team, alleging that he had been forced to practice against medical advice.[9] Wray was fired. The Quaker edifice was now beginning to crack, as weaker teams and the onset of the Depression cut attendance and earnings. Ivy opponents, who had grown tired of being beaten up, again dropped the Quakers. By 1930, only Cornell remained on the schedule.

Part of Pennsylvania's problem had always been a lack of control at the top. By 1930, the university had been without a president for eight years until the trustees decided to restore order by appointing Thomas Sovereign Gates to the job. Gates, an alumnus of both the Wharton business school and the law school, had gone on to make a fortune as a senior partner at J. P. Morgan & Company and Drexel & Company. He was a Penn insider, the man who had underwritten the huge Franklin Field loan.

Gates was also a businessman who recognized the financial bind the athletic program and university had gotten themselves into. One of his first acts was to commission a study of the situation. Four months later, on February 2, 1931, Gates put his stamp on a revolutionary report that went further than anything that had yet been done among the Ivies to curb big-time football.

The Gates Report, as it came to be known, did away with the athletic dormitories, shortened the season, ended under the table payments to athletes, made coaches members of the faculty, and capped their salaries at $7,000. (Wray, in his final year, had gotten $12,000 and was scheduled to earn $14,000 in 1931.) The

A group of exuberant Yale students *ride through the streets of New York City on Thanksgiving morning, 1893, en route to the Princeton game. Carriages rented for as much as $125 a day and had to be booked a year in advance. The wealthy drove theirs right into the stadium and opened picnic lunches on the roof, anticipating the modern tailgate. (Manuscripts and Archives, Yale University Library)*

A group of Dartmouth students plays *"Old Division" in 1876. All the Ivy colleges staged some variant of these interclass rushes, combinations of soccer and rugby that predated the development of football. (Dartmouth College Library)*

Yale's 1891 national champions, *shown here posing for a team shot, went undefeated and did not surrender a single point in thirteen games. They included some of the greatest names in football history, including "Pudge" Heffelfinger (back row, fifth from right), "Bum" McClung (center, holding ball), Frank Hinkey (front row, second from left), and George Foster Sanford (back row, second from right). (Manuscripts and Archives, Yale University Library)*

Two unidentified Cornell players *take on a tackling dummy marked "P" for Pennsylvania around the turn of the century. (Cornell University)*

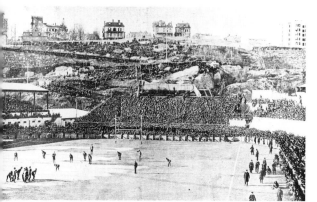

The 1893 Princeton-Yale game *at the Polo Grounds in New York City. "When every other one of those forty thousand human beings stood up and yelled," Richard Harding Davis wrote, "the effect was worth crossing an ocean to see." (Princeton University)*

Harvard demonstrates *the violent tackles back play in a 22-0 victory over Yale in 1901. Mass play, which simply concentrated force on force, was responsible for the shocking rate of injuries that threatened to destroy football. (Harvard University Archives)*

William Clarence Matthews, *one of the first African-American football players, practices with Harvard in 1903. McClure's magazine hailed him as "the best there is in a college athlete." (Harvard University Archives)*

Players plainly needed *the leather helmets and nose protectors they are seen wearing in this violent collision during the 1903 Brown-Dartmouth game. Note the Cornell referee, who was chosen to provide neutral officiating. (Dartmouth College Library)*

Charles Eliot, Harvard's austere *president from 1869 to 1909 and the leading opponent of football. When asked to write Eliot's biography, William James replied, "I'd like to, but to tell the truth, I'm skeered of him." (Harvard University Archives)*

An unidentified Yale player *punts to Harvard in 1911, a game that ended in a 0-0 tie. Forty-two thousand people watched the contest at Harvard Stadium; many of them had to be seated along the sidelines. Note the extra chalk lines painted the length of the field. A rule requiring that passes be thrown at least five yards on either side of the center made the lines necessary but turned the gridiron into a checkerboard. (Manuscripts and Archives, Yale University Library)*

Fritz Pollard, *star of Brown's 1915 Rose Bowl season. (Brown University)*

Dartmouth students follow *the 1929 Cornell game on a Grid-Graph while a band, to the right of the illuminated football field, plays fight songs. As accounts of the game came in by telegraph, operators indicated the type of play and the names of the players involved while moving a lightbulb up and down the field to mark the position of the ball. (Cornell University)*

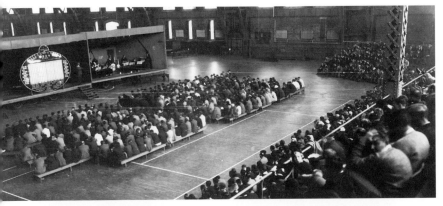

Yale's Clint Frank *(left) and Larry Kelley, the first two winners of the Heisman Trophy.*
(Yale Athletic Department)

Harvard's Barry Wood, *summa cum laude graduate and winner of ten varsity letters between 1929 and 1931, was perhaps the greatest student-athlete ever. Shown here in later life, Wood playfully suggests a different Ivy League philosophy.*
(Harvard University Archives)

Penn runs around end *against Cornell in this Thanksgiving Day game at Franklin Field during the 1930s. (Cornell University)*

George Larsen, the mysterious "Twelfth Man" *(center, in white), runs out of the stands and throws himself into the line during 1935 Princeton-Dartmouth game. (Princeton Athletic Department)*

Columbia's trick play, *the KF-79, springs Al Barabas free for the Lions' lone touchdown in their upset victory over Stanford in the 1934 Rose Bowl. (Columbia Athletic Department)*

Mud-soaked Columbia *players take a break during the team's 15-0 victory over Dartmouth in 1947. (Columbia University)*

Penn's George Munger *coaches from the sidelines at Columbia's Baker Field in 1948. (Penn Athletic Department)*

Brown's Joe Paterno (38) *returns a kickoff twenty-six yards against Princeton in 1949. (Brown University)*

Princeton's Dick Kazmaier, *winner of the Heisman Trophy in 1951, on the cover of* Time.

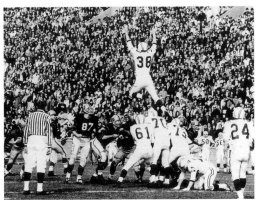

Dartmouth's Samuel Hawken *leaps off a teammate's back in an attempt to block a 1965 field goal by Princeton's Charlie Gogolak, one of the first soccer-style kickers. Hawken was ruled offside, but Gogolak missed the kick on his second attempt. (Dartmouth College Library)*

Yale's Calvin Hill (30) *waves for a pass from quarterback Brian Dowling (10) in the 1968 Harvard game. The Crimson rallied for sixteen points in the last three and a half minutes to gain a 29-29 tie in perhaps the most exciting game in Ivy League history. (Yale Athletic Department)*

Cornell running back *Ed Marinaro exults after scoring a touchdown in a 19-8 victory over Princeton in 1971. Marinaro was the runner-up for the Heisman Trophy that season. (Cornell Athletic Department; photo by Larry F. Baum)*

Quarterback Jay Fiedler *of Dartmouth scores in the snow against Princeton in 1993. In one eight-minute stretch, Fiedler passed for two touchdowns, ran for a third, and scored a two-point conversion to lead a 28-22 Big Green victory. (Dartmouth College Library)*

Brown quarterback James Perry, *one of the best Ivy players of recent years, drops back to pass against Cornell in 1999. (Brown Athletic Department; photo by Tom Maguire)*

Quakers were forced to cancel games already scheduled against Notre Dame. Football was taken away from the alumni and placed under the aegis of a new Department of Physical Education, Intercollegiate Athletics, and Student Health, its budget and expenses supervised by the university. "*In other words*," McKenzie exulted, "sports were to be given back to the students, teaching to the Faculty, and the deficit to the Treasurer." [10]

The *New York Sun* called the Gates Plan "an athletic earthquake." What other schools had talked about, Penn had done. It was "the most astounding blow at intercollegiate athletics that has ever been made by a university important in the athletic world. ... It is a banker's dream and athletic Utopia." [11] "Hail Pennsylvania," added the *Cornell Daily Sun*. [12] Gates was so adamant about uprooting commercialism that he even refused an invitation from President Herbert Hoover's commissioner for unemployment relief to have the Quakers play in a round-robin series to raise money for those out of work. [13]

It took a few years for the effects of the Gates Plan to be felt on the football team, but those effects were predictable. The Quakers collapsed to 2-7 in 1933, their first losing season since 1915, and a year later lost to little Ursinus College on a blocked extra point. Attendance slumped from a high of 530,000 in 1927 to just 257,000 in 1933.

Penn was not alone, however, in reexamining its athletic structure. In 1931, Reed Harris, editor of the *Columbia Spectator*, let loose a broadside in which he labeled intercollegiate football a "semi-professional racket." Harris alleged that "probably 80 per cent of the men who play college football in the bigger institutions are semi-professional athletes hired by assistant coaches who make annual pilgrimages to prep schools." His solution was to let the alumni "pay a good living wage to every football man, openly and not underhandedly. Let all scholastic requirements be waived for football players." [14] Notwithstanding Harris's suggestion that they be paid, two members of the Columbia varsity, captain Ralph Hewitt and William McDuffee, strode over to the Spectator offices and threatened to beat him up. [15]

The Carnegie Report only added to Princeton's woes, as in 1930 they suffered through their worst season to date, finishing 1-5-1 while scoring only forty-six points. They could still rouse themselves for Yale, though, which came into town for the final game of the season, Bill Roper's last as Princeton coach. Despite their record, Princeton had played competitively in almost every game, with the exception of a 31-0 pasting by Navy. It was still a surprise, though, that the Tigers led the Elis at halftime.

Part of the reason for Princeton's success was the weather. It had poured for most of the afternoon, reducing Albie Booth's ability to maneuver. When the rain subsided in the fourth quarter, a thick fog rolled in, so dense that even players on the field had trouble following the action. Yale had pulled ahead on a Booth field goal when Princeton mounted its final drive. Quarterback Trix Bennett, playing with a sore knee, mixed short passes with runs by Jack James and A. W. Armour. With time running out, the Tigers faced fourth down at the Eli two-yard line. Bennett made a lunge for the end zone and was buried under a mass of blue and black jerseys. When the players were unpiled, it was determined that he had been stopped less than a foot short of a winning touchdown—so close that the referee later said that had he been carrying the ball horizontally rather than vertically, he would have made it.

The dramatic ending inspired George Trevor of the *New York Sun* to compose what Grantland Rice later insisted was the best lead of Trevor's career. It was the custom then for Princeton freshmen to ring the school's bell following a football victory. "The mud-stained pigskin is four inches short of the yard pole, chain stretched taut," Trevor wrote, capturing the scene for the following Monday's paper. "That's why the big bronze bells of Nassau Hall are silent as the dazed crowd slowly trickles out of Palmer Stadium, but Yale can hear the ghostly echoes of those muted chimes, and so can William Warren Roper. They never rang so loudly as the night they never rang at all." [16]

Desperate to get back to winning, Princeton flirted with Knute Rockne before hiring Herbert O. "Fritz" Crisler from the University of Minnesota. The move was a break with tradition and reflected how seriously Princetonians viewed the decay of their football program; Crisler was the first Big Three coach who was not an alumnus of that school. To appease disgruntled old guarders, he personally visited all eighty-five Princeton alumni clubs around the country in order to sell himself and his program.

Typical of the advice the new coach received was the following, which he later repeated in an article for the *Saturday Evening Post*: "Our center will block their center. Our guards will block their guards. Our tackles will block their tackles. Our ends will block their ends. Three of our backs will knock down three of their backs. Now, if your one remaining back isn't good enough to dodge the one remaining opposing back and go for a touchdown, you deserve to lose." [17]

One alum who liked to put in his two cents' worth was F. Scott Fitzgerald, Class of 1917, who had quit the freshman team with an ankle injury after only three days of practice. Fitzgerald liked to phone Crisler from the West Coast, often late at night, to suggest plays. Once, Fitzgerald called Princeton's graduate athletic manager, Asa Bushnell with "some suggestions for Crisler" on how to beat Yale. "Princeton must have two teams," Fitzgerald urged. "One will be big—all men over two hundred. This team will be used to batter them down and wear them out. Then the little team, the pony team, will go in and make the touchdowns." Bushnell passed the suggestion on to Crisler, who shrewdly replied that he would try it only if Fitzgerald publicly put his name on the scheme and took credit for its success or failure. In that case, Fitzgerald demurred, perhaps the plan ought better to be held "in reserve." [18]

He remained a fan, however, until the very end of his life. When Fitzgerald was stricken with a fatal heart attack in Hollywood on December 21, 1940, he was seated in a chair scribbling notes on an article in the *Princeton Alumni Weekly* about the Tigers' football prospects for 1941.[19]

Crisler's first days were not auspicious. He arrived in Princeton on March 1, 1932, to discuss his contract and left early the next morning for the train station. Unbeknownst to him, the infant son of Charles A. Lindbergh had been kidnapped the night before in Hopewell, about ten miles away. Driving around at dawn on unfamiliar roads in a borrowed car, Crisler was stopped by police and taken in for questioning. He was not released until the car's owner, Hack McGraw, a prominent alumnus and partner in the McGraw-Hill publishing company, came down to the station to vouch that Crisler was indeed the new head football coach.[20]

Crisler introduced Princeton to the single wing offense they would use for almost two generations and also brought an innovative helmet design. Helmet logos came into fashion after the NCAA noticed that defenses had trouble distinguishing a brown leather ball from a brown leather helmet. Starting in 1931, they decreed that helmets have at least two broad stripes of a contrasting color. Crisler's design, which is usually associated with the Michigan Wolverines, whom he left Princeton to coach after the 1938 season, depicts an art deco-ish tiger with its ears pinned back, a vivid pattern that he also believed helped quarterbacks find their receivers. Princeton, however, soon switched to something else and did not put the logo back on its helmets until 1998.[21]

Helmets helped make the game safer, despite another rash of highly publicized injuries. One tragedy occurred in the Yale Bowl on October 24, 1931, in the Elis' game against Army. Returning a fourth-quarter kickoff, Yale's Bob Lassiter was tackled hard at the twenty-two-yard line by Cadet Richard B. Sheridan. Lassiter jumped back up, but Sheridan, who had been kneed in the head, suffered two broken vertebrae and a severed spinal cord. Although medical staff, including at least one doctor in the stands, tried to resuscitate Sheridan, he died two days later in a New Haven hospital.

Distracted though the Bulldogs must have been, Albie Booth played brilliantly the following Saturday against Dartmouth, scoring three touchdowns on a ninety-four-yard kickoff return, a fifty-four yard run from scrimmage, and a twenty-two-yard pass reception. Dartmouth's Bill McCall managed to match him, scoring three touchdowns of his own. Overconfident, the Bulldogs squandered a fourteen-point lead and had to settle for a 33-33 tie.

Barry Wood, who as a junior had thrown two touchdown passes in Harvard's 1930 victory over Yale, had one of the best afternoons of his career a year later against Army. The Cadets jumped to a 13-0 lead before Wood went to work, connecting on long passes that led to Harvard's first touchdown, running in the extra point after a botched snap, scoring the second touchdown, and kicking an extra point to give the Crimson the lead. When Army's star halfback broke off a reverse that seemed sure to go for a touchdown, Wood raced almost the length of the field to drag him down from behind, then snuffed Army's last drive with an interception that sealed the upset victory.

Harvard was protective of its star. A week earlier, Bill Bingham had fired off a note to William S. Paley, president of the Columbia Broadcasting System, informing him that broadcaster Ted Husing would no longer be admitted to Harvard Stadium because Husing had criticized Wood's play against Dartmouth. "No announcer can come into the Stadium and call the play of any boy on the Harvard team or any other team 'putrid,'" Bingham scolded, setting off a storm in the press, most of which took Husing's side. [22] Heywood Broun (an alumnus, no less) denounced the ban as "another aspect of the menace Harvard offers to human liberty." As it was, on the play after being described as putrid, Wood lofted a touchdown pass and kicked the extra point that won the game.

It was fitting that Wood and Booth met for the last time in 1931, the fiftieth playing of The Game. Both teams entered undefeated, the first time that had happened since 1913. Evenly matched in records, the Crimson and Bulldogs were evenly matched on the field, as well, playing scoreless football through three quarters, although Booth had missed a fifteen-yard field goal.

Such a tight game deserved a terrific ending. In the fourth quarter, Yale moved down to the Harvard four-yard line. Writer Tim Cohane later described what happened next: "Pat Sullivan, who had alternated with Dud Parker, was in the game now. It was the first time he had ever played in the same backfield as Booth. He was calling the plays. He turned to Albie in the huddle and smiled grimly.

> "Can you kick a field goal, you little bastard?"
> "Sure," said Little Boy Blue.
> "And he did. And that was the game." [23]

Wood tried to rally the Crimson from terrible field position, but the Bulldogs smothered him inches from a safety as the game ended with a 3-0 Yale victory. Yale may have respected their distinguished rival, but that did not dampen their celebration. On the train back to New Haven that evening, the cars rang with shouts, "Wood on his ass on the one-yard line! Wood on his ass on the one-yard line!" [24]

Booth was forced to miss his final game, against Princeton, with pneumonia but still managed to make his presence felt from his hospital bed. Shortly before halftime, a telegram was delivered to the Yale bench. It read:

> Ed. Rotan
> Yale team, Yale Bowl, New Haven, Conn.
>   Keep up the good work. Remember I am on my back but fighting in spirit. Do not forget the Dartmouth tragedy.
>   Signed, Albie 2:28 p.m. [25]

Forever joined on the gridiron, Wood and Booth followed very different paths off it. Wood declined an offer to play on a team of Big Three graduates in an exhibition football game at the 1932 Olympics. He got married that summer instead, somehow also finding time to write a book to earn money for medical school. Booth, on the other hand, "almost temperamentally without ambition" in the words of Thomas Bergin, stayed in New Haven, married his high school sweetheart and, when not serving as a part-time assistant coach at Yale and NYU, managed the ice cream division for a dairy.

With their graduation, though, the era of the drop kicker ended in college football. Two rules changes were responsible. In 1927, the NCAA moved the uprights from the goal line to the back of the end zone, making kicks ten yards longer. And in 1934, it reduced the circumference of the ball from 22 1/2 inches to 21 1/2 inches. The smaller ball was easier to grip with one hand, aiding passers, but it no longer bounced true, effectively eliminating drop kicks from the game forever.[26]

The problem with Columbia football, observers concluded, was a lack of talent on the field and insufficient support from the administration. "There is a curious mixture at Columbia today," Paul Gallico wrote in 1930. "The school wants to maintain its athletic and scholastic integrity, and still play schools like Dartmouth and Cornell at football on an even footing. And this apparently cannot be done."[27]

After several mediocre seasons, things were about to change with the hiring of Lou Little. The son of Italian immigrants, he had been a tackle at the University of Pennsylvania before going off to World War I, where he became a captain in the infantry. Upon his return, Little played on the Quakers' 1919 team, a cradle of coaches that also included Bert Bell and Lud Wray. After a few years in the fledgling National Football League and coaching at Georgetown, he turned down an offer to return to his alma mater in order to accept the job at Columbia, which made him one of the highest-paid coaches in the country.

Little looked like a professor and dressed like a movie star. He wore pincenez glasses and boasted that he owned forty suits, dozens of pairs of shoes, and five hundred ties. A screamer until he ruptured his voice and was forced to speak in a raspy, Al Smith growl, he rarely used profanity, typically moaning "Oh, my, my, my, my, my," after a bad play.[28] It was a point of pride that every one of his Columbia starters graduated. "Some of the finest teaching at Columbia College," Dean Herbert E. Hawkes once remarked, "is done at Baker Field by Lou Little."[29]

A good part of that teaching was also hands-on. Trying to demonstrate a play during a scrimmage before the Dartmouth game, Little broke a vertebra in his neck. He coached that Saturday from a specially built swivel chair, his neck immobile in a heavy leather brace.[30] Columbia, which had lost to the Indians 52-0 the year before, won that game for their first victory over Dartmouth since 1899.

Suddenly, Columbia was good again, losing only one game a year during the

1931 through 1933 seasons. Princeton would have gone to the Rose Bowl in 1933 but for the Big Three prohibition against postseason contests. Instead, Columbia got the invitation, despite having been whitewashed by the Tigers, 20-0, and having barely escaped Cornell, the only other Ivy school they faced.

Little informed the team of the invitation one day before practice. As the Lions' star quarterback, Cliff Montgomery, recalled years later, "For a moment we just stood there, gaping. Then pandemonium broke loose as we pounded each other's backs, danced on the rubbing tables and yelled like kids." [31] The administration still had to approve the trip and many thought Columbia ought to beg off, fearing they might be embarrassed by their opponent, Stanford. It remained for an old alumnus, General "Wild Bill" Donovan, to speak up.

"I'm afraid we're overlooking an important point," Donovan said. "To you and me, this may be an invitation, but to the team and the student body it's a challenge. It will be difficult to explain to them that we ran from it. I think we should accept it. I think we *must*." [32]

The Lions did accept, though few took them seriously. A Los Angeles sportswriter dismissed them as "Pomona High in light blue jerseys." [33] Some oddsmakers installed Stanford as a four-touchdown favorite. The campus newspaper, staying far off the bandwagon, scorned the university for having "repudiated its own standards."

Like Harvard, Penn, and Brown teams years earlier, Columbia took a leisurely route to Pasadena. Along the way, they spent a week practicing in Tucson, where Little perfected a little piece of deception. The play, run out of the single wing, was known as KF-79. Montgomery would take the snap, pivot and hand off to halfback Al Barabas, spin the other way and fake to the other halfback, Ed Brominski, would then pretend to keep the ball himself and plunge into the line. It was, Montgomery noted, just a variation on the old hidden ball play but in order for it to work everyone had to execute perfectly and Montgomery needed good footing.

The latter seemed increasingly unlikely as the team drew closer to California. Los Angeles suffered its heaviest twenty-four hour rainfall in its history, more than seven inches in a single day. [34] Because the drainage pipes under the turf were clogged, water backed up, covering the playing field and rising to the level of the box seats. On New Year's Eve, the day Columbia arrived, the field was under eight inches of water. Benches floated around like driftwood. Sportswriters took to calling Columbia the "Sea Lions." [35]

When the downpour subsided later that evening, city officials commandeered local fire trucks to help pump out the water so that by game time on New Year's Day (in a light, sporadic drizzle, which helped keep attendance to only half of capacity) the field was soggy but playable.

Referees in those days did not change the ball when it got wet, with the result that the sodden football became heavy and difficult to throw. The game devolved into a battle of field position, the teams sometimes punting on first or second down and chasing after numerous fumbles. Columbia tried their trick play early, but it did not work. Then, in the second quarter, Montgomery fooled the Stanford defense with a pass down to the seventeen-yard line. He decided it was time to spring KF-79 again.

Montgomery made the handoff and completed his fakes perfectly. "In that instant before I dove after [Barabas]," he recalled, "I saw what must remain one of the most thrilling sights of my life—the entire Stanford team in suspended animation waiting for a clue as to who had the ball. We had fooled them!" [36] No one was near Barabas as he sauntered into the end zone.

With former president Herbert Hoover in the stands (rooting for Stanford, his alma mater), Columbia pulled off what many have called the greatest upset in college football history. Stanford ran up 272 yards in total offense to just 114 for Columbia and sixteen first downs to five, but when the final gun sounded, the Lions had all the points and a 7-0 victory.

Upstarts no more, the victors took a tour of Hollywood and received congratulations from movie stars Ginger Rogers and Edward G. Robinson. Upon their return to New York, they were feted at a civic dinner attended by new Mayor Fiorello LaGuardia, who promoted himself as another upset winner. Five hundred riotous students later crashed the Nimmo Theater on Upper Broadway where the audience was watching a newsreel of the Rose Bowl game, damaging property and running through the aisles shouting "Fire!" Ten were arrested for disorderly conduct. [37]

Their exuberance, if excessive, was well-founded. Little had succeeded in raising the Lions to a height they would never reach again, and the distant memory of Barabas's dash through the Pasadena muck would have to comfort aging boosters during Columbia's nightmare losing streak fifty years later. Nineteen thirty-three remains the pinnacle of Columbia football.

Football continued to operate in the black even during the worst of the Depression, but the surpluses were much smaller than before and thus much less able to mop up the red ink being spilled in other sports. More than 99 percent of the Cornell athletic association's entire net income now came from football, yet receipts fell from $250,000 in the 1920s to less than $100,000 by 1934. [38] At Princeton, all sports except football had posted a combined deficit of more than $102,000 for the 1929-30 school year, but because football had posted a $125,000 profit, the athletic association as a whole had managed a small surplus. By 1931-32, the deficit from other sports had shrunk to $92,000, but football revenues had dropped to less than $85,000. [39]

Schools tried to trim expenses wherever possible. Although Princeton fielded the same number of teams in 1931-32 as it had in 1930-31, the number of games those teams played was cut almost in half. Dartmouth dropped all freshman sports except football in November 1932, and a year later eliminated the varsity tennis, lacrosse, golf, and gymnastics teams entirely. Many colleges cut their football schedules from eight games to seven (Harvard debated cutting it to six) and reduced ticket prices to boost attendance, which only compounded a vicious cycle of declining revenues.

"This, then, is the dilemma which the universities and larger colleges of the United States face," the *Harvard Alumni Bulletin* explained; "Shall football go on as it is now conducted, and its surplus be used for other kinds of intercollegiate athletics, or shall the latter be abandoned or at least materially curtailed?"[40]

Financial necessity forced schools to take control of their athletic departments. The alumni-dominated Cornell University Athletic Association, for example, had run the football program throughout the twenties, when times were flush. Dobie's strong teams and a larger stadium enabled the organization to pay off old debts and build a sizable surplus. Rather than conserve this money, the CUAA spent it and more, using $275,000 (most of it borrowed) to further enlarge Schoellkopf Field and taking over the cost of the intramural athletic program that had previously been paid by the university.

This was manageable so long as the money kept coming in, but when the economy soured and the Big Red stopped winning, it became a crisis. At the depth of the Depression, the CUAA was forced to cut off payments to all sports except football, basketball, wrestling, and baseball. In response, more than a thousand students signed a petition demanding a change in the athletic structure, forcing the Cornell trustees to assume the CUAA's debts in exchange for transferring all of its property and responsibilities to the university under the guise of a new Department of Physical Education and Athletics. In an attempt to instill a little business discipline, they chose James Lynah, a former purchasing agent for General Motors, as the department's first director.[41]

Harvard's new president, James Bryant Conant, took a more innovative approach and looked into creating an endowment that would support all sports and thus break the "vicious connection" between football and the budget.[42] "As long as the athletic budget is drawn in terms of expected revenue, all concerned must keep a weather eye on the football income," Conant warned. "A hand-to-mouth policy is no solution."[43]

It was easier for college authorities to de-emphasize football if fewer people cared. Somewhere around this time, Ivy football began to lose its long hold on the campus imagination. Much of this was simply a cyclical change in styles; other campus traditions, such as the wearing of freshman beanies or organized cheering at baseball games also passed away during these years as hopelessly juvenile. Attendance at the Yale Bowl for the Harvard-Yale game peaked in 1930 at 74,700, a figure that has not been matched. "As we round the corner of this decade we find on the campus a general revolt against the typical collegiate attitude of a few years ago, and especially against that mythical something known as "college spirit," wrote one Princeton senior in 1931. "The present-day undergraduate has concluded that it isn't a matter of life and death whether Princeton defeats Yale, or, in fact, whether Princeton defeats anybody." [44]

Such a change in tastes, however, had serious implications for the financially precarious athletic structure. Even Harvard, which invented apathy, was concerned. "Interest in football seems to be at a low ebb in Cambridge," the *Alumni Bulletin* fretted. "Harvard undergraduates, as well as the alumni, pay less and less attention each succeeding year to what was once the absorbing topic of conversation during the autumn months, namely, the progress and prospects of the eleven." [45] When Yale scored its first touchdown against the Crimson in the 1934 game, Harvard students held up a placard that read, "Who Gives a Damn?" [46]

The Depression and changing student attitudes made some sort of football affiliation among the Ivy colleges desirable. Intersectional games were more expensive than contests against older, regional rivals and the risk of competing against bigger schools with lower standards made it necessary for the Ivy colleges to find an athletic sinecure. Lacking any sort of national organization possessed with the authority to impose standards, the trend, many thought, was toward a series of groupings across the country among colleges with similar athletic standards. [47]

All of the Ivy colleges had grown rapidly, struggling to become research universities without losing their historic character as small colleges. They were something new, writes historian John Thelin— "university colleges"—bigger and more academically diverse than pure colleges such as Amherst or Williams, but smaller and more oriented toward the liberal arts than the major state universities. [48] Although the process was far from complete, the university college ideal, as reflected athletically in the Ivy League, became a way of sewing together institutions as geographically and culturally diverse as Dartmouth and Cornell, Princeton and Pennsylvania.

There could be no affiliation, however, until Princeton and Harvard declared a truce. As early as the spring of 1930, both student papers had begun calling for an "entente cordiale." [49] The following year, the captains of all Princeton teams sent a petition to Harvard urging that athletic relations between the schools be resumed in all sports except football. Harvard's student council immediately approved the petition, and Princeton's athletic department began making arrangements for a resumption. As long as Harvard refused to accord Princeton equal status on its football schedule with Yale, however, the Tigers would not meet the Crimson on the gridiron.

Rather belatedly, Yale tried its hand at balance of power politics by announcing a five-year experiment in which it would alternate the last game of its season between the two schools. Losing the Bulldogs as their climactic game hit Harvard where it hurt. "Yale is obliged to explain this action," the *Crimson* demanded. [50] In a wry column titled "Et tu, Elihu?" Stanley Woodward wrote, "It is reported unofficially...that 60,000,000 codfish in Massachusetts Bay have turned over and expired; and that the Cabots and the Lowells in their excitement have been speaking indiscriminately to all men." [51] Others seemed saddened. "For some time it has been patent that Yale men foster a penchant for Princeton," wrote one Crimson alumnus. "Harvard men are accorded respect. But Princeton evokes Yale's love." [52]

Yale itself tried to play this up. Sounding like an overcourted girl at the ball, the *Yale Daily News* explained that the school loved both suitors equally. "By giving Harvard the most favored nation's right, Yale has discriminated against Princeton. She now considers Princeton as a legitimate rival on the same basis as Harvard." [53]

In order to help their finances, Yale also tried to change the division of gate receipts with its ancient rivals. Because the Yale Bowl seated almost 80,000 people while Palmer Stadium and Harvard Stadium seated less than two-thirds that number, Yale suffered a considerable financial loss when it played Princeton and Harvard on the road. Accordingly they proposed that the home team keep all the receipts rather than divide them evenly, as had long been done. Not surprisingly, the other two members of the Big Three objected strenuously and consulted with each other to plan their attack. Yale withdrew its proposal, but noted a little sourly that Harvard and Princeton could certainly get along when there was money at stake. [54]

With relations resumed in all other sports, football could not be far behind. According to one account, the break came in January 1933 when a prominent Harvard alumnus called on Edward W. Duffield, president of the Prudential Life Insurance Company and acting president of Princeton. Duffield indicated that Princeton no longer cared about her status in Harvard's eyes, other than being an "honored rival." Arrangements were finalized within weeks. "An absurd situation will end," pronounced the *Yale Daily News*. [55]

The first game of the revived series was played at Cambridge in 1935, a hard-fought, 19-0 Princeton victory. The *Harvard Lampoon* and *Princeton Tiger* published a joint humor magazine for the occasion to prevent a repeat of what had happened the last time in 1926, and before the game the Harvard band paraded across the field playing "Auld Lang Syne" before giving a rousing Princeton cheer, which the Tiger crowd reciprocated. Ironically, given the Crimson's old accusations of dirty play, Princeton's first touchdown came after Harvard was called for unnecessary roughness. [56]

Peace between Harvard and Princeton may have made an Ivy League possible, but the league also owed much to the breach itself, which fractured the unity of the Big Three and forced them to consider a broader set of rivalries, emulating in football what they had already done in baseball, basketball, track, and other sports. Throughout the early thirties there were rumors of such alliances, such as Nicholas Murray Butler's "Academic League of Nations" consisting of the nation's top schools. Penn urged the formation of a new "Inter-Collegiate Football Association" comprised of the Quakers' "traditional rivals," by which it meant Cornell, Columbia, Yale, Dartmouth, and Princeton. [57] There were rumors of a "Big Four" alliance between Harvard,

Yale, Princeton, and Dartmouth, and another alliance among of Columbia, Cornell, Penn, Brown, Colgate, and Syracuse.[58]

By the beginning of World War II, Cornell, Dartmouth, Harvard, Princeton, and Yale were playing as many as five or six games a season against Ivy opponents. "The rush of the Eastern ivy colleges into each other's arms," Stanley Woodward wrote in the *New York Herald Tribune*, "no doubt is attributable to hard common sense. It has been discovered through experimentation that there is no substitute for ivy as customer-bait. The clientele rise like a starving brook-trout for a Pamachini Belle when a touch of ivy is trailed across its path."[59]

It was the students, though, who took the first decisive step. On December 2, 1936, the editors of student papers at Columbia, Cornell, Dartmouth, Harvard, Penn, Princeton, and Yale published a joint editorial, titled "Now Is the Time," in which they called for the creation of a football conference. "The Ivy League already exists in the minds of a good many of those connected with football," they argued, "and we fail to see why the seven schools concerned should be satisfied to let it exist as a purely nebulous entity where there are so many practical benefits which would be possible under a definitely organized association.[60]

Unofficial reaction was favorable. Dartmouth coach Red Blaik was quoted as saying, "I am greatly in favor of the formation of an Ivy League because I think it would tend to put all of the teams on the same standards of football."[61] President Livingston Farrand of Cornell and E. LeRoy Mercer, Penn's dean of physical education, were also reported in favor.[62]

But Yale and Princeton dissented, hoping to preserve the hegemony of the Big Three. "I see no health in the Ivy League proposal," Princeton's new president, Harold Dodds, wrote.[63] Bulldog coach Ducky Pond told the press, "The scholastic requirements of the seven universities involved vary to such a degree that regulations unifying these would have to be drawn up before such a League would be fair to all concerned, and I do not think such a stabilization could be effected." That, as some have pointed out, was a thinly veiled swipe at the other schools that were not considered to be of the same academic caliber as the Big Three.[64]

Others, on the other hand, were suspicious of entering into an alliance with the Big Three, which had so long disdained them. "If the marriage ever does take place, I fail to see how the Columbia, Cornell, Penn, and Dartmouth forces can ever expect any happiness from it," one Dartmouth student wrote. "This group may always be in the position of outsiders who have been invited into a family quarrel and are expected to feel honored by the invitation."[65]

For the time being, at least, Brown's place in the proposed group was uncertain. Although they scheduled an average number of Ivy opponents and intermittently produced good teams—quarterback John Buonano almost led them to a second Rose Bowl in 1932 with an offense that scored only eighty-two points—they seemed never to enjoy the highs their rivals did and so tended to remain afterthoughts. By 1935, Brown posted what may have been the worst offense in Ivy history, scoring just twenty-one points in nine games while getting shut out by all four Ivy opponents they played. "Brown must make a radical change in her football department if she isn't to sink completely from sight in an athletic way," one concerned alumnus wrote a few years later. "Something's got to be done—and done now. The Bruin that once trod the sward as bravely as any of them has wasted away to a timid and apologetic sort of little honey-bear that its former foes now merely shoo out of the yard, instead of running for the muzzle loader and yelling for help." [66]

There were also financial impediments to the creation of a league, chiefly the Big Three's refusal to play their smaller Ivy rivals on the road. Yale, for example, would play Cornell at Ithaca only once in four games, and gave the Big Red barely more than a third of the gate when they played in New Haven. Princeton was willing to split its receipts for games at Palmer Stadium, but would not go to Ithaca at all.

Six weeks after the joint Ivy League editorial, the athletic directors of the seven colleges sent their own letter to the student papers. A football league, they wrote, "has such promising possibilities that it may not be dismissed and must be the subject of further consideration." However, "the time has not yet come when the seven suggested members feel ready to establish a definite and formal organization." [67]

Unbeknownst to them, however, the Ivy presidents were considering a much broader association. In December 1936, Harvard's James Bryant Conant received a letter from Howard Savage of the Carnegie Foundation proposing that the foundation create a "board of audit" to investigate athletics each year at thirteen northeastern colleges and universities and act as final arbiter on all questions of eligibility. Savage proposed including all eight Ivy schools, as well as Amherst, Lehigh, New York University, Wesleyan, and Williams. Two meetings were held in January 1937 (the second at Conant's house) to see if agreement could be reached on common principles of eligibility as well as how to split the costs. [68]

The group did not envision a formal league—there would be no round-robin scheduling or championship. The purpose, Conant explained in a letter to Yale's incoming president Charles Seymour, was to create "some outside spokesman who would guarantee the public we are running things in an open manner." [69] Ultimately, the colleges could not agree whether the foundation should control the oversight board or whether they should appoint their own board, and the proposal went no further.

Yale, which had slumped to an unthinkable record of 2-2-3 in its first season after Albie Booth's graduation, tried to restore its lost glory by bringing back Ducky Pond as head coach. Pond relied heavily on his assistants, Earl "Greasy" Neale, Ivan "Ivy" Williamson and, in 1935, the most famous assistant coach in Ivy history, Gerald R. Ford.

The future president had been an All-America center at Michigan and wanted to go to law school there but could not afford the tuition. When his coach passed along the tip that Yale was looking for an assistant coach, at $2,400 a year, he took the job. As assistant coaches do, Ford handled a little of everything—acting as advance scout, and coaching the linemen, the junior varsity, even the boxing team—all the while saving up money to apply to Yale's law school. The law school admissions office, however, did not think Ford's college grades were good enough and Yale's athletic director was not happy about having a coach who studied, so Ford took two summer classes at Michigan without telling anyone.

When he returned to New Haven, Ford presented his grades—a pair of B's — to the law school and was admitted provisionally for the spring semester. He continued the following fall without telling Pond that he was taking law courses and without telling the law school that he was also coaching full-time. "Well, Jerry, you have handled the job," Yale's athletic director said when Ford finally broke the news. "If you will do your job, you can stay on." Ford took light loads during football season and supplemented them with summer courses at the University of North Carolina.[70] Nevertheless, he graduated in the top quarter of a class that included Potter Stewart, Cyrus Vance, and Sargent Shriver.

Although the Bulldogs improved only slightly in Pond's first season, the year before Ford arrived, they gave an indication of better things to come when they upset Princeton. The Tigers entered the 1934 contest with a seventeen-game winning streak, begun the year before when they had outscored their opponents 217-8 and fielded what is arguably the best Ivy team of all time. The weather in Princeton was warm, but when Yale entered their dressing room, they found that someone—they suspected Princetonians—had built a fire in the coal stove, making the room unpleasantly hot. During warm-ups, Princeton tried more psychological intimidation. The team wore unusually prominent shoulder pads, which made the players look bigger than they really were. Their drills over, the Tigers gathered in a semicircle around Coach Crisler at midfield and began silently staring at the Elis. After a while, the Bulldogs noticed.

"What are they trying to do?" asked Jimmy DeAngelis. "Scare us?"

In the locker room, Crisler tried to rally his troops. "Gentlemen," he said, "I have not the honor to be a Princeton man, so I do not feel that I can intrude myself upon the sanctity of this moment. I leave you with your own thoughts. It is your choice to make. What is it to be? Sixty minutes of redemption or a lifetime of regret?"[71]

The Tigers chose regret. Despite the Big Three ban on postseason play, Princeton students had passed out petitions before the game to let the team go to the Rose Bowl if they won. But the Tigers were tense and tentative, as the pregame mind games had suggested. They fumbled seven times in the first ten minutes, prompting Yale's Paul Grosscup to crack to Princeton quarterback John Kadlic, "Hey, Kaddie, I hope the Rose Bowl has handles on it."[72]

The Eli starters played all sixty minutes and won, 7-0, on a pass to Larry Kelley, a sophomore who would soon become much better known. Kelley grabbed the ball at the twenty-nine-yard line and angled toward the end zone. A pair of Princeton defenders, Ken Sandbach and Gary LeVan, almost had him at the five. "Here for the first time [Kelley] broke stride," the *New York Times* reported. "For a fleeting fraction of a second it almost seemed he stood stock still. Then he started again, and half-twisted, half-danced through these two men as though he were a ghost to cross the line standing up and unscathed." [73]

Kelley was one of the most colorful players in college football history. He had, as one writer put it, "a glib Irish wit, stage presence, and the knack of improvising wisecracks on the spur of the moment." [74] The press nicknamed him "Laughing Larry" and the "Rhapsody in Blue." He played end, though he was never much of a blocker, returned punts, and even kicked an extra point against Brown in his senior year. He is also the only player for Harvard, Princeton, or Yale to have scored a touchdown against both Big Three rivals in every game he played against them.

Kelley confessed that he coasted during games, saving his best efforts for the tight spots—something many players probably do, but not the sort of admission that endears a young man to his coaches. "He was a bit of a free-lancer," Ford recalled with a laugh. [75] In his own words, he was "Too radical; too unorthodox; too crazy! You see, when the spirit moved me, I'd quit my post against orders, and gamble on getting the tackle on the other end of the line." [76] Teams could bank on it. Princeton was so sure Kelley would follow a decoy that they devised a play, called the "Cousin Kelley Special," which they ran for a touchdown with Kelley far out of position. [77]

He may have been lazy, but he was tough. In a game against Princeton, Kelley caught a deep pass ahead of Jack White, who had been a high school track star. A step ahead of his pursuer, Kelley nevertheless turned, leveled White with a straight arm, then continued into the end zone. "Gangway for grace and speed and skill! Let genius have its flare!" one sportswriter wrote in a bit of doggerel. "A goddess kisses Kelley when the ball is in the air." [78]

He also had a knack for being involved in freak plays. Against Harvard in 1935, Kelley caught a thirty-five-yard touchdown pass that bounded off a Crimson helmet. A year later, Kelley kicked a fumbled Navy punt from the twenty-five-yard line to the three where he fell on it, leading to what proved to be the winning touchdown. When asked if he had done this deliberately (which would have been illegal), Kelley cracked, "I'm not that smart." [79]

In 1936, Kelley won the first Heisman Trophy, which had just been renamed to honor the great coach. [80] Kelley passed up both professional football and Hollywood, declining an offer to play himself in a movie that was to have been called *Kelley of Yale*, going on instead to teach history and coach football at his old prep school. Three years after graduating, however, he wrote an article for *Look* magazine titled "Poison Ivy League" in which he criticized Yale for forcing players, himself included, to play with injuries. Tragedy dogged Kelley in his final years. Old and sick, he decided to sell his Heisman Trophy in order to provide some money for his family. Although the Yale athletic department bid for it, the trophy went to a sports bar in upstate New York. Kelley killed himself in the summer of 2000.

Like Butch Cassidy and the Sundance Kid, Kelley is seldom mentioned apart from his teammate, quarterback Clint Frank, who won the Heisman the following year. Unlike Kelley, Frank was a two-way star, who also excelled in the defensive secondary, where he specialized in breaking up passes. He was known for his willingness to play hurt, being called "the most taped player of our time."[81]

Frank prepped at Lawrenceville, just down the road from Princeton, but said he went to Yale because "my dad liked it, and he was paying the bills."[82] In three consecutive weeks during his junior season, Frank set up all three Yale touchdowns in a 23-0 rout of Cornell, threw for a touchdown and intercepted two passes in a 7-0 win over Penn, and scored two more touchdowns despite a broken finger in a 12-6 win over Navy. When the Bulldogs met Princeton, Greasy Neale (who constantly called him "Cliff") wrote the signals for thirty-six plays on the knee of Frank's uniform pants so he could read them when he bent over in the huddle. Frank got so worked up during the game that he forgot to look at the pants and called only nineteen of them.[83]

He was even better as a senior, scoring seven touchdowns in four games against Maine, Penn, Army, and Cornell. Frank's thirty-five-yard touchdown pass on fourth down with three seconds remaining gave Yale a 9-9 tie with Dartmouth. Two fans suffered heart attacks. "It was a wonder," someone wrote, "their names were not Ducky Pond and Red Blaik."[84] Against Princeton, Frank erased an early 16-0 deficit with four touchdowns on the way to a 26-23 victory.

Frank closed his career against Harvard at Soldiers Field. Again, Herbert Hoover was in attendance, this time rooting for Harvard. "There is no neutral in football," said the old Quaker."[85] Playing with an injured knee, Frank nonetheless ran for seventy-four yards and scored Yale's only touchdown, though Harvard prevailed, 13-6. "The image of the embattled and dauntless Frank," wrote Thomas Bergin from the Eli perspective, "fighting to the end in a lost cause, would linger in the memory of many spectators long after the score was forgotten."[86] He won the Heisman that fall with almost twice as many votes as Colorado star and future Supreme Court Justice Byron "Whizzer" White. Like Kelley, Frank passed up the NFL for the business world.

When Harvard decided to join the trend away from alumni coaches, it looked to the University of Western Maryland, of all places, where it found Dick Harlow, a coach only the Ivies could have loved. As a lineman at Penn State, he had once cut practice to hunt for birds' eggs.[87] When he wasn't on the sidelines, Harlow continued to pursue his hobbies, collecting stamps, growing rare ferns and rhododendrons, and assembling a collection of at least 850 types of eggs worth more than $40,000.[88] So impressive was Harlow's knowledge that

President Conant gave him additional duties as curator at Harvard's Museum of Comparative Zoology.

He was as innovative at football as he was varied in his interests. Harlow pioneered the shifting, stunting defense, a tactic that befuddled many an opposing offensive lineman who would find the man he was assigned to block suddenly jump to the other end of the line. One year, he used twenty-eight different defensive formations.[89] In 1936, such ingenuity earned him the extraordinary honor of being voted Coach of the Year by the Football Coaches Association of America with a 3-4-1 record.

Harlow's style also seemed suited to Harvard. Despite an otherwise ornery nature, Harlow would call recalcitrant players short gently. "Do it my way, dear boy," he would suggest or "Patience, dear boy, it will come."[90] The night before the 1938 Yale game, Harlow tried to lead the team in singing "Fair Harvard," but was outraged to learn that hardly anyone knew the words after the first verse. "The eleven men representing Harvard University tomorrow afternoon are representing the greatest institution of its kind in the world, and in that capacity, they can be expected to know the words of 'Fair Harvard,' all three verses! Nobody plays tomorrow until they prove to me this lesson is learned!"[91] The Crimson apparently sang to their coach's satisfaction and won the next day, 7-0.

In Ithaca, the reign of Gloomy Gil Dobie finally came to an end. In 1934, Cornell had endured its first losing season in twenty-eight years, an indignity they compounded the following year by going 0-6-1, being embarrassed by St. Lawrence and Case Western Reserve. Dobie did not take losing—or anything else—cheerfully. After a 54-0 whipping by Princeton, he openly suggested that the team absolve him of any blame, saying, "After all, I'm just the coach."[92] Before the Dartmouth game, he took his squad on a tour of the field. "You kick off here," he sneered, pointing at the forty-yard line. Next he walked to the bench. "This is where you sit when you're not playing." Now he walked back to the ten-yard line. "Here," he concluded, "is where you'll be all afternoon with your backs to the wall."[93] (He was right; they lost, 41-6.)

Cracks like that, on top of the miserable record, persuaded Cornell to buy out the last two years of Dobie's contract. "You can't win games with Phi Beta Kappas," he groused.[94] Some alumni agreed, noting that being held out by the Carnegie Foundation as one of the only "lily-white" football programs in the country was not necessarily a blessing. They resolved to intensify recruiting and raised at least the possibility of awarding athletic scholarships, an idea that was eventually dropped.[95]

Hampered by a tight budget and an uncertain philosophy, the Big Red nonetheless managed to improve. Dobie's successor, Carl Snavely, did things differently. One year he forbade his team from riding in automobiles and insisted they go everywhere by bicycle, even during summer vacation.[96] Snavely was also one of the first coaches to make extensive use of film in preparing for games, often having his wife operate the camera from the roof of the stadium. Every Sunday night during the season, he would write each player a personal note outlining what the young man had done well and what needed improvement.[97] "Signals mean nothing to you," a typical one to a tailback read. "You run wild and leave your blockers with no idea as to where you expect to run."[98]

Although Snavely's record in his first season was only 3-5, one of his star players was Jerome "Brud" Holland, the first African-American to play for Cornell and the first to play at any of the Ivy schools since 1919. One of thirteen children ("Brud" was short for "brother"), Holland was born with slightly deformed legs which his grandmother straightened with daily massages. In a 40-7 pasting of Colgate in 1937, he scored three touchdowns in the fourth quarter, two on end-arounds. When Cornell visited Penn, more than four thousand black fans jammed Franklin Field to watch him play.

The Hearst Newspaper chain did not pick Holland for its All-America team, reportedly for fear that southern papers would refuse to print his picture, but the *New York Daily News* did, making him the first black All-American since Paul Robeson.[99] Holland won All-America honors again in 1938, but despite his qualifications never played in the NFL owing to an existing "gentlemen's agreement" against signing blacks. No campus recruiter would offer him a job or even interview him, despite his membership in both the junior and senior honor societies.[100] Instead, Holland earned his Ph.D. at Penn and became a college president. In 1970, President Richard Nixon named him Ambassador to Sweden, a post he held for two years until he resigned to become the first African-American director of the New York Stock Exchange. Ronald Reagan awarded Holland the Presidential Medal of Freedom posthumously in 1985. His son, Joe, followed his father to Ithaca, was named an academic All-American in 1977, and is still the Ivy League record holder for carries per game.

When Red Blaik took over as Dartmouth's coach in 1934, fans in Hanover were less concerned with national rankings than with the more elusive goal of beating Yale, something the Indians had never done in seventeen meetings over a fifty-two year period. They had tried almost everything, including carrying lucky rabbits' feet in their pockets for the 1931 contest (a 33-33 tie), and the streak had come to wear heavily on some fans, especially President Hopkins. "If and when we beat Yale," he wrote privately, "our crowd can not only tear down the goal posts but can lug off a portion of the Bowl so far as I am concerned."[101]

They had come close, losing three games from 1932 and 1934 by a total of twelve points. One spectator at the 1934 game was author Gertrude Stein, who attended as a guest of publisher Alfred Harcourt, a Dartmouth alumnus, before being hounded out of the Bowl by autograph seekers. "We did see them playing football," Stein recounted in one of her autobiographies, "not very well it must be said not very well."[102]

In 1935, Dartmouth went to New Haven undefeated. For all the burden of history pressing down on them, cocky was a better word to describe their attitude. Their band marched into the Bowl playing "Who's Afraid of the Big, Bad Wolf," while at halftime students in warpaint pretended to tomahawk another student impersonating the jinx.

The Indians finally laid the curse to rest, 14-6, on a pair of touchdown passes from Frank "Pop" Nairne to Carl Ray. On this afternoon, at least, the Dartmouth crowd fully earned their reputation as wild men from the North. Several times, officials had to stop play in order to clean up empty liquor bottles that had been thrown onto the field. Exuberant fans began to spill onto the field with five minutes left to play, and with three minutes remaining started in on the goal posts. Both players and officials tried to wave the masses back, but without success. "Three plays before the close it was difficult to see the teams, for the crowd was now edging over the end lines and milling onto the field," the *Herald-Tribune* noted. There was no goal post riot "because there were no goal posts left to battle over." [103]

Dartmouth enjoyed less success but even more excitement three weeks later when they met undefeated Princeton in a game remembered for one of the oddest plays in football history.

Morning flurries had turned into a freak fall blizzard, turning the field at Palmer Stadium into a morass of snow and mud. John Handrahan scored first for Dartmouth, but Princeton fought back behind the running of Ken Sandbach and by the start of the fourth quarter led, 20-6, gaining huge chunks of yardage on the ground. After each big Princeton gain, Dartmouth defensive back Jack Kenny would bellow across the line for the Tigers to "Come on through here again!" After a while that prompted his teammate, tackle Dave Camerer, to turn on Kenny. "Dammit, Jack," he said, "don't forget the sons of bitches are coming through me before they get to you!" [104]

In the fourth quarter, the Tigers took another march down to the Dartmouth two-yard line. Although what happened next was captured on newsreel films, it remained a mystery to almost everyone in the stadium. Just as the teams lined up, a man jumped out of the stands and took his place in the Dartmouth defensive backfield. When the ball was snapped, he rushed into a gap and threw himself in front of the Princeton ball carrier, who was brought down short of the end zone. At this point, everyone seems to have noticed the intruder's appearance and he was grabbed by police and tossed out of the stadium.

Accounts of the game over the next few days scarcely made mention of the incident (Princeton went on to score and won, 26-6). However, sportswriters at the *New York Times* looking for a story began to speculate on the man's identity, or at least allegiance. "I don't think he was a college man," Camerer told them. "At least what he yelled was 'Kill *them* Princeton bastards.'" [105]

The following Tuesday, they thought they had their man when Mike Mesko, a hamburger flipper at a Rahway, New Jersey, diner, confessed that he was the elusive Twelfth Man. He had gone into the game, Mesko told reporters, because he "never did like them Princetons." [106] The press ate it up, dubbing Mesko the "Horatius of Dartmouth's Goal Line." A group of Dartmouth alumni offered to take him to New Haven the following weekend for the Princeton-Yale game as their guest. There were rumors that he would be awarded a mock Dartmouth football letter.

While Mesko was enjoying his fame, another man stepped forward to claim that he, in fact, had been the real Twelfth Man. George Larsen, a twenty-six-year-old architect from Cranford, New Jersey and a University of Cincinnati alum, said he had rushed onto the field "because Dartmouth was taking it on the chin and I always feel sorry for the underdog." [107] He had kept quiet for fear of losing his job, but he also had proof—the films showed the intruder has been wearing a short jacket with writing on it. Larsen produced a short coat covered with autographs, including his nickname, "Guzzie."

Mesko began to backtrack. "Maybe I went on the field and maybe I didn't. I don't remember," he said, just before he was to board the Yale Special at Grand Central Station (a memory loss the *Times* attributed to his "having been too lavish in quaffing bacchanalian nectar"). [108] Mesko confessed later that day and never made it to the game.

With the repeal of Prohibition in 1933, the lavish quaffing of bacchanalian nectar had become an even bigger problem at football games and was generally blamed for all manner of fan misconduct. To an extent remarkable today, fans and spectators seemed to drink to excess in the thirties. Two truckloads of empty liquor bottles were carted out of Palmer Stadium after the Princeton-Dartmouth game in 1936 and as many as five hundred bottles after the Williams and Rutgers games, which had drawn considerably smaller crowds. [109]

Typical of the general public outcry was a letter sent to President James Angell of Yale in the fall of 1936. "Last Saturday we attended the Yale-Dartmouth game," a woman wrote. "In all our twenty years of attending football games we have never seen such a vulgar, revolting spectacle as last Saturday, where girls were laid out flat on the seats and their drunken escorts not able to give them a helping hand. Young men fell down between the seats, when they tried to stand, and there they lay with legs and arms in the air .... Can nothing be done to stop this evil?" [110]

Drinking probably had much to do with the goal post riots, which were now commonplace. Just as in the Dartmouth-Yale game, crowds had surged onto the field during the fourth quarter of the Yale-Princeton game (a 38-7 Princeton triumph) and torn down both goal posts. Princeton players were forced to attempt their final extra point while officials tried to clear the field, then had to wade into a crowd of several hundred spectators in order to get their ball back.

In October 1936, Princeton President Harold Dodds took a decisive step by banning the consumption of alcohol at Palmer Stadium. "Indulgence in alcoholic beverages at football games has assumed proportions which seriously menace the future of the sport as an intercollegiate activity," Dodds declared in a message that was sent to all persons who had ordered tickets for the upcoming Princeton-Navy game.[111] To the surprise of many, even students greeted Dodds' ban with nearly unanimous approval. "We are proud of the fact that Princeton is willing to bear the thankless burden of the pioneer," declared the *Daily Princetonian*.[112]

The ban seemed to have a positive effect. Princeton authorities said the fifty-five thousand fans at the Navy game were well behaved and that they found only ten "dead soldiers" in the stands afterward. At halftime of the Yale game a few weeks later, a truck belonging to the *Princeton Tiger* drove across the field bearing a sign urging fans to "Drink Milk Instead."

Blaik's Indians kept right on going. When they finished 7-1-1 in 1936, Dartmouth students proclaimed them the first champions of the still mythical "Ivy League." Many writers promoted them for the Rose Bowl a year later, but university officials quashed the idea, a decision that cost them $90,000 they surely could have used. With midterms approaching, athletic director William McCarter declared, it was "not fair to the boys to extend the football season."[113] In 1938, they were ranked as high as fourth in the country in the Associated Press poll.

Halfback Bob MacLeod, nicknamed the "Wildfire Scot," led the offense. He played every minute of every Dartmouth game for three consecutive seasons, averaging six yards per carry. The Thursday before the Yale game in 1937, McLeod and eleven other Dartmouth players, five of them starters, contracted food poisoning. Although he lost eighteen pounds in three days, McLeod played anyway and returned an interception eighty-five yards for a touchdown in a 9-9 tie. During the winters, he also led the Indians to two league basketball championships.

Blaik called Harry "Heavenly" Gates the best blocking quarterback he had at Dartmouth. Certainly, he was the most unusual. Gates belonged to something called the Legion of God, a fundamentalist Christian organization otherwise known as the "Holy Ghost and Us" society. He quit the team without explanation before the start of practice in 1938 but two months later was seen peeking in at practice through a window in the field house. Gates asked if he could rejoin the team and that Saturday was in uniform against Yale. During the train ride home, however, he disappeared, showed up on campus several days later denouncing football as "Godless," and never played again.[114]

Columbia fans, meanwhile, watched their team slide farther and farther from their magical Rose Bowl season. Their only highlight was the emergence of tailback Sid Luckman, the first Ivy star in modern professional football. As a quarterback, Luckman led the Chicago Bears to four NFL championships in seven seasons on his way to the Hall of Fame.

Luckman grew up in Brooklyn, but was heavily recruited by forty colleges around the country. He wanted to go to Navy, and when the Midshipmen played the Lions in New York, accepted the Navy athletic director's invitation to meet Columbia coach Lou Little. "I had never met anyone in my life who had such a tremendous effect on me," Luckman later recalled. "There was something about him, his stature, his dress, and those pinched glasses like Roosevelt's. ...I felt my life and my destiny was to go to not only a school where I would play football, but a marvelous academic school." So much so that he chose Columbia even though it could not offer him a scholarship and he had to work his way through college at jobs ranging from babysitting to waiting tables to chauffeuring Mrs. Little.[115]

Luckman could run as well as pass, and once booted a seventy-two-yard punt. In his best game, he rallied the Lions from a twelve-point halftime deficit, throwing one touchdown and setting up another, to beat Army, 20-18. Unfortunately, he was all the Lions had, and they finished with losing records in two of his three varsity seasons.

Penn's Harvey Harman was another coach with a talent shortage. Anyone would have struggled under the Gates Plan, but Harman fought against it. After a miserable 2-4-1 season in 1933, rumors buzzed that Harman had gone behind the administration's back to recruit four star prep school players. The four, who came to be known as the "Destiny Backfield," led the Quakers to a surprising resurgence in 1936, when they finished the season ranked tenth in the country. Their most satisfying win was a 7-0 shutout against Princeton. In what was later called the "Stalingrad of Penn football," the Quakers stopped the Tigers five times inside the Penn ten-yard line, three times in the fourth quarter.

The next year, Harman and some wealthy boosters made plans to circumvent the late starting date for practice by holding summer workouts in Canada. The players recognized that Harman was trying to evade the rules, and with that sort of internal dissention, Penn collapsed. Divine retribution came in the form of a 0-0 tie against lowly Georgetown, when Ed Fielden's twenty-five-yard field goal with thirty seconds left was nullified because Penn had too many men on the field. Harman had sent a substitute out to argue with the referee that it was really third down. The university replaced him with George Munger, who would lead the Quakers to some of their best seasons after World War II.

College football in the late 1930s, if perhaps less popular than it had once been, nevertheless remained a huge source of entertainment for the sporting public, a continuing source or unease for college officials. The Yale Bowl, for example, still lacked such amenities as a time clock. When the Graybar Electric Company suggested installing a public address system, Yale's athletic director, Mac Farmer, turned them down. "Personally, I feel that loud speaking equipment detracts from the atmosphere of college sport, which we try so hard to maintain," he wrote.[116]

Technology, however, and what might be termed commercialism continued to creep in. Almost a dozen games a year could now be heard on the radio, featuring not only the Big Three but Penn, Cornell, and Dartmouth, as well. In

1932, the Eastern Intercollegiate Association, of which Harvard, Yale, Princeton, Penn, Brown, Columbia, and Dartmouth were members, had voted to take their games off the radio in order to boost attendance during the Depression. Under a storm of protest, much of it coming from far-flung alumni, Harvard athletic director Bill Bingham persuaded the association to let schools decide for themselves. Columbia, Harvard, and Yale immediately voted to broadcast their games, though still without charge or sponsorship.

For the 1936 season, though, Yale broke with precedent by selling the rights to six of its games to the Atlantic Refining Company for $20,000. "Civilization has come to Yale University," Ring Lardner wrote. "Yale insists on refinement, and oil is very refined." [117] Athletic officials warned broadcasters that they would not sell the rights to any sponsor that might bring ridicule upon the school.

Within days of Yale's announcement, Brown, Columbia, and Penn began lining up their own sponsorship deals. Nonetheless, Harvard and Princeton continued to resist the commercial aspects of the new world of broadcasting, although they remained willing to make the games available for free. Yale, in the meantime, made even better deals for itself, selling the rights to its 1937 home games for $30,000, followed by a two-year, $75,000 deal to broadcast all its games. Not that fans in the Bowl could enjoy them; Yale banned portable radios at games in 1939, declaring them a "nuisance." [118]

Conant and Dodds tried to resist the growing pressure on them to cash in by sending a letter to the presidents of CBS and NBC in which they offered to continue giving away their games if they could be broadcast without commercial sponsorship. The networks accepted, but such a plan was not financially sustainable. With gate receipts declining, money had to come from somewhere. Harvard's student council soon adopted a resolution calling on Conant to accept commercial sponsorship as a way to avoid large cuts in the athletic budget. In 1941, both schools succumbed, and Harvard sold its rights to the Yale game for $15,000.

In December 1938, spurred by another editorial in the *Daily Princetonian*, the athletic directors of six Ivy schools—Cornell, Dartmouth, Harvard, Penn, Princeton, and Yale—again took up the idea of a football conference, going so far as to draft a proposed constitution, which they then submitted to their presidents for approval. In substance, it was the Three Presidents' Agreement with a broader membership.

The principles of that agreement had now gained broader support. Cornell adopted its own version in 1937 and Dartmouth adhered to most of its terms as well. Under the Gates Plan, Penn now was also compatible. Only Columbia, which refused to accept it, and Brown, which was ignored, remained outside.

It is possible that a league might have been adopted then, but Harvard and Yale remained holdouts, preferring to keep membership in the Big Three closed. In a memorandum to President Seymour, Mac Farmer listed eight reasons against forming a league. Chief among them was his fear that "it would be assumed by the general public that all members of this league were conducting their football on an even basis, and interpreted as an indorsement of the practices which have been in effect at all the member colleges, which would not be the case." [119]

That was enough to sink the students' proposal, although the Big Three adopted their own revised agreement in 1939, which expanded their mutual policies on eligibility, financial aid, and recruiting. A formal Ivy League would have to wait until the end of World War II.

CHAPTER EIGHT

Medium-Time Football

If Hobey Baker was the typical Ivy football player of an earlier generation, a characteristic player on the eve of World War II might have been Alva Kelley, Cornell's star end and later the head coach at Brown. Kelley was an exceptional athlete who also graduated Phi Beta Kappa with a degree in engineering. Hardly a prep school product like Baker, Kelley was the son of a soft drink bottler and had to work his way through college. Years later, he recalled his schedule for a typical day:

6:00 A.M.	Awake, shower, dress, and hurry to work
7:00 A.M.	Set up tables for breakfast at Chi Phi House and eat on the fly
8:00 A.M.	Report for first class in engineering and go through the rest of the morning classes
Noon	Wait table at the Chi Phi House and grab lunch in the kitchen
1:30–4:30 P.M.	Laboratory periods
4:30–6:30 P.M.	Football practice
6:30–7:30 P.M.	Wait tables at Chi Phi House and eat dinner
7:30–8:30 P.M.	Try to take a nap
8:30 P.M.–1:00 A.M.	Study
1:30–6:00 A.M.	Sleep

Classes ran until noon on Saturdays and players were not excused for home games. Many times Kelley had to bolt from the lecture hall in order to get taped before kickoff.[1]

His teammate, tackle Nick Drahos, was, as one Cornell historian has put it, a "rugged individualist extraordinaire." The son of Czech immigrants, Drahos was enormous—six-foot-three and 215 pounds—but insisted later that he had played football only because it got him a scholarship. He also worked his way through college, cooking meals and stoking furnaces at the fraternity houses. During the summer he worked for the federal Soil Conservation Service and majored in wildlife and fish conservation.

A working-class team produced a perfect record for Cornell in 1939, including a 23-14 win over Ohio State, the Big Ten champions. The Buckeyes broke to a 14-0 first quarter lead before the Big Red climbed back on two touchdowns by 158-pound tailback Walter "Pop" Scholl. President Edmund Ezra Day declined a Rose Bowl invitation on their behalf, though they finished the season ranked fourth by the Associated Press, the highest year-end ranking ever attained by an Ivy school in the AP poll. [2]

Coach Carl Snavely lost almost no one to graduation, keeping expectations high for 1940. They seemed to be justified, as the Red won their first six games, four of them by shutout. When the AP rankings were released on November 4, 1940, Cornell was the number one team in the United States, a rank they held for four consecutive weeks.

The Big Red saw little to concern them as they took their eighteen-game winning streak to Hanover. Dartmouth was sliding through a disappointing season, Red Blaik's last, and Cornell's eyes were turned ahead toward their traditional end of the year matchup with Penn the following week. Only eight thousand people even bothered to show up at Memorial Stadium. Blaik, who feared he had primed his men too hard for Cornell the year before, a 35-6 defeat, tried a lighter touch this time, serenading them with jazz records in the locker room. The Indians were helped even more by the weather: a cold, misty rain that turned to snow later in the game and grounded Cornell's passing attack. The mighty Big Red spent the entire first half bottled up inside their own thirty-three-yard line.

Both teams slogged through a stalemate for more than three quarters before Dartmouth's Bob Krieger kicked a field goal with four and a half minutes to play. Facing a devastating upset, Cornell began to move, mixing passes from Scholl and Mort Landsberg until they had marched to the Indian six-yard line with less than a minute left.

On first down, Landsberg bucked into the line for two yards. On second down, Scholl carried for three more. Landsberg then dove for what looked like a touchdown, but he was ruled down just short of the goal line. Cornell captain Walt Matuszak called a timeout—one he didn't have—in order to stop the clock, willingly accepting the five-yard penalty for delay of game. That made it fourth and goal from the Dartmouth six.

A field goal would have tied the game but poets say Fortune favors the brave, so the Big Red decided to play for a win. Scholl looked to the end zone for

Bill Murphy, who had just come into the game, but his pass was batted away by Ray Hall. Under the rules at the time, an incomplete pass in the end zone on fourth down was a touchback, and so head linesman Joe McKenney took the ball and trotted out to the twenty-yard line, prepared to turn it over to Dartmouth. Matuszak ran after referee William H. "Red" Friessel, arguing that both teams had been offside on fourth down, nullifying the play and giving the Big Red one more chance. After the two consulted for a moment, Friessel took the ball from McKenney and returned it to the six-yard line.

Indian captain Lou Young screamed in protest but Friessel ordered him back to his position. There were six seconds left. On his second fourth down, Scholl threw another pass to Murphy, who caught this one in the corner of the end zone. Drahos added the extra point and Cornell ran off the field with an apparent 7-3 victory.

Dartmouth, which had lost four games already that year in the last minutes, was enraged. In the Cornell locker room, players argued over just what had happened. Only Drahos seemed willing to admit that his team had scored illegally. Blaik and President Hopkins drove Friessel to the train station, where the referee admitted that he might have made a mistake. Not knowing this, Day and Cornell athletic director James Lynah issued a statement. If after reviewing game films, the officials determined that the touchdown had come on fifth down, the score would stand as Dartmouth 3, Cornell 0.

But Asa Bushnell, head of the Eastern Football Association (and Friessel's boss) refused to accept the burden, pointing out that a game ended with the final whistle and that neither he nor the officials had any authority to change the score afterward, no matter how grievous the error. Any action would have to be taken by the schools themselves.

It was Monday morning before Snavely and his assistant, Bob Kane, could review the films in a tiny office underneath Schoellkopf Field. After running the reel a few times, the coach turned off the projector. "No question," he said, "it was a fifth down."

In Pittsburgh, Friessel was doing the same thing. He then wired Bushnell. "I am now convinced beyond shadow of doubt that I was in error in allowing Cornell possession of the ball for the play on which they scored.... This mistake was entirely mine as the game's referee, and not shared in or contributed to by any of the three other officials." Friessel also had the grace to wire Dartmouth's captain. "Lou, I am so sorry, for you were such a grand captain and leader." [3]

Day and Snavely agreed that Cornell should refuse the victory, although Day predicted that Dartmouth would decline the offer. "In view of the conclusions reached by the officials that the Cornell touchdown was scored on a fifth down," Lynah wired his counterpart, William McCarter, "Cornell relinquishes claim to the victory and extends congratulations to Dartmouth." McCarter immediately wired back. "Dartmouth accepts the victory and your congratulations and salutes the Cornell team, the honorable and honored opponent of her longest unbroken football rivalry."

Thus, Cornell voluntarily surrendered the victory, their winning streak, and a chance at the national championship. There was some grumbling in the Big Red locker room until Matuszak quelled dissent by speaking in favor of the decision. Snavely, for one, took the reversal in remarkably good spirits, telling a campus rally that it was the first game he had ever lost through arbitration.[4] Nonetheless, bookmakers refused to pay off on Dartmouth, which had been a 15-1 underdog on some boards.

Hanover exploded with parades and bonfires, but in defeat Cornell won much more in the eyes of the sporting public. Newspapers around the country lauded their noble gesture and Day received a blizzard of letters, almost all supportive. "I want to congratulate you on the fine sportsmanship of Cornell re the now famous Dartmouth game," one alumnus wrote. "I hope the Rome and Berlin papers will cover the story. There is a great need for similar fair play in those towns."[5] Even Norman Thomas, Socialist candidate for president, who happened to be in Ithaca on a campaign swing, told a cheering crowd that Cornell's decision had given him renewed confidence in America.[6]

Credit was also due to Friessel, who forthrightly admitted his mistake. Bushnell sent him a probably unappreciated telegram of encouragement: "Don't let this get you down ... down ... down ... down ... down." A week later, Friessel was refereeing a game at Sing Sing prison when one of the inmates approached him. "We all make mistakes," the convict said. "That's why we're up here."[7]

Both teams, though, still had another game to play. The Indians followed their upset by rolling over Brown, 20-6, but Cornell's season continued to fall apart. They were ambushed in Philadelphia, where Francis X. Reagan, Penn's All-America tailback, scored three touchdowns (despite losing two teeth) to give the Quakers a 22-20 come-from-behind victory. "Our hearts weren't there, just weren't there," Kelley remembered later.[8] When the AP released its final poll of the season, Cornell had fallen out of the top ten.

Harvard's 5-2-1 record in 1941 was good enough to spark talk of invitations to both the Rose and Sugar Bowls. Endicott "Chub" Peabody, their unlikely leader, was an All-America guard and future governor of Massachusetts. Few cities revere lineage more than Boston, and few in Boston had a longer lineage than Peabody. His grandfather had founded the Groton School and corresponded with Theodore Roosevelt about the problems facing college football two generations earlier. Dubbed the "Babyface Assassin" for his crushing blocks, Chub had his own respect for tradition. When Coach Harlow put the team up in a Cambridge hotel the night before the 1941 Yale game, he was given special permission to sleep in his own bed, where he would be more comfortable.

Peabody's antithesis, in practically every way two men can be different, was attending Columbia. Jack Kerouac was a highly recruited wingback from Lowell, Massachusetts, who showed up on Morningside Heights in the fall of 1940 with his ne'er-do-well father, Leo, along for the ride in the back seat.

Both father and son had trouble getting along with Lou Little from the beginning. Kerouac sparkled in his first freshman game, returning a punt ninety yards with what he called his "jack-off" style of running. On the next punt, however, he fractured his leg. The Columbia trainer diagnosed it as a sprain and Little accused Kerouac of malingering, ordering him to practice all week before x-rays proved the truth. He spent the rest of the fall at a campus restaurant, gorging himself on steak, ice cream, and Thomas Wolfe novels.[9]

Kerouac might have gotten a second chance the following fall, but when he showed up a day late for the start of practice, he was back in Little's doghouse. The coach continued to ride his mercurial wingback in front of the team when Kerouac was slow to pick up Columbia's trademark trick play, the KF-79. "As if I'd joined football for 'deception' for God's sake," Kerouac moaned.[10]

He quit the team a week before the Army game, joined both the Marine Corps and the Coast Guard on the same afternoon before signing on with the merchant marine the next day and shipping out on the S.S. *Dorchester*.[11] Deception may have started to look better with German submarines trailing them, for during lulls aboard his ship (which would be sunk on its next voyage), Kerouac practiced the KF-79.

When he returned to New York in October 1942, there was a telegram waiting from Little inviting him to rejoin the team. Rosters were thin during wartime and the coach was in no position to turn away headstrong writers who could return punts. Unfortunately, Kerouac still couldn't make the KF-79 work, so Little demoted him to second string. With another big Army game approaching, Leo Kerouac did his part to make matters worse by haranguing the coach that he had reneged on a promise to find Leo a job as a condition of Jack's return. The Cadets waxed the Lions, 34-6, but Kerouac did not play a single down.

The following Monday afternoon, Kerouac lay in his room listening to classical music when it came time to leave for practice. He looked out the window at dreary Harlem. It was cold. It was snowing. The choice seemed easy. "Scrimmage my ass," Kerouac later told a friend, describing the afternoon on which he said he decided to become a writer. "I'm gonna sit in this room and dig Beethoven, I'm gonna write noble words."[12] That was the end of Jack Kerouac's football career, and after the withdrawal of his scholarship, of his college education, as well.

Signs of transition were abundant in the months before Pearl Harbor. After sixty-nine years of playing football, Yale hired its first nonalumnus coach in 1941, Emerson "Spike" Nelson, a graduate of the University of Iowa. That same fall, Princeton fans who had sat on the east side of Palmer Stadium since it was built in 1914 abruptly switched to the shadier west stands, leaving the visitors henceforward to squint into the afternoon sun. "The home crowd at Tigertown is always the majority, and since when have minorities been pampered in a democracy?" the *New York Times* wanted to know.[13]

A much more significant change that fall was the NCAA's decision to relax the substitution rule in order to compensate for the many young men who had already enlisted in military service. The measure was supposed to be temporary, but like all temporary measures proved much more difficult to repeal than it had been to enact.

A liberal substitution rule meant that players need no longer play both ways, that teams could develop (as they soon did) separate squads to play offense and defense. A few years later, while coaching at Army, Red Blaik named these units "platoons" and so the term "platooning" entered the American athletic lexicon.[14] Two-platoon football was another nail in the Ivy coffin, as indeed it was for most small schools, because they now had to find twenty-two skilled players instead of just eleven. The Ivies continued to produce talented players, but their era of producing nationally ranked teams was coming to an end.

With players now shuttling in and out, someone had to direct traffic. Thus, free substitution also brought the end of the old rule against coaching from the sidelines, erasing the last vestiges of the student-run game. Although the rule was widely subverted, sideline coaching had long been scorned as poor sportsmanship under the sound theory that saw coaches as teachers, practices as lectures, and games as examinations—opportunities for players to demonstrate what they had learned rather than simply execute orders. As late as 1940, Ohio State's charge that Carl Snavely had called plays by shifting his rolled-up scorecard from one hand to the other provoked an angry flurry of letters from Cornell officials.

Three hundred and fifty colleges dropped football during the war, but the Ivy schools tried to keep playing. Short of manpower, the Big Three permitted freshmen to play on the varsity for the first time since 1906. Columbia's quarterback Paul Governalli (whom Kerouac might have replaced, had he stayed) was runner-up for the Heisman Trophy in 1942, but it clearly was not the same game. Because of gas rationing and restrictions on travel, only twenty-six thousand people showed up for the Harvard-Yale game, the smallest crowd of the twentieth century. A year later, the big Princeton-Yale game drew just 13,000 fans.

The Big Three played a normal schedule in 1942, but in early 1943 concluded that the maintenance of "athletics as usual" was no longer feasible. Each of the three colleges was left to decide its own course. Harvard dropped intercollegiate football altogether and fielded only an "informal" team whose opponents were drawn from nearby colleges. That did not include Yale, thus interrupting their rivalry for the duration. The Bulldogs played a full schedule throughout the war, while Princeton held on until 1944, when it too fielded only an informal team.

With so many regular students enlisted in the armed forces, campuses were swelled with outsiders such as enrollees in the Navy's V-12 officer training program, who at Princeton came to outnumber regular undergraduates by almost two-to-one. (During the war, Old Nassau awarded its first diploma to an African-American, a V-12 trainee.) More than three-quarters of the players for Princeton and Penn in 1943 were either sailors or Marines. Dartmouth that year used V-12 trainees from sixteen colleges to help post a 6-1 record.

The war also brought about a quirky scrambling of allegiances. Penn's captain Ralph "Cleo" Calcagni, for example, helped beat Cornell in 1943, was sent to Ithaca on a military assignment, and lined up for the Big Red against the Quakers the following year. Wayne Johnson played for Harvard in 1942 and Yale in 1944, becoming the only player to earn a varsity football letter from both schools.

Buoyed in part by its success on the field, Cornell began to push for the creation of a football league, or at least its own inclusion in the Three Presidents Agreement. The Big Three politely declined, on the grounds that to do so would require them to open the club to others, as well. "I like the Harvard-Yale-Princeton Presidents' Agreement because it is personal and informal," Yale President Charles Seymour wrote privately to his counterparts. [15]

It was Seymour, though, who reopened the matter more than two years later. After a meeting of the Yale Board of Control just before Thanksgiving 1943, the president and a group of old Eli football men enjoyed a long dinner in which they discussed the future of Yale's program. To Seymour's surprise, no one wanted to go back to big-time, big-budget football after the war. Opinion was divided, though, as to what ought to be done instead. Some favored the development of a formal league while others, including Seymour, preferred to remain within the looser confederation of the Three Presidents Agreement.

Seymour latched on to a suggestion that the best way to forestall a league was to broaden the Three Presidents' Agreement to include "a few of our other natural rivals and friends." In a letter to Conant and Harold Dodds, Seymour proposed that Dartmouth, Columbia, and Brown be added to the group. [16] Conant liked the idea, but felt bad about omitting Cornell, "because of the institution's standing" and his own friendship with President Day. [17] Dodds wanted Penn added, too, brushing off insinuations that Penn's standards were too low. "We can find no difference in methods between this institution and at least one other on the list," he wrote to Seymour, "except perhaps that they have been more successful." [18]

Princeton joined Seymour's plan without much enthusiasm, however. "I wish the three of us could go it alone," Dodds wrote to him in the winter of 1943, "but it would not work and from other than the standpoint of convenience has little to recommend it." [19] The following spring, Seymour, Conant, and Dodds met to draw up a new agreement, borrowed liberally from the Three Presidents' Agreement, which they would ask other colleges to join. [20]

While the presidents planned, they were being undercut by their own athletic directors, who held their own annual meetings and were drawing up the bylaws for a formal league, which they intended to submit to the presidents for approval. Further complicating matters, the athletic directors (minus Brown, as always) had invited representatives from Army and Navy to join their discussions, forming something they called the "nonagonal group." Compatible with the Ivies in their academic standards and having developed long football rivalries with most of them, there was a good argument to be made for including the service academies. The presidents opposed them, however, on the grounds that Army and Navy were committed, for political reasons, to playing a national schedule and once the war ended would field better teams than the others could hope to match. [21] Army and Navy were quietly dropped from consideration.

If the service academies were out, it was still not clear that Brown was in, a point alumni of that college read with alarm. The nonagonal group did not include them because of concerns that Brown could not schedule enough games with the other members, a polite way of saying that Penn, Cornell, and Navy regarded the Bears as a weak box-office draw. [22] In December 1944, the Brown Club of Providence called on President Henry Wriston to do what he could to secure Brown's inclusion in any Ivy League that might be formed. [23] Although Brown appears to have been on Seymour's list from the beginning, some held to the belief that it was added to provide the Big Three with another vote against creating a formal league. [24]

The eight presidents finally met at the University Club in New York on November 15, 1944, where they argued late over a dinner of oysters, chicken, potatoes, and ice cream, but could not reach agreement. Ernest Martin Hopkins again found himself in the position of being the lone voice in favor of re-emphasizing football, the last disciple of Theodore Roosevelt. "I believe quite definitely," the Dartmouth president insisted, "that in a generation like ours where nothing in the way of physical hazard, to say nothing of physical effort, is demanded under ordinary circumstances, the physical contact games have a definite merit and that up to the limit of permanent injury it is advantageous to a man to have some knowledge of the fact even of what physical pain is. I have never been one who wanted to see games played gently.... Life just isn't made that way." [25]

With his exception, though (and Hopkins was retiring), all the presidents hoped to prevent a return to big-time football—expensive, attention-diverting football—as had happened after World War I. They simply disagreed on how best to achieve that end. After more than a decade of depression and war, everyone was cash-strapped. Cornell's athletic department found itself weighed down under an accrued debt of more than $72,000 by the end of the decade, while Harvard's $60,000 athletic deficit in 1948 forced the abandonment of several junior varsity teams.

To proponents, a league was the way to cut costs by providing a schedule of philosophically compatible opponents as well as a way to ensure that their own

interests were represented in a broader group. Dartmouth and Cornell, in particular, were suspicious of continued hegemony by the Big Three, which, as Day
noted, were "not given to making concessions to their sister institutions of lesser
status and prestige." [26] Hopkins held out hope that Dodds, at least, might be lured
away from Seymour and Conant, observing acidly that "the Big Three is actually
the Big Two with Princeton left to take what is left over in any of the arrangements.
The Princeton alumni, however, I do not think have ever fully appreciated their
position in the whole matter." [27]

The Big Three, on the other hand (with Princeton's place secure), were convinced that a league would re-emphasize football and marry them to a group of
colleges about whose commitment to amateurism they still had doubts. "My chief
objection to the League," one former Yale player explained, "is that you will be in
the minority (that is, Yale, Princeton and Harvard will be) so that eventually the
majority will knock Yale, Princeton and Harvard down to their level; and the
majority will not be brought up to the level of Yale, Princeton and Harvard." [28]

Unlike their predecessors, these Big Three presidents did not talk of setting
a national example. Their aim was not to shape modern football but to escape
from it. In background and temperament, this was a different group of men from
those who had made the first Big Three agreement in 1906. Dodds, for example,
was not a Princeton alumnus. Seymour had gone to Yale, but found himself
bogged down with universitywide budget troubles that made an expensive football program unthinkable. Conant was a Harvard alumnus, though of the distinctly non-Brahmin variety, a chemist by training for whom "contests of muscu-
lar skill ranked low on his list of priorities." [29] Hopkins, for one, considered him
effete, writing to Day that Conant "had graduated in three years with no more real
knowledge in regard to what constituted normal undergraduate concerns at
Harvard than as though he had gone to [MIT]." [30]

Underlying the question of whether or not to create a formal league was the
more important one of who would oversee any such grouping. Cornell and Penn
favored "a minimal code of standards without an effective enforcement mecha-
nism, an eligibility committee of athletics directors without presidential or faculty
oversight, and the establishment of a competitive league." [31] The Big Three, on the
other hand, believed any affiliation would be futile without the presidents' personal participation. "I know that if the HYP agreement had been concluded by the
athletic directors, speaking in the name of the university, my own interest and
activity would have been far less," Dodds acknowledged. "It was the fact that it
was a Presidents Agreement that made me feel that my own honor was involved
and not that of an anonymous athletic council." [32]

The eight remained deadlocked, four in favor of a "hard and fast league"
(Columbia, Cornell, Dartmouth, and Penn) and four opposed (Harvard,
Princeton, Yale, and Brown). During the spring of 1945, Day drafted a new plan
that incorporated most of the proposals the nonagonal group had agreed to but

stopped short of establishing a league. The presidents pledged to support a common set of principles, chief of which was that all Ivy football players would be "truly representative of the student body and not composed of a group of special recruited and trained athletes." Eligibility decisions would be made by a joint faculty committee, while the athletic directors would head a committee on administration. Other thorny issues, such as whether to permit practice in the spring and when to start it in the fall, were deferred.

If the new plan was, as one reporter later dubbed it, a return to "medium time" football, it proved enough of a compromise to reconcile the two groups. As with all successful compromises, both sides believed they had gotten something of value. Though Hopkins grumbled that the agreement was "one for which I have no enthusiasm and in regard to whose stipulations I have only minor confidence," he nevertheless submitted it to his trustees for approval, arguing that "declination on our part along among the so-called Ivy League colleges to sign it would place us in an ambiguous position so far as public judgment is concerned and would give the ungodly too good a chance to scoff for me to be willing to accept the alternative." [33] Yale was confident the agreement could be a vehicle for exporting its own standards of amateurism to Cornell and Penn.

On November 20, 1945, the presidents publicly announced what they called simply the "Intercollegiate Agreement." Although there was no requirement that any of the signatories play each other, the agreement was significant as the first formal affiliation of any kind among the eight colleges in football. By the end of the decade, Harvard athletic director Bill Bingham could declare, "The Big Three no longer exists." [34]

In 1946, Dartmouth became the first to play all seven of its Ivy sisters in the same season, but final membership in that club remained an open question in the minds of some. Cornell was approached that fall by Michigan State (which had not yet joined the Big Ten) with a proposal that the two join Penn State and Syracuse in forming their own football conference. [35] A group of small colleges, led by Washington University in St. Louis, sounded out Harvard and Yale about establishing two affiliated Ivy Leagues, one in the east and another in the midwest. [36]

These proposals went nowhere but did serve to highlight the fact that the presidents had not created an Ivy League. At the Big Three's insistence, that term was never used in the Intercollegiate Agreement. Much as Seymour had anticipated, however, in the public's eye the new association was an Ivy league in fact, if not in name. As columnist Arthur Daley observed, the colleges "produced the baby, but they haven't christened him." [37]

The war ended a few weeks before the 1945 season was to start. Princeton had already decided to return to action, but Harvard was forced to scramble in order to field a team with which to take on Yale. New Haven hotel rooms were booked weeks in advance of the teams' first postwar meeting as students briefly imitated their fathers' enthusiasm, singing the old songs at torchlit pep rallies. That evening, more than a thousand undergraduates and their dates danced to the music of Eddie Wittstein's orchestra at Payne Whitney gym.

Yet everyone knew it was not the same. "There was no evidence of the old do-or-die spirit," one Yale football historian observed.[38] The student body at colleges around the country was an odd mix of green freshmen and jaded servicemen, usually several years older. At Yale and Harvard, Thomas Bergin records, "the influx signified the end of the gracious living in the colleges and houses; dormitories were forced to accommodate twice the numbers they were built for, the elegant dining halls became cafeterias, with self-service and trays replacing the civilized service of old."[39] In 1947, almost two hundred Harvard freshmen were forced to sleep on cots in the gymnasium because the university had no room for them. Freshman classes at Cornell were delayed until barracks could be transported to Ithaca from Sampson Air Force Base.

Among the first returning veterans was Dartmouth's cocaptain, Meryll Scott, who had been severely burned when his plane was shot down over Italy. Although he had been hospitalized for eighteen months, during which he required numerous skin grafts to restore his face, Scott managed to score two touchdowns for the Indians against Penn in 1945 and earned a standing ovation from the crowd at Franklin Field when he was removed from the game.

Crusty Dick Harlow, an old school man if ever there was one, returned from service overseas in ill health and found he could not communicate with the new breed of student. "Most were combat veterans," Harvard's football historian writes, "many had been wounded and some had been prisoners of war. They wanted no part of the old 'rah rah' spirit."[40] Harlow resigned after the 1947 season.

Coaches who could accommodate returning veterans, on the other hand, thrived, few as well as George Munger, who produced some of the best teams in the country. Penn had led the entire nation in attendance from 1938 through 1942, the first five years of his tenure. The quiet, professorial Munger, who was only thirty-five when the war ended, had enough confidence in his players that he let the captains pick the starting lineup each week. Those players, who became known as "Munger Men," responded with devotion. As Jack Welsh, one of his stars, recalled, "George could tell you, 'Hey, you know, I think you ought to go through that wall, maybe head first. It's only two feet thick,' and you'd almost say, 'I think you're right, George.'"[41]

Tactically, Munger's teams played aggressive defense in which members of the secondary were taught to play the ball rather than the receiver, leading to a large number of interceptions. In 1940, Welsh himself picked off four passes in a game against Princeton and nine for the season, both of which are still Quaker records. Penn's postwar teams were built around returning servicemen. These included three All-Americans: tackle George Savitsky, running back Tony "Skip"

Minisi; and center Chuck Bednarik. Savitsky had suffered a severe head injury in the Marine Corps and wore a special helmet with foam padding. Minisi had come to the Quakers twice. Admitted to the Naval Academy out of high school, he had to sit out a year because he was too young and in the interim enrolled in Penn's Wharton School, where he also played football as a freshman in 1944. A year later, he transferred to Annapolis and played for the Midshipmen against Penn, scoring the winning touchdown. Minisi then quit the Naval Academy after fourteen months and returned to Philadelphia.

Bednarik became known as "Concrete Charlie" although he came from the Pennsylvania steel country. By the age of twenty, he had already flown thirty bombing missions over Germany. On one mission, Bednarik's plane crashed after being hit by enemy fire. He escaped the burning wreckage by kicking out a window and jumping twenty feet to the ground.

When Bednarik's high school coach called to recommend him, Munger almost turned him away. "I don't need him," Munger is reported to have said. "I've got five centers." [42] Only one of them would win the Maxwell Award as the nation's best college player, as Bednarik did in 1948. When *Sports Illustrated* selected its collegiate team of the century, Bednarik, the third-team center, was the only Ivy League player named. [43] He went on to a Hall of Fame career in the NFL with the Philadelphia Eagles.

In 1945, the Quakers finished the season ranked eighth in the country. By the end of October the following season, their first with the full veteran complement, they were ranked as high as third and had rolled over their first four opponents, averaging more than forty-four points per game. Princeton came to Franklin Field with a much more modest 2-2 record. Each time the heavily favored Quakers scored, the Tigers matched them. With only a minute and a half to play, Princeton's Ken Keuffel, in as a replacement, kicked a twenty-nine-yard field goal to give the Tigers what the *New York Times* called "an almost unbelievable upset." [44]

Penn's only other loss that season was a 34-7 pounding by Army, the third year in a row the Quakers had been run over by the Cadets. They sought revenge a year later but had to settle for a 7-7 tie when Minisi was tripped and deprived of a sure touchdown on a sloppy field. Nevertheless, the Quakers finished seventh in the country.

With the exception of Penn, the world of big-time college football was one in which the Ivy colleges no longer cared to compete. In 1948, for example, Cornell declined an invitation to play Notre Dame that had been passed along by New York's Francis Cardinal Spellman. "An effort to make room for any play with Notre Dame has seemed to the members of the Board to involve more of a load than Cornell can wisely assume for the present," President Day wrote in reply. [45]

Ivy teams could still, however, play the role of spoiler—none so well in the early postwar years as Columbia. Lou Little's teams had managed a winning record in only two of the ten years since 1934. In 1943, they finished 0-8, becoming the first Ivy team in more than half a century to lose every game they played.

A year later, they revived, stocked with a group of transfer students, including fullback Ventan Yablonski, from crosstown Fordham and receiver Bill Swiacki, from Holy Cross. Halfback Lou Kusserow also had enrolled at Columbia for a year in order to gain math credits necessary to matriculate at West Point, but decided he preferred the smaller school.

New York took to a winner. These were the days of Columbia's Taxi Cab alumni, which counted among its members baseball star Joe DiMaggio, comedian Milton Berle, and restauranteur Toots Shor. Membership was open to anyone who was not actually an alumnus and who professed undying loyalty to Lou Little, whose celebrity was captured in one delightfully apocryphal story. Two Columbia players were waiting outside the coach's open office door one afternoon when they heard his phone ring. Little answered and called out in his raspy voice, "God Almighty! How are you?"

"Holy smokes," one of the players gasped. "It's true!" [46]

The loyalists' faith was tested when Army marched in to Baker Field on October 25, 1947, carrying a thirty-two-game winning streak. The Lions, who were only 2-2, were decided underdogs, especially for those who remembered the 48-14 pounding they had suffered at the hands of the Cadets the year before. It looked as though another rout was unfolding when the Cadets broke to a 14-0 lead in the first quarter, but quarterback Gene Rossides completed two long passes to Swiacki, leading to a touchdown by Kusserow, the first points that had been scored on Army all season. Kusserow almost ran for another touchdown late in the second quarter, only to have it nullified because an official had stopped the clock to give the coaches the two-minute warning.

Army held a 20-7 lead at halftime, but the Cadets spent the intermission griping about the officiating while Blaik tried to keep them focused on the game. Beneath the opposite stands, the Columbia locker room was quiet. "We felt they weren't any better than we were," Yablonski recalled. "We really thought we could beat Army." [47]

Columbia outplayed their opponents in the third quarter but could not score. Early in the final period, as Army's defense poured in, Rossides just had time to heave a fifty-three yard pass into the end zone, where Swiacki made a diving, full extension catch that pulled the Lions to within six points. When the Lions got the ball back, it took their recharged offense only a minute and a half to march sixty-six yards. In order to stop Rossides' passes, Army had shifted an extra man into the backfield, but the alert quarterback took advantage by mixing in running plays before hitting Swiacki again on a twenty-six yard pass to the Army three-yard line. Kusserow ran for the go-ahead touchdown, then sealed the upset by intercepting an Army pass, after which the Columbia line staged a ball-hogging six-minute drive to eat up the clock.

The Lions won the rest of their game and finished their season ranked twentieth in the country. Little, who had twice turned down generous offers to coach in the NFL, was tempted that winter when Yale offered him the job of athletic director, but Dwight Eisenhower, the new Columbia president, persuaded him to stay and build on his success. Sadly, however, it was then back to losing for the Lions, who lost to the Cadets the next two times they played them by a combined score of 97-6.

College officials may have been successful in quelling the anticipated riot of overemphasis on the gridiron, but they had considerably less success controlling their new students off it. The combination of overcrowded dormitories, older students, and access to automobiles proved a volatile mix. Postwar pranks took on a more violent nature, and like the goal post riots of a generation earlier, football enthusiasm was usually only a pretext.

Penn tried to ban pep rallies in 1946 after a "rowbottom" the night before the Dartmouth game in which a policeman was injured and several thousand raucous students snarled traffic for an hour. A month later, a group of Princeton students tore through the Penn campus, painting "P's" on dormitory and class building walls and pouring a gallon of orange paint on the statue of Benjamin Franklin in the main quadrangle. Anticipating retaliation, squads of Princeton students helped proctors patrol the campus the next night, while the university radio station, WPRU, coordinated the defense over the airwaves.

Philadelphia police warned Penn officials to expect trouble that Saturday afternoon and were ready when hordes of Princeton students stormed the Franklin Field goal posts after the Tigers' upset victory. Patrolmen, "determined to save $15 worth of lumber at the risk of life and limb," as the *Princeton Alumni Weekly* put it, clubbed anyone within reach. Thirty mounted police surrounded the field to cut off escape, dodging soda bottles thrown at them from the stands. Two policemen and a Princeton student had to be taken to the hospital, while four people were arrested. Outside Houston Hall, the Princeton band was set upon by a gang of Penn students.

Both schools exchanged formal apologies. "Our traditional friendly relations with Princeton University on the field of sport are worth far more to us than a pair of goal posts or the turf of the entire football gridiron," J. Roy Carroll, Jr., president of the Penn Alumni Society, wrote in an open letter to Princeton alumni.[48] Yet two weeks later, with Army coming to town, three hundred policemen and two fire companies were called out to quell another Penn rally in which students overturned two automobiles and set fires on the trolley tracks.

That was hardly the last of it. The Tuesday before the Yale-Princeton game, a group of Princeton students with some military training drove to New Haven and used a flame-thrower to burn a fifty-foot "P" in the sod of the Yale Bowl. Although the Princeton student council quickly sent a note to President

Seymour "deploring" the conduct of their classmates, they were not quick enough to stop a gang of Yale students who descended on the Princeton campus the following night.

Exhibiting a better strategic sense than the Penn students had, the Yalies first gained entry to the WPRU studios on the pretext of requesting a song. Once inside, they barricaded the door, tied up the student announcers and broadcast "Boola Boola" and derogatory comments about Princeton. Within minutes, a "horde of aroused undergraduates" rushed to the defense, forcing the invaders to flee, but other Eli commandos arranged a large "Y" in the middle of the Palmer Stadium field with shards of the goal posts and smeared blue paint on the tiger statue in Palmer Square. [49]

Each year seemed to bring a fresh crop of outrages, some at least redeemed by a bit of Ivy League wit. In 1947, Columbia students flew a blimp over New Haven, raining down five thousand leaflets that urged the "hungry and bewildered Bulldog" to disregard his leaders' "empty promises of victory" and promised "safe conduct" for any who crossed enemy lines to surrender before the game. Columbia students posted lookouts in the chapel bell tower the next night to keep watch during the Lions' pep rally.

A much less inventive group of Brown students, displaying unwonted cockiness, raided Cambridge in 1948 to decorate the front of Widener Library and burn the now customary letter at midfield. Unlike almost all the other student vandals, these unlucky few were suspended. "We urge that all Brown men take heed of the punishment meted out in this instance," the student paper moralized, "and yet exhort them to even new heights of spirit rechanneled into humorous but harmless outlets ... not to mention lusty songs and cheers." [50]

A different verdict was pronounced by Princeton's dean, Francis R. H. Godolphin, after Quaker raiders defaced their rival campus in 1947 and were caught by police following an eighty-mile-an-hour car chase. "I don't mind the painting of the tigers and the cannon," he said, "but this business of being waked up at 3:30 and 5:30 every morning is getting on my nerves." [51]

A more salutary consequence of the war was a broadening of the student body. At the turn of the century, for example, more than a third of Yale's undergraduates came from the state of Connecticut. By 1951, that was down to one-fifth, with a corresponding increase in the percentage of students from the South, Southwest, and Pacific Coast. [52] Newer immigrant groups from Eastern and Southern Europe were represented in greater numbers, thanks in part to the SAT (one of James Bryant Conant's projects), which was first administered in 1943. Yale teams after the war included players named Barzilauskas, Prchlik, Jablonski, Nadherny, and Pivcevich. George Munger's great Quaker teams featured All-American players from at least eight ethnic backgrounds.

A broadening of the student body coincided with, and contributed to, a toughening of the curriculum, which further reduced the amount of devotion students could give to football. For Princeton students near the turn of the century, "real study was almost altogether optional"; at Yale, undergraduates required only an hour a night to prepare for all their classes.[53] The postwar undergraduate's schedule more and more began to resemble Al Kelley's, a daily juggling act.

The popular stereotype of the collegiate football player, which had evolved over the years from thug to blond-haired god, shifted again after the war as the new stereotype of the hulking, square-head with a multisyllabic surname emerged. On Ivy campuses, at least, the prep school WASPs of yore turned increasingly to other sports.

Joe Paterno, who was raised in Brooklyn and entered Brown in 1946 after a brief stint in the Army, was one who felt the strain of the new social order. He was recruited by Everett "Busy" Arnold, a comic book publisher, who offered to help pay Paterno's way to attend Brown (a form of assistance that became illegal when the Bears signed the Presidents' Agreement). College Hill seemed an alien place, not least to the Paterno family's parish priests, who denounced sending the boy to a non-Catholic school.

Coach Rip Engle started him in the defensive secondary, where he returned fourteen interceptions during his career for 290 yards, both still Brown records. Asked to return punts, as well, Paterno proceeded to lead the team in runback yardage, including a game against Princeton in which he returned four punts and four kickoffs for 146 yards. For his last two seasons, Paterno was the Bears' quarterback, leading them to an 8-1 record in his senior year. In his final game, against Colgate, Paterno engineered three touchdowns in the last four minutes of a 41-26 victory. When Engle left Brown for Penn State the next season, Paterno went with him as an assistant, and was later the highly successful head coach of the Nittany Lions.

Being an athlete helped ease Paterno's introduction to college, but he never forgot the feeling of insecurity when he attended his first fraternity party, an experience he shared with many other new arrivals at Ivy campuses. "At home, if I ever felt I was better than another kid, it was because I could play better or think better—not because I was better," he wrote. "This time I caught a whiff of people who put themselves in a higher echelon for starters, without a contest. I soon understood, but never learned to accept, that in those days a typical Brownie instinctively needed to sniff out who your family was and how rich you were."[54] The experience gave him, he said, a sense of how black people felt when they walked into a crowd of whites and the room fell silent.

Race had never been an important issue in Ivy football, if only because there had only been a handful of black players. Those who had played—Matt Bullock, Fritz Pollard, and others—had been accepted, if not always warmly, by teammates, opponents, and fans. The chance of racial problems grew, though, as the Ivy colleges began playing intersectional games against southern colleges, even more so when they began to play those games on the road. There had been some concern in 1941, for instance, whether Cornell would use two of its black players, Samuel Pierce (later secretary of Housing and Urban Development) and Cliff Robinson in a game against Navy at Baltimore, but the midshipmen voiced no objection.

In 1947, Harvard's Chester Pierce became the first African-American to compete against a white college in the South when the Crimson traveled to Charlottesville to play the University of Virginia. A few weeks before the game, a Virginia athletic official called Bill Bingham to suggest that Pierce not make the trip, lest there be any disturbances in the stands. To his credit, Bingham made it clear that either the whole Harvard team went or no one went. A few Harvard players, including captain Kenny O'Donnell, later an aide to President John F. Kennedy, wrote to the Virginia players reiterating that Pierce was a member of the team and would play. The Cavaliers, many of whom came from the Northeast anyway, unanimously voted their agreement.

If the Virginia players were not a problem, the Virginia citizenry was. When a Charlottesville hotel manager insisted on lodging Pierce in a black hotel, Harlow moved the rest of the team there, as well. When a local restaurant owner made Pierce use the rear door, the entire Harvard team followed. When the Crimson entered the stadium on Saturday afternoon, Harlow ran in next to Pierce, staying on the side closest to the stands so that any debris thrown might hit him instead. Despite catcalls from the bleachers, the game passed without incident except that Harvard absorbed its worst defeat in twelve years, losing 47-0.

Levi Jackson, the first black player in Yale's football history, also became the first black captain of an Ivy League team in 1948. The great-grandson of slaves, Jackson had gone to high school in New Haven, where his father had worked for a time as a butler to Frank Butterworth, Bulldog football hero in the 1890s. He joined the Army and played on a service team during the war, declining collegiate scholarship offers as well as a pro contract from the New York Giants. Instead, the G.I. Bill enabled him to attend Yale, paying $500 of his $600 tuition. He was one of only three African-Americans among more than eighty-five hundred undergraduates.

Public reaction to Jackson's election as captain, which was reported on the front page several national newspapers, was overwhelmingly favorable. "In honoring Jackson they honored themselves and they honored Yale," the *New York Times* editorialized.[55] The white press lionized him in its clumsy way, with nicknames like "the Ebony Express." New Haven took to him as the first townie to captain the Bulldogs since Albie Booth.

Jackson himself was perfect for the role of racial pioneer, saying all the right things, insisting that he would not turn pro because he didn't like to play football for money, and letting it slip that his boyhood hero had been Clint Frank. When he was tapped for Skull and Bones, as was traditional for Yale football captains, Jackson slyly alluded to that secret society's lingering anti-Semitism by noting that if his first and last names had been reversed, he would not have been admitted. [56] Already married and living off-campus, he turned them down.

Anyone who objected to Jackson's presence was quieted by his coach. Herman Hickman hailed from Chattanooga and had been an All-America tackle at the University of Tennessee and an assistant coach to Red Blaik at Army. At five-foot-ten and more than three hundred pounds, he was practically square and affected a sly, Smoky Mountain wit, remarking one year that the Bulldogs would probably lose just enough games to keep the alumni "sullen but not mutinous." To another audience, he advocated a "three platoon" system: "One platoon for offense, one for defense, and one to go to class." [57]

For all the good-ol'-boy routine, Hickman had completed high school when he was only sixteen, and loved Kipling and Edgar Lee Masters. He pursued several outside interests (too many, some grumbled, noticing his propensity to forget players' names), including his own radio show (the first Ivy coach to have one) and a spot on a TV quiz program. Still the transition from West Point to Yale was difficult. His first year in New Haven, Hickman nicknamed his slight offensive line the "Seven Dwarfs." (Jackson promptly dubbed himself "Snow White.") "Somewhere in the world God must have made a couple of tackles, six-feet-four, 230 pounds, who had enough intelligence to attend Yale, and they were agile, mobile, and hostile," Hickman liked to moan. [58]

Yet he embraced Bulldog traditions, keeping a bust of Walter Camp in his front hallway (which he would salute after victories with, "Hey, Walter, we win another!"), and even boarding Handsome Dan, the team mascot. A man sensitive to the poetry of a moment, Hickman was overcome before his first Harvard game in 1948. Standing in the tunnel with Jackson and his teammates before the kickoff, he stared silently at the green turf and gray columns of Harvard Stadium. Suddenly he began reciting, from memory, Spartacus' oration to his gladiators: "O comrades! Warriors! Thracians! If we must fight, let us fight for ourselves!... If we must die, let it be under the clear sky, by the bright waters, in noble, honorable battle!"

Spartacus lost, of course, and so did the Elis, 20-7. There was only so much that inspiration could do. [59] Hickman left Yale after five seasons to become a commentator for NBC, one of the first coaches in any sport to leave the sideline for the broadcast booth.

Cornell was another school that had difficulty adjusting to the postwar world. No one was hit harder than Carl Snavely, who lost his only son in the South Pacific in 1943. He moved back to North Carolina after the 1945 season (one in which his quarterback, Al Dekdebrun, was named All-American) and was succeeded by Ed McKeever, the interim wartime coach at Notre Dame during Frank Leahy's absence. Cornell's boosters wanted a big-name coach for a big-time program, but McKeever proved a disastrous fit for a smaller school with a different attitude.

For one thing, McKeever was an old-fashioned coach, and it was difficult to play drill sergeant to men who had been real sergeants just a few months earlier. When McKeever tried to lure many of his old Fighting Irish stars to transfer (because of the wartime disruptions, the rule requiring transfer students to sit out a year was suspended), he was dismayed to find they couldn't get into Cornell. "Don't they want a football team here?" he griped. "I can't believe this place. I had some of the best guys in the country all set to come." [60]

Unlike Hickman, McKeever was unwilling to play by the Ivy rules. A few weeks before the end of the 1946 season, Bob Kane, now athletic director, learned from an alumnus that certain Big Red boosters had been paying players under the table, with the coach's knowledge. President Day decided immediately to buy out the rest of McKeever's contract, but to let him resign at the end of the season rather than make a stink in the press.

The defrocked coach stood on the sidelines as Cornell beat Dartmouth, even though his assistant, George "Lefty" James, a Snavely disciple, was the one actually calling the plays. McKeever let the cat out of the bag before the Penn game, prompting a flurry of excitement as angry alumni threatened Kane while a group of sullen players were reportedly ready to jump McKeever after the final whistle because of all the abuse he had given them. [61] Not surprisingly, the Big Red lost, 26-20.

James brought the soft-spoken, more approachable manner that seemed to define all successful Ivy coaches in the early postwar years. He eschewed pep talks, saying of his players, "I want them loose and relaxed. That's when you give your best efforts." He was also more typical of the modern Ivy coach, a professor of physical education, as well. McKeever had taught Cornell the T formation that most big-time teams played in the forties, but James combined it with the power blocking techniques of the old single wing to produce an offense he called the "scrambled T." He coached the Big Red for fourteen years.

After a slow first year, James's tactics (combined with many of McKeever's leftover players) began to show results. The Big Red went 8-1 in 1948, led by halfback Hillary Chollet, in the opinion of some the greatest all-around athlete Cornell has ever produced.

As a prep school star in New Orleans, Chollet was assiduously recruited by both Louisiana State and Tulane. When Chollet chose Tulane, someone leaked to the newspapers that LSU had not wanted him anyway because he had Negro blood. The Chollets were Cajun, but because of the rumors the family was shunned socially and even made to feel unwelcome in their church. Tulane quietly suggested that Chollet might find it difficult to go there. Fortunately, a Tulane booster knew that Chollet hoped to study medicine and recommended Cornell, and so the entire Chollet family left New Orleans for upstate New York. Arriving in Ithaca after the season had begun, Chollet did not see any action until the Yale game when he dropped a sure touchdown pass in the end zone on his first offensive play.

That inauspicious debut notwithstanding, he soon became a starter and, in the winter, led the basketball team in scoring. An ankle injury forced Chollet to sit out the entire 1947 season, but he was back in uniform to lead the Big Red renaissance in 1948. Given another chance against Yale, he personally amassed 242 yards in total offense in the following manner: 54 yards rushing, 45 yards receiving, 57 returning a pair of interceptions, 31 returning two punts, and 55 returning the opening kickoff.

Halfback Frank Bradley was another returning serviceman who played a key role in the Cornell offense, but he had broken his jaw against Colgate and was not expected to be available for the expected showdown against Dartmouth. A few days before the game, a Cornell alumnus, who also happened to be vice president of the National Cash Register Company, called James and offered to fashion a steel facemask for Bradley to wear for protection. Thus outfitted, Bradley took a pitchout the first time he entered the game and ran eighty yards for a touchdown, almost collapsing in the end zone because he could barely breath with his jaw wired shut.

That put Cornell ahead for the moment, but Dartmouth led, 26-14, as the teams entered the fourth quarter. The Big Red closed the gap, then got a break when Joe Quinn forced a Dartmouth fumble. Quarterback Pete Dorset, a former bomber pilot and prisoner of war, connected on several passes while substitute fullback Bob Dean not only scored the tying touchdown but added the extra point that gave Cornell a 27-26 victory. A week later, the Big Red beat Penn for the first time in nine years.

Although an ankle injury forced Chollet to miss much of the 1949 season (another 8-1 finish in which the team was ranked as high as sixth in the country), Grantland Rice still named him a second-team All-America halfback, behind Heisman Trophy winner Doak Walker. Chollet became a doctor after all, founding a chain of cancer treatment clinics until he was diagnosed with Lou Gehrig's disease. Still fighting, he learned to use a word processor with his toes, but died on Christmas Eve 1989.

On November 12, 1949, W. Thacher Longstreth, a junior advertising executive for *Life* magazine, attended the Princeton-Yale game at Palmer Stadium, a 21-13 Princeton victory. The following week, he returned to see the Tigers defeat Dartmouth. Longstreth attended all nine Princeton games the next year, and then all nine games the year after that. By the end of the 2000 season, he had not missed a Princeton varsity football game, home or away, in more than half a century, a streak of 461 games.

If Longstreth was perhaps the most extreme example of the fanatical football alumnus, he was by no means the only one. For years, Dartmouth's Les Godwin used to rent a room in a Hanover hotel each summer to watch preseason practice. Judge Amos Blandin, chief justice of the New Hampshire Supreme

Court, was so much a fixture at Dartmouth practices from 1951 until the early eighties that players used to assume that if he was not at practice, it had been canceled. Al Ostermann snuck into the Yale Bowl for the first game ever played there in 1914 and attended more than 522 Eli home games thereafter, missing only a blowout of Alfred College in 1930. His fondest boyhood memory was meeting Walter Camp, who gave him a football.[62]

None, though, quite compares with Longstreth. As an end for the Tigers in the late thirties and early forties, he had made honorable mention All-American despite eyesight so poor he could not see balls thrown to him downfield. A primitive pair of contact lenses, which had to be inserted and removed using tiny suction cups, only partially alleviated the problem. In a game against Navy, Longstreth took an end-around and hurled a deep pass to his halfback, not seeing that the man had tripped at the line of scrimmage. His loyalty was unshaken despite being kicked off the team late in his senior year for having broken training by taking the first—and only—drink of his life. As a member of the undergraduate honor committee, the conscience-stricken Longstreth turned himself in to Coach Tad Weiman, who took an inflexible view of the rules and asked him to turn in his uniform.

Fanaticism can only partially explain a man who invited his entire senior class to his wedding (more than a hundred attended) or who insisted that his own daughter change her wedding date because it conflicted with the Yale game. Neither bad weather, bad teams, nor the waning days of two unsuccessful campaigns for mayor of Philadelphia kept Longstreth from his seat among the Tiger faithful.[63] When the new Princeton Stadium was built in 1998, Longstreth donated the visitors' locker room. To his disappointment, the university rejected his suggested inscription for the plaque that honors him: "Abandon hope all ye who enter here."

CHAPTER NINE

The Ivy League

During the hot summer of 1948, Philadelphia played host to three major party presidential conventions. The Republicans met first, and although New York's Thomas E. Dewey walked away with the nomination, his rival, former Minnesota governor Harold E. Stassen, stayed behind for a consolation prize of sorts. A few weeks after the convention, he was offered the presidency of the University of Pennsylvania.

A lumbering six-footer with thinning hair and a bland, toothy smile, Stassen still looked like the midwestern farmboy he had once been. He had become the darling of Republican liberals during the primaries that spring and although he had no experience as an educator, he did bring a most impressive resume for a man who was only forty years old. Elected to the first of three terms as governor when he was thirty, Stassen had also served as chief of staff to Admiral William "Bull" Halsey in the South Pacific and helped write the United Nations charter, accomplishments that earned him the nickname "Young Man Going Places." The place Stassen most wanted to go was the White House, but with that avenue closed for the time being, academia seemed a good spot in which to wait.

In addition to the publicity his selection brought, Stassen also possessed one political talent the university badly needed. He was an accomplished fund-raiser and Penn, having set out on another ambitious capital campaign after the war, was short of cash. It was also still saddled with an outstanding mortgage of more than $1.6 million on Franklin Field, as well as an accumulated deficit of $200,000 from minor sports that could not pay for themselves. The new president recognized his football team's potential as a cash cow and set out to milk it.

Stassen's lack of an academic background caused many of his presidential colleagues to view him with suspicion. He had few eastern connections, let alone Ivy ties. Where men such as Conant and Dodds were scientists or administrators by training, Stassen was a lawyer and a politician—just the sort of man, many of them must have thought, that an upstart place like Penn would pick for its president. He was, in short, an outsider in a very clubby world.

Dwight Eisenhower, another outsider (albeit one with far greater celebrity), had taken care to ingratiate himself with the Ivy presidents when he had taken over at Columbia. In his first months in office, he sent each a letter assuring them that he was "in complete accord with all the provisions and regulations" of the Intercollegiate Agreement.[1] Stassen, on the other hand, seemed oblivious to matters of diplomacy.

He was a product of the University of Minnesota and brought with him a Big Ten faith that good academics and successful football teams need not be mutually exclusive. He openly rooted for the Quakers, visited them at training, attended practices, and threw out the first ball at their home opener. (He also integrated the team, clearing the way in 1950 for Edward Bell and Robert Evans to become the first black players to wear a Penn uniform.) Shortly after taking office, Stassen scheduled a game with mighty Notre Dame for the 1952 season, despite an unwritten Ivy prohibition against playing the Irish, whom they considered the epitome of a big-time program. That Penn's highly successful football team slacked off during the first two years of Stassen's tenure, to a 5-3 record in 1948 and 4-4 in 1949, did little to allay fears around the Ivies.

Despite the Quakers' mediocre record, they had feasted on their Ivy opponents. As a result, neither Harvard nor Yale had played them since the war, rankling the ancient insecurities of Penn alumni about their college's place among the elite. Shortly after the end of the 1949 season, Stassen went on a speaking trip to New England, where he also hoped to persuade Harvard officials to put Penn back on the Crimson football schedule. Before Stassen could ask, Harvard athletic director Bill Bingham doused the idea. "We can't compete with their state scholarships," he said in an interview with the Associated Press.[2]

The reference must have been obscure to most readers. Although Penn was not a state institution, under Pennsylvania law each of the fifty state senators could nominate three high school students a year for a scholarship to the university. Stassen tried to explain that Penn did not decide whom to put up for the scholarships and that a nomination did not guarantee admission. In fact, only a dozen of the 558 Penn students who received these senatorial scholarships played football, and only seven of the scholarships—barely one percent of the total—went to lettermen.

Bingham would have been on firmer ground had he broadened his criticism. As one study of Quaker football at this time has shown, Penn and Cornell awarded more scholarships of all kinds to football players, and for a greater average dollar amount, than either Harvard or Princeton, a figure that reflected the socioeconomic background of Penn football players.[3] Three-quarters of the members of the Princeton team were public school graduates by the early fifties, and received scholarships at twice the rate of the undergraduate body as a whole.[4] Penn, which recruited less successfully from the top prep schools anyway, would have had a higher percentage of public school boys on its football team, and hence a higher percentage of scholarship recipients.

Yet Stassen did not make these arguments, boasting instead about revising afternoon class schedules at the Wharton Business School that made it difficult for athletes to attend practice.[5] Penn also continued to find jobs for needy players and the school's admissions standards did appear to be among the most lenient in the Ivies, as evidenced by one Quaker letterman who received a scholarship despite scoring in only the eighth percentile on the SAT.[6]

When Paul Buck, Harvard's provost, apologized to Stassen for Bingham's impolitic remarks, the Penn president took advantage of the opening to propose that the two schools schedule a football game for a particular Saturday in 1952. Buck was politely noncommittal but Stassen took his answer as an acceptance and directed his athletic director, H. Jamison Swarts, to clear the date. Informed that the Quakers had already scheduled a game against Columbia for that date, Stassen told Swarts to break the engagement, which the embarrassed athletic director did, much to the dismay of Penn's New York alumni. But when Swarts then tried to nail things down with Cambridge, he learned that Harvard regarded a 1952 contest as much more of a theoretical proposition than did Penn. Swarts was forced to go back to Columbia and ask to be put back on the schedule.[7]

As the Notre Dame contest suggested, Stassen intended to upgrade Penn's football profile. He needed to—with mediocre records, attendance at Franklin Field had dropped from an average of seventy thousand in 1946 to just over fifty-five thousand in 1949. The following August, just before the start of the 1950 football season, Stassen fired Swarts, who had many friends around the league (this in spite of being colossally boring; behind his back, he was called "the collegiate Coolidge"). Stassen replaced him with Francis T. "Franny" Murray, a brash radio sportscaster, promoter, and former Quaker star from the controversial "Destiny Backfield." Where Swarts had been getting by on $8,500 a year, Murray was handed a five-year contract at $20,000 a year. Murray was also to head a new department of intercollegiate athletics that, in a reversal of the Gates Plan, would again be separate from the department of physical education—a troublesome indicator of Stassen's intentions. One of Murray's first acts was to jazz up the marching band, quickening their steps and adding drum majorettes, just the sort of Big Ten-itis many puritans around the league had their eyes open for.

At the press conference called to announce the switch, Stassen outlined what he called the "Seven Commandments" that would henceforward govern Quaker football. For the most part they were bromides dressed up in corny biblical syntax: "Thou shalt not take unfair advantage of thy opponents by improperly recruiting athletes contrary to the rules," was a representative example.

Stassen's sixth commandment was the most innocuous but caused the greatest trouble. "The goal of the player and of the team," the president declared, "shall be victory, but only if it can be won with honor. Defeat shall be accepted cheerfully and good sportsmanship shall characterize thy conduct in victory or defeat."

That euphonious slogan, "Victory with Honor," instantly came to characterize Penn football. The "victory" part was obvious, but many on other Ivy campuses had their doubts about the "honor." Stassen gave them further cause for doubt when he went on to assert that Penn could produce winning teams by skirting the edges of the rules.

In its own effort to curb football abuses, the NCAA had in 1948 adopted what became known as the "Sanity Code." It was strict by national standards but lax compared to the Ivy agreements, permitting athletic scholarships and the like. The first time the NCAA tried to enforce it by expelling several schools, their own members voted them down. After that, most observers, and certainly the Ivy presidents, considered the Sanity Code a dead letter.

Yet Stassen announced that this would provide the mark against which Penn would measure itself. "We are going to take full advantage of the [NCAA] code in order to bring top athletes to Penn," he told a press conference. "We can live up to the [NCAA] Code without bending over backwards to follow it.... Moving with ingenuity and resourcefulness...we can have great teams at Penn in football and other sports."[8]

The press scorned the seven commandments as hucksterism. Penn managed to finish only 6-3 in 1950, with lopsided victories over three of the four Ivy rivals on its schedule, as well as Navy and Wisconsin. But when it came time to draw up the 1953 schedule that winter, Columbia, Dartmouth, and Princeton all informed Murray that they would no longer play the Quakers. Left with only Cornell, Murray was forced to look elsewhere for opponents, although the details of that 1953 schedule remained a secret for the time being even from Munger.

It was obvious to everyone at Penn that the other Ivy schools were staging a boycott, in the grand old Ivy tradition. In keeping with another tradition, it remained a whispering campaign until a sportswriter finally broke the story on January 15, 1951. The following day, Stassen suggested publicly that Penn was being snubbed because it had scheduled the Fighting Irish. "I do not believe in boycotting Notre Dame or any other American college team whether they are weak or strong, North or South, East or West," the president declared to the press.[9]

Some suspected Stassen was using the opportunity to ingratiate himself with Roman Catholics around the country, but from the standpoint of Penn's relations with the other Ivy colleges his statement was politically foolish. Columbia and others rushed to affirm their high respect for Notre Dame and everything it stood for, all the while seething at Stassen for having held them out as elitists. When Stassen added that Penn would "never drop a team from its schedule because the team has beaten Penn consistently," he made Harvard and Yale out to be sore losers, as well.[10]

Stassen tried to climb out of the hole he had dug, writing an imploring letter to Princeton's Harold Dodds. "I come to you for counsel and advice as a personal friend and as the President of a great University with which Pennsylvania has had a long tradition of relationships," he wrote. "If there is anything which either Pennsylvania or I have said or done which has offended the other Universities, I respectfully apologize personally and officially."[11] Dodds denied knowing anything about a boycott, explaining Princeton's decision to drop Penn as part of its policy of periodically rotating opponents—the same excuse Harvard had given twenty-five years earlier for snubbing Princeton.[12]

Although Penn was in the midst of another identity crisis (the alumni magazine went so far as to poll its readership on the desirability of changing the school's name to Franklin University, to end its age-old confusion in the public mind with Penn State), the feelings of Quaker alumni broadly mirrored those of their president. They wanted to belong to the Ivy League, but with freedom to play a more ambitious schedule, as well. In early 1953, the *Pennsylvania Gazette* polled twelve hundred alumni on which teams the Quakers ought to play on a regular basis. The two leading vote getters were Cornell (named by 95 percent) and Princeton (named by 94 percent). Two faux Ivy rivals, Navy and Army, followed, named by 93 and 92 percent, respectively. From there, it was a long drop down to Yale (62 percent), Columbia (60 percent), Penn State (57 percent), and Dartmouth (51 percent). Only 36 percent named Harvard as a team they would like Penn to play, just ahead of Notre Dame and Michigan. Brown came in near the bottom, at 8 percent.[13]

In another attempt to repair the damage, Stassen wrote again to Dodds in March proposing that the eight Ivy presidents meet to begin a "reappraisal" of intercollegiate athletics. The presidents, many of whom wanted to create a formal league, agreed, and met in New York on April 3, 1951, for the first time since they signed the Intercollegiate Agreement. They undertook a complete overhaul of the 1945 agreement and promised to meet again in December. Little did Stassen anticipate that before the group would reconvene, Penn's membership not only in the Ivy League, but in the NCAA itself, would be cast into doubt.

The issue was television. In the fall of 1938, technicians from the Philco Company conducted an experiment, taking their new cameras to a Penn football game and beaming the pictures to their laboratory across town. There were only six television sets in Philadelphia at the time, all of them at Philco and all presumably tuned to the game, thus giving it, if one wants to look at it that way, the highest rating of any sporting event ever.[14]

Their experiment was such a success that two years later, Philco beamed Penn's 51-0 whipping of the University of Maryland to some seven hundred sets in the Philadelphia area, making it the first publicly broadcast football game. Although the technology was still jerry-rigged—cameras perched atop the Franklin Field stands provided the pictures while sound had to be piped in from the radio broadcast—because there were more television sets in Philadelphia than in almost any other city in the country, Penn was ideally situated to take advantage of the new medium. "In the emerging world of televised sports," one historian has written, "Pennsylvania was a pioneer without peer." [15] The Quakers quickly announced that they would televise their entire slate of home games.

Broadcasts continued throughout the war. When Stassen took over, he recognized the revenue potential, not to mention the fund-raising and publicity potential, that Penn could tap by televising its football games, particularly at a time when stadium attendance was falling. Here was a good way to plug the athletic department's deficit. In 1950, Penn sold the TV rights to its games to the American Broadcasting Company for $150,000, a figure Murray thought he could double in 1951.

Not everyone had a contract with ABC, however, and many of the schools that did not blamed television for their losses at the box office. The NCAA was their vehicle for doing something about it. In 1949, the NCAA hired a New York research firm to study TV's effects on game attendance in four northeastern cities. When that study proved inconclusive, delegates to the NCAA's annual convention in 1950 voted to undertake another study, this one by the National Opinion Research Center, a nonprofit research group.

The research center's report also was inconclusive, but it found enough of a link between television and gate receipts to convince most NCAA delegates, very few of whose schools were yet getting much TV exposure, that something had to be done. Egging them on was Fritz Crisler, now Michigan's athletic director, who had a ninety-seven thousand-seat stadium to fill. Fearful that Notre Dame would dominate midwestern airwaves, Crisler persuaded the Big Ten to ban all television broadcasts of its games, then urged the rest of the NCAA to follow. At the association's next convention in Dallas, the delegates voted 161-7, with forty-five abstentions, to prohibit any live TV broadcast of college football games during the 1951 season. Although their names were not mentioned, it was clear who the targets of the resolution were. "We had to act to keep Penn and Notre Dame from being on every week," a University of Alabama official explained. "That would have been so damaging to college football." [16]

Murray phoned Stassen from Dallas to ask for instructions and was told to fight. "I am not a lawyer," Murray declared on the convention floor, "but there is serious doubt in my mind about the legality of this." [17]

No sooner had the NCAA voted to ban television than public outcry forced it to retreat. The NCAA's television committee instead approved a program to allow one national broadcast each week. No school could appear more than twice (once at home and once on the road) and the NCAA, not the schools, would negotiate the network contract and divide the proceeds. Any college that tried to defy the ban would be declared "a member not in good standing" and could be expelled from the NCAA altogether.[18]

For several months, Penn argued against the decision in NCAA meetings without success. Finally, on June 6, 1951, Murray notified NCAA President Dr. Hugh C. Willett that Pennsylvania would not comply with the television ban. To punctuate the point, he also announced a few days later that the Quakers had signed a new $200,000 contract with ABC to broadcast all eight of its home games in 1951 and would split the revenue with its opponents. True to its plan, the NCAA immediately announced that Penn was no longer a member in good standing. The Quakers would go to war.

Stassen and Murray quickly discovered that none of their Ivy brethren wanted to be in the foxhole with them. Being a member not in good standing was a public relations black eye, but only that. There was no legal prohibition against playing such a college, if one did not mind the stigma attached. Within days, Army, Navy, William and Mary, and Wisconsin all announced that they would honor their commitments to play the Quakers that fall. But Dartmouth, Columbia, Cornell, and Princeton (which had already dropped Penn for the 1952 season) announced that they would cancel their scheduled games for 1951, as well. "We do not believe that any institution should capitalize an opportunity to go it alone during this experimental period," Dodds wrote to Stassen.[19]

Perhaps sensing a need to clean up the record, Stassen drafted a letter to Murray restating Penn's athletic policy and had it inserted into the trustees' minutes. It included a pledge that the "letter and the spirit of the codes of eligibility and conduct set forth by the Ivy Group presidents" as well as the ECAC and NCAA "should be adhered to at all times." He also stated that Penn "shall at all times endeavor to maintain the closest and most constant relationships, athletically as well as academically and scientifically, with the Ivy Group."[20]

Beyond that, Stassen did what he could to salvage relations. "We are extremely anxious, John, to maintain our relationship with Dartmouth and will go to almost any lengths to do so," he wrote to John Dickey.[21] The Dartmouth president, no doubt speaking for all of them, firmly informed Stassen that, although they "genuinely regret that the matter has reached the position it has," it was "not a 'trading position.'"[22]

If Stassen possessed any illusions about the reception he could expect around the league, he need have looked no further than the membership of the NCAA's TV committee. One of its three members was Ralph Furey, the Columbia athletic director, whom Stassen had crossed up in his botched attempt to schedule Harvard. In 1952, the committee was chaired by Ralph Hall of Yale and also included Princeton's Asa Bushnell, who went on to become the NCAA's television director until 1970. When Hall stepped down, he was succeeded by Bob Kane of Cornell. Not only had the Ivy League supported the NCAA's television policy, its members had practically drafted it.

Stassen also appears to have misunderstood the NCAA's stake in the battle. The NCAA had a bad track record as an enforcement agency. Having been rebuffed when it first tried to discipline colleges for violating the Sanity Code, it could not back down from another fight, especially one against a college as isolated as Penn now found itself. This time, the NCAA drew a line in the sand and intended to enforce it. Ironically, by presenting a united front in defense of the NCAA, the other Ivy colleges helped strengthen the power of an organization they had long viewed with distrust.

Nevertheless, Penn continued to keep up its public relations offensive against the ban. Speaking to a group of alumni, Stassen sounded like a man running for something. He denounced the NCAA's "central controlitis" and defended blanket television coverage by invoking the wounded servicemen at Philadelphia veterans hospitals, as well as the "thousands of shut-ins [who] follow the Red and Blue.... Boys clubs, Scouts, school play-ground groups, follow these wholesome sports with their great spirit over television." [23] Notre Dame's Father Theodore Hesburgh, however, a better politician than Stassen, let it be known that the Irish would accede to the NCAA despite its objections to the TV plan.

In no mood to trifle, the NCAA demanded that Penn change its mind by July 19 or be suspended, subject to formal expulsion at the next general meeting. This was a different matter. Quite apart from the damage to the school's reputation, if Penn became an intercollegiate pirate it would have a hard time finding anyone to play. It would also have a hard time interesting anyone in televising its games. Football revenues, on which the entire athletic department depended, would disappear.

As the deadline approached, Murray tried to maneuver by agreeing to comply in some respects but not in others. [24] Willett immediately wired back, demanding to know whether Penn agreed to "conduct its live broadcasting of 1951 football games in accordance with whatever arrangements may be approved by our television committee?" [25] Stassen and Murray mulled this over, and on July 19, the day of the NCAA's deadline, capitulated.

For 1952, the NCAA adopted an even more restrictive plan, limiting each school to only one TV appearance per season. Murray made a special plea to televise the Quakers' opener against Notre Dame, which would not affect attendance because the game was already sold out, but was told that only the NCAA could negotiate the contract. Penn dropped the request and did not appear on TV at all. Only two Ivy games were televised that year: Princeton at Columbia and Cornell at Yale.

Stassen was practical enough to recognize the financial effect the ban would have on Penn's finances. But he was also nothing if not a man unembarrassed at tilting at windmills, as his six future runs for the White House amply demonstrated. He considered the NCAA's ban an illegal restraint of trade and a violation of the Sherman Antitrust Act, an opinion buttressed, he claimed, by the opinion of the university's general counsel.

Early in 1952, a chastened but undeterred Penn tried another assault on the television policy, as Murray offered a resolution at the NCAA convention that the group ask the Attorney General to issue a formal opinion, known as a declaratory judgment, as to the legality of the NCAA's program. The delegates rejected the motion by a vote of 163-8. Undeterred, Stassen submitted the same proposal to the other Ivy presidents before the start of the season. If the program were upheld, he promised in a round-robin letter, Penn would acquiesce. "Do you see any objection to such a proceeding by Pennsylvania with the NCAA to obtain such a ruling?" Stassen asked. "Will our endeavor to ascertain the answer to this legal question with the NCAA affect our relationships with [your school] in any manner?" [26]

Most made clear that it would. "Princeton will not join you in any such action; and I do not believe that we need the help of the Sherman Act to solve our athletic problems," Harold Dodds shot back. [27] Grayson Kirk, then vice president (and later president) of Columbia, let it be known that "such a proceeding ... would not, in my judgment, be helpful in strengthening the spirit of solidarity among Ivy Group institutions which, I am sure, is our common goal." [28] Henry Wriston sounded encouragement but added, "I am afraid the whole business is somewhat theoretical, as far as Brown is concerned. No one would be interested in televising our games." [29]

In fact, there was broader support for Penn's position than was apparent. Some commentators, such as Shirley Povich of the *Washington Post*, called for a federal investigation of the NCAA. In coming years, Yale would decline to join the national television program, questioning its legality, and in 1954 Harvard, through its dean, McGeorge Bundy, refused the NCAA's offer of $30,000 to televise the Yale game. (Conant alone had called Stassen's declaratory judgment proposal "a logical one.") [30] Even Princeton was said to favor a more lenient policy. But they would not buck the NCAA and they would not help Pennsylvania.

Stassen may have been foolish, but he was not wrong. When the University of Oklahoma challenged the NCAA's television policy in 1984, the U.S. Supreme Court ruled that it did indeed violate the antitrust laws. But by then it was far too late for the Quakers.

When the eight Ivy presidents met again in December 1951, they looked back on one of the bleakest years in college sports history. Besides the showdown with Penn, ninety Army cadets, including most of the football team, had been expelled for cheating. William and Mary was found to have altered academic transcripts in order to keep athletes eligible. Several football games had been marred by a periodic upsurge in violence. Most shocking of all were revelations that basketball players at City College of New York and six other schools had shaved points at the instigation of gamblers. Against all this, the NCAA had been powerless, its new TV policy a rare exception.

Since signing the Intercollegiate Agreement in 1945, the Ivy group had done little. The presidents themselves had not met as a group for almost six years. Some schools, most notably Penn, Cornell, and Dartmouth, had also interpreted the agreement to provide more latitude in recruiting than purists thought acceptable. In a confidential memorandum to his trustees, Conant baldly stated that "in retrospect it was certainly a great error on Harvard's part to have entered this new so-called Ivy League arrangement, and particularly to have given up the proselyting clause." [31]

Conant's solution was to return to the tight collegiality of the Big Three, either as a counterweight to the other Ivies or, if need be, as an independent group. In the fall of 1950, he, Dodds, and President A. Whitney Griswold of Yale met secretly to formulate strict policies on recruiting and admissions practices that would at least insulate themselves against backsliding by the others. All were aware of the delicacy of their maneuvering. "Let's be sure of what we're doing," Dodds warned Griswold, "and let us be very careful that we are not caught red-handed selling the Ivy League down the river." [32]

It was not until almost a year later, just after the Penn imbroglio, that the "Joint Statement of Scholarship Policy by the presidents of Harvard, Yale and Princeton Universities" was published in booklet form. It condemned athletic scholarships in all forms and reiterated that only college officials could commit the college on either admission or financial aid. [33] Although the ostensible reason for printing the document was to distribute it to Big Three alumni, several of the other Ivy colleges saw it as an attempt to put public pressure on them.

Given Penn's intransigence and the general fragility of the alliance, it was far from certain, as the presidents' December 1951 meeting approached, whether the whole Ivy structure would simply fall apart like the old Intercollegiate Football Association. "I will lay you two to one that neither Pennsylvania nor Cornell will go along with us," Griswold predicted to Conant, "and I will give you even money that Dartmouth won't either. I think it is worth making a try for all of them... but I also come with profound feelings of futility for any true Ivy group solidarity that reaches beyond Harvard, Yale, Princeton, Columbia, and Brown." [34]

Instead the others did come around, recognizing perhaps that they could not afford to stand apart and fearing that the Big Three would cut them out. They appointed Conant and Dickey to redraft the Intercollegiate Agreement and later that winter adopted an eight-point code of amateurism that served as an unintended but unmistakable counterpoint to Stassen's seven commandments. In addition to tightening even further the eligibility, recruiting, and subsidization rules, they prohibited players and coaches from participating in postseason contests, shortened the season by setting a late date for the start of fall practice, and banned spring practice altogether.

Because it was an issue on which the Big Three themselves disagreed, spring practice proved to be the final snag. Yale had been the first to ban it, a unilateral decision that prompted eleven members of the board of athletic control to resign.[35] Conant praised Yale's act, while his football coach, Lloyd Jordan, called it a disaster. Cornell and Princeton promptly announced that they would continue spring practice, while Penn went so far as to extend it to six weeks.

Schools that favored spring practice defended it as essential both to competitiveness and to safety, citing studies that showed ill-prepared players were more likely to get hurt. They also argued that it would actually undermine reform by increasing pressure to recruit top athletes, who would need less training. The *Daily Princetonian* derided the ban as "little more than a clumsy attempt to gild the Ivy League's amateur lily."[36] To opponents, though, practice out of season was emblematic of overemphasis and incompatible with the ideal of a student-athlete.

Under the rules that governed Ivy presidents' meetings, six votes were needed for a motion to carry. With Princeton and Cornell strongly in favor of continuing spring practice, proponents of a ban found themselves one vote short. Incredibly, as low as Penn's standing was, it now found itself the crucial swing vote. His political experience at last coming to good use, Stassen recognized that he was in a position to demand a concession. In exchange for Penn's support for ending spring practice (a position his own athletic department vigorously opposed), the other Ivy colleges agreed to play the Quakers at least once every five years. "We had to decide whether we were going to be in the Ivy League," Stassen explained later. "It was a matter of going along with the others." When he submitted the agreement to Penn's board of trustees, the chairman congratulated him "on his effective leadership in reaching a highly satisfactory solution to a once difficult problem."[37] With a stroke, the Ivy boycott of Penn was lifted.

In July 1952, the presidents signed what they officially titled the "Ivy Group Agreement." Besides fleshing out the points they had agreed to in February, it created a Presidents' Policy Committee having "full and final responsibility for the determination of all agreed policies of the group" and committed the presidents to meet twice a year thereafter to provide direction for the new entity.[38] College presidents around the country hailed the announcement, though few expressed interest in imitating it.

The practical effects of the spring training ban did not become apparent for another year, however. Back when the other Ivy colleges had begun their boycott, Franny Murray had filled the open dates on Penn's 1953 schedule with three national powerhouses, Notre Dame, Ohio State, and Vanderbilt, to round out a slate that already included California, Penn State, Navy, Army, and Michigan—a big-time schedule for big-time revenues. ("What the hell was I supposed to do, play Swarthmore and Drexel?" Murray later barked. "We had a good football team.")[39] No one, however, had bothered to tell George Munger until a newspaper reporter broke the scoop a year and a half later. The coach bluntly told Stassen, "We can't play teams like that with our material." Stassen assured Munger that he would "have the horses." [40]

By the time the 1953 season rolled around, though, Stassen was gone, having left Penn for a post in the Eisenhower administration. Then the NCAA surprised everyone by adopting a resolution offered by former Princeton coach Tad Weiman to end two-platoon football, which many had come to criticize as too expensive. Starting that fall, players would once again have to play both ways.

Over time, such a rule should have helped the Ivy League by reducing the number of good players a college needed in order to field a successful team. Its immediate effect, however, was disastrous. Players who had played only, say, the offensive line the previous fall would now have to learn how to play the defensive line as well, and quickly. There would be a scant six months in which to do this. But by banning spring practice and limiting fall practice, the Ivy League had cut its teams' preparation time to just days.

No one felt the effects of this change more than Penn, which was now saddled with one of the toughest schedules ever assembled. The Quakers would have little enough chance of beating these teams under any circumstances, but none at all when their opponents would also have several extra months of practice in which the relearn the new game.

Penn players, who recognized this as well as anyone, met among themselves to discuss what to do. On March 4, 1953, they sent a joint letter to acting university president William H. DuBarry, fifty-eight members of the university trustees, and leading alumni, taking Murray to task for having assembled their schedule without consulting Munger. Although they expressed their belief that Penn should remain a part of the Ivy League, they complained that the university had set them up with a suicide schedule against teams "to which we are vastly inferior in conditioning and organization." [41] Finally, they pleaded for permission to hold spring practice, even if it meant allowing the players to organize it on their own.

Murray called the team together for what he called a "harmony dinner" but which was in fact a trip to the woodshed. Reading from a prepared speech, he first attacked Munger, and criticized the coach's suggestion that the schedule be lightened by canceling Vanderbilt, saying such a move would be "a cowardly act." Sounding like a tin dictator, Murray continued that "A coach has no more right to question my administration...than I have to question the presidents' undertaking." He called the players' petition "unfortunate" and suggested that they were quitters. "We're here to help you, to try to get you off the hook in the impression you made on the general public."

As soon as Murray sat down, Munger sprang to his feet. "That was an unfair and unjust attack on a fine bunch of college athletes," he leveled at Murray, in a rare show of anger. "The boys' courage shouldn't be questioned. 'Off the hook' could be applied more to our athletic authorities." [42]

News of the feud leaked to the press, as DuBarry tried to finesse the situation by announcing the he was appointing former U.S. Supreme Court Justice Owen J. Roberts to undertake "a searching study" of Penn's athletic policies. But without Stassen's backing, Murray's days were numbered. Two months later, Penn bought out the remaining two years of his contract, and eventually he went off to rejoin Stassen at the Office of Foreign Operations.

A week later, Munger and his entire staff submitted their resignations, unwilling to supervise a university-sponsored massacre. Responding to a letter of condolence from Lou Little, Munger laid out his views. "The present Ivy Agreement makes it impossible I think, to compete in football except among our-selves in the Ivy League and with smaller teams like Franklin and Marshall, Swarthmore, etc."[43] Only after much pleading did he agree to stay on for one more year, before moving upstairs to become director of intramural athletics.

With hat in hand, DuBarry then approached the other Ivy presidents with a request that a special exception be made to permit the Quakers to hold spring practice before the 1953 season; a necessity, he tried to explain, lest the boys get hurt.[44] If he anticipated a break, he got none. "The problem which you present faces all the Ivy Group Universities who play schools outside that League," Cornell's President Deane Malott lectured him in reply. "It happens to present a problem of particular force at Pennsylvania because of the very strenuous sched-ule you have undertaken."[45] The Quakers having made their bed, in others words, the rest of the league was happy to let them lie in it.

All things considered, the Quakers performed heroically that fall, defeating Vanderbilt, Penn State, and Navy, and coming close against Notre Dame, Ohio State, and Army. It was Munger's only losing season, but in light of their per-formance under such conditions, Penn football historian Dan Rottenberg suggests that the 1953 eleven can lay claim to the title of the Quakers' best ever.[46]

A year later, though, the bottom fell out. The Quakers lost every game they played in 1954 and again in 1955, their program decimated. When they finally snapped their twenty-four game winless streak against a mediocre Dartmouth team, fans sacked the Franklin Field goal posts.

Harvard was another Ivy college that televised its home football games in the late 1940s, but the athletic situation in Cambridge could not have been more differ-ent from that in Philadelphia.

The Crimson, who had gone 4-4 in their first campaign under coach Arthur Valpey in 1948, began the 1949 season on a disastrous note after Conant approved a cross-country road trip (their first since the 1920 Rose Bowl) to Stanford. Not only were the Crimson embarrassed, 44-0, several starters were injured playing with the wrong size cleats. They followed by falling to Columbia, Cornell, Army, and Dartmouth on their way to a 1-8 record. One local columnist pronounced Harvard the "champion of Middlesex County only because they did-n't meet Arlington High this season."[47]

Fingers were pointed all around. Many alumni criticized Valpey, most vocally former All-American Hamilton Fish, who insisted that the coach be fired "at all costs." [48] Others were aimed at Bingham, who in turn pointed them at the players, whom he accused of having poor spirit. The Crimson blamed the alumni for poor recruiting. Boston sportswriters blamed the administration, complaining that the school's insistence on student-athletes was "gradually smothering what remains of its football prestige." [49]

The solution, according to Bingham (who was nominally in charge of the whole mess), was retreat. A week after the 1949 season, he announced that Harvard would discontinue "big-time" football—which, of course, assumed that they had been playing big-time football. There would be no more intersectional games. "We are not going to compete with the West or the South," Bingham declared. "We are going to try to play in our own class. We are going to stick to the Ivy League." [50]

Even many among the Old Guard approved. "We want to win," the alumni magazine explained, "but if we are not so fortunate as to attain the victories which we feel important, we should at least lose gracefully." [51] Harvard undergraduates also deplored any subsidization of football. More than three-fifths favored restricting the schedule to Ivy opponents, although some favored giving up the sport entirely. As one wrote, "More harm can be done by producing poor teams than by eliminating athletics entirely." [52]

That winter, the administration did its own soul-searching. At the beginning of February 1950, Provost Paul Buck submitted a report to Conant, which became the blueprint for Harvard football for the rest of the decade. [53]

Buck presented four options. The first, and most radical, was to give up football altogether. More than four dozen colleges around the country had done just that, in one of the periodic surges of dropouts. Buck, however, quickly dismissed the option, quoting the dean of the college that such a step would damage Harvard as an educational institution by "increas[ing] our already strong, and possibly dangerous, tendencies toward over-intellectualized and narrowly-intellectual student body."

The second option, pursing a big-time schedule in the hopes of reestablishing Harvard as a national football power, was no less palatable and even less attainable. Buck rejected this out of hand, as well, as a "betrayal of Harvard ideals" that would "involve Harvard in a vicious and steadily declining circle with lowering of standards the constant price of such a course."

Having dispatched the two straw men, Buck next turned to a pair of more realistic options. The first, and more popular among students and alumni, called for Harvard to pursue an "aggressive policy within Ivy League rules." This entailed adhering to the letter of the Ivy Code, but increasing efforts to identify good players and lure them to Cambridge. Buck criticized the Athletic Association for being "passive and even opposed to activity on the part of alumni groups to assist in the recruitment of athletes." What really was required was keeping up with Princeton, Dartmouth, and Yale, but Buck painted a more lurid picture. "It means frankly joining a frenzied competitive scramble for a limited number of 18 year olds whose chief qualification is athletic ability."

He called his final option "operations 'purity.'" This entailed continuing football "as a significant but relatively minor" part of college life, giving no special consideration to athletes either in recruiting or admission, confining the schedule to teams that shared Harvard's values (mostly small, eastern liberal arts colleges), and cutting expenses. Buck concluded with a rhetorical flourish. "Do the lovers of a fine and manly sport wish to save it...And do the Colleges...seriously wish to disentangle themselves from a "game" which has caused so much hostility, suspicion and distrust among them? And do the players want to continue under a distorted set of values...? No one knows the answers to these questions. They are only straws in the wind."

Conant believed he knew the answer—sharp de-emphasis along the lines Buck had presented, a course dubbed "Operation: Strictly Amateur." The first step was to beg off games against better opponents. In keeping with this new policy, Harvard backed out of a rematch with Stanford for the 1950 season, although Army remained on the schedule to avoid antagonizing Eisenhower, its most prominent alumnus. It was a blow for what one Harvard historian referred to in somewhat different circumstances as "gentlemanly mediocrity." [54] (The Cadets won, 49-0.)

Conant also consolidated control over intercollegiate athletics in the hands of the university, doing away with the three-headed Committee on the Regulation of Athletic Sports, which had existed since 1888, and replacing it with a Faculty Committee on Athletic Sports. Students and alumni would have no official role in the governance of Harvard football. The alumni-dominated Athletic Association was also folded into the Department of Athletics, controlled by the faculty of the College of Arts and Sciences.

De-emphasizing football meant that Harvard could no longer support its athletic program with gate receipts, which had been declining anyway. Fans had stayed away in droves from lousy football and as a consequence, the athletic deficit had quadrupled, from $108,200 in 1949-50 to $466,500 in 1950-51. [55] Henceforward, games would be scheduled without regard to their potential at the box office. Football expenses, Conant declared, were "not to be regarded as an athletic deficit, but as much a proper charge against the resources of the Faculty as the maintenance of a library or a laboratory." [56] The university itself would make up any deficits out of general funds.

Harvard was now free to build a lighter schedule. In 1952, their opponents included Davidson, Ohio University, and Washington University, but soon even they were weeded out lest the Crimson have to play intersectional games, and replaced with the University of Massachusetts and Bucknell. Cornell was also added, as "the lesser evil than Pennsylvania." [57] Nevertheless, when Conant had the bleachers at the open end of Harvard Stadium dismantled in 1951, reducing its capacity by nineteen thousand seats, many Crimson faithful regarded it "as if the walls of Jericho had come tumbling down again." [58]

Gentlemanly mediocrity is not achieved overnight, and so Harvard's first year under its new program was just as disastrous as its last year under the old one. Quarterback Carroll Lowenstein was drafted after the first game of the 1950 season and Harvard finished 1-7. Fellow students jeered the team. "Two powerful elevens will take the field in Princeton's Palmer Stadium this afternoon," the *Crimson* wrote one Saturday. "In a few minutes they will be joined by Harvard's football players." [59]

Nevertheless, even Buck had recognized that Harvard could not remain in the Ivy group without winning at least its fair share of games. Thus, the administration also revised the university's financial aid programs and directed the admissions office to identify prospective students "who were both intellectually and athletically proficient." Slowly, things began to improve on the field. By 1952, behind fullback John Culver, later U.S. Senator from Iowa, the Crimson again posted a winning record, and in 1953 beat Yale for the first time in six seasons thanks to five touchdown passes by Lowenstein, who had returned from Korea.

Harvard banned alcohol from the stadium for the 1954 season but somehow managed to beat Yale for the second year in a row on a dramatic juggled catch by Bob Cochran that also gave them their five hundredth football victory. Although they lost to the Elis a year later in a New Haven snowstorm, their lone touchdown that afternoon was memorable because it was caught by future U.S. Senator Edward M. Kennedy.

All four Kennedy brothers had played football for Harvard, with varying degrees of success. Joseph, Jr., had played on the 1935 and 1937 teams. John, a Princeton transfer, never made it past the junior varsity. He enjoyed telling of the time he approached his freshman coach and asked to be put in for a few plays of the Yale game. "Who the hell are you?" the coach replied.

Robert Kennedy was a rangy receiver who frequently teamed up with quarterback Kenny O'Donnell. He scored his single varsity touchdown as a senior in 1947, only to see his career end a week later when he crashed into an equipment cart during practice. Kennedy limped around at drills for three days until he collapsed and it was found that he had been playing on a broken leg. When Valpey substituted him into the Yale game for a minute so he could qualify for his varsity letter, Kennedy threw himself into a tackle on the first play, leg cast and all. [60]

Ted, though, was the athletic star of the Kennedy family, a six-foot-two, 200-pound tight end who had also scored a touchdown earlier in the 1955 season against Columbia. His play was good enough to warrant attention from the Green Bay Packers, who sent him a form letter asking him to fill out a questionnaire that would help them evaluate him for the professional football draft.[61] He chose politics instead.

The Ivy giant during the late forties and early fifties was Princeton, which achieved national rankings while clinging to an outdated offense. Unlike Harvard, Princeton was successful. Unlike Penn, it was successful without trying to play a big-time schedule. More than either, Princeton provided the model for a successful Ivy team in the modern era.

Princeton's success began with the hiring of Charlie Caldwell as head coach in 1946. A member of the 1922 "Team of Destiny," Caldwell might have seemed destined for a career as a football coach, but baseball was his first love. As an undergraduate, his batting average was higher than Lou Gehrig's at Columbia. The New York Yankees signed them both and, just a few weeks after graduation, Caldwell found himself pitching in the major leagues, a career that unfortunately lasted only three games.

Caldwell planned to go back to work in his father's peach orchard until Princeton asked him to coach its freshman football team. Three years later, he took over at Williams, where he remained for seventeen years, winning three "Little Three" titles and coaching the basketball and baseball teams in the off-season. When Williams dropped football during the war, Caldwell moved to Yale as an assistant coach before returning to Princeton.

Bucking the national trend toward the T formation, he relied on the quirky, increasingly forgotten single wing, refining it with the touch of a master. Traditionally the single wing was a power formation, but Caldwell added complicated fakes and reverses, lining up his offense in twenty-four different formations and his defense in thirty-six. Before the snap, as many as three Princeton linemen called out blocking signals in cadence with the quarterback, who called out the play.

"I didn't recognize his damn offense," Munger complained after the Tigers upset his Quakers in Caldwell's first season. "Everything was different. He had two flankers out. He had men in motion. He moved an end and played five men on one side of the center."[62] When everything worked, as it did that afternoon, the result was a powerful, efficient offense that kept defenses confused and ate up the clock. In one 1951 game, Princeton controlled the ball for 101 of 137 plays.

Tradition-minded though the coach may have been, this was still the campus of Einstein and Oppenheimer. Caldwell admitted after the 1951 season that for two years the Princeton athletic department had been using a computer (which a delighted press called an "electronic brain") to help determine opponents' tendencies and prepare game plans. He had cooked up the idea with the help of a Princeton mathematics professor and an ends coach who was also assistant to the chairman of the Physics Department. In a process that grew more elaborate over time, the group spent as many as eight hours each week studying film, dissecting each player on each play, jotting down information that would then be put onto punch cards by secretaries in the registrar's office and run through the university's giant mainframe. Their product was a thirteen-foot long printout that was used to devise the next week's game plan. "There's no story," Caldwell bluffed when reporters came snooping around. "It's just one of those things we don't talk about." [63]

In 1947, Princeton won the first of six consecutive Big Three titles, surpassing the old record of four held by Percy Haughton's Harvard teams. By decade's end, playing no major non-Ivy opponents but Navy, they were nationally ranked for the first time in a decade. Cornell upset them in late October 1949, but after that the Tigers did not lose again until the 1952 season, a span of twenty-two consecutive games. During that stretch, they scored forty or more points in a game eight times, fifty or more points six times, and sixty or more points three times.

Any successful single-wing offense relies on its tailback. Fortunately, Caldwell had Dick Kazmaier, who in 1951 became the first Princetonian and last Ivy Leaguer to win the Heisman Trophy. Both his father's boss and the head of the local school board were Princeton alumni—just the sort of recruiting network that made Paul Buck quake—so Kazmaier's college choice was settled when he was still a junior in high school. A true triple threat who could run, throw, and kick, Kazmaier excelled as an option passer, rolling either left or right after each snap, setting up in a pocket that was never in the same place twice. If defenses played back, Kazmaier would zip around the end. If they pursued him, he would loft a pass over their heads. Yet he weighed only 155 pounds, prompting Princeton's admissions director to note on his interview card, "Fine boy. Excellent record.... Probably too small to play college football." [64]

Apparently Caldwell thought so, too, for he played Kazmaier only part-time during his sophomore season, during which he still managed to lead the entire Ivy League in total offense. In twenty-seven varsity games from 1949 through 1951, Kazmaier rushed for 1,964 yards, threw for almost 2,400 more, and scored fifty-five touchdowns—twenty on the ground and the rest through the air. He also averaged more than 36 yards per punt.

In 1950, Princeton finished second in the nation both in total offense and in rushing, amassing more than twice as many total yards as their opponents. They ended the season ranked sixth by the AP, which also named Caldwell coach of the year. Harvard fell by a score of 63-26, as did Yale the following week, 47-12, when Kazmaier and halfback Bill Kleinsasser scored touchdowns of fifty, sixty-three, and fifty-four yards in twelve plays.

They capped the season with a 13-7 win over Dartmouth in a game played during Hurricane Flora, in conditions the New York Times called "so miserable as almost to defy description." [65] Only five thousand people were foolish enough to brave the eighty mile-an-hour gales that had shattered windows at Dartmouth's hotel that morning and howled so fiercely through

Palmer Stadium an official had to hold the ball while the teams were in their huddles, lest it blow away. The one time Kazmaier tried to punt into the wind, the ball sailed back over his head.

No one expected Princeton to enjoy a similar level of success in 1951, having lost ten of eleven offensive starters and six of eleven defensive starters to graduation. Yet for the second year in a row they did not lose a game and again finished sixth in the country. At times, Kazmaier seemed to will them to victory. When he became dehydrated in an early-season game against Navy, he had fullback Homer Smith spit in his hands between plays so he could pass. In a showdown against undefeated, nationally ranked Cornell, Kazmaier led the Tigers in a 53-15 rout, passing for three touchdowns, rushing for two more, and outgaining the entire Big Red team, 360 yards to 210. He even scored a safety for good measure.

In a year of national disgust with collegiate sports, Kazmaier became a symbol of all that many wished they could be, idolized as much for what he represented as for what he had done. The Eastern press, especially, rhapsodized over Kazmaier in a way they had not done over an Ivy athlete since Barry Wood. *Time* magazine, which put him on its cover, called him "a refreshing reminder, in the somewhat fetid atmosphere that has gathered around the pseudo-amateurs of U.S. sports, that winning football is not the monopoly of huge hired hands taking snap courses at football foundries." [66]

The AP named him their Athlete of the Year, ahead of Stan Musial, Ben Hogan, Otto Graham, and heavyweight boxing champion Jersey Joe Walcott. He won the Heisman by the largest margin in history up to that time. Kazmaier received the news when he was called in to the dean's office on a Tuesday afternoon. "Wonderful," he said, then went back to class. [67]

Like every Ivy Heisman winner before him, Kazmaier declined to turn professional, preferring to enroll in Harvard Business School instead. "I don't see anything I could gain from it," he said of the NFL. [68] After a stint in the Navy, he went on to become president of the Voit sporting goods company, president of the National Football Foundation and Hall of Fame, and president of the U.S. Field Hockey Foundation (he had six daughters). His memory lingered on at Old Nassau, which has always held its idols dear. Princeton's trainer would not allow any athlete in any sport to wear Kazmaier's number 42 for more than ten years, until Bill Bradley arrived to play basketball. [69]

Even without Kazmaier, the Tigers, under captain Frank McPhee, rolled on the following season, rising to as high as tenth in the AP poll before an upset loss to Penn ended their winning streak. McPhee was succeeded by Royce Flippin, nicknamed "the Yale killer," who accounted for eleven of the twelve touchdowns Princeton scored against the Elis in his career. Before the start of the 1957 season, Caldwell requested a leave of absence and was replaced by his assistant, Dick Colman. Two months later, he died of pancreatic cancer at the age of fifty-six.

In 1954, the Ivy League, which had existed in the public imagination for a generation, at last became a fact when the presidents announced a round-robin football schedule. Considering that everyone but Penn now played at least five Ivy games a year, the announcement was something of an anticlimax, but one that, for the sake of pride, could not be put off any longer. That fall, the Ivy colleges played a total of twenty-seven games against outside opponents and won only eight.

Once again, students applied some well-timed public pressure. In January 1953, six of the eight Ivy papers had published a joint editorial calling for members to play at least five league games each year "to promote a spirit of loyalty and competition within the League." Princeton even came to the defense of the beleaguered Quakers (who had not joined the appeal). "Either these schools should agree to formulate an Ivy League in reality," the *Daily Princetonian* added, "or they should cease condemning each other for deserting a non-existent league." [70]

The presidents took up the subject at their next meeting. Despite the Big Three's historical coolness toward the idea, a league with a round-robin schedule passed without much disagreement. By committing themselves to play each other every year, the presidents inked in seven of the nine games on their schedules, making it impossible for any of them to build another suicide slate. Penn suggested splitting the League into two divisions—a northern division comprised of Harvard, Yale, Dartmouth, and Brown, and a southern division comprised of Cornell, Columbia, Penn, and Princeton—which would have committed each of them to fewer league games, but no one else seems to have been interested. [71]

Although the presidents tried to keep the plan secret until their trustees could vote on it, the news quickly leaked and by the time the Ivy athletic directors attended the annual NCAA convention, it had already hit the New York papers. Ralph Furey ungraciously commented that the presidents would have acted sooner had it not been for Penn. "Now that there has been a change in administration," he said, "and they have shown a sincere desire to go along with the Ivy group, the way has been opened for a round-robin." [72]

Grayson Kirk made the formal announcement on February 11, 1954. Because schedules were to be arranged no more than two years ahead of time, round-robin play would not commence until the 1956 season. Teams were to be limited to six home games a year, meaning that Princeton, for example, would now have to make the long journey to Dartmouth for the first time. [73] (For the first time also, visiting teams also had to wear white jerseys.) Travel, road games, absence from class, long the administration's chief objections to intercollegiate football, now were mandated.

The Big Three had long balked at the idea of a league champion. But as a gesture of conciliation, Penn donated the new Ivy trophy. Presented by the Class of 1925, it was capped by a sculpture of a scene from a painting called *The Onslaught*, which depicts a Penn-Harvard game from the 1890s, when the two teams had clashed in violence and in glory and the Ivy colleges had bestrode the football world. [74]

1955-2000

CHAPTER TEN

A Well-Rounded

Class

Only twelve thousand people turned out at Baker Field on September 29, 1956, to watch Brown defeat Columbia, 20-0, in the first-ever Ivy League game. Dick Bence earned the distinction of scoring the first Ivy touchdown when he reeled in a twenty-nine-yard pass from Frank Finney, a nineteen year-old sophomore who had not played high school football because of polio. Those twenty points, however, proved to be more than a quarter of Brown's output for the season against its seven Ivy rivals, so it is not surprising that the Bears also recorded the league's first loss a week later, despite a brawl between Bence and Yale quarterback Dean Loucks that cleared both benches. The only bright spot in Providence was tackle Gil Robertshaw, who became the only Ivy Leaguer selected in the 1958 NFL draft.

University President Barnaby Keeney complained that Brown teams were "unnoticed in victory and castigated in defeat."[1] Indeed, in their first seventeen Ivy seasons, Brown would have a losing record against league opponents sixteen times. Not even the return of Tuss McLaughry's son, John, as head coach from 1959 through 1966 could turn things around. In such a universe, only an Ivy League professor could charge, as one Brown English instructor did, that it was necessary to "get rid of this bourgeois game of football and get down to the real business of being a university."

The new conference was the subject of great curiosity in the press, as newspapers and magazines profiled the first season. Not everyone was enthralled. George Marshall, president of the Washington Redskins, told reporters, "The Ivy League is destroying the game it created." An alumnus of one of the Big Ten schools was less polite. "Ivy League football stinks."[2]

Although a few players transferred before they were consigned to round-robin play, little on the field had changed. Yet there was a sense of transition, heightened by Lou Little's announcement that he was retiring after twenty-seven years at Columbia. President Eisenhower, Little's old boss, lauded him as a "national symbol of fair play and good sportsmanship."

But not of winning. An old profile of Little in the *Saturday Evening Post* had been titled, "He Doesn't Have to Win," a sinecure in which the aging coach seemed increasingly to take advantage as the years rolled on.[3] In the two seasons immediately before the start of league play, the Lions had gone 2-16 and been outscored by more than four hundred points. When Army visited Baker Field in the fall of 1956—the last time the two state rivals would play each other for almost thirty years—the Cadets presented Little with a plaque as a memento of the old times, and a 60-0 defeat as a reminder of the new.

Yale won the first Ivy trophy, a crowning success for coach Jordan Olivar, who could not have begun under less promising circumstances. Born Giordano Olivari, the son of a Genovese prizefighter, Jordan was coaching Loyola of Los Angeles when Herman Hickman hired him as an assistant in the spring of 1952. A few months later, Hickman resigned, leaving Jordan the head-coaching job even though he needed to study photographs of his players before their first practice in order to identify them.

In some ways, Olivar was the last of the old coaches, men from Walter Camp to Bill Roper for whom football was only a part-time occupation. Olivar insisted that he be permitted to return to the West Coast after each season to attend to his insurance business, spending enough time in New Haven to transform the Elis' record from 2-7 to 7-2. That made it easier for alumni to swallow a little of his California showmanship, even the heretical one of putting gold trim on the Bulldogs' blue jerseys.

Olivar also pulled one of the great pranks—if a doubtful act of sportsmanship—in Yale's 1953 rout of Harvard. Leading 40-7 in the third quarter, Yale set up to attempt the extra point when the holder, quarterback Ed Molloy, rolled out and threw to a mysterious number 99 in the end zone for two points. Number 99, who was not listed in anyone's program, turned out to be Charlie Yeager, the team manager, who stood only five-foot-five and weighed 140 pounds. Olivar had been planning the stunt for weeks after watching Yeager shag passes in practice and had been careful to have him sign eligibility papers. At least some took the trick in good spirit. In a note to Yeager, Heylinger deWindt, manager of the 1910 Crimson team, expressed what many in that fraternity must have felt. "Every former Harvard manager envies you."

By the time the round-robin Ivy schedule began in 1956, Olivar's Bulldogs rolled through to a perfect league record behind Dean Loucks, end Vernon Loucks (no relation), halfback Dennis McGill, and fullback Steve Ackerman. They stumbled the following year, but upset Princeton and capped their season with a 54-0 pounding of Harvard, the worst loss the Crimson have ever suffered in the series. In 1960, with All-America center Mike Pyle, Yale was ranked thirteenth in the AP poll and achieved first perfect season since 1913, one of only two teams in the country with an unblemished record. Average attendance at Yale home games in those years continued to exceed that at Oklahoma, Purdue or Wisconsin, and was almost five times that at Brown home games, speaking to the continuing imbalance within the league.

The emerging Ivy dynasty, however, was in New Hampshire. Bob Blackman had never been to New England before he arrived in Hanover for a job interview in 1955. Like Olivar, he had spent his coaching career in the west, at Denver University, although he was widely rumored to be under consideration by the Los Angeles Rams, as well. Blackman's own college career at Southern California had been cut short by polio, which left him with a limp, but he was a workaholic (in the days before that term was used) who might celebrate a victory by staying late in his office to review game films. Although his teams were known for their raw power, Blackman liked trickery, as well; in 1956, the Indians recovered eight of eleven onsides kicks. Under his direction over the next fifteen seasons, Dartmouth would win or share seven Ivy titles.

But Dartmouth, Blackman soon discovered, was nothing like the Rams, or for that matter Denver University. On the team's first road trip, the coach looked around the train in disbelief. "They were reading the *Wall Street Journal*," he related in wonder. "I wouldn't even know how to read it, myself. When I was coaching at Denver University, the first time we went on the road the kids either pulled out decks of cards or comic books."[4]

In 1957, Blackman led Dartmouth to their best record in twenty years, although they lost the Ivy title to Princeton in a snowstorm on the last day of the season. A year later, the Indians gained their revenge. Princeton tailbacks Dan Sachs and Hugh Scott staked the Tigers to an early 12-6 lead before Indian quarterback Bill Gundy (who was also one of the nation's leading punters) and star halfback Jack Crouthamel came through for a 21-12 victory. Crouthamel, who succeeded Blackman as Dartmouth coach in 1971, was lucky not to have gotten thrown out of the game after tearing off his helmet and confronting the referee when an interference call went the wrong way.

Dartmouth was assiduous about recruiting, a point Harvard and Yale viewed with misgivings—ignoring, as always, the advantages their own reputations always gave them in attracting students. Blackman, for example, kept a thick notebook on prospects and mailed letters touting Indian football to high school coaches around the country. He also encouraged alumni efforts to subsidize campus visits by prospective students (not only legal, but tax deductible), which helped lure many to the North Woods.[5] Yale's dean of admissions, Arthur Howe, complained to President Griswold about permitting coaches to recruit football players. "At the moment," he wrote in 1957, "I detect that Harvard and Yale say it is not [acceptable]; that Penn, Columbia, and Cornell say with reservations it is acceptable; and Princeton, Brown, and Dartmouth encourage the practice."[6]

While Dartmouth was improving, Penn was almost deliberately getting worse, demonstrating its own belief in Ivy ethics. Harold Stassen, who seemed as happy to leave Penn as the trustees were to be rid of him, was succeeded by Gaylord Harnwell, a physicist much less prone to embarrassing exploits. "Doctor Harnwell, unlike Harold Stassen, talks the same language as the other Ivy presidents," one writer put it.[7] One senses that, whatever language was used, they did not discuss football. Harnwell, who once informed the varsity club that "winning half our games is plenty," had little interest in the sport. He made his obligatory appearances at Franklin Field, shaking hands as he worked his way up the rows, only to duck out a fire escape when he reached the top.

The man who really did the talking was the new athletic director, Jeremiah Ford, who as an undergraduate had been voted "that member of the class who most closely approaches the ideal Pennsylvania athlete."[8] His assignment was to convince the rest of the league that the university was sincere in its promises to abandon big-time football. Ford's way of doing that was to produce terrible teams—something Penn now did with regularity—sentencing the Quakers to a term in Ivy purgatory to atone for Franny Murray's sins.

Steve Sebo, the backfield coach at Michigan State, replaced George Munger in 1954, bringing with him a complicated "multiple offense" that fit poorly with players used to the single-wing. Under new command, the Quakers set an Ivy futility record that lasted until Columbia broke it in the eighties. Students hung Sebo in effigy under a banner that read "Heave Steve," but in fealty to Ivy principles, Harnwell ignored a vote by sophomore and junior letterman to fire him (the margin reportedly was 20-2) and reappointed the coach for three more years. "We don't ask our students what they think of their instructors," Harnwell sniffed.[9]

The losing continued. When Ford finally resolved to fire Sebo in 1958, he secretly hired John Stiegman from Rutgers, with the proviso that Stiegman would not start until 1960, when Sebo's contract expired. As Quaker luck would have it, Sebo proceeded to win the Ivy title in 1959, behind backs Dave Coffin and Fred Doelling, but was let go anyway.

Stiegman went back to the single wing and Penn went back to losing, Ivy doormats for most of the next decade. By the early Sixties, Quaker football was uniformly awful. Stiegman tried to counter this by throwing bodies at the problem, awarding varsity letters to thirty-eight players at the end of a 3-6 season in 1962. Bored upperclassmen made their own fun by throwing cartons of orange drink from the upper deck onto freshmen and their dates. "We had a conga offense," recalled future Philadelphia mayor Ed Rendell. "One—two—three—kick."[10] Following a 34-0 pasting by Princeton in 1963, students published a mock obituary. "Pennsylvania football, a living legend who had thrilled millions over three-quarters of a century, died Saturday at the age of 87," they wrote. "He is survived by Coach Stiegman, several cheerleaders, and Franklin Field." [11]

Balancing purity and victory was the eternal Ivy dilemma, a measure each school tried to strike in its own way. Under mounting pressure, Harnwell decided to change the way Penn struck the balance by hiring Dr. Harry Fields in 1965 to fill a new position called assistant to the president for athletic affairs. The move was troubling in several respects. Fields—a gynecologist, former professional wrestler, and Penn booster—had no experience as an administrator and occupied a position that had no counterpart at any of the other Ivy colleges, thus muddying the chain of athletic command and freeing him from direct responsibility for upholding league rules. [12]

Where Ford had kept alumni out of football matters, Fields invited them back in, sounding very much like Stassen when he declared that he was "willing to bend the league rules, but I won't break them." He hired one assistant to be in charge of academic tutoring and another to handle advertising and promotion, an indication of the direction in which intercollegiate athletics was headed. The new football coach, Bob Odell, appeared on fourteen radio and television shows during his first season in an attempt to boost interest in the team.

Ford, who correctly saw the appointment as an attempt to undercut his authority, charged that Fields winked at illegal spring practices and the existence of an athletic slush fund (although he did not provide details), thereby "jeopardiz[ing] the most important educational asset Pennsylvania has acquired in the last ten years—membership in the Ivy League." [13] Fields, however, was the boss and Ford was out, succeeded by Fred Shabel, who continued to pursue an aggressive course, working closely with the dean of admissions and director of financial aid, winning for the athletic department the right to raise its own funds again, and improving recruiting. Other Ivy colleges never apologized for winning, Shabel liked to point out, so why should Penn?

Overall, Penn athletics thrived under Shabel, rising to national prominence in a number of sports, though not football. Odell produced a few memorable seasons, most notably a 7-2 record in 1968 in which the Quakers won five Ivy games by a total of twenty-two points. Other that that, Penn seemed resigned to being, as Odell once put it, "the best of the have-nots." [14]

Some Penn supporters muttered that the Ivy League had become a vehicle for Big Three hegemony, a bargain in which Harvard, Yale, and Princeton lent their academic prestige to the others in exchange for the "luxury of fielding winning intercollegiate teams without apology or suspicion." [15] This would have been news to Harvard.

If Lloyd Jordan had pulled the Crimson back from the brink, he had not made them winners. As Harvard's football historian notes with icy politeness, "By the autumn of 1956 there was a question whether some of those boys who had come to Harvard looking for an education first, plus an opportunity to play football, were getting the same fine level of instruction from their football coach that they were entitled to, and received, in a Harvard lecture hall." [16] Although Harvard had not sacrificed its athletic purity, there were indications that Nathan Pusey, who succeeded James B. Conant as president, would not be so doctrinaire about the commercial aspects of football, as evidenced by his decision to allow the Boston Patriots of the fledgling American Football League—professionals!—to play their home games at the stadium in 1960.

When Harvard began looking for someone to replace Jordan, Dick Harlow recommended John Yovicsin, the coach at Gettysburg College. Yovicsin was an austere man who could have passed for an economics professor; indeed, someone once described him as "an abbreviated Galbraith, except that Yovicsin looks less rumpled and more scholarly." [17] He took over a team that had only four returning seniors and little support on campus. "I don't mind if we lose, so long as we lose interestingly," one Harvard undergraduate said, in words that must have brought the coach to tears. "I kind of love it when we fumble on the goal line. It gives the team character. It's not getting near the goal line that bores you." [18]

Yovicsin's teams were boring to watch—defense, kicking, and then offense were his stated priorities—but they did succeed, posting ten consecutive winning seasons and claiming at least part of three Ivy titles. In the early years, their plucky star was Charles duFort Ravenel. His friends called him "Pug" (thanks to a broken nose as a boy), but the short, slight quarterback was enough of a gambler on the field that he came to be known as "Riverboat" Ravenel, after the dashing Captain Gaylord Ravenal in Edna Ferber's novel *Show Boat*.

Although he came from one of the oldest Charleston families, neither his father nor his grandfather had attended college. Ravenel went north to Exeter Academy on a newsboy scholarship and held down five jobs as an undergraduate, including basketball referee, waiter, and campus sales representative for a men's clothing store. His arm was not especially strong (he completed only thirty-four of eighty-seven passes during his junior season), but he was quick and fearless. And as all Crimson stars should, he seemed to save his best performances for Yale. The 1958 game meant nothing in the standings, but Ravenel scored Harvard's first touchdown and set up the next two in a 28-0 victory. The following year, he and halfback Chet Boulris sparked the Crimson to twenty-seven points in twelve minutes on their way to a 35-6 walloping. A leg injury cost him most of his senior season, but he still returned in time to score Harvard's only touchdown in a 39-6 loss to Yale. In a gesture of respect and admiration, the Elis invited him to speak at their annual football banquet.

The Crimson did not win their first Ivy League title until the year after Ravenel's graduation, when they had to share it with an unlikely claimant—Columbia, which surprised everyone, including coach Aldo "Buff" Donelli by winning what remains their only Ivy football crown. Donelli's background had been in soccer, not football—he was the only American to score a goal in the

1934 World Cup—but he learned the game well enough to coach both Duquesne University and the Pittsburgh Steelers football teams simultaneously in 1941. In his first few years on Morningside Heights, the Lions had suffered their usual share of indignities, as well as some new ones, such as having their wallets stolen from their dressing room at Brown in 1959. When someone once asked to watch practice, Donelli replied, "We've got nothing to hide. I wish we did." [19]

Yet in 1961, a balanced team in a balanced league put the Lions on top. Fullback Al Butts and kicker Tom O'Connor helped Columbia end Yale's eleven-game winning streak. A week later, when the Lions polished off Harvard, it marked the first time in ten years that they had won back-to-back games.

When writer Roger Angell wandered around the Harvard campus during the 1962 Yale weekend, he counted at least sixteen other contests being played—junior varsity and freshman football, soccer, crew, cross-country, even touch football between the residential houses—testimony to the success with which "athletics for all" had taken hold. [20] In a view of Eastern society written at around this time, writer Stephen Birmingham observed the decline of football's popularity. "At Yale today," he wrote, "the men who consider themselves the college's social leaders have never met members of the Yale football team. They indulge, instead, in a sport that would horrify their grandfathers—touch football." [21]

It is difficult to determine exactly when football became a financial drag, as well, but it seems to have been around this time. Football remained profitable at Dartmouth, at least, into the early fifties, while by the middle of that decade Columbia, with considerably weaker teams, had begun to lose money. Certainly, football was no longer able to support the rest of the athletic department. Despite winning teams and large crowds, Princeton's athletic department recorded deficits of almost $200,000 a year by 1956, deficits that had to be made up from general university funds. [22]

Demoted from its former position of importance, football nevertheless remained the chief attraction of autumn Saturdays. Tailgating was by now firmly established as a pregame ritual. An article in one Columbia game program informed readers that "the flask is becoming obsolete, surpassed in popularity by the bar case with monogrammed glasses." [23]

A *New York Times* reporter took a stopwatch to the 1961 Princeton-Harvard game and discovered that although the whole show ran for two hours and twenty-three minutes, between times out and other stoppages of play there was only eleven minutes and forty-five seconds of actual action (for which the teams had put in a combined six hundred man hours of preparation). [24] One thing that made games longer was a greater emphasis on passing. College offenses took their cue from the pros and began to abandon the old, conservative split-T formation in favor of the more freewheeling wing T. Some attributed the high-scoring games to the now universal use of game films, which made it possible to dissect defenses with new precision. Others, not entirely tongue in cheek, gave credit to the Soviet Union for launching Sputnik in 1957, which prompted public high schools to improve their science curriculums and enabled more good athletes to meet Ivy admissions standards.[25]

Whatever the reason, it was a good time for quarterbacks. Three of them—Cornell's Gary Wood, Columbia's Archie Roberts, and Dartmouth's Bill King—dominated the league in the early sixties.

Wood led the Big Red to a remarkable streak of comebacks as a junior in 1962. He had given notice the year before, entering the Princeton game as a mop-up with his team down by twenty points, and ending it with them down by only five and driving as time expired. Coach Tom Harp made Wood the starter in 1962, then chewed his nails as Cornell squeaked out wins over Harvard, Princeton, and Brown by a total of five points. In the 35-34 win over the Tigers, Wood, playing with badly bruised ribs, helped his team retake the lead four times, the last time on an eleven-play, eighty-five-yard drive. In the Big Red's season-ending win over Penn, Wood participated in fifty-four of Cornell's seventy offensive plays and personally accounted for 387 of their 418 total yards, even catching one of his own batted passes.

Everyone fell before Dartmouth, though, which recorded its first perfect season since 1925 and was ranked fourteenth in the country. King and center Don McKinnon became the first Ivy players since Dick Kazmaier to be named first team All Americans, but the Indians' defense could be even more overpowering, holding Penn, for example to minus four total yards of offense and not a single first down in a 17-0 shutout.

Blackman organized the squad into three units: the "Green Team," composed of the two-way starters; the defensive specialists, known as the "Savages," and a spare offensive unit called the "Tomahawks." Demonstrating his faith in his quarterback, Blackman would send in only half a dozen per game, leaving King to improvise the rest. That faith included the authority to overrule the coach. In the Indians' finale at Princeton, with a perfect season on the line, King faced third and nine from deep in his own territory, clinging to a 31-27 lead. Blackman ordered a quick kick, but King instead audibled a pitchout to halfback Tom Spangenberg, who gained twenty-nine yards and set up a touchdown that iced the victory.

King threw for 324 yards against Columbia in a duel with Archie Roberts, the latest star quarterback to play for the Lions. Roberts, the best pure passer of the group, had been widely recruited but chose Columbia because he wanted to become a doctor. He seemed too good to be true; a polite, three-sport athlete who also belonged to the Premedical Society and Citizenship Council, delivered newspapers, and worked with poor children in Harlem. Roberts was a precise passer, but given the Lions' lack of blocking, was also quick enough to lead the team in rushing, as well. Sometimes, though, nothing helped; Brown sacked Roberts fourteen times for a total of eighty-nine yards in losses in the final game of his collegiate career in 1964.

Wood led the Big Red to three more come-from-behind victories in 1963 (while also leading the nation in kick return yardage), but it was a game he could not pull out—a 12-7 loss to Dartmouth—that kept his team out of the title picture. A few weeks earlier, Dartmouth had carried its fifteen-game winning streak into Cambridge, the first sellout of Harvard Stadium for anyone except Yale in thirty-two years. The Crimson spotted Dartmouth seven points, then took off behind quarterback Bill Humenuk, flanker Scott Harshbarger, and ends Tom Stephenson and Frank Ulcickas to win, 17-13. Illustrating the unpredictability of Ivy play, Harvard was itself upset the following Saturday at Franklin Field, losing 7-2, as Bruce Mulloy downed punt after punt deep in Crimson territory, scored Penn's only touchdown, and for good measure accounted for all of Harvard's points as well by allowing himself to be tackled in the end zone rather than try to kick into a stiff wind.

Dartmouth was to play Princeton for the championship on November 23, 1963, but that game, like all the other Ivy contests that weekend, was postponed after the assassination of President Kennedy.[26] When the teams finally met a week later, Dartmouth prevailed, 22-21, after recovering a fumble on Princeton's two-yard line that John McLean took in for a touchdown. The two teams shared the crown with identical 5-2 records.

Princeton did not have to share the title with anyone in 1964, going 9-0, the last perfect season they have ever achieved. Dick Colman was the only major college coach who still used the single wing, but where Charlie Caldwell had relied on quickness, Colman depended on the single wing's traditional power, in the form of straight-ahead fullback Cosmo Iacavazzi, who was also an aeronautical engineering honors student. A less-used weapon was cornerback Hayward Gipson, who became Princeton's first black football player—seventy-one years behind Harvard and only seven years ahead of the University of Alabama. A timely move, some thought, in the year Congress passed the Civil Rights Act.

As Princeton got bigger, its teams got better, so much so that by 1965 their starting line was fifteen pounds heavier than it had been only five years earlier. Tackle Paul Savidge and All-America linebacker Stas Maliszewski, who had been born in the Soviet Union and came to America as a child from a displaced persons camp, led the defense. They held opponents to only six touchdowns in eight games and posted four consecutive shutouts. A generation earlier, that might have brought national acclaim, but skepticism about the old-fashioned offense and an Ivy-dominated schedule cost them the Lambert Trophy as best team in the East (which went to Penn State instead) and kept them from cracking the AP's Top Twenty.

If Princeton demonstrated the difficulty an Ivy team faced in achieving national recognition, those difficulties were compounded that winter when the NCAA again did away with two-way football and brought back unlimited substitution. Not only were the Ivy colleges at a disadvantage because of their smaller enrollment, unlimited substitution compelled larger rosters, which in turn required bigger budgets for everything from training to equipment, a trend the Ivy League had no interest in following. Recognizing this, the League considered adopting its own rule but finally agreed to go along with the NCAA.

Ironically, however, unlimited substitution encouraged specialization, something the Ivy League quickly took advantage of, most visibly in the persons of two Hungarian refugees who introduced soccer-style kicking to the United States. Charlie Gogolak kicked for Princeton, while his older brother, Peter (whose middle name, serendipitously, was Kornell), kicked for the Big Red.

The brothers were also beneficiaries of the NCAA's decision in 1959 to promote kicking by widening the goal posts, perhaps to offset the two-point conversion, which had been introduced the previous year. With the demise of the drop kick more than a generation earlier, the field goal had all but disappeared from college football. Only three had been kicked in thirty-two Harvard-Yale games played between 1931 and 1966, while Cornell had kicked only three in the entire decade from 1950 to 1960. Peter Gogolak matched that total in his first game.

The brothers introduced a revolutionary European flair, lining up at an odd angle to the ball and striking it not straight on, but with the instep. Their family had fled Budapest during the Soviet invasion of 1956, settling in upstate New York. Because their town had no soccer team, the boys took up football, where Peter was discovered by the Cornell hockey coach. At the time, no team, either collegiate or professional, carried someone on the roster whose duties were just to kick, so Peter made the Cornell freshman squad as an end. The intricacies of pass routes and blocking were still alien to him but kicking was not, as he demonstrated by hitting a forty-eight-yard field goal against Yale in his second freshman game. By the time he made the varsity, the coach had found a spot for a place kicker.

Harp did not try his new weapon until five games into the 1961 season, when Peter kicked a forty-one-yarder against Princeton. He went on to set a new collegiate record by making forty-four consecutive extra points and by his senior year was also one of the top punters in the country, averaging more than forty-five yards per kick. After graduation, he kicked for the Buffalo Bills of the American Football League before jumping to the NFL's New York Giants, where he became their all-time leading scorer.

His younger brother, Charlie, recruited himself to Princeton, writing an unsolicited letter to Colman in which confided that, "although I cannot kick as far as Pete, I am very accurate inside the 30." The one time the two faced each other, in 1964, Charlie kicked a chip shot fifteen-yard field goal and six of seven extra points in a 51-14 Princeton romp.

Soccer style kicks tended to follow a lower trajectory than toe kicks, enticing defenses to think they could block them. Dartmouth tried something called the "human steps," in which a player leapt onto the backs of two linemen, who wore foam rubber padding under their jerseys. The obvious way to defeat the trick was to delay the snap, although Gogolak missed when he did attempt the kick.

Cornell went one better when they played the Tigers in 1965, building a human pyramid by stacking two backs on the shoulders of two linemen. Facing a human wall, Gogolak shanked his thirty-six-yard attempt, but the play was nullified by a penalty and Princeton proceeded to score a touchdown. Charlie went on to kick field goals of fifty-four and forty-four yards in the 36-27 Princeton victory and the following winter the NCAA outlawed the "piggy back" defense.

Princeton lost Iacavazzi in 1965, Charlie Gogolak's senior season, but gained tailback Ron Landeck, who had been actively recruited by Ohio State's Woody Hayes. Like Dartmouth, Princeton's aggressive recruiting aggressively (no fewer than sixty-eight members of its sophomore class had been high school football captains) irritated some Ivy coaches, who grumped that the Tigers should be playing in the Big Ten. When undefeated Princeton met undefeated Dartmouth in the last game of the season, they carried a seventeen-game winning streak. "There is a popular misconception that The Game, as Harvard and Yale like to call their annual contest, is being played tomorrow afternoon in New Haven," the Dartmouth paper wrote. "It isn't—the site for The Game is Princeton, New Jersey." More than 1,800 students and their dates traveled south from Hanover, many wearing tags that read simply: "KILL." [27]

"The Game" 1965 was close for one quarter, but quarterback Mickey Beard passed for 229 yards and accounted for three touchdowns to provide a 28-14 Dartmouth victory and what the Daily Princetonian called "a bitter, bitter end." [28] Perhaps because they were a better-known commodity, the Indians claimed both the Lambert Trophy and the national ranking that had eluded Princeton's undefeated team a year earlier.

In 1966, there was another three-way tie for the title, this time between Dartmouth, Princeton, and Harvard, which had the best overall record in the league despite losing Yovicsin for several months after heart surgery. The Crimson had gone to Princeton as the leading rushing team in the nation behind halfback Bobby Leo and fullback Tom Choquette, only to lose, 18-14. But Leo personally helped Harvard claim a piece of the title by scoring two touchdowns against Yale, becoming the first Harvard player ever to score against the Elis in three straight seasons and helping Harvard to its first three-game winning streak in the series since Barry Wood's day.

When members of the Students for a Democratic Society stormed the Columbia president's office in April 1968, they taunted authorities with an old football cheer:

> Who owns New York?
> Why, we own New York!
> Why, we own New York!
> Who?
> C-O-L-U-M-B-I-A! [29]

Many campus athletes, however, were conspicuous counterrevolutionaries. A group calling themselves the Majority Coalition (which included several football players) blockaded Low Library in an attempt to starve the demonstrators into retreat, until a group of their black classmates broke through. "That's Columbia for you," one reporter was heard to say. "Never could hold on fourth and one." [30]

The only thing Lion fans found worth cheering on the field was quarterback Marty Domres, whose 5,345 total career yards was the fifth-highest in major college history at the time of his graduation. In a game against Cornell in 1968, Domres either ran or passed on sixty-six of the Lions' eighty-one offensive plays, snapping a nine-game losing streak. He later was the first round draft choice of the San Diego Chargers.

All the things football represented—discipline, aggression, territorial conquest—came in for scorn in the sixties, further depressing the sport's already diminished popularity on campus. Although most were protected by student draft deferments, at least one Ivy player, Yale's Woody Knapp, was killed in Vietnam. Two Bulldogs who wanted to wear black armbands in 1969 to protest the war were tersely informed that the Yale uniform was not open for political advertisement.

Occasional run-ins over hair length notwithstanding, little of the sixties rebelliousness showed on the field. Five black players quit the Princeton varsity and freshman teams at the end of the 1968 season, alleging that they had been kept out of the starting lineup because of Dick Colman's "racist tendencies." True or not, that must have contributed to Colman's decision to resign a few weeks later to become the athletic director at Middlebury, thus spelling the end of the single wing in college football.

Yale, Princeton, and Dartmouth all admitted women at around this time, thus changing both the atmosphere on campus and the composition of their athlete pool. Although Cornell and Penn had been co-ed for years, women had been welcome in the Big Three grandstands only as dates. Harvard, for example, had tried to ban women from the cheering sections of the Stadium after World War II, only to retreat under heavy protest by male undergraduates, while a group of Yale students who recruited a small contingent of "girl cheerleaders" from Connecticut College for Women in 1965 were forced to drop the idea after just one game. [31]

Students no longer wrote fight songs but they did write satire, the most famous of which, "Fight Fiercely, Harvard," had been composed in 1945 by a seventeen-year-old undergraduate and later math professor named Tom Lehrer. By the 1960s, it had become a band staple, a rousing example of self-mockery:

> *Fight fiercely, Harvard, fight, fight, fight,*
> *Demonstrate to them our skill,*
> *Albeit they possess the might, nonetheless we have the will!*
> *Oh, we will celebrate our victory,*
> *We shall invite the whole team up for tea.*

Most of the Ivy bands abandoned their old marching routines for the "scramble" style in which they ran around aimlessly before reassembling into formation. Columbia added joke instruments, including something called an Australian didgereedoo that no one knew how to play. Harvard's band created a scandal when they appeared on the pages of *Playboy* forming a bunny head.

Halftime performances were now accompanied by a script read over the public address system, usually featuring "social commentary and avant garde wit," which often was being generous. Older alumni hated it, which of course was a large part of the point. Bands could be clever—depicting a Shakespearean sonnet, for example, by arranging themselves into fourteen lines or, as the Brown band once did, the electronic circuitry of a hydrogen bomb—but more often were too willing to settle for vulgar. When ABC agreed to televise the Princeton-Harvard game in 1968, they blocked out the sound during the halftime show (in retaliation, the Princeton band formed the letters "ABC" for the national TV audience, then morphed into "NBC," the network's rival).

With tradition changing everywhere, it was somehow reassuring that Ivy football closed the sixties with primacy restored to its most storied rivalry, Yale versus Harvard. Football spirit had dimmed in New Haven, as indeed it had almost everywhere, enough that some Yale alumni proposed singing "Bright College Years" right after the national anthem because so few stayed around for the end of the games.[32] Olivar resigned in 1963 when Yale insisted that he give up his off-season business interests and was succeeded by John Pont, who himself left for the Big Ten two years later. Carmen Cozza, one of Pont's assistants and arguably Yale's greatest coach of the century, succeeded him, ironically just weeks after Amos Alonzo Stagg died at the age of 102.

Cozza had played for Ara Parseghian and Woody Hayes at Miami of Ohio, then spent a few years as a minor league baseball player. Like Blackmun at Dartmouth, Cozza's first visit to New Haven had also been his first trip east of Pittsburgh. After two seasons as a line coach, he was going to accept the head job at the University of New Hampshire until Yale's athletic director, DeLaney Kiphuth, asked him to succeed Pont. (Joe Paterno, who had been offered the job first, declined.) By the time he retired in 1996, Cozza was Yale's all-time winningest coach, surpassing even Walter Camp. His teams won ten Ivy titles, sent two dozen players to the NFL, and boasted five Rhodes Scholars.

All that, however, lay in the future. In the present, Cozza's Bulldogs lost his first two games, including their first-ever loss to the University of Connecticut, traditionally a creampuff, on the way to a 3-6 record. A year later, they improved slightly to 4-5—not a pair of records that generally enables a coach to keep his job. Fortunately for Cozza, better troops were on their way.

Brian Dowling had never lost a football game he had finished since the seventh grade. Notre Dame wanted him badly, as did Woody Hayes, who asked the governor to try to recruit him for Ohio State. A leader in the mold of Barry Wood (although Dowling was notorious for taking gut courses), he was one of those athletes who could excel at anything, leading the freshman basketball team in scoring and for a time playing tennis and baseball, as well. "He had the smooth muscles and relaxed carriage of a country club athlete," Jack McCallum wrote, "dark eyes and black, slightly curly hair, plus poise and an affable manner."[33] A generation after he graduated, *Sports Illustrated* named Dowling the sixth best college quarterback of all time, ahead of Troy Aikman, Joe Theisman, and Doug Flutie. He would also be one of the last All-Americans at the college that invented the idea.

One student who piggybacked on his fame was an art major named Garry Trudeau, who worked Dowling—as perpetually helmeted quarterback "B.D."—into his comic strip, "Bull Tales," later "Doonesbury." Like Trudeau, his fellow students idealized him, in that mocking way of the times, as "a swashbuckling pirate in a sea full of cod fishermen." When it began to drizzle during the Princeton game in Dowling's junior year, a decidedly wry cheer went up from the Yale student section, "Make it stop, Brian, make it stop."

He was, however, less a throwback than a transitional figure. "They entered the old Yale, the last gasp," wrote A. Bartlett Giamatti, a Yale man himself (Class of 1960) and later university president. "They entered the Yale I had, but they left campus under completely different assumptions than the ones they'd arrived with. It was the extension of a time that was gone...only nobody knew it was gone at that time."[34]

Unlike Harvard or Princeton, to say nothing of Columbia or Penn, President Henry Griswold had bucked the trend toward a standardized-tested meritocracy in favor of the "well-rounded" young man who had always been the Yale type. "Well-roundedness" leavened academic achievement with athleticism, good character, and a traditional background; thus, twenty percent of Yale's freshman class in the early sixties came from just five prep schools and two-thirds of the alumni sons who applied were accepted. As soon as the more diverse GI Bill classes had cleared out in the early fifties, Griswold had instituted a dress code as a remedy for "disorderliness" and "sloppiness."

His successor, Kingman Brewster, set out to change things, declaring, "I do not intend to preside over a finishing school on Long Island Sound." Although Yale's geographic balance had begun to change under Griswold, Brewster turned it in a different direction, recruiting more heavily from the inner cities, hiring the college's first black admissions officer, and instituting the first truly need-blind admissions policy in the country.[35] The Class of 1970 arrived on campus in 1966 with the highest SAT scores in Yale's history, but also the highest percentage of public school students and African-Americans. As Brewster liked to observe, the new policy was no less elitist than the old one had been, but it was elitism differently defined.

With it, though, the conception of what an Ivy League student should look like also changed, carrying drastic implications for athletics. Harvard's freshman dean, F. Skiddy von Stade, Jr., summed it up nicely. "What we're after is not the well-rounded boy but the lopsided boy who will make up a well-rounded class. You don't get the whole college doing any one thing and that simply is extended to athletics, football included." [36] A few of those lopsided boys, however, could still be athletes, whom Harvard routinely stuffed into the bottom quartile of its entering classes along with alumni children and prep school legacies. A committee that revised Penn's admissions policies in the late sixties recommended that 5 percent of each class—roughly eighty-five students in a typical Penn class of seventeen hundred—be reserved for athletes, half of whom were expressly permitted to be "academic risks." [37]

Though little appreciated at the time, lopsidedness was also a recognition of the continuing American trend toward specialization. If excellence, whether or not tempered by balance, was the ideal, it invited a separation of athletes from the rest of their class. The implications of this change in philosophy would become more apparent over time.

Calvin Hill, Dowling's teammate, was representative of the new Yale. Like Dowling, Hill had never played in a losing football game. He had been raised in Baltimore but had gone to tony Riverside Country Day School in New York on a scholarship for black students from the South. On senior visiting day each year, Riverside granted excused absences to students making college visits, so Hill and a friend decided to spend a day in the city on the pretext of visiting Columbia. Upon their return, one of the assistant coaches asked why the two had missed practice. "If you're thinking about the Ivy League and football," the coach (a Yale man) said when told of the Columbia visit, "I think there are four schools you ought to consider: Harvard, Yale and Princeton, because in terms of football, one of those schools is always going to be there, and Dartmouth." On that recommendation, Hill applied to Yale and was accepted.

"Is that a good school?" his father, a construction worker, asked months later when his son told him the news.

"Yeah, it's gotta be one of the tops," Hill answered.

"Well if it is, you gotta go for it."

Hill went for it expecting to be the quarterback, as he had been in high school, but with Dowling in the same entering class, Cozza moved Hill to linebacker and fullback. Several of his black classmates, attributing the switch to racism, proposed picketing the athletic department until Hill dissuaded them. Hill himself said later that he considered transferring, but did not want to lose a year of eligibility by doing so.

The tandem was slow to get started, as Dowling missed most of his sophomore season with of a knee injury, then broke his right wrist in the third game of his junior year (but insisted to Cozza that he could still pass with his left hand). He returned in time to lead a 56-15 rout of Dartmouth (gunning for their fifth Ivy title in six years), the most points a Yale team had scored in almost forty years. Two weeks later, the Bulldogs humbled Princeton for the first time in six years, 29-7, including a sixty-yard touchdown pass from Hill to Dowling on a reverse. In New Haven, the dining halls that week had been forced to stop selling oranges, which looked too much like Princeton's helmets and were being turned into missiles.

Although Yale had already clinched the Ivy title, more than sixty-eight thousand people jammed the Bowl for the traditional finale against Harvard, the largest crowd in fourteen years. Yale broke to a 17-0 lead after Dowling, trapped seventeen yards behind the line of scrimmage, uncorked a fifty-three-yard bomb to Hill, who had managed to get open. (I knew he would see me," Hill said afterward). But the Crimson would not go quietly, taking advantage of four interceptions to forge a 20-17 lead late in the fourth quarter on a pass from Ric Zimmerman to Carter Lord. A Harvard defender slipped, allowing Del Marting to haul in a Dowling pass (one of only five he completed all day) three plays later, to give Yale a 24-20 victory, iced when Harvard fumbled on its final drive.

They kept rolling in 1968, providing a few hours' respite each weekend for a divided campus. "At a time when an understanding gap has frequently separated alumni from students," the *Yale Alumni Magazine* wrote, "football had provided a bridge of common interest." [38] Yale was scarcely challenged through their first eight games, winning all of them by an average margin of more than three touchdowns.

Harvard lacked Yale's talent, but they matched its record—a perfect 8-0 as the two headed for their climactic game in Cambridge. It was the first time both schools had entered The Game undefeated since 1931 and they have not done so since. Yet as a mark against the Ivy League, neither earned even a sniff from the AP poll voters, Yale's sixteen-game winning streak—the longest in the nation—notwithstanding.

John Yovicsin had a good team, perhaps his best, but in an age of discord, many of his seniors had almost quit before the season started, feeling underappreciated. The election of halfback Vic Gatto as captain quelled the mutiny, at least temporarily. One of those mutinous seniors was Tommy Lee Jones, an All-Ivy offensive tackle, cum laude English major, dorm mate of future Vice President Albert Gore, and aspiring actor, who would go on to become one of the biggest stars in Hollywood. Jones had gone to prep school in Dallas instead of traveling to Africa when his father, an oil executive, was transferred there, and said he chose Harvard because it was "the furthest away and had the strangest name." [39] Too small to hope for a pro career, Jones knew the Yale game was the last he would ever play.

Tickets were impossible to get. Harvard alumni who had been out less than twenty years were shut out completely and had to do the best they could with students, who were scalping their two complimentary tickets (face value: $6) for $100 apiece. "I found my turkey for Thanksgiving," one Yale undergraduate bragged. "He's fat and Old Guard and rich." [40]

November 23, 1968, in Cambridge was chilly but clear—a great day for a football game, actually—and the stadium was charged with an atmosphere that had not been felt in years. Extra seats had to be put on the field level behind the benches in order to accommodate the overflow crowd. Once Cozza yelled into his headphones for someone to tell him what yard line the ball was on, and several spectators seated directly behind him answered. In the Harvard stands, one middle-aged woman was overheard reminiscing that she had first gotten drunk at a Harvard-Yale game when she was only fifteen. Her escort asked which side she had been sitting on. The Yale side, she replied. "Thank God," he exhaled.[41]

Showdowns often turn out to be dud games, and for fifty minutes this one appeared to follow that trend. Although Hill had spent most of the week in the infirmary after biting his tongue in the Princeton game, he and Dowling jumped all over the Crimson to put Yale up 22-0 with almost eight minutes left until halftime. Mordant Harvard students began chanting, "We're number two!"

Desperate to try something, Yovicsin yanked starting quarterback George Lallich and replaced him with little-used Frank Champi, a high school javelin thrower, who engineered a sixty-four-yard drive in his first possession to put the Crimson on the board before halftime. Many of his teammates, however, were not pleased. "Frank surprised me," Jones recalled. "He looked scared to death. It all looked overwhelming to him.... But he didn't know our playbook well, which was a very demanding one. There were ten guys on the field who knew it better than Frank did."[42]

To some of the Crimson seniors, it was just the sort of high-handed move that had caused so much trouble before the season. "Yovicsin had given up on us," one groused. "All he wanted us to do was go out there and get the rest of the afternoon over as quickly as possible. But we weren't playing for him and we weren't playing for the school, we were playing for ourselves."[43]

Nevertheless, when the teams returned from the locker room, Lallich was back under center. Another futile series, though, and he was done. Three plays after re-entering the game, Champi got Harvard into the end zone again, but Yale answered the score and led 29-13 with three and a half minutes to play. On the sidelines, it briefly crossed Cozza's mind to try for two points, but he chose to kick for one instead. "After the fourth [touchdown], I figured what difference does it make?" he said after the game. "There was no way they could come back."[44]

Indeed, Dowling and Hill—"the Two Horsemen of the Apocalypse," someone called them—seemed to guarantee victory. They were grinding out the clock until Harvard recovered a Yale fumble (their sixth of the day) on their own fourteen-yard line with 3:31 left to play. Although Hill could not have known it, he had just played his last down of college ball.

John Ballantyne, Bruce Freeman, and Champi moved the ball down the field until Champi found Freeman in the end zone for a touchdown that cut the deficit to 29-19. Luck—and some said the officials—were smiling on Harvard.

Champi's pass for the two-point conversion was incomplete, but he got another chance when Yale was called for interference. This time he found tight end Pete Varney and suddenly Harvard trailed by only eight.

Earlier in the season, Dowling had begged Cozza to let him return a kickoff. The coach picked this moment to honor the request, but the ball never reached B.D. Instead, Harvard's onsides squib bounced twice, hit Brad Lee (who was a pitcher on the baseball team and used to fielding bunts) in the chest, and rolled on the turf where Bill Kelley of the Crimson fell on it. Worse, the scoreboard operator had not started the clock on the kickoff, so no time had expired. Down by eight, Harvard had the ball again with forty-two seconds to play.

Now Dowling and Hill both rushed up to Cozza and asked to be sent in on defense—anything to stop the bleeding. To his credit, Cozza refused, saying that he could not embarrass the men they would replace by yanking them in such a crucial situation.

Although a facemask penalty improved Harvard's field position, they could not move the ball on their own. On third and ten, Yovicsin called for a fullback draw—the same play on which the Crimson had fumbled away a chance a victory a year earlier—but this time it was good for fourteen yards to the six-yard line. Yale's defense broke through to sack Champi on first-and-goal.

Now there were only three seconds left. As Champi rolled out, he could not find Gatto, his intended receiver. "I knew I was free," Gatto recalled, "but I didn't want to wave because I didn't want to call attention to the fact that I was open. Then Champi threw to me, and the ball came so slow and big."[45] Touchdown, Harvard, which trailed now by two points as the teams lined up one last time. The clock read zero. The conversion would be tried in a timeless limbo, a place in which most of the Yale fans must have felt they had been trapped for hours.

Yale jumped offside but Champi found Varney in the end zone for two points. "The Stadium exploded," the *Harvard Alumni Bulletin* described the scene. "Strangers embraced, full professors danced and the Yale people put their handkerchiefs to the uses they were intended for."[46] As Monday's *Crimson* gleefully declared: "Harvard Beats Yale, 29-29."

The Dallas Cowboys drafted Hill in the first round the following spring, but Dowling—who had another year of college eligibility—was still on the board when the Minnesota Vikings took him in the eleventh round, then cut him before the season started. He rode the bench for a few years in understudy duty for the New England Patriots and two teams in the World Football League. Champi, who spent the summer teaching English to prison inmates, gave up football altogether the following year saying, in true sixties fashion, that the game had "lost its meaning" to him.[47] "I didn't quit a football squad," he wrote, criticizing what he felt was big-time pressure at Harvard, "I quit a firm."[48] He dropped out of sight and became a high school teacher.

Tommy Lee Jones insisted he took no consolation from the tie ("It was not satisfying. Not to me. Not to anyone"), but many other Harvard faithful did. "Who will remember the team that lumbered ahead to a lopsided lead in the first half? No one," the *Crimson* predicted. "A draw in name only then. By every other reckoning, a magnificent victory." [49]

CHAPTER ELEVEN

What Is This Thing Called "Winning"?

Intercollegiate football celebrated its hundredth anniversary when Princeton and Rutgers met again in New Brunswick on September 27, 1969. More than one hundred black radicals interrupted pregame ceremonies by parading across the field with clenched fists raised to protest university policies. They were booed lustily by the crowd of thirty-one thousand.

Just as they had a century before, the Tigers lost, this time 29-0. "Today," one reporter wrote, "Princeton set football back 100 years."[1] Once they returned to the comfortable confines of the Ivy League, though, Princeton recovered under new coach Jake McCandless, who dropped the single wing in favor of a "pro set" T formation and, fittingly, marked their centennial season by sharing the title with Dartmouth and Yale.

Although Princeton dropped from sight for the next decade or more, Dartmouth and Yale remained the league's powerhouses. Dartmouth's 1970 team in particular was Bob Blackman's best, and also his last, as he left after the season for Illinois in the Big Ten. They finished 9-0, their third perfect season in nine years, with an offense led by quarterback Jim Chasey (who had competed in high school against future NFL standouts Jim Plunkett and Dan Pastorini) and running backs Brendan O'Neill and John Short. It was the Big Green's defense, though, that set records, surrendering only forty-two points all season, the fewest by any team in the country, and holding opponents scoreless six times. Not once did a Dartmouth opponent take possession of the ball beyond its own forty-yard line, and the team never trailed. Some resented Blackman's take-no-prisoners approach, however, such as attempting a fourth quarter onsides kick against Penn with a twenty-eight-point lead.

Yale was also nationally ranked and undefeated when they met the Indians before sixty thousand fans in the Bowl on the season's sixth week, surging behind senior quarterback Joe Massey and sophomore fullback Dick Jauron, who had rushed for 116 yards in his first varsity game against Connecticut. In an act of divided loyalty unimaginable a generation earlier, Dartmouth played the first half without their kicker, Wayne Pirmann, who remained in Hanover to compete in a varsity soccer game, then flew to New Haven immediately afterward on a private plane. He arrived in time to kick a field goal in a 10-0 victory that denied Yale a fourth consecutive Ivy title.

Boasting an invitation to play in the Gator Bowl (which Ivy rules forbade them from accepting), Dartmouth finished the season ranked fourteenth in the country and again won the Lambert trophy as best team in the East. When Joe Paterno, whose Penn State team finished second for the Lambert, suggested that the two schools play each other to settle the question of regional supremacy, Blackman cheekily replied that, considering the Nittany Lions' 7-3 record, Dartmouth deserved a better opponent.

In such circumstances, there was little enough to criticize about Indian football, though it wasn't the football that bothered some Dartmouth students, but the Indian. They wanted the college's mascot eliminated, declaring that it was "based upon insensitivity to the culture of Native American peoples."[2] Dartmouth's history as a training institution for Indians notwithstanding (overstated, it turned out), the nickname itself was hardly ancient, invented in the 1920s by a Boston sportswriter. The Indian head logo—a severe looking brave with a feather in his hair—did not appear on Dartmouth's road football uniforms until 1965, or on home uniforms until 1970, in the midst of the controversy.

Native American students, who began protesting the symbol in 1969, won an immediate victory when the buckskinned and feathered student mascot disappeared from the sidelines. The cause was taken up by committees and countercommittees, but it was not until the fall of 1972 that Dartmouth's athletic authorities recommended retiring the Indian. Henceforth, college teams would be known as the "Big Green," another common Dartmouth nickname, albeit derivative of Cornell. Eventually, old college songs such as "Eleazer Wheelock," with its reference to tempting the native tribes with "500 gallons of New England rum," and "As the Backs Go Tearing By," with its savage war whoop, were also mothballed.

However, because the Indian had never been officially adopted as Dartmouth's mascot, the athletic committee reasoned, it could not be officially revoked. But because it was not officially revoked, the issue was not officially put to rest. Every few years, attempts were made to restore the Indian, which polls always showed to be the overwhelming preference of students and alumni, although other suggestions included the "Woodsmen" and, more puckishly, the "Animals."

Along the way to Dartmouth's perfect 1970 season, they had held Cornell's junior fullback, Ed Marinaro, to only sixty yards rushing, his lowest total of the year, in a 24-0 victory, but Marinaro was the league's best player—arguably the best player on any Ivy team since the league's creation. The son of a New Jersey sign painter, Marinaro had been pursued by dozens of other colleges, whose interest cooled when a hand injury spoiled his senior year. He chose Cornell because he liked its program in hotel administration, asking only that he be given three different helmets to use; one for practice, one for home games, and one for road games. Big Red trainer Doc Kavanaugh cheerfully promised Marinaro as many helmets as he wanted.

He served notice as a sophomore, rushing for 281 yards and five touchdowns in a 41-24 pasting of Harvard, a performance good enough to get him named Back of the Week by the Associated Press and *Sports Illustrated* and eventually finishing second in the country in rushing. "There are only two Italians I ever lost sleep over," joked Yale defensive coach Bill Narduzzi after a 17-0 defeat. "The first was my wife and the other was Ed Marinaro." [3]

On many afternoons, he simply was the Big Red attack. "Our offense is that old three yards and a cloud of dust," Cornell's backfield coach admired. "But with Ed running the ball, it becomes five, six or even twelve yards and a cloud of dust." [4] Illustrating the extent to which they relied upon him, Marinaro led a late drive against Columbia in 1971 by carrying the ball on nine consecutive plays and ten times in eleven downs, gaining forty-eight yards to set up the winning field goal. In his final game, against Penn, running out of the I formation, Marinaro carried the ball forty-two times for 230 yards, scored five touchdowns and a two-point conversion in a 41-13 victory. The Big Red that year shared the Ivy title, their first, with Dartmouth, which ground out a 24-14 victory when the two teams met at Hanover.

Playing on one of two artificial turf fields in the Ivy League, which Cornell president Dale Courson dubbed "Marinaro's Meadow" (Franklin Field had the other), Marinaro became the first player ever to rush for more than 4,000 yards in a three-year varsity career and averaged almost 175 yards per game. [5] A consensus All-American, he won the Maxwell Award and finished second in the Heisman Trophy balloting behind Pat Sullivan of Auburn after finishing eleventh in the voting a year earlier. When the Ivy League selected its Silver Anniversary team, Marinaro was named the outstanding Player of the Era (his teammate, linebacker Bob Lally, was also selected). After several seasons with the Minnesota Vikings, Marinaro went on to a successful acting career.

Despite the loss of Dowling and Hill, Cozza had enough returning talent to produce some of Yale's best teams throughout the seventies. In 1972, Yale's centennial season, they fell half a game short of Dartmouth when Harvard upset them, 35-16, on the last day of the season, but captured what in retrospect was a more significant honor. When the weekly AP poll was released on November 7,

1972—the day Richard Nixon buried George McGovern in the presidential election—Yale was ranked twentieth in the nation, the last time any Ivy team would ever be nationally ranked among the major colleges.

Two Eli starters that season went on to the NFL. Jauron, a junior in 1972, grew up a few miles from Cambridge and as a high school student was in Harvard Stadium, rooting for the Crimson, the day of the infamous 29-29 tie. He set a new Yale single game rushing record with 186 yards against Connecticut, then broke it against them a year later with 196 yards, scoring touchdowns of 80, 64, and 18 yards. As a senior in 1974, he became the first Yale player ever to rush for 1,000 yards in a season. After a nine-year playing career in the NFL, most of them with the Detroit Lions, he went on to become head coach of the Chicago Bears. Gary Fencik was an All-Pro defensive back for the Bears during their Super Bowl season in 1985 but a wide receiver at Yale, setting a school record as a junior by catching eleven passes for 187 yards in a loss to Harvard. A year later, in 1975, he caught the longest touchdown pass in Eli history, 97 yards, on a halfback option from Don Gesicki, who had taken the pitch from quarterback Stone Phillips, later an anchorman for NBC news.

Although Yale regularly found itself battling Dartmouth for the Ivy title during these years, Harvard also emerged to provide a three-way battle for the top. Yale rooters had known for decades that no championship was ever won without getting past the Crimson, contests that also provided a fascinating contrast in coaching styles between Carm Cozza and Harvard's Joe Restic. "Fanciful philosophers might see in these mentors a kind of incarnation of the spirit of the institutions they serve," wrote Eli football historian Thomas Bergin, "Yale, steady, traditional, perfectionist; Harvard, adventurous and inventive."[6]

When ill health forced John Yovicsin to retire after the 1970 season, Harvard, which could claim to have stolen football itself from Canada, raided north again by hiring Restic, head coach of the Hamilton Tiger Cats of the Canadian Football League. Spiritually, Restic seemed like a man Dick Harlow, the ornithologist, would have liked, a former philosophy major fond of quoting St. Augustine, whose favorite writer was the Catholic theologian Jacques Maritain.

Restic's satori was something called the "multiflex" offense, a wide-open system as unpredictable as it was entertaining (the term was an amalgamation of its two core attributes, "completely multiple and totally flexible"). "Restic might have dreamed it," the Harvard Bulletin once speculated, "like Coleridge and Xanadu and Kekule and the benzene ring."[7] Awaiting the snap, Harvard's offense might jump into three different sets, out of a hundred in its playbook, while the quarterback barked one of three kinds of verbal signals in two different cadences, rhythmic and nonrhythmic. The multiflex also had a defensive component, with shifts in response to the opposing team's sets. "They bend over, call signals, look up, and we're not there," Restic said with thinly disguised glee.[8]

Once, when an ingratiating reporter asked Restic to state the major and minor premises of the multiflex, the philosopher-coach shot back with, "That's a false basic premise, so I'm not going to answer you in syllogistic form." [9] He was by no means, though, philosophical when it came to success. "To get maximum enjoyment out of football, you have to win, because that's the object of the game," he once said. "A loss, well, a loss is a week taken out of your life." [10]

The multiflex could be baffling to defenses, which was its stated purpose. At other times, though, it could be baffling to Harvard's offense, which was not its purpose but which probably accounted for breakdowns such as the 111 yards the Crimson once were assessed in penalties during a single game against Cornell, most on illegal procedure calls or ineligible receivers downfield. Nothing was out of bounds. In the 1971 Yale game, Restic sent his *quarterback* in motion, leaving no one under center, and had the ball snapped directly to an end who had moved into in the fullback slot. The fullback then threw to the quarterback for a touchdown. In 1975, Crimson quarterback Larry Brown offered a for-credit course called "Fundamentals of the Multiflex Offense," which was attended by twenty students, including three members of the Harvard defense.

If Restic was more imaginative than Yovicsin had been, some whispered that he seemed more interested in tweaking his prize offense than in devising a game plan that addressed an opponent's weaknesses. Many complained that its impenetrable trickery cost the Crimson games it might otherwise have won. In 1982, almost all the seniors on the team sent a letter to the *Crimson* blasting the coach as "inept" and aloof. [11] "I don't think he ever motivated anybody," one former player complained. [12]

Nevertheless, Harvard adapted to the multiflex and reasserted themselves at the top of the league. In 1973, they entered The Game with a chance to tie Dartmouth for what would have been Harvard's first Ivy League title but Jauron, playing his final game, helped the Elis overcome a 17-0 first quarter deficit to win, 28-17, and claim a share of second place. In 1974, the year of Harvard's football centennial, the Crimson came to the finale needing a victory to tie Yale at the top. The Bulldogs had the stingiest defense in the country, surrendering fewer than six points per game, while Harvard had split end Pat McInally, their first All-American since Chub Peabody in 1941. McInally, who had caught ten passes against Penn the previous season (including a one-handed game winner in the corner of the end zone with thirty seconds to play) was also the team's punter, and would go on to an All-Pro career at that position with the Cincinnati Bengals.

Four hundred and fifty Yale fans chartered seven railroad cars for a tailgate from New Haven. Cambridge, meanwhile, was graced by a host of Democratic potentates, as well as Argentine stripper "Fanne Fox," who had just gained infamy by being caught with Congressman Wilbur Mills in the Tidal Basin. Restic stacked four tackles and two ends on the line, daring the Elis to beat him through the air, but it was McInally who hit split end Jim Curry on a fifty-yard flea flicker just before halftime. White-shoed quarterback "Pineapple" Milt Holt from Hawaii then led a late drive through the ostensibly impregnable Yale defense to seal Harvard's victory.

A year later, Harvard won the title outright for the first time and again the Yale game was decisive. Quarterback Jim Kubacki, who succeeded Holt, played well, as did captain and offensive tackle Dan Jiggetts, who would later play for the Chicago Bears. Mike Lynch kicked a twenty-six-yard field goal with thirty-three seconds left for a 10-7 win. "I just kept telling myself not to shank it in front of 70,000 people," he said afterward.

Almost overlooked in Harvard's 1975 championship season was Brown, which fell a game short in their bid for a first Ivy title. Theirs had been a tale of mediocrity during the "Rock Bottom" years since Ivy play began. There had been good players, such as quarterback Bob Hall and John Parry, who from 1961 to 1964 set the school career record for pass receptions, but a good year, one observer wrote, meant finishing at the top of the second division, while a bad year meant battling Columbia "for the distinction of being the stepchild of Ivy football.[13] Nineteen seventy-five was the first year since the league's creation that they had finished higher than fourth.

There were several reasons for the Brown's historic ineptitude. It had never really established a strong football tradition; its enrollment was among the smallest in the league; it lacked Yale's status, Penn's zeal, Cornell's size, or Dartmouth's organization; and it usually had less scholarship money to offer students in need, whether athletes or not. Unlike Princeton, which has always kept its graduates close, thereby reaping untold financial and recruiting rewards, Brown did not hire its first alumni secretary until after World War II.

In other respects, however, Brown's athletic program was diverse and a successful example of "athletics for all." Like Penn, they achieved national success in the early seventies in less visible sports, including ice hockey and soccer. But when the university's new president, Donald F. Hornig, declared in 1971 that football, like anything else at Brown, should be first-rate, the team backed him up by losing eighteen of their next nineteen games.

As frequently happens, a coaching chance seemed to spur the Bears in a new direction. John Anderson, the successful coach at Middlebury, arrived in Providence in 1973 at the age of forty-one promising an Ivy championship within four years. If nothing else, he seemed to have luck, as Brown rallied to tie Rhode Island on a batted pass in his first game. If Brown had trouble developing its own talent, Anderson could import it, such as quarterback Bob Bateman, who in 1975 transferred from the University of Vermont, which had dropped football. That fall, ABC decided to televise the Bears' game against Harvard (the undefeated Crimson were the attraction), an event that caused considerable excitement on campus, but Brown was not quite ready for prime time. Kubacki killed them on play action fakes as the Crimson romped to a 45-26 victory; revenge of sorts against the Brown band members who had stolen the famous Harvard drum a year earlier by posing as representatives of ABC sports who claimed they needed it for publicity photos.

Despite losing thirteen starters, Brown improved in 1976, notwithstanding a shaky kicking game that succeeded on only two of ten field goal attempts during the season. Paul Michalko replaced Bateman at quarterback, relying on speedy receiver Bobby Farnham, who was nicknamed "the rabbit." They opened the season by beating Yale for the second year in a row then, after falling to Penn, 7-6, on a disputed fumble in a driving rainstorm, gained revenge against Harvard by forcing a fumble deep in Crimson territory late in the game. A headline in the student paper on Homecoming weekend asked, "What is this thing called 'winning'?"

Brown's finale at Columbia, the most overlooked season-ending rivalry in the country, took on critical importance, yet most of the campus seemed to greet success with a yawn. A student reporter, taking in the scene on College Hill that afternoon, came upon a likely-looking apartment with a "BRUNO NUMBER I" banner hanging outside. "I'm watching Harvard and Yale," the rooter called down. "Are you kidding? Brown and Columbia? What boredom!"

Boring, it was not. Brown began their biggest game in decades by fumbling on the Columbia one-yard line and throwing two interceptions. When the Lions jumped to a 17-7 halftime lead, students who had remained in Providence, glued to their radios, grew despondent. "If they blow it against Columbia, that would be so pitiful," one moaned. But halfback Billy Hill rallied the Bears with two fourth quarter touchdowns, for a 28-17 victory and a share of the title with Yale. Back on campus, according to the reporter, a handful of exultant diehards paraded a Brown pennant through Wayland Arch, "but finding only a few lacrosse players, they shuffled away."[14]

The Bears remained in the Ivy title race for the next three years, falling a game short each time. In two of those years, they effectively lost the championship on the opening week of the season with one-point losses to Yale, which stopped them four times from the two-yard line in 1977 and scored a late touchdown in 1979. Anderson resigned in 1983, three years after his last winning season, citing the pressures of recruiting. "Everyone expects you to win all the time," he said, "and we just can't do it."[15]

Harry Gamble, a Ph.D. and amateur arborist, was a "teacher-coach" in the model of George Munger, in the words of Dan Rottenberg, Penn's football historian.[16] He had been an assistant to John Steigman in the early sixties, returning to Penn several years later to succeed Bob Odell as head coach. Aggressive recruiting, sound coaching, and a high-powered offense helped the Quakers to three consecutive winning seasons from 1972 to 1974 for the first time in more than twenty years.

Penn surprised everyone in 1972 by vaulting back into Ivy contention behind speedy sophomore tailback Adolph "Beep Beep" Bellizeare, who graduated as the Quakers' all-time leading rusher, and quarterback Marty Vaughn, who broke Quaker passing records. Together with end Don McClune, who set receiving records, the Quakers scored ten points or more in twenty-four consecutive games, yet were always just a step behind the top of the league. In other respects, however, they could be a step ahead of it, such as the 1973 game against Brown in which Vaughn and the Bears' Dennis Coleman became the first black quarterbacks to face each other in major college history (a 28-20 Quaker victory).

Little was heard from Cornell after Marinaro's departure. Football season ticket sales in Ithaca fell from almost eight thousand in 1971 to fewer than five thousand four years later and by 1974, just three years after sharing the Ivy League title, Bob Kane, the dean of physical education, had a hard time finding someone willing to take the head-coaching job. While attending the NCAA convention in Washington, D.C., he found himself eavesdropping in horror to a conversation in the adjoining room between Joe Yukica, a leading candidate for the job, and several other Ivy football coaches, all disparaging Cornell as a place to work. Yukica, who had almost joined the Cornell coaching staff a few years earlier, withdrew his name from consideration, only to become head coach at Dartmouth later.

Kane attributed Cornell's problem to a vicious cycle in which declining football revenues contributed to weaker teams, compounded by a national economic recession, which reduced funding the university as a whole, had become dependent upon from the state and federal government. Another culprit in Kane's opinion was the Cornell University Senate, an oversight body composed of students and faculty that controlled the athletic department's budget and bedeviled its officials with a series of investigations. Students complained about a bloated football budget as well as Cornell's compulsory physical education requirement, much as earlier generations at other colleges had complained about compulsory chapel. Despite cutting off several minor sports from funding, by the mid-seventies the athletic department had accumulated a deficit of almost $350,000. When the university's board of trustees recommended writing off the deficit, one professor dissented, insisting that "Athletics are neither integral, nor important, nor an educational opportunity ... athletics are peripheral." [17]

Eventually, Kane found a better coaching candidate, but he could not keep him. George Seifert was the highly regarded defensive coordinator at Stanford when he accepted the job in Ithaca, but he did not take over until February and managed to win only one game in his first season. In 1976, he won only two. When the Red won the second of those two games, their season finale against Penn, Seifert's players carried him off the field on their shoulders, unaware that he had already been fired by athletic director Dick Schultz, who would go on to become head of the NCAA itself.

Schultz thought he had a coup, luring Bob Blackman back to the Ivy League, but Blackman's magic had stayed in Hanover. Over the next six years, he won just seventeen games, lost twenty-five, and tied one, the lowest winning percentage of any Cornell football coach lasting more than two seasons. As for Seifert, he returned to Stanford as an assistant to coach Bill Walsh, then followed Walsh to the San Francisco 49ers, where he won four Super Bowls at a salary twenty-two times what he had been earning in Ithaca.

Except for occasional interruptions by the Crimson or Bears, the Ivy League during this time remained mostly a matched battle between Yale and Dartmouth, one of which claimed at least a piece of nineteen football titles in twenty-one years between 1962 and 1982. Cozza was named Yale's athletic director in the summer of 1976 with the understanding that he would resign as football coach at the end of the season. But five days after doing so (and after tying for yet another Ivy title), Cozza changed his mind and relinquished his new administrative duties in order to return to the sidelines, where he remained for another twenty years.

Demonstrating a successful program's ability to perpetuate itself, Yale, which had replaced Dowling and Hill with Jauron and Fencik, now filled their places with running back John Pagliaro (from Derby, Connecticut, about ten miles from the Yale Bowl), guard Kevin Czinger, and end Curt Grieve. In 1977, the Bulldogs defeated Harvard, 24-7, for the Ivy title when on fourth-and-twenty, Mike Sullivan ran a botched punt sixty-six yards for a touchdown. In 1978, Yale beat the Crimson again when tight end John Spagnola, who would later star for the Philadelphia Eagles, scored a decisive touchdown by yanking an errant pass back from the Harvard defender who had intercepted it.

Although Yale had already clinched the Ivy title in 1979, Bulldog fans anticipated their first perfect season in nineteen years when they met Harvard in the season's last game. The Crimson limped in with a dismal 2-6 record, having suffered so many injuries during the season that Restic had been forced to shelve the multiflex for simpler formations. Midway through the season, Yale's defense was ranked number one in the country (Nebraska was second), while tailback Kenny Hill, a biochemistry major who had gone to Yale after committing to Louisiana State, chewed up yardage on the ground. Ten thousand tickets were sold in a single day, a record for the series, but the underrated Crimson handed the Bulldogs a crushing disappointment when they cruised to a surprisingly easy 22-7 victory, the third time in twelve years that Harvard had spoiled an otherwise perfect Yale season.

Three-time All-Ivy linebacker Reggie Williams helped Dartmouth win a league title in 1973, but spent his remaining varsity seasons on disappointing squads that, not surprisingly, given his presence, continued to boast strong defenses. Williams, who had attended three years of elementary school at the Michigan School for the Deaf, went on the become an All-Pro for the Kansas City Chiefs, whose humanitarian work off the field later earned him *Sports Illustrated*'s designation as one of its "Sportsmen of the Year."

Coach Jake Crouthamel continued to field mediocre teams despite efforts to get alumni and parents involved by hosting a coffee hour (known as the "Pregame Jitters") before home contests.[18] Joe Yukica succeeded Crouthamel in 1978 and proceeded to win the Ivy title in his first season with Buddy Teevens, the man who would eventually replace him as coach, at quarterback. In a show-down against Brown on the next-to-last week of the season, Dartmouth saw a 21-7 lead evaporate, but held on to win thanks to three touchdowns by sophomore fullback Jeff Dufresne. The Big Green won two more titles in 1981 and 1982 with an offense that featured two prominent sons—receiver Dave Shula, son of Miami Dolphins coach Don Shula (and later an NFL coach in his own right) and quarterback Jeff Kemp, son of presidential aspirant Jack Kemp, who would play for several NFL teams.

In order to boost revenue, the Ivy League voted to add a tenth game beginning with the 1980 season (the NCAA allowed as many as eleven), the first time Ivy football schedules had been that long since 1936.[19] Harvard, Princeton, and even Columbia used the extra game to put Army and Navy back on their schedules for the first time in decades while Yale, ever-adventurous, added the Air Force Academy, only the second time it had ever played a college located west of the Mississippi River. In the post-Vietnam era, it was again acceptable to schedule service academies, but though popular in theory, the rivalries usually resulted in lopsided defeats and were discontinued after several years. On top of being shut out, 34-0, in 1981, Princeton suffered the added indignity of having its marching band banned from West Point because of its halftime shows.

Student attitudes toward football did seem more positive, which had more to do with a change in styles—an inevitable reaction against the rebelliousness of the previous decade—than with anything that had transpired on the field. When Dartmouth traveled to Cambridge in 1972, the student paper had printed a tongue-in-cheek guide for road-tripping undergraduates. Tip number one: "Do not under any circumstances wear your Dartmouth warm-up jacket around Harvard Square. The sight of hundreds of uniformly attired post-adolescents just is not considered cool by anyone in Cambridge, especially Radcliffe girls."[20] True, perhaps, but just a few years later Cozza said he noticed that "athletes are wearing their varsity jackets again.... Athletes and other students are dressing neatly again."[21]

Notwithstanding successful teams and standout players, including several future professionals, the 1970s marked the end of the days in which good Ivy football teams could hope to win national attention. The league had always been a conglomeration of haves and have nots, but by the early eighties, even successful programs such as Yale or Dartmouth were struggling to hold their own in non-conference games.

It was perhaps not so much that the quality of play in the Ivy League declined, but that they fell even further behind as major college football grew bigger and richer. Some blamed the lack of spring practice, which made it hard for Ivy teams to compete against colleges that permitted it, but that had not stopped Princeton, Yale, or Dartmouth from winning national acclaim. Coaches complained that they could not force good athletes to turn out for football or to stick with it once they did, which several attributed to the younger generation's desire for instant gratification but which Cozza probably correctly recognized as a by-product of the broader range of extracurricular activities now available.

Certainly, the colleges took pride in their status as football puritans. Although Yale permitted the NFL's New York Giants to use the Bowl while Yankee Stadium was being renovated, the Ivy League remained a place where a 1974 freshman football game between Harvard and Dartmouth was delayed two hours so members of the Crimson could take an economics exam in a Dartmouth classroom (the change of venue being the faculty's only concession). That fall, the Crimson's best defensive back, Mike Page, missed a varsity game against Columbia in order to take the law school board examination.

The last Ivy team that might have won national recognition lost its chance at glory in one of the league's great upsets, a game that has been hailed as the most exciting ever played in Palmer Stadium.

Despite highpoints, like halfback Walt Snickenberger, a third team All American in 1974, Princeton had suffered through the worst decade in its history. After years of uncommon stability, the Tigers lurched from McCandless to Bob Casciola, both alumni coaches, before hiring Frank Navarro, a move that must have made sense to someone at the time as Navarro had led Columbia to only one winning season in his six years on Morningside Heights. In 1980, tired of being beaten up, they once again dropped Rutgers from the schedule, this time for good. (A 1974 game had ended in a 6-6 tie when Princeton was unable to attempt an extra point after a last-second touchdown because fans had ripped down the goal posts. That winter, the NCAA was forced to require the home team to keep a portable goal available for just such an exigency.)

By 1973, Princeton was offering discounts on tickets in a bid to fill Palmer Stadium's empty seats with townies. Average home attendance had fallen from thirty-two thousand per game in 1965 (not far below the mid-thirties peak of thirty-nine thousand) to a few more than ten thousand by 1980. Blame was given to everything from the introduction of fall break, which let students go home on two football Saturdays, to the greater availability of beer at eating clubs, which reduced the importance of football parties.[22]

Emblematic of the Tigers' futility was its inability to beat its oldest rival, Yale. Entering the 1981 contest, the Tigers had lost fourteen straight to the Elis, a streak unprecedented in Princeton football history. None of the previous nine defeats had been by less than two touchdowns. In 1976, Princeton economics professor Uwe Reinhardt (a Yale graduate) undertook an elaborate, if fanciful, mathematical analysis of the team's chances of beating Yale that fall and concluded that they had none.[23] A year later, Reinhardt professed to have changed his mind, but the best reason he could come up with for a Tiger victory was the law of averages.[24]

Stymied on the field, Princeton students sought what victories they could off it. In 1979, a group of undergraduates dognapped Yale mascot Handsome Dan XII (the first female ever to serve) by posing as Yale cheerleaders. Dan was spirited out of town, but returned to her rightful owners at halftime (of a 35-10 Yale victory), decked out in orange and black.

To further dim the Tigers' chances, Yale's 1981 team was its best in almost a decade. Fullback Rich Diana, a molecular biology major, was the team's leading punt and kickoff returner and second-leading receiver, in addition to being the league's best rusher since Marinaro. As a junior, he had ranked second only to Heisman Trophy winner Marcus Allen in all-purpose yardage, with nearly 175 yards per game. After the Elis upset Navy on network television, speculation grew that they might even crack the Top Twenty.

Princeton's 1981 season had not been altogether unsuccessful. They had beaten Brown for the first time in nine years and extended their unbeaten streak against Harvard to five. But halfway into the season, injuries had rendered the Tigers' already weak running attack impotent. Against Army, they had run the ball twenty-four times for twenty-five yards. Two weeks later against Maine, they carried the ball sixteen times and went backward—for minus nine yards.

Yet in football, as in so many other areas of life, despair is the true mother of invention. With nowhere else to go, quarterback Bob Holly took to the air, all but abandoning his nonexistent running attack. In the two games before Yale came to town, Holly averaged almost fifty passes per game and threw for almost nine hundred yards, while the team scored seventy-four points.

It appeared that Yale, a twelve-point favorite, would continue the streak when it jumped to a 21-0 lead midway through the second quarter, controlling the ball for twenty-eight out of thirty-two plays during one stretch as Diana carried again and again. But Cozza began to play conservatively, enabling Princeton to climb to within 21-15 by halftime. To everyone's surprise, the Tigers pulled ahead, 22-21, shortly after the second half began, but Diana, who was playing with two broken fingers and bruised ribs, and quarterback John Rogan reestablished a lead of 31-22.

With less than nine minutes to play there was no point in even pretending to run. Princeton running backs would not touch the ball again for the rest of the game. It took only three minutes to cut the deficit to 31-29, but Rogan marched the Bulldogs on a time-consuming drive that culminated in a missed field goal attempt with just over a minute and a half to play. Holly took over at his own twenty-four-yard line with no times out left.

His first three passes were incomplete, but on fourth and ten, Scott Oostdyk, Holly's high school teammate, caught the ball just inches beyond the first down marker. With fifteen seconds left, Holly's pass to Derek Graham in the end zone was knocked away, but Yale was called for pass interference, giving the Tigers first and goal at the one-yard line. Although Holly kept trying to go to the sideline for instructions, Navarro waved him back, fearful of being penalized for delay of game. The coach passed up a field goal attempt into a stiff breeze at a sharp angle to run one more play, a dangerous decision given that if Princeton was stopped short of the end zone, it could not kill the clock. Rolling to his left, Holly dove for the winning score, only the second time in twenty snaps that he had not thrown the ball.

Holly, whose thirty-six completions (in fifty-five attempts) and 501 passing yards set new Ivy League records, was named *Sports Illustrated*'s offensive player of the week, while United Press International tabbed Navarro as its Coach of the Week. Graham's fifteen pass receptions also set an Ivy record. Diana's exceptional game—forty-six carries for 222 yards and three touchdowns—was lost amid the din, and Yale's shot at glory was ruined. Holly and Diana would face each other, as backups for the Washington Redskins and Miami Dolphins, respectively, in Super Bowl XVII. The Bulldogs, for their part, would return the favor in the Bowl three years later when Mike Curtin engineered a 98-yard drive in the last minute and a half with no times out remaining to steal a 27-24 victory from the Tigers.

Their metal goalposts reduced to scrap, the Princeton athletic department erected temporary wooden goal posts, which also fell the following week when the Tigers beat Cornell. An overexuberant Princeton band led an impromptu (and illegal) parade down Nassau Street, which got their leader, Steve Teager, arrested. He received an official pardon from New Jersey Governor Brendan T. Byrne, Class of 1949, who declared "it is impossible to have criminal intent so shortly after a Tiger victory."[25]

While Princeton was upending Cornell, more than seventy-two thousand fans filled the Yale Bowl to see the Bulldogs shut out Harvard, 28-0, thus capturing a piece of the Ivy League title (which it shared with Dartmouth). It was, however, to be the last game of its kind. Thirteen days later, at a special meeting of the NCAA in St. Louis, the delegates voted, by a show of hands, to institute criteria that expelled the eight Ivy League teams and twenty-nine others to second-tier Division I-AA.

The Ivies had been dodging this bullet since the NCAA created Division I-AA in 1978. The issue was money. Major college teams, which were battling the NCAA over television revenues and eligibility rules, resented the influence exerted by smaller schools, particularly the sanctimonious Ivy League. Henceforward, in order to remain in Division I-A, a football team would have to draw an average of at least seventeen thousand fans to home games over the preceding four years or play those games in a stadium that could seat at least thirty thousand people. As Ivy Cassandras had warned all along, the NCAA now defined big-time football not in terms of a college's commitment to athletics, but in terms of spectators and revenue.

Relations with the NCAA had never been close, notwithstanding the Ivy League's refusal to back Penn during the TV dispute in the early fifties. Just as the Big Three had long feared allying with colleges they believed had lower standards, the Ivy League as a whole now resisted efforts by the NCAA to redefine the student-athlete. Yet as Geoffrey Kabaservice has written in a study of Yale's role in the formation of the Ivy League, "The Ivies continued to delude themselves that they could exert a beneficial influence on the NCAA, and that the organization was forever teetering on the brink of redemption." [26]

The Ivy colleges scorned the letter of intent and the requirement that athletes maintain a 1.6 grade point average, arguing that they created distinctions between athletes and other students and interfered with their own autonomy. When the league refused to comply with the grade point threshold, they were stripped of eligibility for all NCAA championships. A few years later, the other Ivy presidents stood by Yale when it insisted on using a basketball player who had competed in the Maccabiah Games, refusing to be a party to the NCAA's attempt to wrest control over amateur athletics from the Amateur Athletic Union, even though this drew the Elis a two-year suspension in all sports.

Many also chafed at a regulation limiting the number of players who could dress for home games (Cozza referred to it as "that stinking rule"), and when the NCAA permitted freshmen to play on varsity teams in 1970, thus reducing the number of students given an opportunity to participate in intercollegiate athletics, the Ivy League insisted on maintaining freshman football. More than once, the eight Ivy colleges had considered withdrawing from the NCAA, but such a move became less and less tenable as the financial benefits of NCAA membership increased.

At Penn's instigation, when the NCAA created the new Division I-AA in 1978 it spared the Ivy League by permitting colleges to remain in Division I-A if they fielded teams in at least twelve varsity sports. But as television revenue became even more important to the major colleges, which constituted themselves as the College Football Association and prepared a legal challenge to the NCAA's longstanding TV monopoly, they dropped the Ivy League exemption. Schools that could not sell tickets would have to get out.

As usual, the press waxed eloquent in defense of Ivy ideals, but if the Ancient Eight waited for help from the other colleges, they waited in vain. Even Joe Paterno scorned them. "The Ivy League is in another world all by their own," the Brown alumnus said. "They are in another world. I'm in the real world." [27]

Although NCAA rules permitted schools affected by a decision to request a waiver, the eight declined to do so. "I guess the Ivy presidents just won't go with hat in hand begging," the league's director said. [28] Half the league—Harvard, Yale, Princeton, and Penn—met the NCAA's criteria and thus could have stayed in

Division I-A, but remained loyal to their ancient rivals and followed them into obscurity.

Cut adrift, the Ivy League considered expanding by as many as six schools to include Army, Colgate, Holy Cross, Navy, Northwestern, and William and Mary, but concluded it should stay as it was. Some of their prospective members were less than eager to affiliate, also. "We'd love to join the Ivy basketball league," Army athletic director Carl Ullrich told the press, "But we couldn't afford to join them in football." [29]

Yet having committed to a ten-game schedule but with only seven league games possible, Ivy football squads had to schedule at least some outsiders, usually games in which they were prohibitive underdogs. In 1983, Brown served themselves up against Penn State and despite betting odds that made them thirty-five point underdogs, escaped with a respectable 38-21 defeat in which they amassed more yards of offense than the Nittany Lions in the first half. Three years later, Princeton hosted Ivy-aspirant Northwestern, the first time one of the Ancient Eight had played a Big Ten team since 1953. ("A duel of eggheads and bigger eggheads," *Sports Illustrated* joked.) [30] The Wildcats whipped them, 37-0.

These games continued intermittently. More than a decade later, Cornell agreed to visit Stanford in 1991 to commemorate that school's centennial and lost, 56-6. Commenting on Stanford's massive linemen, one sportswriter wrote, "The Cornell Big Red was not only playing out of its league, it was playing out of its species." [31] Yale, always the Ivy evangelist, has played in a different Soldier Field— Chicago's—against Valparaiso, at San Diego, at Central Florida, and in 1987 halfway across the Pacific against the University of Hawaii. More realistically, Columbia returned to California in 1995 to play little St. Mary's—and still lost by twenty points.

Given Ivy restrictions, however, it had become apparent that there were not many teams outside the league with which they could compete, and few Division I-A teams cared to schedule I-AA teams for fear of weakening their chances at a bowl bid. Concern about Brown's Penn State game prompted the presidents to explore the possibility of creating a companion league among philosophically compatible and athletically beatable colleges. In 1983, they asked Tony Maruca, a vice president at Princeton, to identify potential rivals. Maruca met with the presidents of Holy Cross and Lehigh and helped them recruit other northeastern colleges. [32] The resulting conglomeration, known as the Colonial League, included Bucknell, Lafayette, and Colgate—once cannon fodder, now partners—whose statement of athletic principles echoed those of the Ivy League almost verbatim.

Even this drew complaints, however, as the Colonial League permitted both spring practice and an NCAA-maximum eleven-game schedule. Yale objected to the alliance from the standpoint of the box office when William and Mary, which was supposed to join League, withdrew and was replaced by Davidson. Over the first five years of the agreement, Ivy League teams won barely more than a third of their games against Colonial League opponents. Eventually, the Colonial League became the Patriot League, which now rounds out the non-conference part of most Ivy schedules, though it remains an informal arrangement, one teams can pursue or not as they choose.

Within their own group, the Ivy League basked in the rays of national attention in 1983 when Harvard and Yale met for the one hundredth playing of The Game. Athletically speaking, the contest meant little—both teams were coming off poor seasons—yet twelve hundred Harvard students made the trip down from Cambridge. Ticket prices were raised from $15 to $20, and programs from $1 to $5, all contributing to the $5 million windfall reaped by the New Haven economy that weekend. In a display of merchandising that would have been scandalous to an earlier generation, souvenir sellers hawked commemorative sweaters, T-shirts, glassware, tote bags, stickpins, and other memorabilia at exorbitant prices. Nonetheless, the Bowl was not sold out and attendance was actually slightly less than it had been two years earlier when Yale had fielded a good team.

Not even the hundredth game, though, could hope to match what had happened the year before, when a group of MIT students pulled perhaps the greatest prank in college football history. Midway through the second quarter, the forty thousand spectators in Harvard Stadium were stunned when a six-foot wide, electronically controlled weather balloon, emblazoned with "MIT," sprouted from the sod at the forty-yard line and exploded in a cloud of white dust. The scheme had been cooked up by members of the Delta Kappa Epsilon fraternity, who had been working on it for four years. Their stunt drew national attention as sportscaster Brent Musberger breathlessly, though inaccurately, announced on CBS that a bomb had blasted a three-foot deep crater. Unable to contain themselves, the Dekes called a press conference the following Monday to claim credit. [33]

For the one hundredth Game, thirty-two former captains from each school met at midfield to conduct the coin toss, led by ninety-four-year-old Hamilton Fish. (A touch football reunion that morning between veterans of the 1968 classic was declared a forfeit when only Brian Dowling showed up for the Elis.) As they had in their first meeting, Harvard prevailed, 16-7. [34]

"Harvard-Yale isn't just a football game. It's a social event built around a football game," explained Robert Pickett, head of the Harvard Varsity Club (yet a Yale alumnus). [35] Yale President A. Bartlett Giamatti was more philosophical, calling it "probably the last great nineteenth century pageant left in the country." The Game, he said, "has all the tradition and texture and color of a coming together of rival families. In many ways, the game is a celebration of the comradeship of competition." [36]

CHAPTER TWELVE

The Modern Game

The eight Ivy colleges moved down in classification in 1982 but took their principles with them, refusing, for example, to participate in the Division I-AA playoffs. Two years earlier, Yale president A. Bartlett Giamatti had warned alumni that "some students, and not a trivial number, spend far, far too much time, with the encouragement of the institutions, on athletic pursuits." If the Ivy Group wanted to be "more than a set of financial aid policies and a concatenation of schedules," he said, it had to return to its "first principles." Toward this end, Giamatti called upon the colleges to curtail recruiting, end postseason play in sports that allowed it, shorten the football season, and encourage coaches to diversify their interests by working in more than one sport.[1] A few years later he undertook an even more quixotic fight, asking Ivy League athletic directors to explore the possibility of once again banning coaching from the sidelines.

Only Dartmouth responded favorably to Giamatti's call for still more de-emphasis, although even the Big Green were uncomfortable with his proposal to restrict recruiting, arguing that to do so would perpetuate the advantage already enjoyed by the Big Three. Still, as Giamatti's warning demonstrated, small-time status had neither eliminated nor even mitigated concerns about the proper role of football in college life. Those concerns remained acute as the Ivy presidents wrestled with how to structure both the league and the game in the face of declining importance and growing costs.

Quite unlike the Harvard-Yale anniversary, Ivy League football achieved notoriety of a very different sort when Columbia embarked upon a titanic losing streak in the mid-eighties.

Ivy losing streaks had never been long before the start of round-robin play. Between 1888 and 1954, only two teams had gone through even a single season without a victory: Cornell in 1935 and Columbia in 1943. Only with Penn's self-imposed collapse in the mid-fifties did the concept begin to creep in. Brown recorded winless seasons in 1961 and 1971 (and would again in 1988 and 1992) while Penn endured another in 1979. None, though, compared with Columbia's agony.

The string of losses did not sneak up on Columbia, which had not won more than once in a season since 1978 or enjoyed a winning record since 1971. In the first thirty years of the league's existence, in fact, the Lions won less than a quarter of their league games. Some attributed the problem to the size of its undergraduate enrollment, the smallest in the league. Others blamed the big-city atmosphere, which dampened school spirit and athletic involvement. It may just have been the ethos of the place. "It takes a brutal and aggressive personality to be good at football," wrote Leonard Koppett, a Columbia alumnus, in the *New York Times*. "That personality has always been welcomed in its own context at Harvard, Yale and Princeton because of their different traditions. It's much more easily absorbed in larger places like Cornell and Pennsylvania. It has always been put down at Columbia."[2]

Put down or not, the Lions defeated Yale, 21-18, midway through the 1983 season behind senior quarterback John Witkowski, the latest in a string of excellent Columbia quarterbacks. The following week they tied Bucknell, and after a 77-28 shellacking by Holy Cross, tied Dartmouth, 17-17. That was the last game that would end up anywhere other than in the loss column for almost five years.

When the Lions lost all their games in 1984, it spelled the end for Coach Bob Naso, who departed with a record of 4-43-2 over five seasons. He was replaced by Jim Garrett, a fiery-tempered taskmaster hired to bring some discipline to a disorganized program. For the previous twenty years, Garrett had been a scout and assistant coach for three NFL teams. Before that, though, as head coach at Susquehanna College, he had been forced to resign two games into the 1966 season when he expressed his displeasure at a bad play by slapping one of his players on the helmet.

That surely was not what Columbia officials had in mind for their own program, but Garrett did not take losing well. In his first game, he watched his team jump to a 17-0 lead over Harvard, then collapse as the Crimson scored on seven consecutive possessions for a 49-17 victory. Afterward, Garrett exploded. "They are drug-addicted losers," he said, describing his team to reporters. "Once adversity comes, and bang! They're right back in the sewer again."

He had not meant to suggest that his team was addicted to drugs, rather that they were addicted to losing, but as if this statement were not bad enough, Garrett went on to single out his punter, senior Pete Murphy, for special blame. "The punting absolutely killed us," Garrett ranted. "Absolutely killed us." Murphy, who had been honorably mentioned for the All-Ivy team the previous year, had averaged thirty-eight and a half yards on eight punts, three yards more than his average during the two previous seasons. "I want to see him when he graduates and goes to work downtown on Wall Street and does the things that he did today," Garrett continued, refusing to let the matter drop. "See how long he is gonna work for that company, how long Merrill Lynch or Smith Barney is gonna have him around. I'm no different than anybody else." [3]

Predictably, the coach was jumped on from all corners, including a *New York Times* editorial. "I'm from Sooner Country—Norman, Oklahoma, and I came here to get away from that rah-rah spirit," one student complained. [4] Columbia officially reprimanded him, Athletic Director Norman Mintz saying, "Winning is extremely important to us, but not at any cost." [5] Murphy accepted Garrett's apology (though he declined to receive it in person), but quit the team anyway, the tenth player to walk away from the Lions in little more than a month.

The loss to Harvard had been Columbia's twelfth in a row, setting a new school record for futility that was nowhere near ending. Garrett limped through the rest of the season, losing the nine remaining games by an average of almost thirty points before resigning. He was replaced by Larry McElreavy, a former Penn assistant, but the new coach could do no better, suffering even more indignities and beginning to draw national attention. When winless Columbia faced winless Colgate seven weeks into the 1986 season, Colgate was nonetheless a thirty-point betting favorite, which, as it turned out, was being charitable. The Red Raiders covered, 54-8.

Into 1987 the losing streak continued, week after unhappy week. "With so much attention currently focused on the football team," one sportswriter suggested, "it is an ideal time for the Columbia administration to consider moving to Division II or III, where victories would not be so elusive." [6] On October 10, the Lions fell to Princeton, 38-8, their thirty-fifth game in a row without a victory, thus establishing the longest winless streak in NCAA Division I history. Princeton issued 120 press credentials for the game, about 100 more than usual, as reporters from around the country came to watch the powder blue train wreck. Adding insult to injury, the Tiger starters that afternoon included Jim Garrett's three sons, who had transferred from the purgatory of Morningside Heights when their father left. At season's end (a 19-16 squeaker to Brown), eleven Columbia seniors took off their jerseys for the last time without ever having won a varsity game.

If Princeton clinched the record, however, Princeton also ended it. In a happy twist of fate, the streak was broken exactly a year later, having grown to forty-four games, when Columbia upset the Tigers, 16-13, on a fourth quarter touchdown by Solomon Johnson. "Columbia Wins! That's Right, Wins!" exulted the *New York Times*, which noted the event on its front page. The few thousand Lion fans inside Wien Stadium, their numbers swelled as news of the impending upset spread, carried off both goal posts, not to mention the first down markers, yardage chains, and end zone pylons. Incredibly, it was Columbia's first game without a fumble in sixteen years.

On campus, where most students had remained that afternoon, stereos blasted "Dancing in the Street" out open apartment windows. A few, however, could not shake their sense of irony even on such a momentous day. "It was a welcome relief to have a really bad football team," one junior said.[7]

Victory or no victory, the young man still had one. Although the Lions rallied to win a second game that season for the first time in almost a decade, they had hardly been transformed. McElreavy resigned over the winter amid charges of personal misconduct, though worse were allegations that some Columbia players had been using steroids. Players, who had chafed under his harsh criticism, did not rally to their coach's defense. "The decision itself is not one that I and most of my teammates regret," said Terry Brown, a senior receiver.[8]

In a sense, Columbia was only a particularly vivid illustration of a broader problem the league was forced to address—how to balance the fundamental Ivy principle that athletes should be representative of the student body with the necessity that teams win at least some of their games; how to balance, in other words, purity and victory. This was a problem the teams had wrestled with almost since football was invented, but as the Big Three had long been aware, it had always been difficult to agree on an objective measure of purity that could compare athletes at schools of different sizes and standards.

One solution was something called the Academic Index, devised in 1981 by James Litvak, the Ivy League director and a Princeton economics professor. Using a complicated formula involving each entering student's standardized test scores and high school class rank, the index generated a numerical average for each entering class at each of the eight colleges. Athletes had to have a score within a certain range of their college's average and in the case of football, that range was further subdivided into smaller bands, with only a certain number of players permitted to fall within each. No athlete could be admitted whose score fell below a league-wide floor unless the college had a nonathletic reason that it could justify to the others. Finally, the league also set a limit on the number of football players each college was permitted to admit over any four-year period.

Shortly after the Academic Index was created, however, the Ivy presidents quietly agreed to suspend it in order to enable Columbia to admit athletes whose scores fell slightly below the league minimum. Where the average index of Columbia freshmen in 1987, for example, was 195 and the league floor was 161, the waiver enabled the athletic department to recruit players whose index was as low as 153. "They don't think it's a good thing for the league that Columbia loses all the time," explained the dean.[9]

When news of the waiver leaked two years later in the middle of the losing streak, many Columbia students were outraged. "I thought I was at an institution that would never lower its standards for anything," said Roger Rubin, sports editor of the *Spectator*. School officials viewed it differently. "The league ... saw it undesirable to have one school lagging so far behind," explained Columbia's dean of students, Roger Lehecka. "The fact is that an uncompetitive program is not a fair thing to do to students." [10]

In all, the Lions enrolled a total of eleven football players during the two-year waiver, helping the freshman football team post the best record in school history, although they had little impact once they reached the varsity. Columbia went back to abysmal, if not record-breaking, football under new coach Ray Tellier, winning no more than three games in each of the next five seasons after the streak ended, and going 8-42 during that period.

By 1994, though, the Lions posted their first winning record in twenty-three years. Although they slipped in 1995, they did upset Penn, 24-14, behind two touchdowns by quarterback Mike Cavanaugh, ending the Quakers' twenty-four-game winning streak. Finally, in 1996, after two generations of misery, the Lions surprised everyone by finishing 8-2, their best record since 1945, and placing second behind Dartmouth.

Many gave credit to the new university president, George Rupp, an ordained Presbyterian minister and former Harvard Divinity School professor, who willingly made changes to help athletics, such as extending cafeteria hours so players returning from practice would not miss meals. The real secret to the Lions' success, though, was their renewed emphasis on recruiting. Conceding the Northeast to their Ivy rivals, Columbia focused its attention on the Southwest, a decision that reaped benefits beyond the playing fields. By 1996, applications for admission universitywide were up 69 percent from their level five years earlier. [11] Twenty-nine of the ninety-three Lion football players, meanwhile, including eleven starters, came from California.

Marcellus Wiley was the prize of that group, a Los Angeles native who had passed up UCLA to attend Columbia. At six-foot five-inches tall and 255 pounds, Wiley was bigger and faster than most of the other players in the league, powerful enough that Tellier moved him from running back, where he played his first two seasons, to defensive end, where he later became a second-round draft pick of the Buffalo Bills. Wiley proved versatile enough to play both ways occasionally. In a 42-16 victory over Holy Cross in 1996, he scored three touchdowns, leading the Lions to the most points they had scored in a game in twenty-one years.

Even so, there were disturbing questions about what Columbia had to do in order to keep him. Wiley was expelled for poor grades after his junior season and told he would have to earn at least a B+ average at an academically comparable school in order to be readmitted. He returned to California, where he attended West Los Angeles Community College. When he applied for readmission a year later, Columbia reportedly accepted his community college credits in full. [12] As soon as Wiley graduated, the Lions slid back to losing football.

Although the Academic Index was intended to level the playing field, so to speak, the Big Three often complained that it worked against them because it only compared football players against the class within each college, not between colleges. Thus, Harvard, Yale, and Princeton, with the most rigorous academic standards, can only admit athletes with higher scores than can colleges with lower indexes, most notably Cornell and Penn. What this argument overlooked, however, was that other colleges had always been less selective, relatively speaking. In fact, the Academic Index gave the Big Three a means of monitoring what those other schools were doing and restraining how low they could dip.

Nevertheless, the Quakers became a handy target for those critical of the Academic Index. It had, in fact, been Penn's basketball team, not its football team, that inspired the index in the first place, when the Quakers went to the Final Four of the NCAA basketball tournament in 1979 with players whose academic qualifications were questioned in other corners of the league. Penn's football resurgence, which began at about the time the index was put into place, owed as much to an aggressive pursuit of victory within the rules as it did to lower admission standards. In that sense, the Quakers could claim to be a model for the rest of the Ivy League.

Harry Gamble had coached them to winning records in three of his first four seasons, but the bottom had dropped out in the late Seventies as the team won only three of twenty-eight games. Penn replaced him with Jerry Berndt, the head coach at DePauw University in Indiana, who ditched Gamble's wishbone offense as well as the traditional uniforms with red and blue stripes down the sleeves. "They were completely out of style," one player complained. "I wore them and I felt old." [13]

Berndt also placed a new emphasis on training, increasing the number of Quakers who could bench press three hundred pounds, for example, from twelve to thirty in one season. He restored ties to Quaker alumni who could promote the old winning spirit and help support the team financially, while promoting recruiting by continuing the tradition of inviting Philadelphia-area high school coaches and players to Penn home games free of charge.

Nineteen eighty-one, Berndt's first season, opened on a promising note with an upset over Cornell, which now opened the season in alternate years. But that was the Quakers' only victory. The season slid downhill from there, reaching its lowest point when four players were suspended before the Harvard game for smoking marijuana in their Boston hotel room.

No one expected anything better in 1982. *Penthouse* magazine, in the ultimate insult, ranked the Quakers as the third-worst team in the country, but Penn shocked Dartmouth, 21-0, on the opening Saturday as quarterback Gary Vura broke the school passing record by completing twenty-three passes for 254 yards and three touchdowns. Penn proceeded to win its first four games for the first time since 1968. When they beat Harvard in the next-to-last week of the season—on a second-chance field goal as time expired—the Quakers clinched a share of their first Ivy championship since 1959.

Proving that this was no fluke, the resurgent Quakers shared the Ivy League championship again the following year and claimed it outright in 1984, 1985, and 1986—the first time an Ivy football team had ever won three consecutive league championships outright. In 1985, Penn overcame a 21-0 Princeton lead (built on two touchdown passes from Doug Butler, the Tigers' all-time leading passer), for a 31-21 victory that extended their winning streak to thirteen games. Although Harvard ended the streak a week later, the Crimson lost their own chance at the title when Yale upset them. Penn, meanwhile, playing without quarterback Jim Crocicchia and running back Rich Comizio, eked out a 19-14 win over Dartmouth. Students chanting, "Four, four, four," tore down the goalposts and dumped them in the Schuylkill River.

In 1986, the Quakers not only recorded their first perfect season since 1904, but also beat Division I-A Navy with three Crocicchia touchdown passes, one of the rare Ivy victories against a Division I-A opponent. Their meeting with Cornell on the last weekend of the season marked the first time two unbeaten teams had decided the Ivy League title since Harvard and Yale in 1968. Comizio rushed for 162 yards as Penn cruised to its fifth consecutive title, having lost only four league games during that period.

As frequently happens, athletic improvement also coincided with a change in administration, in this case the hiring of Sheldon Hackney as university president. Hackney had been credited with helping revive Tulane's football program while president of that university and set out to do the same at Penn, arguing that, given the increase in donations from happy alumni, it cost the university more money to lose than it did to win. Much as Stassen had thirty years earlier, Hackney became a football evangelist, increasing the athletic budget, spending more than half a million dollars on new AstroTurf for Franklin Field, speaking to alumni groups, and even contacting recruits. Unlike Stassen, however, Hackney was content with success on the Ivy League's terms.

Hackney's enthusiasm paid off in other areas, as well. Thanks in part to the pro-business mentality of the times and the prominence of Wharton graduates such as Donald Trump and Michael Milken, applications to Penn soared. In 1979, only 15 percent of Penn students came from outside the northeastern United States; ten years later, more than half did. By the mid-nineties, *U.S. News & World Report* ranked Penn as the seventh-best national university in the United States.

After a one-year slump in 1987, Berndt continued to win, claiming a share of still another Ivy title in 1988 with Cornell, which beat the Quakers on the last game of the season with sixteen fourth-quarter points. The game was ugly by Ivy standards. A year earlier, Penn had brought its "barking dog" defense, which took itself perhaps too literally. Quaker linebacker Brad Hippenstiel, who had once been found bow-hunting squirrels on the Penn quad, declared before the game, "I hate Cornell and every other team in the Ivies, and every year my hatred for these dweezils grows deeper. People say Penn players are human, but we're not. We're not quite cannibals, because they eat meat and we just spit at it." [14]

Cornell spat right back and won, 17-13, but the Big Red, who had finished second in the league the year before, could do no better than 5-5. A year later, in the season's final week, the battle resumed. Coach Maxie Baughan prepared his team for more barking dogs by having his second team grab and curse the starters during practice. "We knew we weren't preparing for the Little Sisters of the Poor," said Cornell linebacker Mike McGrann. [15]

Penn's defense tried intimidation by running out onto the field carrying a red and blue sledge hammer, known as the Big Stick, which was awarded each week to the player making the hardest hit. Attitude the Quakers had in abundance ("Their guys were grabbing us in the pile, spitting in our faces whenever they could, and mouthing off," Cornell quarterback Aaron Sumida complained), but it came at a price. They were penalized five times for personal fouls (Cornell was penalized four times), the most costly when the defense was backed up at their own nine-yard line. The Big Red prevailed, 19-6, enough to claim a tie with Penn atop the league.

Berndt left Penn for Rice University after the 1985 season and was succeeded by his assistant, Ed Zubrow, who had previously been the football coach at Philadelphia's William Penn Charter School. Only thirty-five years old, Zubrow was the youngest coach in Penn history and the first Quaker assistant to step up since George Munger, but the team continued to win. Three years and two more Ivy championships later, Zubrow himself resigned to take a job fighting drug abuse and truancy in the Philadelphia public schools.

The Quakers posted three straight losing seasons under Zubrow's successor, Gary Steele, but have rebounded under Al Bagnoli, formerly coach at Union College, who took over in 1992 and has twice been voted Division I-AA Coach of the Year. In 1993, the Quakers hosted Princeton at mid-season in a battle of unbeatens, the first time the two schools had faced each other in that position since the Battle of Trenton in 1894. This time, it was Princeton's mohawk-sporting fullback Keith Elias who was doing the talking, belittling Penn's admissions standards. The Quaker defense held him to only fifty-nine yards on twelve carries and benefited from eight fumbles, four of them on the simple exchange from center to quarterback, and won convincingly, 30-14. Elias's opposite, Terrence Stokes, rushed for 272 and was in no mood for generosity after the game. Again, the Quakers kept rolling, repeating as champions in 1994 and extending their winning streak to twenty-one games, a Division I-AA record.

"Everybody thinks we're breaking some rules," Quaker quarterback Mark DeRosa boasted in 1995. "I'm sure we're bending some rules, but everybody else better start bending some, too." [16] Two years later, it was discovered that rules had indeed been bent and that All-Ivy tackle Mitch Marrow had played in eight games while academically ineligible. According to two Penn history professors, someone in the athletic department approached a junior professor asking that an independent study course be devised for Marrow late in the season in order to restore his eligibility. When that request was rebuffed, another independent study was arranged in the Wharton School just seventeen days before the end of the semester. The course was canceled after the story hit the papers, but the league presidents pursued the matter vigorously. After an investigation, Penn agreed to forfeit all the victories in which Marrow had played, the first such forfeiture in the history of Quaker football.

Cornell's 1988 triumph over Penn's barking dogs proved to be the last hurrah for Maxie Baughan. A former all-pro linebacker with the Philadelphia Eagles, Baughan had been the defensive coordinator for the Detroit Lions when he was approached for the Cornell job, which he accepted without ever visiting the campus. His first three seasons in Ithaca were dismal, despite the presence of tailback Derrick Harmon, a future NFL star who maintained an A average in engineering physics and later pursued a master's degree in Chinese. Although the Big Red tied for the league title in 1986 and 1988, Baughan was forced to resign amid allegations of personal misconduct.

His replacement, Jim Hofher, a Cornell alumnus, managed to sustain Baughan's success, sharing the Ivy crown with Dartmouth in 1990. When running back John McNiff went down with an injury that season against Yale, backup Scott Oliaro, who entered the game without even being called, rushed for a 69-yard touchdown on his first play, and 288 yards for the day, breaking Ed Marinaro's single game record in a 41-31 victory.

Midway through the 1994 season, the undefeated Big Red were ranked twenty-fifth in the country in the Division I-AA poll (Penn was thirteenth) despite playing before half-full crowds. Upon investigation, it turned out that the reason Cornell had made the list was because its own coaching staff ranked themselves first in the country, thus giving them the extra votes they needed.[17] It all proved a mirage, as the team proceeded to lose its last four games.

The Big Red and Quakers were not the only ones who continued to thrive in Division I-AA. Ivy League football, like the Ivy League colleges, was sufficiently self-referential that games could still be appreciated on their own merits—and in fact had to be, considering the League's refusal to participate in the Division I-AA playoffs.

Harvard defeated Yale for the title in 1987, Restic's last, when Tom "Yo-Yo" Yohe bested Kelly Ryan, the Bulldogs' all-time leading passer. As good a passer as he was, though, a knee injury had turned Ryan into a statue in the backfield (he *lost* nearly one hundred yards rushing in his career), so two years later Cozza installed an obsolete offense—the wishbone—to take advantage of Ryan's fleet but diminutive successor, Darrin Kehler, whom Cozza had recruited from Yale's baseball team. When the undefeated Bulldogs visited the undefeated Tigers on the next-to-last week of the season, Palmer Stadium was crowded with than thirty-seven thousand fans, the biggest Princeton crowd in twenty-four years. Yale converted a blocked punt (their fifth that season) into a touchdown and a 14-7 victory. Harvard upset them the following week, forcing the Elis and Tigers to share what proved to be Cozza's last title.

Though he won Ivy League championships in 1978, 1981, and 1982, Dartmouth fired coach Joe Yukica after a disappointing 2-7-1 season in 1985. Rather than submit, Yukica sued the college, citing the sanctity of his contract, which still had a year to run. A New Hampshire judge promptly enjoined Dartmouth from firing the coach or hiring a replacement. When the case went to trial, Joe Paterno and Bob Blackman were among the fellow coaches who testified on Yukica's behalf. He eventually agreed to a settlement in which he was paid $70,000 and allowed to remain coach for another season.

Given the turmoil, it was not surprising that Dartmouth sank from sight for several years thereafter, finishing among the Ivy also-rans. By the early 1990s, however, they rose again behind quarterback Jay Fiedler, who later succeeded Dan Marino as quarterback of the Miami Dolphins. Fiedler had been recruited by Stanford as a decathlete, but chose Dartmouth instead. As a junior in 1992, he led all Division I-AA quarterbacks in passing efficiency and by the time he graduated, his 7,249 total yards in offense had set a new Dartmouth record, almost half as many again as the old mark. Fiedler's final game, against Princeton in 1993, was perhaps his best. In one eight-minute span in the fourth quarter, he threw two touchdown passes, ran for a third, and scored a two-point conversion to lead a 28-22 victory.

Every great player needs a great rival, and Fiedler found his in Keith Elias.[18] As it had in the mid-sixties, the annual end-of-season meeting between the Big Green and Tigers decided the Ivy title three years in a row in the early nineties.

Princeton finished second in the league in 1991, posting their best record since the days of Cozmo Iacavazzi, but lost the championship when Al Rozier, the Big Green's all-time leading rusher, ground out 190 yards in a 31-13 victory at Hanover. A year later, Elias set a new Princeton single-season rushing record with 1,368 yards and receiver Mike Lerch doubled as a defensive end on passing downs, joining Columbia's Dan Werthman as rare two-way players. But under John Lyons, who succeeded Yukica as coach, Fiedler led Dartmouth through a snowstorm to a 34-20 victory that forced Princeton to share the league crown. Ironically, Dartmouth's offensive coordinator, Roger Hughes, whom Fiedler credited with developing him as a quarterback, would become Princeton's coach in 2000. Although Princeton won its first outright Ivy title since 1964 a year later, they backed into it, losing to Yale in an upset on the next-to-last weekend and then salvaging a 10-10 tie with Dartmouth on a last-second field goal by Alex Sierk.

If reverting to Division I-AA insulated the Ivy League from the pressures of big-time competition, it did not insulate it from the pressures of modern collegiate athletics. One by one, many of the old rules and prohibitions that had long been regarded as central to the Ivy code passed away, victims not only of changing attitudes and financial necessity, but of a continuing effort to find the proper place for athletics in college life. More remarkable still was the ease with which the changes were made.

Freshman, who had been kept off Ivy varsities since the turn of the century on the theory that they should be given time to adjust to college life, were made eligible in 1993. Although the Big Three strongly objected, the move was made in order to reduce the number of football recruits admitted in each class, thus making room for students with other interests. The decision killed the Ivy League's freshman football teams, which had for generations offered a less-pressured introduction to the game and given students who lacked varsity talent a chance to play.

Spring practice, the issue that had split the colleges in the early fifties, also returned. Well-roundedness having long before given way to specialization, the ideal of promoting a variety of athletic interests came to seem quaint to students who now started concentrating on a single sport year-round in high school. By the mid-1990s, none of Harvard's thirteen hundred varsity and junior varsity athletes played three sports and only about 10 percent played even two.[19] The day of three-sport athletes such as Barry Wood is over.

Even the ban on postseason play, one of the oldest Big Three traditions, has been attacked by those who cited the success of Ivy teams in NCAA-sponsored post-season basketball, hockey, soccer, and lacrosse tournaments. Although the league has voted against it twice in the last ten years, pressure will certainly continue, and seniors and coaches are now allowed to participate in postseason showcase contests such as the Blue-Gray game.

Far from underwriting the rest of the athletic program, as it once had, football now lost money, and lots of it, at every Ivy League college. Yale's football team for example, finished more than a million dollars in the red in 1996 and accounted for more than a quarter of the athletic department's total deficit.[20] Different colleges approached these deficits in different ways. Harvard and Princeton have sufficiently large endowments to support their athletic programs entirely from general university funds, while football teams at Penn and Cornell must raise as much as a third of their own funds. In an attempt to help Cornell and Brown, which had suffered large athletic deficits, the Ivy presidents decreed in 1996 that each college cut one assistant coaching position in order to save money.

Shortfalls have increased the pressure to find new sources of revenue. Gate receipts are hardly sufficient. A ticket to a Princeton home game costs $5, much cheaper, in real terms, than sixty years earlier. Instead, most Ivy athletic departments now have fundraising and marketing directors. Yale, which rents its baseball field to a minor league team and has named its tennis center after the tea company that paid for it, recently unveiled a new logo to help boost sales of its athletic apparel. One may safely assume that Charles Eliot would turn over in his grave at the idea of Harvard encouraging people to walk around with the college's name emblazoned on their clothes, but even they now do this. Coaching salaries throughout the Ivy League are now paid from endowments. In 1988, Cozza became the first occupant of an endowed chair for the Yale football coach, created with a million-dollar donation from a wealthy alumnus who cited football's ability to motivate "persons with the potential to become tomorrow's leaders." [21]

Ironically, the Ivy League benefited from the triumph of the CFA and the demise of the NCAA television monopoly, returning to the airwaves, albeit on a much more limited scale. In 1984, one Ivy game each week was broadcast on public television to an audience of approximately seven hundred thousand. By 1988, the league got its first national contract, with cable upstart ESPN, a deal that ended after two disappointing seasons when ESPN picked up the Big Ten instead. Each team is now permitted to arrange its own contracts. Cornell negotiated a deal with Sportschannel America in 1991 to televise all of its games nationwide, which collapsed when Harvard and Yale refused to allow the cable station's cameras in its stadiums. "These moves reflect the arrogance that Harvard and Yale have expressed towards us for years," one Cornell booster complained. "I mean, how can you tell a twenty-one year old young man that he can't have the opportunity to play on national TV, just because of some ridiculous college politics?" [22]

Although many of these changes have been decreed by financial necessity, they also reflect a new generation's acceptance of commerce. While some Ivy colleges continue to eschew the gaudier manifestations, such as selling advertising space on their scoreboard, others do so without embarrassment. "If we are to maintain broad-based programs, there's a price to pay," Cornell athletic director Charles Moore has said of scoreboard advertisements. "If I have my way there'll be more. I don't see it as commercialism, I see it as support for programs." [23] Harvard may still be the Ivy League's purist, in part, because Harvard can afford to be.

Those seeking evidence of creeping commercialism—and the Ivy League's helplessness to keep it out—need have looked no further than something called the Ivy Bowl. In the late eighties, the Japanese American Football Association approached the International Management Group, a marketing firm, with the idea for a college all-star game to be sponsored by the Epson Computer Company. William and Mary traveled to Tokyo the first year before someone hit on the idea of inviting the Ivy League, which offered a level of academic excellence that promised to be good advertising and a level of athletic talent not likely to run up the score on their hosts. Rebuffed by the league presidents, IMG simply went around them, hiring Maxie Baughan, the ex-Cornell coach, who in turn contacted graduating seniors. The rogue eleven whipped a Japanese all-star team, 47-10, on national television.

A year later, IMG went back to the Ivy presidents, who now recognized that the game could go on without them and decided to jump on board. Players—again graduating seniors, to ensure their eligibility—were chosen from the annual All-Ivy balloting, their coach rotated each year in order of seniority. Eschewing the Ivy League sanction against advertising, the team wore their school helmets on top of blue jerseys with the computer company's name emblazoned on front. The Ivy Bowl was discontinued after six years when the Japanese economy slumped, the Ivy all-stars having won each time.

The most visible manifestation of the Ivy League's struggle to adjust to its diminished status was the problem of its stadiums, now far too large for modern crowds. Columbia's decrepit Baker Field was the first to go. It had been falling apart for years, whole sections of the stands blocked off as unsafe (Larry McElreavy, when a Quaker assistant, had once put his foot through a plank on his way up to the press box). In 1982, it was torn down and replaced by Wien Stadium, named for a wealthy alumnus who donated the money. In 1995, the university added Astroturf in order to make the field usable by the women's field hockey team.

Princeton abandoned Palmer Stadium, the second-oldest football stadium in the country, after the 1996 season, concluding that the old concrete structure was too far gone to be saved and too big to be needed. The Tigers played their entire 1997 schedule on the road, including a game against Yale in Giants Stadium before 6,500 fans, the first time they had met the Elis in the New York area since 1896, but a sad echo of old times. Palmer Stadium, meanwhile, was razed and a new $40 million structure erected in its place. It is called simply Princeton Stadium and will remain so until someone donates the money the university is asking for the naming rights.

Harvard was forced to spend nine million dollars to salvage its stadium— thirty times what it had cost to build it in the first place. Thirteen years later, when the university completed its new athletic center at the open end of the stadium, observers from the third floor windows made a startling discovery. For ninety-five years, the gridiron had been off-center, situated ten feet closer to the visitors' grandstands than to the home side. The explanation, it turned out, was that the cinder track that had once encircled the field had extra sprint lanes on one side, and the gridiron had been centered within the track, not within the stadium. It was quickly moved, at a cost of $50,000 to regrade and recrown the field.[24]

By the early 1990s, even the Yale Bowl had fallen into disrepair. Trees could be seen growing out of the walls in places and concrete adornments were often water-stained and crumbling. This led to the heretical suggestion that the Bowl be demolished and replaced with something smaller. Although that has so far been resisted, Yale tried to aid the bowl's upkeep by exploring the possibility of allowing the University of Connecticut to play its home games there, as well.

Both Wien Stadium and Princeton Stadium were considerably smaller than the structures they replaced, acknowledging that neither Columbia nor Princeton would ever routinely draw 50,000 fans again. Attendance continued to drop leaguewide, from almost 20,000 per game in the mid-sixties to about 9,400 three decades later. Although Yale boasted the second-highest average attendance in all of Division I-AA in 1999, the number of season tickets sold to students at Dartmouth has plunged by 79 percent over the last decade.[25]

That is not necessarily a bad thing, reflecting instead of the number of other activities, including athletics, available to students on any given Saturday. Football is no longer the exclusive focus of intercollegiate athletics. At some schools—basketball at Penn, for example, or soccer at Columbia—it may not even be the primary focus. Harvard boasts that 20 percent of its student body participates in intercollegiate sports, as compared with about 2 percent in much of the Big Ten. Brown fields teams in more than twice as many sports as Nebraska, although its undergraduate enrollment is almost one-tenth the size. In 1997, *Sports Illustrated* named Princeton the number ten "jock school" in America, defined as "any college or university in which sports are central to campus life."[26] When junior varsity, club sports, and intramurals are included, more than three-quarters of the students on most Ivy campuses participate in some form of athletic activity. "It is of far more importance," Theodore Roosevelt once wrote, "that a man shall play something himself, even if he does it badly, than that he shall go with hundreds of companions to see someone else play well."[27]

A broad-based athletic program has its costs, however, especially at small Ivy League colleges. If Princeton has more varsity athletes than Ohio State, for example, it is also under correspondingly greater pressure to admit athletes in order to fill the rosters for all those teams. Former Princeton president William Bowen argues that Ivy athletes, as a group, have lower grades than non-athletes, and because of specialization in a single sport and the year-round focus that requires, are less representative of their classmates than were athletes half a century ago.[28] Why, then, Bowen asks, should any preference be given to athletes in admission? The debate over the proper role of athletics, which has gone on since the first student ball games, remains far from settled.

Although the league as a group is much more harmonious than it once was, significant differences remain between its members, differences that continue to cause a certain muted resentment. Brown and Cornell, with much smaller endowments than Harvard or Princeton, for example, find themselves at a perpetual funding and recruiting disadvantage, one exacerbated by the Big Three's decision to change its financial aid policies to provide more money in grants and less in loans. Princeton and Yale offer applicants "early decision," which some think gives them a recruiting advantage over Brown and Harvard, which do not.

One way of compensating for such differences has been the pursuit of transfer students. Although the NCAA requires students transferring from one Division

I-A program to another to sit out a year (an idea Walter Camp first pushed through the Intercollegiate Football Association to stop tramp athletes like Snake Ames), a student transferring from Division I-A to Division I-AA can play for his new school immediately. Cornell and Penn aggressively pursue transfer students, many of them good athletes in big programs such as quarterback Gavin Hoffman, who switched from Northwestern and led the Quakers to the 2000 title. Princeton, in contrast, does not accept any transfer students, athletes or not.

These differences mitigate imbalances on the field. In the first forty seasons of the Ivy League's existence, Harvard and Princeton combined to win almost half the total championships in all men's sports. Brown and Columbia on the other hand, each won only 4 percent of the men's titles during that period. That may be changing; every team except the Lions won at least one football title during the nineties and no one, with the exception of Penn, has enjoyed sustained dominance.

In 1996, for example, Dartmouth, under Coach John Lyons finished their first perfect season since 1970, compiling a twenty-two-game unbeaten streak, longest in the nation. By 1998, the Big Green were in the cellar, as Penn finished on top for its ninth title in seventeen years.

Joe Restic retired after the 1993 season with the Crimson in the midst of their worst stretch since the early 1950s. The losing continued under his successor, Tim Murphy, so much that by 1995, Harvard won only one league game (fortunately, it was against Yale). Only two years later, the Crimson went undefeated in the league and posted their best record since the 1919 Rose Bowl season.

Carm Cozza stepped down in 1996, five years after his last winning season. Like Murphy at Harvard, his successor, Jack Siedlecki, the successful Amherst coach, went down before going up. In his first season, the Bulldogs won only one of their ten games, a tie for Yale's worst record ever, but two years later, they too, shared a piece of the Ivy title. At the start of the 2000 season, Yale recorded its eight hundredth victory, more than any other college, but Michigan will likely overtake them in 2001.

The Elis shared their 1999 title with Brown, which was in the midst of a surprising resurgence, due in part to the support of President Gordon Gee, who had come to Providence from Ohio State. In 1998, the Bears came out of nowhere to finish second behind a barnburner offense that outlasted Penn, 58-51, in the highest-scoring game in league history. Each of the last eleven possessions by both teams ended in touchdowns, but Brown's James Perry found Stephen Campbell in the end zone with four seconds left to win. In 1999, the Bears nipped Yale in the season's opening week when, playing for a tie with fourteen seconds left, they ran their own blocked extra point attempt for a two-point conversion and the victory.

They would not repeat, however. The Ivy League sanctioned Brown in the summer of 2000 when it was disclosed that athletes had been given financial aid not on the basis of need by the Brown Sports Foundation, a booster club.

Although the NCAA considered the infractions minor, the presidents ruled the Bears ineligible for the 2000 football title and cut the number of recruits for the next two years, the harshest sanctions they had ever imposed in any sport. "The League's prohibition against any special financial aid for athletes is perhaps the most fundamental of all League rules," explained Columbia President George Rupp.[29]

On Sunday, April 18, 1999, Penn's senior tailback Jim Finn drove from his parents' home in Fair Lawn, New Jersey, to New York's Madison Square Garden to watch the NFL draft in person. As the Quakers' fourth leading all-time rusher, Finn had reason to hope he might be selected, but the fourth round passed, then the fifth, then the sixth, and still his name had not been called. Finally, the Chicago Bears took him with the forty-seventh pick in the seventh round—the very last player selected.

A professional afterthought such as Finn would have been a longshot at best to make the team's roster (indeed he was cut in training camp by Dick Jauron, the Bears' coach). Instead, Finn became the center of attention, all of it dripping with irony. He was besieged with interview requests and honored with a parade at Disneyland, where he accepted something called the "Lowsman Trophy," which was capped by a figurine of a football player tripping after a fumble. A nickname, bestowed annually on the last player taken in the draft, was even given to the Ivy League's Player of the Year.

The title was "Mr. Irrelevant."

Finn, a product of Bergen Catholic High School in New Jersey, was representative of the modern Ivy player. Indeed, by the time of the hundredth Harvard-Yale game in 1983, only seventeen of the sixty-nine Eli players had gone to prep school, and the percentage has not grown. "Football," Keith Elias observed, "doesn't fit the Ivy mold. It's not an Ivy League sport; it's not rowing."[30] More than a century after William Henry Lewis, ten African-Americans were on the Crimson roster, although the athletic department was criticized because only four of the university's 130 coaches and assistant coaches were black (only Cornell had fewer). The Ivy League has never had an African-American head football coach. Always a step ahead of the demographic curve, however, Harvard's captain and star running back in 1996 was Eion Hu, the son of Chinese immigrants, Hu became their all-time leading rusher (thanks in part to an extra year of eligibility) and certainly the most prominent Asian-American football player in Ivy history.

Though it seems hard to believe, many people early in the twentieth century were concerned that football had become a grind. "It is a very interesting fact to me that the game of football ... has ceased to be a pleasure to those who play it," Woodrow Wilson declared in 1909. "Almost any frank member of a college football team will tell you that ... he does not play it because of the physical pleasure and zest he finds in it, which is another way of saying that he does not play it spontaneously and for its own sake."[31] Despite specialization and commercial pressures, the same could not be said of Ivy football players today, perhaps the greatest and least appreciated advance the league has made.

There has been a trend toward the retro in Ivy League football, as there has been throughout the culture. Princeton and Yale wear essentially the same jerseys they have worn for more than a hundred years. The Tigers have brought back their logo from Fritz Crisler's days, while Dartmouth has restored the distinctive helmet design it wore under Bob Blackman. In Hanover, students still light bonfires, and the strains of "Give My Regards to Davy," the old, obscure Cornell fight song, or "Going Back to Nassau Hall" can still be heard on chilly autumn Saturdays. Even the Crimson still flout their indifference. "Most of us could rattle off Harvard football statistics with no more skill than we could communicate with the urban poor," one student has written, with more than a little pride.[32]

A modern-day Richard Harding Davis, wandering through the tailgates outside Harvard Stadium before the Yale game, would see much that was reminiscent of the old: a sea of sport utility vehicles, Volvo station wagons, and rented U-Haul trucks the modern manifestations of the carriages and tally-hos that once clogged the streets around the Polo Grounds. There are tailgate picnics on linen-covered card tables, and cakes decorated with gridirons trimmed in blue and crimson icing. As the ragtag Harvard band marches by playing "Rule Britannia," bed sheet banners flutter in the November breeze, ranging from the clever ("Lux sux") to the ribald:

> *Your*
> *Asses*
> *Look*
> *Enormous*

Hundreds of fans remain in the parking lot long after the kickoff, many engaged in their own games of touch football.

Several years earlier, the Yale alumni magazine published a rarity—a new football song—that the marching band had commissioned for $750. If it was not quite Cole Porter, one suspects he might have sung along:

> *Oh, Harvard men have higher SATs,*
> *And the Princeton campus has a lot of trees;*
> *Dartmouth men know about the birds and bees.*
>
> *But Yale's got a better football team,*
> *Yale's got a better football team,*
> *Yale's got a better football team,*
> *And we know that's all that matters.*[33]

Head Coaches

Brown

No official coach	1878-1886
I. E. Walker	1889
J. H. Lindsey	1890-1891
Mr. Howland	1892
William Odlin	1893
Mr. Norton	1894
Wallace Moyle	1895-1897
E. N. Robinson	1898-1901
	1904-1907
	1910-1925
J. A. Gammons	1902
	1908-1909
D. S. Fultz	1903
D.O. "Tuss" McLaughry	1926-1940
J. N. Stahley	1941-1943
C. A. "Rip" Engle	1944-1949
G. G. Zitrides	1950
A. E. Kelley	1951-1958
John McLaughry	1959-1966
Len Jardine	1967-1972
John Anderson	1973-1983
John Rosenberg	1984-1989
Mickey Kriatkowski	1990-1993
Mark Whipple	1994-1997
Phil Estes	1998-

Columbia

No official coach	1870-1898
George F. Sanford	1899-1901
William F. Morley	1902-1905
No team	1906-1914
T. Nelson Metcalf	1915-1918
Fred Dawson	1919
Frank O'Neil	1920-1922
Percy Haughton	1923-1924
Paul Withington	1924
Charles F. Crowley	1925-1929
Lou Little	1930-1956

Aldo "Buff" Donelli	1957-1967
Frank Navarro	1968-1973
William V. Campbell	1974-1979
Robert J. Naso	1980-1984
James W. Garrett	1985
Larry McElreavy	1986-1988
Ray Tellier	1989-

Cornell

No official coach	1887-1893
Marshall "Ma" Newell	1894-1895
Joseph Beacham	1896
Glenn "Pop" Warner	1897-1898
	1904-1906
Percy Haughton	1899-1900
Raymond Starbuck	1901-1902
William Warner	1903
Henry Schoellkopf	1907-1908
George Walder	1909
Daniel Reed	1910-1911
Al Sharpe	1912-1917
No team	1918
John Rush	1919
Gil Dobie	1920-1935
Carl Snavely	1936-1944
Ed McKeever	1945-1946
George "Lefty" James	1947-1960
Tom Harp	1961-1965
Jack Musick	1966-1974
George Seifert	1975-1976
Bob Blackman	1977-1982
Maxie Baughan	1983-1988
Jack Fouts	1989
Jim Hofher	1990-1997
Pete Mangurian	1998-2000
Tim Pendergast	2001-

Dartmouth

No official coach	1881-1892
Wallace S. Moyle	1893-1894
William C. Wurtenburg	1895-1899
Frederick E. Jennings	1900
Walter McCormack	1901-1902

Fred Folsom	1903-1906
John O'Connor	1907-1908
Walter Lillard	1909
William Randall	1910
Frank Cavanaugh	1911-1916
Clarence "Doc" Spears	1917-1920
Jackson Cannell	1921-1922
	1929-1933
Jesse Hawley	1923-1928
Earl "Red" Blaik	1934-1940
D. O. "Tuss" McLaughry	1941-1942
	1945-1954
Earl Brown	1943-1944
Bob Blackman	1955-1970
John "Jake" Crouthamel	1971-1977
Joseph M. Yukica	1978-1986
Eugene F. "Buddy" Teevens, III	1987-1991
John J. Lyons	1992-

Harvard

Coached by captains	1874-1880
	1882-1884
	1887-1889
Lucius N. Littauer	1881
No team	1885
Frank A. Mason	1886
George A. Stewart and George C. Adams	1890-1892
George A. Stewart and Everett G. Lake	1893
William A. Brooks	1894
Robert W. Emmons	1895
Bertram G. Waters	1896
W. Cameron Forbes	1897-1898
Benjamin H. Dibblee	1899-1900
William T. Reid	1901
	1905-1906
John W. Farley	1902
John S. Cranston	1903
Edgar N. Wrightington	1904
Joshua Crane	1907
Percy D. Haughton	1908-1916
Wingate Rollins	1917
Pooch Donovan	1918
Robert T. Fisher	1919-1925
Arnold Horween	1926-1930

Edward L. Casey	1931-1934
Richard C. Harlow	1935-1942
	1945-1947
Henry N. Lamar	1943-1944
Arthur L. Valpey	1948-1949
Lloyd P. Jordan	1950-1956
John M. Yovicsin	1957-1970
Joseph Restic	1971-1993
Timothy Murphy	1994-

University of Pennsylvania

No official coach	1876-1884
Frank Doyle	1885-1887
E. O. Wagenhurst	1888-1891
George Woodruff	1892-1901
Carl S. Williams	1902-1907
Sol Metzger	1908
Andy Smith	1909-1912
George Brooke	1913-1915
Robert F. Folwell	1916-1919
John W. Heisman	1920-1922
Louis A. Young	1923-1929
Ludlow Wray	1930
Harvey Harman	1931-1937
George A. Munger	1938-1953
Steve Sebo	1954-1959
John Stiegman	1960-1964
Bob Odell	1965-1970
Harry Gamble	1971-1980
Jerry Berndt	1981-1985
Ed Zubrow	1986-1988
Gary Steele	1989-1991
Al Bagnoli	1992-

Princeton

No official coach	1869-1900
Langdon Lea	1901
Garrett Cochran	1902
A. R. T. Hillebrand	1903-1905
William W. Roper	1906-1908
	1910-1911
	1919-1930
James B. McCormick	1909

Logan Cunningham	1912
W. Gresham Andrews	1913
Wilder G. Penfield	1914
John Rush	1915-1916
Keene Fitzpatrick	1917-1918
Albert Witmer	1931
Herbert O. "Fritz" Crisler	1932-1937
Elton E. "Tad" Wieman	1938-1942
Harry E. Mahnken	1943-1944
Charles W. Caldwell, Jr.,	1945-1956
Richard W. Colman, Jr.,	1957-1968
J. L. McCandless	1969-1972
Robert F. Casciola	1973-1977
Frank Navarro	1978-1984
Ron Rogerson	1985-1986
Steve Tosches	1987-1999
Roger Hughes	2000-

Yale

No official coach	1872-1887
Walter Camp	1888-1892
William Rhodes	1893-1894
John Hartwell	1895
S. B. Thorne	1896
Frank Butterworth	1897-1898
J. O. Rogers	1899
Malcolm McBride	1900
George Stillman	1901
Joseph Swan	1902
G. B. Chadwick	1903
C. D. Rafferty	1904
J. E. Owsley	1905
Foster Rockwell	1906
William Knox	1907
L. H. Bigelow	1908
Howard Jones	1909
	1913
Edward Coy	1910
John Field	1911
Arthur Howe	1912
Frank Hinkey	1914-1915
T. A. D. Jones	1916-1917
	1920-1927
No team	1918

Al Sharpe	1919
Marvin "Mal" Stevens	1928-1932
Reginald Root	1933
Raymond "Ducky" Pond	1934-1940
Emerson "Skip" Nelson	1941
Howard Odell	1942-1947
Herman Hickman	1948-1951
Jordan Olivar	1952-1962
John Pont	1963-1964
Carmen Cozza	1965-1996
John Siedlecki	1997-

Cumulative and Ivy League Records

Cumulative Record

	W	L	T	Pct.
Yale	806	301	55	.694
Princeton	744	330	50	.662
Harvard	734	359	50	.642
Dartmouth	626	358	46	.608
Pennsylvania	736	436	42	.606
Cornell	585	409	34	.569
Brown	522	498	40	.492
Columbia	343	543	43	.369

Ivy League Record
(1956-2000)

	W	L	T	Pct.
Dartmouth	203	103	9	.644
Yale	185	122	8	.587
Harvard	175	131	9	.556
Princeton	175	135	5	.556
Pennsylvania	151	160	4	.479
Cornell	148	162	5	.470
Brown	123	185	7	.390
Columbia	74	236	5	.235

Ivy League Champions

Year	Team	Ivy Record
1956	Yale	7-0-0
1957	Princeton	6-1-0
1958	Dartmouth	6-1-0
1959	Pennsylvania	6-1-0
1960	Yale	7-0-0
1961	Columbia	6-1-0
	Harvard	
1962	Dartmouth	7-0-0
1963	Dartmouth	5-2-0
	Princeton	
1964	Princeton	7-0-0
1965	Dartmouth	7-0-0
1966	Dartmouth	6-1-0
	Harvard	
	Princeton	
1967	Yale	7-0-0
1968	Harvard	6-0-1
	Yale	6-0-1
1969	Dartmouth	6-1-0
	Princeton	
	Yale	
1970	Dartmouth	7-0-0
1971	Cornell	6-1-0
	Dartmouth	
1972	Dartmouth	5-1-1
1973	Dartmouth	6-1-0
1974	Harvard	6-1-0
	Yale	
1975	Harvard	6-1-0
1976	Brown	6-1-0
	Yale	
1977	Yale	6-1-0
1978	Dartmouth	6-1-0
1979	Yale	6-1-0
1980	Yale	6-1-0
1981	Dartmouth	6-1-0
	Yale	
1982	Dartmouth	5-2-0
	Harvard	
	Pennsylvania	
1983	Harvard	5-1-1
	Pennsylvania	

1984	Pennsylvania	7-0-0
1985	Pennsylvania	6-1-1
1986	Pennsylvania	7-0-0
1987	Harvard	6-1-0
1988	Cornell	6-1-0
	Pennsylvania	
1989	Princeton	6-1-0
	Yale	
1990	Cornell	6-1-0
	Dartmouth	
1991	Dartmouth	6-0-1
1992	Dartmouth	6-1-0
	Princeton	
1993	Pennsylvania	7-0-0
1994	Pennsylvania	7-0-0
1995	Princeton	5-1-1
1996	Dartmouth	7-0-0
1997	Harvard	7-0-0
1998	Pennsylvania	6-1-0
1999	Brown	6-1-0
	Yale	
2000	Pennsylvania	6-1-0

Ivy League Championships (1956-2000)

	Won Outright	*Shared*	*Total*
Dartmouth	9	8	17
Yale	6	7	13
Pennsylvania	8	3	11
Harvard	3	6	9
Princeton	3	5	8
Cornell	0	3	3
Brown	0	2	2
Columbia	0	1	1

Ivy League National Champions

Year	Team
1869	Princeton
1870	Princeton
1872	Princeton
1873	Princeton
1874	Yale
1875	Harvard
1876	Yale
1877	Yale
1878	Princeton
1879	Princeton
1880	Princeton
	Yale
1881	Yale
1882	Yale
1883	Yale
1884	Yale
1885	Princeton
1886	Yale
1887	Yale
1888	Yale
1889	Princeton
1890	Harvard
1891	Yale
1892	Yale
1893	Princeton
1894	Yale
1895	Pennsylvania
1896	Princeton
1897	Pennsylvania
1898	Harvard
1899	Harvard
1900	Yale
1903	Princeton
1904	Pennsylvania
1906	Princeton
1907	Yale
1908	Princeton
1909	Yale
1910	Harvard
1911	Princeton
1912	Harvard
1913	Harvard

1915	Cornell
1919	Harvard
1921	Cornell
1922	Cornell
	Princeton
1923	Pennsylvania
1925	Dartmouth
1927	Yale
1933	Princeton
1935	Princeton
1939	Cornell

Ivy League Silver Anniversary All-Star Team
Selected in 1981 by writers, broadcasters, coaches, and administrators.

Offense

Pos	First Team	Second Team
E	Don McClune, Pennsylvania	John Spagnola, Yale
E	Pat McInally, Harvard	Gary Fencik, Yale
T	Dan Jiggetts, Harvard	John Sinnott, Brown
T	Bob Asack, Columbia	Steve Diamond, Harvard
G	Ben Balme, Yale	Steve Cafora, Yale
G	Mike Guerin, Princeton	Vic Staffieri, Yale
QB	Archie Roberts, Columbia	Brian Dowling, Yale
RB	Ed Marinaro, Cornell	Cosmo Iacavazzi, Princeton
RB	Dick Jauron, Yale	John Pagliaro, Yale
RB	Calvin Hill, Yale	Jake Crouthamel, Dartmouth
KSp	Charlie Gogolak, Princeton	Jose Violante, Brown

Defense

Pos	First Team	Second Team
E	Tom Csatari, Dartmouth	Bob Baggott, Harvard
E	Jim Gallagher, Yale	Clint Streit, Yale
T	Tom Neville, Yale	Carl Barasich, Pennsylvania
T	Gregg Robinson, Dartmouth	John Sponheimer, Cornell
G	Kevin Czinger, Yale	Paul Savidge, Princeton
LB	Reggie Williams, Dartmouth	Paul Kaliades, Columbia
LB	Bob Lally, Cornell	Murray Bowden, Dartmouth
LB	Stas Maliszewski, Princeton	John Woodring, Brown
DB	Keith Mauney, Princeton	Elvin Charity, Yale
DB	Bill Emper, Harvard	Willie Bogan, Dartmouth
DB	Ted Gregory, Columbia	John Cahill, Yale
P	Pat McInally, Harvard	Joe Randall, Brown

The following abbreviations are used in the notes:

BAM	*Brown Alumni Monthly*
CUA	Cornell University archives
DAM	*Dartmouth Alumni Magazine*
DCA	Dartmouth College archives
DP	*Daily Princetonian*
HAB	*Harvard Alumni Bulletin*
HUA	Harvard University archives
NYHT	*New York Herald-Tribune*
NYT	New York Times
PAW	*Princeton Alumni Weekly*
PUA	Princeton University archives
SEP	*Saturday Evening Post*
SI	*Sports Illustrated*
UPA	University of Pennsylvania archives
YAM	*Yale Alumni Magazine*
YAW	*Yale Alumni Weekly*
YDN	*Yale Daily News*
YUA	Yale University archives

Preface

[1] See "Is the Ivy League Still the Best?" *Newsweek*, November 23, 1964, 65.

[2] John L. Powers, "Powers of the Press," *Harvard Crimson*, April 30, 1971.

[3] Howard Patton and W. T. Field, *Eight O'clock Chapel* (Boston: Houghton Mifflin, 1927), 10-12.

[4] "Views of Sport," NYHT, November 21, 1945.

[5] "How The 'Ivy League' Got Its Name," DAM, November 1961, 26. According to the preface of the article, Harron's piece was first written in 1956 but was rejected as "not of national interest."

[6] Harron's story does check out in some respects. Adams did cover Columbia's game against Penn at Baker Field the same day—October 16, 1937—that Woodward covered the Fordham-Pitt game at the Polo Grounds and Adams, a Fordham alumnus, would have had an interest in the other game. Furthermore, Woodward used the appellation "ivy" to refer to these colleges twice in the following week.

[7] "With the College Athletes in Their Diversified Affairs," NYHT, January 15, 1933.

[8] "Navy Eleven Travels to Pittsburgh; Yale Playing W&J," NYHT, October 14, 1933. The *Oxford English Dictionary* cites a Woodward column dated October 16 as the first usage of the term "ivy colleges," but this is incorrect.

[9] "Brown Seen As Charter Member of Ivy League," *Providence Journal*, February 8, 1935.

[10] "Football Here and There," NYHT, October 31, 1935.

11 "'Ivy League' Will Bloom with Three Games Saturday," NYHT, October 29, 1936; see generally John R. Thelin, *The Cultivation of Ivy* (Cambridge, Mass.: Schenkman, 1976), 24.

Chapter 1. *The Big Three*

1 Works Progress Administration, *Connecticut: A Guide to Its Roads, Lore, and People* (Boston: Houghton Mifflin, 1938), 78.

2 Thomas J. Wertenbaker, *Princeton, 1746-1896* (Princeton: Princeton University Press, 1946), 245.

3 Ibid., 138.

4 *A Comedy of Errors*, act II, scene I, lines 82-83; *King Lear*, act I, scene 4, lines 93-94.

5 Kathleen D. Valenzi and Michael W. Hopps, *Champion of Sport: The Life of Walter Camp, 1859-1925* (Charlottesville, Va.: Howell Press, 1990), 40.

6 "Princeton" had come into usage as a formal university nickname only that April, when the college baseball team had taken on the professional Philadelphia Athletics with "Princeton" emblazoned across their shirt fronts. It would not become the college's official name until 1896.

7 The "tiger" in the cheer was of common usage, however, and did not refer to the Princeton Tiger, which was not conceived for another decade.

8 See Ronald A. Smith, *Sports and Freedom: The Rise of Big-Time College Athletics* (New York: Oxford University Press, 1988), 70-71.

9 PAW, December 15, 1909, 186.

10 Richard Goldstein, *Ivy League Autumns* (New York: St. Martin's Press, 1996), 6-7.

11 Parke H. Davis, *Football: The American Intercollegiate Game* (New York: Charles Scribner's Sons, 1911), 40. Ronald Smith states that Schaff learned rugby from visiting English students while attending the Kornthal School in Germany. See Smith, *Sports and Freedom*, 73 and n. 32.

12 "Yale at Columbia," *New York World*, November 17, 1872; "Yale's First Football Game," YAW, October 17, 1924, 126.

13 A. C. M. Azoy, "Desire Under the (New Haven) Elms, 1873," Princeton-Yale football program, November 12, 1938, 15.

14 Goldstein, *Ivy League Autumns*, 8.

15 Henry R. Grant to secretary, Yale Football Association, October 11, 1873, HUA.

16 Alexander M. Weyand, *The Saga of American Football* (New York: Macmillan, 1955), 11. For the second game with McGill, Harvard wore magenta and white striped jerseys. The crimson Harvard "H" first appeared on their uniforms in a game against Tufts in the spring of 1875. Harvard's colors were selected by two students, Charles W. Eliot (later Harvard's president) and Benjamin W. Crowninshield, for a crew race in 1858. Looking for bandanas for their fellows to wear, the two considered blue, orange, green, and yellow, but preferred the red ones. See "Crimson in Triumph Flashing," *Harvard Magazine*, November–December 1996, 88.

17 See John Adams Blanchard, ed., *The H Book of Harvard Athletics, 1852-1922* (Cambridge: Harvard Varsity Club, 1923), 358.

18 Yale at this time was also trying to persuade Harvard to join it in withdrawing from the Rowing Association and may have decided to curry Harvard's favor by yielding on the football rules.

[19] L. H. Baker, *Football Facts and Figures* (New York: Rinehart, 1945), 538.

[20] *New Haven Register*, November 15, 1875.

[21] David M. Nelson, *The Anatomy of a Game* (Newark: University of Delaware Press, 1994), 33.

[22] "Intercollegiate Foot-Ball," NYT, November 19, 1876.

[23] "Remington and the Eli Eleven," *American Heritage*, October–November 1981, 98.

[24] Peggy Samuels and Harold Samuels, *Frederic Remington* (Garden City, N.Y.: Doubleday, 1982), 26.

[25] H. W. Brands, *TR: The Last Romantic* (New York: Basic Books, 1997), 41.

[26] Yale Football Glossary, Yale athletic department.

[27] Benjamin G. Rader, *American Sports: From the Age of Folk Games to the Age of Televised Sports* (Engelwood Cliffs, N.J.: Prentice-Hall, 1996), 88. Others attribute the quote to Frederic Remington.

[28] John Stuart Martin, "Walter Camp and His Gridiron Game," *American Heritage*, October 1961, 50.

[29] John McCallum, *Ivy League Football Since 1872* (New York: Stein & Day, 1977), 29.

[30] "Walter Camp on Sportsmanship," *The American Sporting Experience: A Historical Anthology of Sport in America*, Steven A. Reiss, ed. (Champaign, Ill.: Leisure Press, 1984).

[31] "The Princeton Boys Win," NYT, November 4, 1877.

[32] Ibid.

[33] Walter Camp wrote years later that he had first seen the smock when Yale played Trinity College in 1877. As Baker notes, because Yale also played Princeton later that year, Camp would certainly have been in a position to know which of the two schools first used it. Furthermore, the 1877 Princeton team photo does not show them wearing it. Navy also claims that it developed the smock in 1879. See Baker, *Football Facts and Figures*, 593-94.

[34] See Amos Alonzo Stagg, *Touchdown!* (New York: Longmans, Green, 1927), 44.

[35] Martha Mitchell, *Encyclopedia Brunonia* (Providence, R.I.: Brown University Library, 1993), 232.

[36] Quoted in Thomas G. Bergin, *The Game: The Harvard-Yale Football Rivalry, 1875-1983* (New Haven, Conn.: Yale University Press, 1984), 12.

Chapter 2. *Making the Rules As You Go Along*

[1] "Kicking the Leather Egg," NYT, November 28, 1879.

[2] "An Important Question," *Princetonian*, September 17, 1880.

[3] Nelson, *Anatomy,* 46.

[4] As usual, several people, including Amos Alonzo Stagg and John Heisman, claim credit for having invented the between-the-legs snap. The first Ivy player to adopt the technique was Yale's Bert Hanson, who in 1889 "bent over and bounced the ball back between his legs with his hand." Allison Danzig, *The History of American Football: Its Great Teams, Players and Coaches* (Englewood Cliffs, N.J.: Prentice-Hall, 1956), 84-85.

[5] "Vain Work at Foot-Ball," NYT, November 26, 1880.

[6] Lewis Sheldon Welch and Walter Camp, *Yale, Her Campus, Class-Rooms and Athletics* (Boston: L.C. Page, 1899), 520.

[7] McCallum, *Ivy League Football*, 31.

[8] Henry Bancroft Twombley, *Personal Reminiscences of a Yale Football Player in the Early 'Eighties* (New Haven: Yale University Press, 1940), 32; Weyand, *Saga*, 25.

[9] Goldstein, *Ivy League Autumns*, 15.

[10] Ibid., 13.

[11] Parke H. Davis, "Lamars's Run, Forty Years Ago," PAW, November 18, 1925.

[12] Nelson, *Anatomy*, 53.

[13] Horace Coon, *Columbia, Colossus on the Hudson* (New York: E. P. Dutton, 1947), 299.

[14] Mitchell, *Encyclopedia Brunonia*, 138.

[15] Wiley Lee Umphlett, *Creating the Big Game: John W. Heisman and the Invention of American Football* (Westport, Conn.: Greenwood Press, 1992), 16 n. 27.

[16] Howard M. Tibbetts, "Football at Dartmouth," DAM, May 1915, 259.

[17] Horace G. Pender and Raymond M. McPartlin, *Athletics at Dartmouth* (Hanover, N.H.: Dartmouth College Athletic Council, 1923), 94.

[18] Morris Bishop, *A History of Cornell* (Ithaca, N.Y.: Cornell University Press, 1962), 136.

[19] Bishop, *History of Cornell*, 296.

[20] Robert J. Higgs, *God in the Stadium: Sports and Religion in America* (Lexington: University of Kentucky Press, 1995), 115.

[21] "Yale Outplays Princeton," NYT, November 26, 1886.

[22] Ibid.

[23] Woodman, *"Football in the "Gay Eighties,"* YUA.

[24] W.W. Heffelfinger, *This Was Football* (New York: A. S. Barnes, 1954), 43.

[25] W.W. Heffelfinger, "Nobody Put Me On My Back," SEP, October 15, 1938, 14.

[26] Weyand, *Saga*, 34.

[27] "Poes at Princeton," NYT, April 13, 1933.

[28] McCallum, *Ivy League Football*, 33.

[29] "The Ghost of Poe's Raven," Football collection, PUA.

[30] "The Berkeley Athletic Club," *The Wheel*, October 5, 1888.

[31] Weyand, *Saga*, 35.

[32] Morris A. Beale, *The History of Football at Harvard, 1874-1948* (Washington, D.C.: Columbia, 1948), 46.

[33] Stagg, *Touchdown*, 93-99.

[34] Welch and Camp, *Yale*, 519

[35] James Bryce, *The American Commonwealth* (Indianapolis: Liberty Fund, 1995), 2:1328. Bryce believed that fewer than fifteen schools in the country met this standard, although the "older New England colleges" generally did.

[36] "The Football Match," NYT, November 28, 1886.

[37] "Fighters at Football," NYT, November 29, 1886.

[38] Stagg, *Touchdown*, 79.

[39] *Princetonian*, December 8, 1882.

[40] McCallum, *Ivy League Football*, 30.

[41] Harvard College *Report upon Athletics*, 1888, Athletic Department records, HUA, 12. Nelson observes that Harvard's decision may have had something to do with the 52-0 shellacking Yale had given them a few weeks earlier. *Anatomy*, 55. It is worth noting the social dimension to Harvard's decision. By banning only the intercollegiate games, it implicitly blamed the problem on outsiders rather than on Harvard students themselves.

[42] "Trying to Save Football," NYT, December 6, 1884.

[43] Nelson, *Anatomy*, 54.

[44] Twombley, *Reminiscences*, 45-46.

[45] *Harvard Lampoon*, reprinted in *Princetonian*, October 31, 1884.

[46] Valenzi and Hopps, *Champion of Sport*, 57.

[47] *Report upon Athletics*, 1888, Athletic Department records, HUA.

[48] Walter C. Bronson, *The History of Brown University, 1764-1914* (Providence, R.I.: Brown University, 1914), 417.

[49] *Report upon Athletics*, 19.

[50] Ibid., 52.

[51] Ibid., 50.

[52] Riess, "Sport," 194.

[53] Oliver Wendell Holmes, Jr., "The Soldier's Faith," *The Mind and Faith of Justice Holmes* (New York: Little, Brown, 1943), 23.

[54] Elliot J. Gorn and Warren Goldstein, *A Brief History of American Sports* (New York: Hill & Wang, 1993), 161.

[55] William G. Durick, "The Gentlemen's Race: An Examination of the 1869 Harvard-Oxford Boat Race," *Journal of Sport History*, Spring 1988, 41.

[56] "How Football Men Train," NYT, January 12, 1890.

Chapter 3. *Wonderful to Behold and Terrible to Stop*

[1] *New York Herald* quoted in Michael Oriard, *Reading Football: How the Popular Press Created an American Spectacle* (Chapel Hill: University of North Carolina Press, 1993), 93-95.

[2] Richard Harding Davis, "The Thanksgiving Game," *Harper's Weekly*, December 9, 1893, 1170.

[3] *New York Herald*, November 25, 1887.

[4] Walter Camp, "Intercollegiate Foot-Ball in America," *St. Nicholas*, January 1890, 242.

[5] William Edwards, *Football Days* (New York: Moffat Yard, 1916), 2-3.

[6] L. H. Baker, *Notebooks* ("Baker Book"), 437, Yale Athletic Department.

[7] Goldstein, *Ivy League Autumns*, 21.

[8] "Yale," *World*, November 25, 1892.

[9] The cheer was adapted from the croaking sound the frogs make on the banks of the River Styx. It was first performed at a baseball game that summer when, according to legend, Yale rallied for a late inning comeback victory. Judith Schiff, "The Greatest College Cheer," YAM, May 1998, 88.

[10] "The Orange Above the Blue," NYT, December 1, 1893.

[11] "Princeton 6, Yale 0," *New York Herald*, December 1, 1893.

[12] Ibid.

[13] See "College Boys Drift Away," NYT, November 26, 1892; Oriard, *Reading Football*, 90 (for figures from 1879 and 1889 games).

[14] "A Riot of 'Rahs," *New York Herald*, November 25, 1887.

[15] "Not Red, But Blue, Did They 'Paint the Town,'" *New York Herald*, November 25, 1892.

[16] "A Rip-Roaring Night," *World*, November 25, 1892.

[17] Ibid.

[18] Parker Morell, *Diamond Jim: The Life and Times of Diamond Jim Brady* (New York: Simon & Schuster, 1934), 87.

[19] "A Rip-Roaring Night," *World*, November 25, 1892.

[20] "Wine for Tigers; Beer for Yale," *New York Journal*, November 22, 1896.

[21] "Wine for Tigers; Beer for Yale," *New York Journal*, November 22, 1896.

[22] "Yale and Princeton Paint the Town Blue," *New York Herald*, November 27, 1891.

[23] "A Rip-Roaring Night," *World*, November 25, 1892.

[24] "Justice Koch Was Lenient," NYT, December 2, 1893.

[25] "Dungeon Cells for College Boys," *New York Herald*, December 1, 1893.

[26] *Report of the President of Harvard College and Reports of Departments, 1892-93*, 20.

[27] There were several reasons for the change of date. Yale was also unhappy at having her two biggest games of the year, Harvard and Princeton, bunched only five days apart. Princeton and Yale did not play again in the New York metropolitan area until 1997.

[28] "Another Yale Committee," NYT, February 2, 1890.

[29] *Princetonian* (Supplement), March 7, 1890.

[30] *Princetonian*, March 7, 1890.

[31] One of the first professional football players was Pudge Heffelfinger, who received $500 in 1892 to play for the Allegheny Athletic Association, a sum equal to a school teacher's annual salary. Robert Peterson, *Pigskin: The Early Years of Professional Football* (New York: Oxford University Press, 1997), 16.

[32] Kim Townsend, *Manhood at Harvard: William James and Others* (New York: W. W. Norton, 1996), 106.

[33] Judith Ann Schiff, "Mayhem on the Field," YAM, November 1995, 88.

[34] Umphlett, *Heisman*, 13.

[35] See Weyand, *Saga*, 44.

[36] Heffelfinger, *This Was Football*, 48.

[37] *Biographical Dictionary of American Sports*, David L. Porter, ed. (New York: Greenwood Press, 1987), 265.

[38] Goldstein, *Ivy League Autumns*, 22.

[39] *Biographical Dictionary*, 266.

[40] Heffelfinger, *This Was Football*, 49.

[41] *Biographical Dictionary*, 266.

[42] Dan Rottenberg, *Fight On, Pennsylvania: A Century of Red and Blue Football*, (Philadelphia: University of Pennsylvania Press, 1985), 30.

[43] Danzig, *History*, 25.

44 Heffelfinger, *This Was Football*, 43. Heffelfinger attributes the quote to George Trevor.

45 Ellen Axson Wilson to Anna Harris, November 22, 1892, *The Papers of Woodrow Wilson*, Arthur S. Link, ed., 69 vols. (Princeton, N.J.: Princeton University Press, 1966-94), 8:47-48.

46 "Victory's Meaning to Pennsylvania," *Philadelphia Press*, November 12, 1894.

47 Ibid.

48 Rottenberg, *Fight On, Pennsylvania*, 9.

49 "Pennsylvania Scalps the Tiger," *Philadelphia Press*, November 11, 1894.

50 "Yale Again Triumphant," NYT, November 25, 1894.

51 "The New Football," *Nation*, November 29, 1894, 399.

52 "It's Not So Brutal," *The World*, November 30, 1893, 2. Charles Eliot produced data several years later showing that the success of Harvard's football team had no effect on the number of applications for admission in succeeding years. See *Report of the President of Harvard College and Report of Departments, 1900-01*, 14-18.

53 Stagg, article in SEP, October 23, 1926.

54 "One Solitary Touchdown!" *Cornell Daily Sun*, November 16, 1891. The red in the "Big Red" suffered refinement in 1897, when Heberton L. Williams saw the team defeat Penn at Franklin Field. Williams worked for the Campbell's Preserve Company, which was just beginning to introduce a line of condensed soups. He so liked Cornell's uniform color that he borrowed it for the labels (ironically, they had been orange and black), thus giving Campbell's soup cans their distinctive appearance. Robert J. Kane, *Good Sports: 123 Years of Cornell Athletics*, (Ithaca, N.Y.: Cornell University, 1992), 48-49; Andrew F. Smith, *Souper Tomatoes*, (New Brunswick, N.J.: Rutgers University Press, 2000), 88.

55 Ron Chernow, *Titan: The Life of John D, Rockefeller, Sr.*, (New York: Random House, 1998), 351.

56 "What the Alumni Think," *Springfield (Mass.) Union*, undated, reprinted in the *Dartmouth*, November 26, 1897, 136.

57 Letter, May 2, 1893, Harvard letterpress book, Football file, HUA. By way of comparison, Harvard gave MIT $30 that season, Amherst $110, Dartmouth $160, Wesleyan $175, and Cornell and Williams each $200. Tufts did not accept the offer.

58 See, e.g., *Dartmouth*, January 20, 1899 ("A football deficit is easily possible as the result of a poor season, . . . but payment of taxes . . . should exist as an expression of personal pride and of college loyalty"); see also *Nassau Literary Magazine*, October 1892, 216 ("The college at large is a submissive body. It has a taste for foot-ball and it is willing to pay for the gratification of that taste.... But there are limits to submission, and even patriotism can see no object in uselessly enriching an association whose treasury never lacks an abundant surplus").

59 See "Financial Report of Dartmouth College Football Association—Season 1899," *Dartmouth*, March 23, 1900. It is interesting to look at a smaller school. Dartmouth's football association posted a deficit in 1899 of more than $1,000. Forty percent of their annual revenue came from gate receipts at five home games. Student subscriptions accounted for another third, and guarantees for games at Army, Columbia, Harvard, and Wesleyan, another twenty-seven percent.

[60] "Yale's Football Receipts," NYT, March 25, 1893. Among their expenses that year were $1,004 for cabs and busses, $444 for shoes, $200 for medicine, and $62 for lawyers' fees.

[61] Henry Adams to Mabel Hooper, October 6, 1894, *The Letters of Henry Adams*, (Cambridge, Mass.: Belknap Press, 1988), vol. IV, 220.

[62] Smith, *Sports and Freedom*, 95.

[63] Higgs, *God in the Stadium*, 122.

[64] Poe is widely credited with having stolen the ball, but contemporary game accounts do not support this. Baker states that the stolen ball story first appeared in Big Bill Edwards' memoir, *Football Days*.

[65] "The Princeton Game," YAW, November 17, 1898, 72.

[66] Edwards, *Football Days*, 64-65.

[67] *Nassau Herald (1900)*, 120.

Chapter 4. *More Work for the Undertaker*

[1] Owen Johnson, *Stover at Yale* (New Haven, Conn.: Yale Bookstore, 1997), 135-36.

[2] Michael Oriard, *Sporting with the Gods: The Rhetoric of Play and Game in American Culture* (New York: Cambridge University Press, 1991), 27.

[3] Richard Harding Davis, "Richard Carr's Baby," *St. Nicholas*, November 1886, 50.

[4] Michael Oriard, *Dreaming of Heroes: American Sports Fiction, 1868-1980* (Chicago: Nelson-Hall, 1982), 30.

[5] See Stewart H. Holbrook, "Frank Merriwell at Yale Again—and Again and Again," *American Heritage*, July 1961, 24.

[6] Deification of Ivy football heroes was occurring in other mediums, as well. In 1913, Daniel Chester French, better known for his statue of Abraham Lincoln in the Lincoln Memorial, finished *The Christian Athlete*, which depicts a stalwart youth in a Princeton letter sweater, sleeves rolled up, his school books slung over his shoulder. French's model was W. Earl Dodge, Class of 1879, who had witnessed the historic first Harvard-Yale game and persuaded Princeton to adopt rugby-style rules. In 1930, students tore the statue from its pedestal during Princeton's third consecutive losing season and dragged it around the campus. It now sits in the lobby of the Princeton gymnasium. Although the cinema was just becoming a popular diversion, the Vitascope Company had already offered Harvard and Yale $25,000 for the exclusive rights to make moving pictures of their game. There was one catch: to make filming easier, they proposed that the game be played entirely in the middle of the field, and that someone on the sideline award a touchdown whenever one of the teams gained fifty-five yards. The request was denied, though a few years later Thomas Edison filmed part of the Harvard-Yale game.

[7] Baker Book, 665.

[8] YAW, November 28, 1900, 90.

[9] YAW, November 28, 1900, 84. Supporting the latter theory is the fact that Hirsch wrote another Yale fight song a few years later, known as the "Fijian War Cry," the chorus of which went: "Kahmahti! Korah! Korah! Kah!/ Tenati! Tongati! Facka! Ti! Rah!/Korah! Korah!/Nana i mai for Yale!"

10 Arthur T. Hadley to John O. Heald, January 28, 1907, Arthur Hadley papers, YUA, quoted in Marcia Synnott, *The Half-Opened Door: Discrimination and Admissions at Harvard, Yale, and Princeton, 1900-1970* (Westport, Conn.: Greenwood Press, 1979), 16.

11 "Ten Thousand Men of Harvard," perhaps the best-known Crimson fight song, did not appear until 1914.

12 Theodore F. Green, "Anniversary for Bruno," *Brown Alumni Monthly*, January 1956, 18.

13 Charles Eliot to Arthur Hadley, January 16, 1902, Arthur Hadley papers, YUA.

14 John T. Bethell, "Frank Roosevelt at Harvard," *Harvard Magazine*, November-December 1996, 38.

15 Louis P. Benezet, *Three Years of Football at Dartmouth* (1904), 182.

16 Karl Lindholm, "William Clarence Matthews," *Harvard Magazine*, September-October 1998, 58.

17 Karl Lindholm, "William Clarence Matthews," *The National Pastime*, Society for American Baseball Research, June 1997, 67.

18 Synnott, *The Half-Opened Door*, 48.

19 "Yale's Treatment of Matthews," *Yale Alumni Weekly*, December 7, 1904.

20 McCallum, *Ivy League Football*, 75.

21 Alexander Leitch, *A Princeton Companion* (Princeton, N.J.: Princeton University Press, 1978), 190.

22 YAW, January 9, 1906, 348.

23 PAW, November 17, 1900, 300.

24 *New York Sun*, March 24, 1900.

25 When Yale got wind of Needham's article, the secretary of the Yale corporation, Anson Phelps Stokes, tried to persuade the magazine to squelch it. See John Sayle Watterson, *College Football: History, Spectacle, Controversy* (Baltimore: John Hopkins University Press, 2000), 66.

26 See Henry Beech Needham, "The College Athlete (Part I)," *McClure's Magazine*, June 1905, 118.

27 Needham also alleged that James Cooney at Princeton received a similar scorecard deal. Ibid., 125-26.

28 *Big-Time Football at Harvard, 1905: The Diary of Coach Bill Reid*, Ronald Smith, ed. (Urbana: University of Illinois Press, 1994), 16; cited as Reid Diary.

29 Clarence Deming, "Athletics in College Life," *Outlook*, July 1, 1905, 570-71.

30 Caspar Whitney, "The Sports-Man's View Point," *Outing*, January 1903, 498-510.

31 Legend has it that Roosevelt called the conference after seeing a newspaper photograph of a Swarthmore player being beaten during a game against Penn but, as John Sayle Watterson observes, there is no evidence that this incident was discussed during the White House meeting. Watterson, *College Football*, 65-66. Furthermore, the conference was held just two days after the Penn-Swarthmore game and it seems unlikely that even Roosevelt could have acted so quickly.

32 Moore, "Football's Ugly Decades, 1893-1913," *The Rise of American Sport*, 178.

33 *Harvard Crimson*, January 5, 1906.

[34] Richard Norton Smith, *The Harvard Century: The Making of a University to a Nation* (New York: Simon & Schuster, 1986), 44.

[35] In a letter to his son, Ted, who was playing on the freshman team at Harvard, Roosevelt related an amusing story about his immediate reaction to the game. "This morning at breakfast," he wrote, "I took up the paper and said: 'Oh Lord! It's too bad that Pennsy won.' Whereupon Quentin [Roosevelt's younger son] remarked in a meditative aside: 'I suppose Pennsy's a democrat.'" Theodore Roosevelt to Theodore Roosevelt, Jr., November 12, 1905, *The Letters of Theodore Roosevelt*, Elting E. Morison, ed. (Cambridge, Mass.: Harvard University Press, 1952), 76.

[36] Smith, *Sports and Freedom*, 196.

[37] Dashiell later explained that he had not called a penalty because Quill had hit Burr with his open hand (breaking his nose) rather than a closed fist, a rather formalistic reading of the rules. Thomas H. Pauly, "A Man for Two Seasons," *Harvard Magazine*, November-December 1991, 67.

[37] Nelson, *Anatomy*, 100.

[38] Smith, *Sports and Freedom*, 197.

[40] Edwin E. Slosson, *Great American Universities* (New York: Macmillan, 1910), 452.

[41] "Football Conference at the White House," NYT, December 5, 1905.

[42] "Abolish Football, Says Harvard Bulletin," NYT, October 19, 1905.

[43] "Harvard's Tackle Gives Up Football," NYT, December 5, 1905. Reid doubted Brill had the stuff to be a top player. He noted in his diary that a teammate had overheard Brill saying, "I would much rather get an 'A' in calculus than beat Yale," a sentiment his coach found unfathomable. "This shows how little Brill has thrown himself into this work," Reid wrote. "I don't care how much of a student a fellow cares to be at other times—four days before the Yale game he ought, and I don't see how a man can help feeling that hardly anything is more important than to beat Yale." Reid Diary, 300-301.

[44] Ronald Smith, "Harvard and Columbia and a Reconsideration of the 1905-06 Football Crisis," *Journal of Sport History*, Winter 1981, 7.

[45] Ibid., 15.

[46] Smith, *Sports and Freedom*, 206.

[47] Others credit Princeton with the first successful pass, a week earlier in a game against Villanova. See Watterson, *College Football*, 106.

[48] Baker Book, 847.

[49] Frank Butterworth, "Honesty in Football," *Outing*, November 1904, 141.

[50] Frederick Rudolph, *The American College and University* (Athens: University of Georgia Press, 1990), 393.

[51] Bergin, *The Game*, 96.

[52] See Herbert Reed, "Harvard, Gridiron Deceiver," *Harper's Weekly*, November 27, 1915, 520.

[53] Percy Haughton, *Football and How to Watch It* (Boston: Marshall Jones, 1922).

[54] McCallum, *Ivy League Football*, 68-69.

[55] Ibid., 56.

[56] Bergin, *The Game*, 100-101.

[57] *Harvard Lampoon*, October 28, 1907, 72.

[58] Goldstein, *Ivy League Autumns*, 46.

[59] Robert A. Rosenstone, *Romantic Revolutionary* (New York: Alfred A. Knopf, 1975), 54.

[60] "Effects of Football Reform at Columbia," *American Review of Reviews*, December 1909, 730.

[61] Nelson, *Anatomy*, 141.

[62] Two years later, in 1912, the final pieces were added—requiring four downs to gain ten yards, increasing the value of a touchdown to six points and reducing the value of a field goal to three points.

[63] Henry Aaron Yeomans, *Abbott Lawrence Lowell, 1856-1943* (Cambridge, Mass.: Harvard University Press, 1948), 336.

[64] Ibid., 337.

[65] "Yale and Harvard Meet on Football," NYT, December 10, 1909.

[66] Wilson to Hadley, December 6, 1909, Arthur Hadley papers, YUA.

[67] Robert A. Caro, *The Power Broker: Robert Moses and the Fall of New York* (New York: Vintage, 1975), 42.

[68] "Harvard to Join New College Body," NYT, December 21, 1909.

[69] See Harford Powel, Jr., *Walter Camp, The Father of American Football* (Boston: Little, Brown, 1926), 111-121.

[70] McCallum, *Ivy League Football*, 65.

[71] Powel, *Walter Camp*, 128.

Chapter 5. *The Sign We Hail*

[1] Goldstein, *Ivy League Autumns*, 50-51.

[2] McCallum, *Ivy League Football*, 67.

[3] Tim Cohane, *The Yale Football Story* (New York: Putnam, 1951), 198.

[4] Harold F. Braman, "Dartmouth Songs, Part III (1915-1963)," DAM, April 1961.

[5] Danzig, *History*, 190.

[6] Goldstein, *Ivy League Autumns*, 43.

[7] "Brickley's Five Field Goals Top Yale," NYT, November 23, 1913.

[8] Ibid.

[9] In a remarkable bit of quackery, the director of the New Jersey State Board of Health attributed Brickley's appendicitis to too much meat in the Crimson training table diet. See "Meat Made Brickley Ill," NYT, December 13, 1914.

[10] Bergin, *The Game*, 118.

[11] Matthew J. Bruccoli, *Some Sort of Epic Grandeur: The Life of F. Scott Fitzgerald* (New York: Harcourt Brace Jovanovich, 1987), 33.

[12] NYT, November 5, 1911.

[13] Quoted in Ron Fimrite, "Hobey Baker: A Flame That Burned Too Brightly," SI, March 18, 1991, 78.

[14] Ibid., 79.

[15] *A History of Columbia College on Morningside* (New York: Columbia University Press, 1954), 213.

[16] "Butler Opposes Football," NYT, October 28, 1910.

[17] *Alumni News*, November 20, 1914.

[18] "Report of the Committee on Student Organizations in Regard to the Restoration of Football," reprinted in *Papers Relating to the Game of Football*, February 16, 1915, 2, Columbia University archives.

[19] "The War in the Yale Bowl," NYT, November 21, 1914.

[20] McCallum, *Ivy League Football*, 68.

[21] Letter, YAW, December 18, 1914, 365.

[22] "Record Football Receipts," NYT, November 29, 1916.

[23] Harvard Athletic Association, Income and Expenditure Accounts, FYE July 31, 1911, through July 31, 1922 (Schedule A), Harvard Athletic Association files, HUA.

[24] See Harvard Athletic Association, Expenses of Games, etc. for the Year Ending July 31, 1917 (Schedule B-2), Harvard Athletic Association files, HUA.

[25] Rollo Warren Brown, *Dean Briggs* (New York: Harper & Bros., 1926), 197.

[26] H. J. Ludington, "Football Report for 1914-1915," CUA.

[27] Bishop, *Cornell*, 415.

[28] See *Biographical Dictionary of American Sports*, 1992-1995 Supplement for Baseball, Football, Basketball, and Other Sports, David L. Porter, ed. (Westport, Conn.: Greenwood Press, 1995), 371-72.

[29] Kane, *Good Sports*, 47.

[30] See Rube Samuelsen, *The Rose Bowl Game* (Garden City, N.Y.: Doubleday, 1951), 10-11.

[31] John M. Carroll, *Fritz Pollard, Pioneer in Racial Advancement* (Urbana: University of Illinois Press, 1992), 79.

[32] See "The Needs of Brown Football," BAM, January 1914, 143.

[33] Ernest M. Hopkins to W. A. Green, December 2, 1920, E. M. Hopkins papers, DCA. Hopkins was generous to Cornell and Penn, which did not have black athletes on their football teams until 1936 and 1950, respectively. Yale admitted its first black student in 1854, but did not have a black football player until 1949. Princeton did not graduate its first black student until 1947, and did not have a black football player until 1964.

[34] Carroll, *Pollard*, 60.

[35] Ibid., 67-68.

[36] "Harvard and Brown," BAM, December 1915, 123.

[37] Carroll, Pollard, 87-88.

[38] Ibid., 106.

[39] Goldstein, *Ivy League Autumns*, 57.

[40] "Question Timing in Yale Victory," NYT, December 4, 1916.

[41] See "Penn Players Vote to Oust Football Coach," *Cornell Sun*, December 4, 1914; "Penn Grads Up in Arms," NYT, December 5, 1914.

[42] Samuelsen, *Rose Bowl*, 16.

[43] "Comment on Current Events in Sports," NYT, January 8, 1917.

[44] "Folwell, Deposed Penn Coach, Will Be Given Hearing," *Philadelphia Inquirer*, January 31, 1917.

[45] See "Folwell Cast Off As Coach at Penn," NYT, January 30, 1917; "Flock to Defense of Coach Folwell," NYT, January 31, 1917; "Comment on Current Events in Sports," NYT, February 5, 1917.

[46] "Folwell Signs War Clause in Contract," *Philadelphia Inquirer*, February 8, 1917.

[47] "War Saves Harvard $50,000 on Sports," NYT, April 22, 1917.

[48] Washington and Jefferson had been the first team in the country to number its players, in 1908.

[49] "Yale Teams Play for Yale Only," NYT, March 24, 1916. Captain Black changed his mind after Yale tried the experiment that season in a game against Carnegie Tech, and was thereafter a staunch supporter of numbering.

[50] "Yale Will Number Players in Harvard and Princeton Games," NYT, November 9, 1920.

[51] Address of H. McClenahan, December 28, 1915, reprinted as "Athletic Standards," PWA, January 12, 1916, 325.

[52] "Opposed to Athletic Proselyting," A. L. Lowell papers, HUA.

[53] Lawrence Lowell, for one, attributed Princeton's recruiting success to "one advantage— that her graduates are always lauding their college in preparatory schools, whereas our graduates are always criticizing Harvard." A. Lawrence Lowell to Frederick A. Martin, May 22, 1926, A. L. Lowell papers, HUA. The three presidents' efforts to stop athletic "proselyting" as they called it with an agreeably biblical word, should also be seen in conjunction with other steps to make the admission process more rational and democratic. Beginning after the Civil War, each college administered its own entrance examination to prospective students, a system that permitted many abuses in the recruiting of athletes. In 1904, Harvard decided to join the College Entrance Examination Board, which gave a standardized admission test and sent the results to the colleges. Yale and Princeton soon joined. Penn, however, along with a number of midwestern state universities, continued to accept applicants on the basis of a simple certificate of fitness from accredited secondary schools.

[54] "Big Four May Be Big Three's Rival," NYT, February 12, 1919.

[55] McClellan, "Eliminate Practice Game," *Pennsylvania Gazette*, March 14, 1919, 542.

[56] "No Athletic Aristocracy," NYT, March 25, 1919.

[57] Beale, *Football at Harvard*, 233.

[58] Brown, *Dean Briggs*, 197.

[59] Goldstein, *Ivy League Autumns*, 61.

[60] "Coolidge Sends Greetings," NYT, December 30, 1919.

[61] "The Harvard-Oregon Football Game in Pasadena," *The Literary Digest*, January 17, 1920, 114.

[62] "Harvard Starts on Return Trip," NYT, January 3, 1920.

[63] Samuelsen, *Rose Bowl*, 32.

[64] See "Ban on Football Lifted at Columbia," NYT, October 11, 1919.

Chapter 6. *Team of Destiny*

[1] Mitchell, *Encyclopedia Brunonia*, 402-3.

[2] "Charges Harvard Slighted Holy Cross," NYT, January 23, 1925.

[3] McCallum, *Ivy League Football*, 85.

[4] Leitch, *Princeton Companion*, 418.

[5] *New York World*, October 23, 1921, quoted in Lester, Stagg's University, 118.

[6] "A Princeton Classic—Revisited After Half A Century," 7, PUA.

[7] Quoted in Francis Wallace, *Knute Rockne* (Garden City, N.Y.: Doubleday, 1960), 161. On New Year's Day, 1926, a group of ex-Princeton football players (including Caldwell) met a group of Notre Dame alumni in a charity game in Miami and lost again, 6-0, on a disputed call by referee John Heisman. Wealthy vacationers and beauty queens packed the stands at $25 apiece, including the British ambassador to the United States and Misses New York, Missouri, and Mississippi. The game had been organized by Henry Dutton, a real estate developer, who agreed to pay the Princeton squad $15,000 for appearing. Their cheerful motto that afternoon was "Fighting for dirty Dutton and dear old gate receipts." See Stephen R. Dujack, "The First Superbowl," PAW, October 4, 1976, 16.

[8] Bob Paul, Director of Sports Information, to Edwin Pope, August 19, 1954, courtesy of Dan Rottenberg.

[9] See Cohane, *Greatest Football Coaches*, 66.

[10] Kane, *Good Sports*, 30.

[11] Bergin, *The Game*, 137.

[12] *Biographical Dictionary of American Sports*, 1992-1995 Supplement, 485-86; Cohane, *Greatest Football Coaches*, 100.

[13] NYT, November 25, 1923.

[14] Bergin, *The Game*, 145.

[15] Quoted in Charles E. Widmayer, *Hopkins of Dartmouth* (Hanover, N.H.: University Press of New England, 1977), 54.

[16] See Woody Klein, " Glory Days," DAM, November 1988, 37.

[17] McCallum, *Ivy League Football*, 100.

[18] Goldstein, *Ivy League Autumns*, 72.

[19] See John R. Scotford, Jr., "What It Was Was Grid-Graph," DAM, October 1980, 46.

[20] *The Dartmouth Football Seasons of 1924 and 1925* (Vol. II of II), Scrapbooks of Del Worthington, DCA.

[21] "P. D. Haughton Dies, Stricken Suddenly" NYT, October 28, 1924.

[22] See "Columbia Bad Faith Charged by Rockne," NYT, December 13, 1925; "Anent Knute Rockne," *Columbia Alumni News*, January 8, 1926; Wallace, *Knute Rockne*, 205-9.

[23] Jay Barry, "The Birth of a Brown Legend: Iron Men of 40 Seasons Ago," BAM, November 1966, 38.

[24] "Yale Seeks Curb on Pro Football," NYT, January 8, 1926.

[25] "Yale Punishes Twenty in Ticket Investigation; Says Bootleggers, Fighters, Waiters Saw Game," NYT, December 12, 1930. Ernest Martin Hopkins later alleged that gamblers, some of whom had helped fix the 1919 World Series, had wagered $15,000 against Dartmouth in one game. "White Sox Scandal Gamblers Put $15,000 Against Dartmouth Eleven, Says Hopkins," NYT, April 17, 1926.

[26] "Ticket Probe Is Begun by Harvard," NYT, November 23, 1921.

[27] "The Human Side of Ticket Allotment," HAB, November 23, 1922, 232.

[28] "Football Ticket Distribution for 1927," Yale-Princeton Football Program, November 12, 1927, Princeton Athletic Department.

[29] See "Yale Football Receipts Top $400,000; Is New Record," NYT, November 27, 1922; " Football Receipts at Yale $626,194," NYT, January 30, 1925; "$801,258 Received for Sports at Yale; Football Brings $690,372, Report Shows," NYT, December 4, 1925; "Athletics at Yale Yield $853,369 Gross; Football Alone Drew $740,876," NYT, December 16, 1926; "Athletic Finances for 1926-27," YAW, February 3, 1928, 539; "Athletic Finances for 1927-28," YAW, November 2, 1928, 183.

[30] See Harvard Athletic Association Financial Report, Income and Expenditure Account, FYE July 31, 1920, 1921, Schedule A, HUA; "Harvard Football Took in $584,195," NYT, January 17, 1928.

[31] Spaulding, "Football and Educational Finances," YAW, December 7, 1928.

[32] "News and Comment," YAW, November 2, 1928.

[33] See "Football Only Paying Sport at Cornell; Nets $116,353," NYT, October 31, 1928. The following year, with a considerably more successful team, football profits rose to $145,000, producing an overall surplus of more than $50,000. "Cornell Has $145,000 Profit in Football, Only Paying Sport," NYT, October 16, 1929.

[34] "The Big Scrimmage over College Football," *Literary Digest*, November 9, 1929, 58.

[35] H. T. Marshall, *What the Football Season of 1925 Taught Us About Business Administration*, American Management Association, 1926, 5, DCA.

[36] "Many Stars Work Their Way Through Yale," NYT, November 29, 1923; "18 of 40 Men on Yale Football Squad Are Working Their Way Through College," NYT, November 16, 1924.

[37] Marcia Synnott, "A Social History of Admissions Policies at Harvard, Yale, and Princeton, 1900-1930" (Ph.D. diss., University of Massachusetts, 1974), 49.

[38] Synnott, *The Half-Opened Door*, 20.

[39] Synnott, "A Social History of Admissions Policies at Harvard, Yale, and Princeton, 1900-1930," 49.

[40] Slosson, *Great American Universities*, 363.

[41] Heywood Broun and George Britt, *Christians Only: A Study in Prejudice* (New York: Vanguard Press, 1931), 73.

[42] The previous fall, two more Yale players had been declared ineligible when it was revealed that they had competed previously for other colleges.

[43] "Coach Roper Plans Drastic Measures," NYT, March 30, 1922.

[44] "Scholarship, Then, Does Suffer?" NYT, March 31, 1922.

[45] "Yale News Asks Harvard's Pardon," NYT, November 28, 1923.

[46] *A Treasury of Damon Runyon* (New York: Modern Library, 1958), 122.

[47] "'Exuberance' Frees Columbia Students," NYT, November 24, 1927.

[48] Morton Prince, "For Whom Is Football a Sport?" HAB, November 12, 1925, 188.

[49] Quoted in Widmayer, *Hopkins of Dartmouth*, 129-30.

[50] See ibid., 130-31; E. M. Hopkins to Livingston Farrand, February 7, 1927, E. M. Hopkins papers, DCA.

[51] "Princeton Official Opposed," NYT, March 21, 1927.

[52] "President's Proposals Attract Much Comment," DAM, May 1927, 643-44.

[53] E. Digby Baltzell, *Philadelphia Gentlemen: The Making of a National Upper Class* (Glencoe, Ill.: Free Press, 1958), 326-28.

[54] *Report of the Committee on the Regulation of Athletic Sports*, 4, Harvard College, October 1925, Lowell papers, HUA.

[55] "The real fact is," wrote President Hopkins, "that there has been no college in the country as unfriendly to Dartmouth and her interests nor as caustic in her comments and criticisms as Yale for at least the last twenty years." E. M. Hopkins to J. P. Margesun, Jr., December 1, 1922, E. M. Hopkins papers, DCA. Once, when President Angell (whom Hopkins liked) referred to Dartmouth as the daughter of Yale, Hopkins slyly replied that Yale had always behaved more like a stepmother.

[56] E. M. Hopkins to Alexander Meiklejohn, March 27, 1922, E. M. Hopkins papers, DCA.

[57] E. M. Hopkins to David J. Main, December 20, 1923, E. M. Hopkins papers, DCA.

[58] LeBaron Briggs to A. L. Lowell, January 24, 1924, A. L. Lowell papers, HUA.

[59] "Cornell Attacks Big Three Policy," NYT, February 14, 1919. The Harvard Student Council agreed, adopting a resolution that " any code of rules between Harvard, Yale, and Princeton would tend to give an erroneous impression of the existence of an exclusive triumvirate and is contrary to undergraduate opinion." See "Opposes New Big Three," NYT, March 7, 1919.

[60] George Wilson Pierson, *Yale College: An Educational History, 1871-1921* (New Haven: Yale University Press, 1952), 580, n. 4.

[61] Kenneth S. Davis, *A Prophet in His Own Country: The Triumphs and Defeats of Adlai E. Stevenson* (Garden City, N.Y.: Doubleday, 1957), 108-9. Stevenson graduated from Princeton in 1922.

[62] "Seeks to Restore Athletic Concord," NYT, November 14, 1922.

[63] A. L. Lowell to James Angell, April 6, 1922, A. L. Lowell papers, HUA.

[64] See John G. Hibben to A. L. Lowell, September 29, 1926, A. L. Lowell papers, HUA.

[65] A. L. Lowell to John G. Hibben, September 30, 1926, A. L. Lowell papers, HUA.

[66] See Report of the Committee on the Regulation of Athletic Sports, 2, October 1925, A. L. Lowell papers, HUA.

[67] James Angell to John G. Hibben, September 26, 1926, Smith papers, PUA.

[68] *Harvard Lampoon*, November 3, 1926 (Princeton game issue), 114-15.

[69] Goldstein, *Ivy League Autumns*, 77.

[70] "Harvard and Princeton," DP, November 9, 1926.

[71] *Harvard Crimson*, November 9, 1926.

[72] In a puckish, but humorous, rebuke, Princeton seniors the following spring listed Harvard as their fifth favorite men's college, with 14 votes (first-place Yale had 365). They also ranked all-male Harvard as their third-favorite women's college, ahead of Bryn Mawr and Wellesley. *Nassau Herald*, 1927.

[73] "'Yale First' Policy Rules at Harvard," NYT, November 28, 1926.

[74] W. D. Hubbard, " Dirty Football: A Former Harvard Player Tells Why His University Broke Relations with Princeton," *Liberty*, January 29, 1927, 38.

[75] "Treat 'Em Rough," HAB, February 3, 1927, 490.

[76] Jac Weller, *History of Princeton Football, 1916-1942* (privately printed, 1984), 27, PUA.

[77] NYT , October 26, 1929.

[78] Grantland Rice, NYHT, quoted in "Albie Booth, Yale's Bare-Legged Jumping Bean," *Literary Digest*, November 23, 1929, 50.

[79] Damon Runyon, *New York American*, quoted in "Barry Wood: Harvard's Football Meteor," *Literary Digest*, November 14, 1931.

[80] Herbert Reed, "Harvard—Football Phoenix," *Outlook*, December 12, 1928, 1326.

Chapter 7. Red Ink

[1] The Carnegie Foundation was one of the great philanthropic creations of industrialist Andrew Carnegie who, as a member of the Cornell board of trustees, was startled to learn that university professors earned less than some of the employees in his steel mills. He endowed the foundation to establish a faculty pension system (which it did—the Teachers Insurance and Annuity Association, or TIAA), but its purpose was soon broadened to include the scientific study of education in America, making it one of the country's first think tanks.

[2] Widmayer, *Hopkins of Dartmouth*, 131-32.

[3] Yale considered adding an upper deck to the Yale Bowl, but decided against it because it would cut off the view of fans sitting below.

[4] R. Tait McKenzie, "Physical Education at the University of Pennsylvania—from 1904 to 1931—and the Gates Plan," *Research Quarterly*, May 1932, 19.

[5] See Rottenberg, *Fight On, Pennsylvania*, 44.

[6] Goldstein, *Ivy League Autumns*, 84.

[7] Notes of interview, Dan Rottenberg with P. G. Riblett, July 13, 1976; notes of interview, Rottenberg with Jeremiah Ford.

[8] NYT, November 8, 1930.

[9] Samuel Mitchell Greene, "*Intercollegiate Athletics at Pennsylvania: Corruption and Penitence,*" senior thesis, University of Pennsylvania, 1993, 42.

[10] McKenzie, *Research Quarterly*, 25.

[11] "Pennsy's Bitter Dose and Reducing Diet for Stadium Fever," *Literary Digest*, February 21, 1931.

[12] *Cornell Daily Sun*, February 7, 1931.

[13] Thomas A. Gates to Owen D. Young, September 18, 1931, Athletic Association papers, UPA. Brown, Dartmouth, and Yale participated in the series; Cornell, Harvard, Penn, and Princeton did not.

[14] "College Football Viewed As 'Racket,'" NYT, November 11, 1931.

[15] "Football Men Threaten Columbia Editor; His 'Racket' Charges Upsets Alumni, Too," NYT, November 12, 1931. Harris later elaborated upon his charges in a book, *King Football: The Vulgarization of the American College* (New York: Vanguard Press, 1932), a supercilious attack on big-time football and college administration in general. His youthful editorials, however, were not altogether forgotten. A generation later, in 1953, when Harris was a deputy director of the International Information Administration in the Eisenhower administration, Senator Joseph McCarthy called him before his committee to testify about alleged communist leanings as an undergraduate. Goldstein, *Ivy League Autumns*, 87.

[16] Goldstein, *Ivy League Autumns*, 84.

[17] "Grads Not Bane of Crisler's Existence: In Fact, 'I Like 'Em,' He Says in 'Post,'" DP, November 13, 1935.

[18] Goldstein, *Ivy League Autumns*, 92.

[19] The article Fitzgerald was reading was "Plus and Minus: An Analytical, Long Range View of the 1940 Football Team; the Outlook for Next Year," by Gilbert Lea. PAW, December 9, 1940, 9. "Perfection is naturally something to be strived for and gained if possible, and criticism of non-perfection is the easiest thing in the world," the article stated, in perhaps the last words Fitzgerald ever read.

[20] Jay Dunn, *The Tigers of Princeton: Old Nassau Football* (Huntsville, Ala.: Strode Publishers, 1977), 162-63. Curiously, Crisler was also a tangential figure in another of the great crimes of that era—the murder of Bobby Franks by Richard Loeb and Nathan Leopold, Jr. While an assistant coach at the University of Chicago in the early 1920s, Crisler earned extra money by tutoring the son of a prominent Chicago alumnus, Morris Rosenwald. Loeb and Leopold, two dissolute rich boys, planned to kidnap young Rosenwald, kill him, and try to collect a ransom, but on the day they planned to commit the crime, Rosenwald had a toothache. Crisler took the boy to the dentist and, not finding Rosenwald at home, Loeb and Leopold took Franks instead. See Cohane, *Greatest Football Coaches*, 53; "Playing for Keeps," *People Magazine*, June 14, 1999, 141.

[21] J. I. Merritt, "After 61 years, 'Tiger' Helmet Returns to Princeton," PAW, September 9, 1998, 31.

[22] "Limits on Broadcasting," HAB, November 20, 1931, 246-47.

[23] Cohane, *Yale Football Story*, 269.

[24] Goldstein, *Ivy League Autumns*, 86.

[25] Baker Book, 2140. Booth was still recuperating a few weeks later when the day came to take the team photograph. Another student sat in Booth's place when the photograph was shot, but in the final print his head was deleted and an old shot of Booth inserted in its place. Ibid., 2153-54.

[26] Nelson, *Anatomy*, 204.

[27] Quoted in "Critics Say Lack of Material Handicaps Columbia," *Columbia Alumni News*, October 31, 1930, 5.

[28] Cohane, *Greatest Football Coaches*, 119.

[29] Frank, "He Doesn't Have to Win," SEP, November 16, 1946, 18.

[30] Goldstein, *Ivy League Autumns*, 87.

[31] Cliff Montgomery, "Football's Biggest Upset," *Coronet*, January 1955, 46.

[32] Ibid., 47.

[33] Goldstein, *Ivy League Autumns*, 88.

[34] *College Football's Memorable Games, 1913 Through 1990*, 20.

[35] NYT, January 1, 1934.

[36] Montgomery, *Coronet*, 49. Although KF-79 became an indelible part of Columbia athletic lore, history is often lost on undergraduates. A few years later, a Lions coach asked center Ted Ruberti, "What do you do on KF-79?" Ruberti replied, "I stand at attention and salute." *A History of Columbia College on Morningside*, 224.

[37] Goldstein, *Ivy League Autumns*, 90.

[38] Kane, *Good Sports*, 312.

[39] "Financing Princeton Athletics," PAW, February 3, 1933, 1.

[40] "Football Money," HAB, December 9, 1938, 332.

[41] See Kane, *Good Sports*, 308-12; Bishop, *Cornell*, 504-6.

[42] NYT, April 11, 1935.

[43] Ibid.

[44] Henry M. Kennedy, "These Sophisticated 'Thirties," PAW, March 20, 1931, 583.

[45] "About Football," HAB, October 13, 1933, 67.

[46] YAW, November 30, 1934, 267.

[47] See, e.g., Alan Gould, "Athletic Leaders, Coaches Disavow Sweeping Reforms," *Providence Journal*, December 31. 1934.

[48] See Thelin, *The Cultivation of Ivy*, 21-23.

[49] Marcia G. Synnott, "The 'Big Three' and the Harvard-Princeton Football Break, 1926-1934," *Journal of Sport History*, Summer 1976, 188.

[50] "The Crimson Editors See Red," NYT, February 17, 1931.

[50] NYHT, February 17, 1931.

[51] Walter L. Leighton, HAB, April 2, 1931, 811.

[52] "Rotation Is Hailed by 'Yale News' as Assuring Parity for Princeton," NYHT, February 16, 1931.

[53] Lawrence Perry, "The Football Brahmins Make Peace," *Scribner's Magazine*, November 1934, 291.

[54] NYT, January 10, 1933.

[55] Dartmouth president Ernest Hopkins related a story that illustrated the still submerged rivalry between Harvard and Princeton. According to Hopkins, at a smoker the night before the game, Crisler and Harvard athletic director Bill Bingham exchanged toasts. Bingham took a few humorous shots at Crisler, and when the latter's turn came to speak he "wound up with a brief reference to the game with Harvard next day and admitted his partisanship but asserted in spite of that that he still hoped that the best team might win. Bill Bingham, sitting on the stage, remarked in not so very much sotto voce, "You mean 'better.'" To this Crisler came back without a moment's hesitation, "No, I mean 'best.' I brought over three teams and I don't know which one of them I shall use." E. M. Hopkins to James Angell, November 6, 1934, James Angell papers, YUA.

[57] "New Football Body Urged," NYT, November 25, 1931.

[58] "Conference Rumors Won't Die Down," BAM, February 1933, 191.

[59] "View of College Sports," NYHT, January 20, 1935.

[60] "Immediate Formation of Ivy League Advocated at Seven Eastern Colleges," NYT, December 3, 1936.

[61] "Dartmouth Endorses Idea," NYT, December 3, 1936.

[62] "Schedule Commitments Prevent Immediate Formation of League," NYT, December 4, 1936.

[63] Harold Dodds to James Angell, December 10, 1936, James Angell papers, YUA.

[64] See Thelin, *The Cultivation of Ivy*, 28.

[65] Whitey Fuller, "The World of Sports," *Dartmouth*, December 4, 1936. Others echoed the view. "Harvard, Yale, Princeton, and perhaps Cornell!" grumbled Morris Bishop about the short shrift often given to his alma mater. "Perhaps Cornell! It has

always been the fate of our University to be Perhaps Cornell!" Bishop, "—And Perhaps Cornell," in Raymond Floyd Hughes, ed., *Our Cornell* (Ithaca, N.Y.: Cayuga Press, 1939), 76-77.

[66] Mian Gulian, "A Dossier on Brown Football," BAM, December 1937, 140.

[67] "Plea for an Ivy Football League Rejected by College Authorities," NYT, January 12, 1937; "Action Delayed on Ivy League by Agreement," *Dartmouth*, January 12, 1937.

[68] Howard Savage to J. B. Conant, December 30, 1936; J. B. Conant memorandum, January 27, 1937; J. B. Conant to James Angell, January 28, 1937, J. B. Conant papers, HUA.

[69] J. B. Conant to Charles Seymour, June 8, 1937, J. B. Conant papers, HUA.

[70] "Gerald Ford at Yale: Football Coaching and Law," YAM, October 1974.

[71] Cohane, *The History of Yale Football*, 279.

[72] Larry Kelley, "Everybody There Saw Kelley," SEP, October 23, 1937, 14.

[73] "53,000 See Yale Score Stirring Football Upset by Halting Princeton, 7-0," NYT, November 18, 1934.

[74] McCallum, *Ivy League Football*, 135.

[75] Author interview, April 1998.

[76] Kelley, SEP, October 23, 1937, 14.

[77] McCallum, *Ivy League Football*, 133.

[78] George Daley, "Sport Talk" NYHT, December 10, 1936; quoting poem by J.L. Marks, delivered at Philadelphia Racquet Club dinner.

[79] Goldstein, *Ivy League Autumns*, 96. The rule was later changed to prohibit a player who kicks a loose ball from falling on it, whether or not he did it deliberately.

[80] In 1935, Jay Berwanger of the University of Chicago had won the award presented by the Downtown Athletic Club of New York to the best collegiate football player, but that award was not named the Heisman Memorial Trophy until 1936. Heisman, who was the club's athletic director, had died earlier that year.

[81] John T. Brady, *The Heisman, Symbol of Excellence* (New York: Atheneum 1984), 42.

[82] McCallum, *Ivy League History*, 135.

[83] See Kelley, SEP, October 23, 1937, 14.

[84] Earl H. Blaik, *The Red Blaik Story* (New Rochelle, N.Y.: Arlington House, 1974), 155-56.

[85] Bergin, *The Game*, 172.

[86] Ibid., 174.

[87] Ivan Kaye, "Dick Harlow: Rare Bird," *Harvard Magazine*, November-December 1989, 83.

[88] Ibid., 82-83; Cohane, *Greatest Football Coaches*, 78.

[89] Kaye, "Dick Harlow," 83.

[90] Ibid.

[91] Ibid., 84.

[92] Cohane, *Greatest Football Coaches*, 69.

[93] Goldstein, *Ivy League Autumns*, 100.

[94] Cohane, *Greatest Football Coaches*, 70.

[95] "Cornell to Give Scholarships to Obtain Athletes," *Providence Journal*, December 24, 1934.

[96] "Bike Replaces Auto for Football Squad," NYT, March 30, 1939.

[97] Ibid., 181.

[98] Robert A. Hall, "Cornell Goes to the Movies," SEP, October 26, 1940, 18.

[99] Arthur Ashe, *A Hard Road to Glory: A History of the African-American Athlete* (New York: Warner Books, 1988), 95.

[100] Jerome Holland, *Black Opportunity* (New York: Weybright & Talley, 1969), vii.

[101] E. M. Hopkins to W. J. Bingham, October 29, 1934, W. J. Bingham papers, HUA.

[102] Gertrude Stein, *Everybody's Autobiography* (New York: Random House, 1937), 195-98.

[103] "Nairne-Ray Touchdowns End Eli Jinx over Indians," NYHT, November 3, 1935.

[104] McCallum, *Ivy League Football*, 129.

[105] Ibid., 130.

[106] Donald C. Stuart, Jr., "When Eleven Were Twelve," *Princeton Athletic News*, November 21, 1936, 13.

[107] NYT, December 1, 1935.

[108] Ibid.

[109] "Orderly Crowd of 51,000 at Princeton Game as Ban on Drinking Stands Its First Test," NYT, October 25, 1936.

[110] Marie Zellner to James Angell, undated [Fall 1936], James Angell papers, YUA. While Angell reassured Mrs. Zellner, in effect, that only a few bad apples should not spoil the barrel, he had already asked for a report on incidents of drunkenness at the Yale Bowl each week. Typical was the report issued following the Rutgers game, held October 24, 1936: " Drinking very light but considerable roughhousing occurred especially during last half of game such as throwing papers, etc. This appeared to be somewhat due to fraternity initiation week." Ibid.

[111] "Princeton Bans Liquor at Games; Dodds Calls It Menace to Sport," NYT, October 19, 1936.

[112] "Dr. Dodds Acclaimed for Stand Against Football Fans' Drinking," NYT, October 20, 1936.

[113] "McCarter Declares Rose Bowl Classic Not for Dartmouth," *Dartmouth*, November 13, 1937.

[114] See *The Red Blaik Story*, 157-58.

[115] Jacqueline Dutton, "The Legendary Sid Luckman '39," Columbia College Today, Fall 1990, 24.

[116] Malcolm Farmer to Charles Seymour, September 8, 1938, Charles Seymour papers, YUA.

[117] "Yale's Radio Tie-Up Inspires Broadcast," syndicated article, September 4, 1936, Charles Seymour papers, YUA.

[118] Columbia did the same a year later.

[119] Malcolm Farmer to Charles Seymour, January 6, 1939, Charles Seymour papers, YUA.

Chapter 8. *Medium-Time Football*

[1] Kane, *Good Sports*, 152.

[2] Since the inception of the AP poll in 1936, only four Ivy schools have ever finished the season ranked in the top ten: Penn in 1936, 1945, and 1947; Princeton in 1950

and 1951; Dartmouth in 1937; and Cornell in 1939. Every Ivy school except Brown has been ranked in the AP top twenty at some point during the season.

[3] *Dartmouth*, November 24, 1940.

[4] "Cornell Wants No 'Long Count,' President Tells Students," NYT, November 20, 1940.

[5] Vincent T. Meany to Edmund E. Day, undated, E. E. Day papers, CUA.

[6] "Day Explains Cornell Stand on Indian Game," *Cornell Daily Sun*, November 20, 1940.

[7] Cohane, *Greatest Football Coaches*, 182.

[8] Author interview, August 6, 1999.

[9] Barry Gifford and Lawrence Lee, *Jack's Book: An Oral Biography of Jack Kerouac* (New York: St. Martin's Press, 1978), 26.

[10] Tom Clark, *Jack Kerouac* (New York: Harcourt Brace, 1984), 46.

[11] Ann Charters, *Kerouac* (London: Andre Deutch, 1974), 28.

[12] Clark, *Kerouac*, 54.

[13] "Topics of the Times: Another Tradition Gone," NYT, May 12, 1941.

[14] Nelson, *Anatomy*, 226-27.

[15] Charles Seymour to Harold W. Dodds, January 10, 1941, Charles Seymour papers, YUA.

[16] Charles Seymour to J. B. Conant, November 30, 1943, Charles Seymour papers, YUA.

[17] J. B. Conant to Charles Seymour, December 11, 1943, Charles Seymour papers, YUA.

[18] Harold Dodds to Charles Seymour, September 23, 1944, Charles Seymour papers, YUA. Most likely, Dodds was referring to Cornell.

[19] Harold Dodds to Charles Seymour, December 12, 1943, Charles Seymour papers, YUA.

[20] J. B. Conant to Charles Seymour, March 7, 1944, and attached memorandum of meeting, Charles Seymour papers, YUA.

[21] Harold Dodds to Charles Seymour, September 23, 1944, Charles Seymour papers, YUA; Edmund E. Day to Frank Fackenthal, September 6, 1945, E. E. Day papers, CUA.

[22] William H. McCarter to Ernest M. Hopkins, October 26, 1944, E. M. Hopkins papers, DCA.

[23] Resolution of Brown Club of Providence, December 20, 1944, Henry Wriston papers, Brown University archives.

[24] Memorandum, E. M. Hopkins to Board of Trustees, October 18, 1945, E. M. Hopkins papers, DCA.

[25] E. M. Hopkins to Edmund E. Day, January 4, 1945, E. E. Day papers, CUA.

[26] Edmund E. Day to E. M. Hopkins, January 16, 1945, E. M. Hopkins papers, DCA.

[27] E. M. Hopkins to Edmund E. Day, March 27, 1945, E. E. Day papers, CUA.

[28] John Field to Edwin F. Blair, January 24, 1945, YUA.

[29] Smith, *The Harvard Century*, 173.

[30] E. M. Hopkins to Edmund E. Day, January 4, 1945, E. E. Day papers, CUA.

[31] Geoffrey Kabaservice, "Yale and the Creation of the Ivy League," unpublished ms., August 1998.

[32] Harold Dodds to Charles Seymour, November 21, 1944, Charles Seymour papers, YUA.

[33] Memorandum, E. M. Hopkins to Board of Trustees, October 18, 1945, E. M. Hopkins papers, DCA.

[34] "Bingham on Football," HAB, December 3, 1949, 249.

[35] John A. Hannah to Edmund E. Day, October 28, 1946, E. E. Day papers, CUA.

[36] Arthur H. Compton to Charles Seymour, December 27, 1945, Charles Seymour papers, YUA. Several years later, the Rutgers student paper suggested their school for the Ivy League, too, a proposal Yale athletic officials flatly declared stood "absolutely no chance." Kabaservice, "Yale and the Creation of the Ivy League," 78-79.

[37] Daley, "Sports of the Times: In Search of Utopia," NYT, November 21, 1945.

[38] Baker Book, 3220.

[39] Bergin, *The Game*, 186.

[40] *The Second H Book of Harvard Athletics*, Geoffrey H. Movius, ed. (Cambridge, Mass.: Harvard Varsity Club, 1964), 200.

[41] Rottenberg, *Fight On, Pennsylvania*, 64.

[42] McCallum, *Ivy League Football*, 150.

[43] Red Blaik received an honorable mention among college coaches, primarily for his post-Dartmouth success at Army.

[44] "Last-Minute Princeton Field Goal Upsets Penn, 17-14," NYT, November 3, 1946.

[45] Edmund E. Day to Francis Cardinal Spellman, December 10, 1948, E. E. Day papers, CUA.

[46] *A History of Columbia College on Morningside Heights*, 225.

[47] "Backtalk: When Army Was Caught by Surprise in Lions' Den," NYT, October 19, 1997.

[48] "Apologies Exchanged in Wake of Riot," PAW, November 15, 1946, 10.

[49] "Eli 'Commandos' Raid Princeton and Even the Air Is Painted Blue," NYT, November 15, 1946.

[50] Editorial, *Brown Daily Herald*, November 12, 1948.

[51] "Penn Reprisal Backfires," NYT, October 23, 1947.

[52] George Wilson Pierson, *A Yale Book of Numbers, Historical Statistics of the College and University 1701-1976* (New Haven: Yale University, 1983).

[53] Sykes, "Gentlemen—the 'Nineties," PAW, February 6, 1931, 419; Laurence R. Veysey, *The Emergence of the American University* (Chicago: University of Chicago Press, 1965), 359.

[54] Joe Paterno, *Paterno: By the Book* (New York: Random House, 1989), 51.

[55] "Yale's Captain," NYT, November 24, 1948.

[56] Dan A. Oren, *Joining the Club: A History of Jews at Yale* (New Haven: Yale University Press, 1985), 162.

[57] McCallum, *Ivy League Football*, 157.

[58] Goldstein, *Ivy League Autumns*, 125.

[59] Arthur Daley, "The Fabulous Herman Hickman," NYT *Magazine*, October 28, 1951.

[60] Kanes, *Good Sports*, 323.

[61] Ibid., 321-25.

[62] "Football Record Holder Never Wore a Uniform," NYT, November 17, 1991; "At Yale, After 522 Games, Still Keeping Score at 92," NYT, October 25, 1998.

[63] Thacher Longstreth, *Main Line WASP* (New York: W. W. Norton, 1990).

Chapter 9. *The Ivy League*

[1] Dwight D. Eisenhower to Edmund E. Day, November 17, 1958, E. E. Day papers, CUA.

[2] Joel Sayre, "Pigskin at Penn: A Real-Life Drama," SI, January 28, 1957, 56.

[3] David L. Goldberg, "What Price Victory? What Price Honor? Pennsylvania and the Formation of the Ivy League, 1950-1952," *Pennsylvania Magazine of History and Biography*, April 1988, 227.

[4] "Princeton Proves Good Football Is Possible Without 'Overemphasis,'" SEP, January 5, 1952, 10.

[5] Stanley Woodward, "Is Penn Too Tough for the Ivy League?" *Sport*, November 1951, 36.

[6] Tim Cohane, "The Penn Is Mightier than the Ivy," *Look*, November 20, 1951, 70.

[7] See Sayre, "Pigskin at Penn," SI, January 28, 1957, 56.

[8] Ibid.

[9] "'Boycott' of Penn Laid to Irish Game," NYT, January 17, 1951.

[10] Leo Riordan, "The Football Blues Hit Penn," SEP, November 7, 1953, 25.

[11] Harold Stassen to Harold Dodds, January 22, 1951, Harold Dodds papers, PUA.

[12] Harold Dodds to Harold Stassen, January 23, 1951, Harold Dodds papers, PUA.

[13] See "Football Poll Results," *Pennsylvania Gazette*, April 1953, 6.

[14] "Televised College Football," Hearing before the Subcommittee on Oversight and Investigations, House Committee on Energy and Commerce, Serial No. 98-169, July 31, 1984, Statement of John L. Toner, President of NCAA, 12.

[15] Keith Dunnavant, *The Forty-Year Seduction: How Television Manipulated College Football's Development from Sport to Big Business* (Newnan, Ga.: Sovolox, 1997), Chapter 1.

[15] Ibid.

[16] Ibid.

[17] Murray Sperber, *Onward to Victory: The Crises That Shaped College Sports*, (New York: Henry Holt, 1998), 393.

[18] Harold Dodds to Harold Stassen, June 12, 1951, Harold Dodds papers, PUA.

[19] Harold Stassen to Francis Murray, May 31, 1951, Athletic Department files, UPA, a copy attached as Appendix B to minutes of Meeting of Board of Trustees, June 4, 1951.

[20] Harold Stassen to John Dickey, June 22, 1951, John Dickey papers, DCA.

[21] John Dickey to Harold Stassen, June 28, 1951, Athletic Department files, UPA.

[22] "Television and Freedom and the NCAA," Address of Harold E. Stassen at Alumni Reunion, June 16, 1951, Athletic Department files, UPA.

[23] See Frances Murray to Hugh Willett, July 12, 1951, Athletic Department files, UPA.

[24] Telegram, Hugh Willett to Francis Murray, July 12, 1951, Athletic Department files, UPA.

[25] Harold Stassen to Harold Dodds, September 30, 1952, Harold Dodds papers, PUA.

[26] Harold Dodds to Harold Stassen, October 14, 1952, Harold Dodds papers, PUA.

[27] Grayson Kirk to Harold Stassen, October 10, 1952, Athletic Department files, UPA.

[28] Henry Wriston to Harold Stassen, October 20, 1952, Henry Wriston papers, Brown University archives.

[29] J. B. Conant to Harold Stassen, October 7, 1952, J. B. Conant papers, HUA.

[30] Memorandum, J. B. Conant to Harvard Corporation, February 7, 1950, J. B. Conant papers, HUA.

[31] Harold Dodds to Ernest Griswold, November 20, 1950, Ernest Griswold papers, YUA.

[32] "Joint Statement of Scholarship Policy by the presidents of Harvard, Yale and Princeton Universities," October 22, 1951, Ernest Griswold papers, YUA.

[33] Ernest Griswold to J. B. Conant, November 14, 1951, Ernest Griswold papers, YUA. Griswold was at the same time finishing a report on intercollegiate athletics for the American Council of Education, another response to the scandals of that year. The chief evils of intercollegiate football, the Yale president declared, were "the rewards in money and publicity held out to winning teams…and the desire of alumni, civic bodies, and other groups to see the institutions in which they are interested reap such rewards." *A Report by the Special Committee on Athletic Policy of the American Council on Education in December 1951*, PUA. Charles Eliot could not have said it better.

[35] John Wynne, "The Preservation of Amateur Ideals" (senior thesis, Princeton University, 1998), 41.

[36] DP, February 19, 1952.

[37] Minutes of Meeting of Board of Trustees, June 2, 1952, 364, UPA.

[38] The Ivy Group Agreement was extended to cover all sports in December 1953.

[39] Goldberg, *Ivy League Autumns*, 239.

[40] Rottenberg, *Fight On, Pennsylvania*, 75-76.

[41] George Bosseler and John Dern to W. H. DuBarry, March 4, 1953, attached to W. H. DuBarry to Deane W. Malott, March 13, 1953, Deane Malott papers, CUA.

[42] Rottenberg, *Fight On, Pennsylvania*, 76.

[43] George Munger to Lou Little, May 29, 1953, Athletic Department papers, UPA.

[44] See W. H. DuBarry to Deane Malott, March 13, 1953, Deane Malott papers, CUA.

[45] Deane Malott to W. H. DuBarry, March 21, 1953, Deane Malott papers, CUA.

[46] Rottenberg, *Fight On, Pennsylvania*, 76.

[47] Bill Cunningham, *Boston Herald*, quoted in Joe Bertagna, *Crimson in Triumph: A Pictorial History of Harvard Athletics, 1852-1985* (Lexington, Mass.: S. Greene Press, 1986), 24.

[48] Goldstein, *Ivy League Autumns*, 125.

[49] Harold Keene, "What's the Matter with Harvard Football?" *Boston Globe* [undated], W. J. Bingham papers, HUA.

[50] "Harvard to Discontinue 'Big Time' Football After Poorest Season," NYT, December 2, 1949.

[51] "Bingham Is Back on Harvard Stand," NYT, December 14, 1949.

[52] "Harvard Students Opposed to Subsidizing, But Urge Drive to Bolster Football Team," NYT, December 4, 1949.

[53] Paul Buck, *Report on Harvard Football*, February 1, 1950, J. B. Conant papers, HUA.

[54] Smith, *The Harvard Century*, 185.

[55] *Second H Book*, 30.

[56] Ibid. 37.

[57] Paul Buck to J. B. Conant, November 4, 1952, J. B. Conant papers, HUA.

[58] *Second H Book*, 111.

[59] McCallum, *Ivy League Football*, 169.

[60] C. David Heymann, *RFK: A Candid Biography of Robert F. Kennedy* (New York: Dutton, 1998), 44.

[61] Lisle Blackbourn to Edward M. Kennedy, October 1955, personal papers of Edward M. Kennedy, a copy of which was graciously loaned to the author.

[62] Goldstein, *Ivy League Autumns*, 115.

[63] "Aha! Princeton, Undefeated in Two Years, Admits Use of Electronic Brain on Gridiron," NYT, May 27, 1952.

[64] Goldstein, *Ivy League Autumns*, 127.

[65] "Princeton Beats Dartmouth, 13-7," NYT, November 26, 1950.

[66] *Time*, November 19, 1951.

[67] Interview with author, November 2, 1999.

[68] "Kazmaier Rejects Pro Football Bids," NYT, December 13, 1951.

[69] Brady, *The Heisman*, 98.

[70] "Ivy League Presidents Should Adopt Proposal," DP, January 9, 1953.

[71] "University of Pennsylvania Conference Proposal," December 2, 1952, Athletic Department files, UPA.

[72] "NCAA Group Is Expected to Propose Retaining Limited Football TV," NYT, January 7, 1954.

[73] Dartmouth, however, was given the option of playing all its games against Yale at the Bowl.

[74] The *New York Times* had first offered to create an Ivy League championship trophy, but the league declined.

Chapter 10. *A Well-Rounded Class*

[1] "Is Indifference an Ivy Disease?" BAM, January 1957, 16.

[2] "Still Ivied Autumn?" *Newsweek*, October 15, 1956, 75.

[3] Stanley Frank, "He Doesn't Have to Win," SEP, November 16, 1946, 18.

[4] Murray Olderman, "Ivy League Revolutionary," SEP, November 8, 1958, 31.

[5] Dan Nelson, "Stalking the Student Athlete," DAM, March 1978, 24.

[6] Arthur Howe to Ernest Griswold, January 31, 1957, YUA.

[7] Thelin, *The Cultivation of Ivy*, 33.

[8] Sayre, "Pigskin at Penn," SI, January 28, 1957, 56.

[9] Ibid.

[10] Interview, August 20, 1998.

[11] "Penn Eleven Dead at 87," *Daily Pennsylvanian*, October 14, 1963.

[12] Rottenberg, *Fight On, Pennsylvania*, 94.

[13] "Jerry Ford Out; Penn Seeks a 'New Personality,'" *Pennsylvania Gazette*, April 1967, 33.

[14] See Rottenberg, *Fight On, Pennsylvania*, 93-96.

[15] David William Zang, "Winning and Losing in the Vietnam Era: Redefining Athletic Excellence at the University of Pennsylvania," Ph.D. diss., University of Pennsylvania, 1986, 130.

[16] *Second H Book*, 124.

[17] E. J. Kahn, Jr., *Harvard Through Change and Through Storm* (New York: W. W. Norton, 1969), 203.

[18] Alfred Wright, "Who Loves Harvard?" SI, November 4, 1963, 14.

[19] McCallum, *Ivy League Football*, 191.

[20] Roger Angell, "Just a Personal Thing," *New Yorker*, December 15, 1962, 156.

[21] Stephan Birmingham, *The Right People: The Social Establishment in America*, (Boston: Little, Brown, 1958), 84.

[22] See Harold Dodds, "The Princeton Philosophy of Athletics," PAW, March 1, 1957.

[23] Anne Mullin, "The Compleat Spectator," *Harvard Football News*, October 19, 1963, 9.

[24] "11 Minutes of Football in Collegiate Game," NYT, November 15, 1961.

[25] Wright, "Who Loves Harvard?" SI, November 4, 1963, 14.

[26] Brown's game against Colgate was simply cancelled.

[27] "'Kill' Shouts Herald Coming Weekend; Indians Meet Bengals for League Title," *Dartmouth*, November 19, 1965.

[28] Quoted in David Shribman, *One Hundred Years of Dartmouth Football* (Hanover, N.H.: Dartmouth College Board of Trustees, 1980), 47.

[29] William Manchester, *The Glory and the Dream* (Boston: Little, Brown, 1973), 1131-32.

[30] Roger Kahn, *The Battle for Morningside Heights* (New York: William Morrow, 1970), 171.

[31] See "Columbia Trips Yale, 21-7, for First Victory," NYT, October 17, 1965.

[32] See letter, William Elder Marcus, YAM, February 1963, 4.

[33] McCallum, *Ivy League Football*, 216.

[34] Frank Deford, "B.D.," SI, September 5, 1988, 120.

[35] Geoffrey Kabaservice, "The Birth of a New Institution," YAM, December 1999.

[36] Robert H. Boyle, "The Harvards and the Yales," SI, December 17, 1962, 21.

[37] *Admissions Policy of the Undergraduate Schools of the University of Pennsylvania* [McGill Report], August 1, 1967, 5.

[38] Quoted in Deford, "B.D."

[39] Jon Paulson, "Man of Action," *Harvard Football News*, November 2, 1968, 53.

[40] Pat Putnam, "Unbeatens Met, and What Happened Beats All," SI, December 2, 1968, 75.

[41] Kahn, *Harvard Through Change and Through Storm*, 73-74.

[42] Tommy Lee Jones, "Backtalk: A Star Recalls His Role in a 30-Year-Old Drama," NYT, November 22, 1998.

[43] Putnam, "Unbeatens Met," 75.

[44] Ibid.

[45] Bertagna, *Crimson in Triumph*, 39.

[46] Bergin, *The Game*, 255.

[47] McCallum, *Ivy League Football*, 226.

[48] Philip Nobile, "Forty-Two Seconds over Cambridge," *Esquire*, October 1975, 196.

[49] *Harvard Crimson*, November 25, 1968.

Chapter 11. *What Is This Thing Called "Winning"?*

[1] McCallum, *Ivy League Football*, 225.

[2] "Indian Students Denounce Symbols," DAM, January 1972, 17.

[3] McCallum, *Ivy League Football*, 226.

[4] Goldstein, *Ivy League Autumns*, 177.

[5] Robert W. Smith, "The Greening of Schoellkopf," Cornell-Colgate program, September 25, 1971, 312. Within a few years, however, the turf turned an ugly shade of turquoise, lost many of its fibers, and began to tear at the seams, creating thirty-yard-long wrinkles that had to be cut out. Cornell sued the manufacturer and replaced the surface with AstroTurf in 1979. See "Schoellkopf Field: A History of Changes," *Cornell Daily Sun*, November 21, 1985.

[6] Bergin, *The Game*, 265.

[7] John T. Bethell, "The Radical Theoretician of Soldiers Field," *Harvard Bulletin*, October 1972, 32.

[8] "Multiflexing Its Muscles," SI, October 20, 1980, 59.

[9] Bethell, "Radical Theoretician," *Harvard Bulletin*, October 1972, 32.

[10] Ibid.

[11] "Rebellion at Harvard," NYT, May 16, 1973.

[12] David Smith, interview with author, January 21, 2000.

[13] "By 1978, Brown: Whither?" BAM, October 1969, 30.

[14] *Brown Daily Herald*, November 14, 1976 (Extra).

[15] "Pressure to Win, Even at Brown," NYT, November 18, 1983.

[16] Rottenberg, *Fight On, Pennsylvania*, 98.

[17] See Kane, *Good Sports*, 336-349.

[18] "Coffee Hour Helps Settle Football Jitters," *Dartmouth*, September 23, 1977.

[19] In 1975, the league had declined a proposal from the United Negro College Fund that each team play a tenth game against a historically black college.

[20] "How to Survive Harvard Weekend," *Dartmouth*, October 26, 1972.

[21] "Cozza Expresses Regret at Having to Relinquish Yale Coaching Post," NYT, November 18, 1976.

[22] Scott Oostdyk, "Where Have All the Fans Gone?" PAW, December 15, 1982, 16.

[23] U. E. Reinhardt, "A Bayesian Analysis of Princeton's Chances of Beating Yale," PAW, November 1, 1976, 8.

[24] U.E. Reinhardt, "Why Princeton Will Beat Yale Next Year," PAW, November 21, 1977, 22.

[25] "Zeal Wins a Pardon," NYT, December 16, 1981.

[26] Kabaservice, "Yale and the Creation of the Ivy League," 88.

[27] "Ivy League Is Forced to Lose Major-Team Football Status," NYT, December 5, 1981.

[28] "Demotion by N.C.A.A. Irks Ivy League," NYT, January 17, 1982.

[29] "Army Is Seeking to Join Ivy Basketball," NYT, January 11, 1982.

[30] Rick Telander, "A Wildcat Strike Hits Princeton," SI, October 6, 1986, 53.

[31] Richard Hoffer, "A Real Birthday Bash," SI, October 21, 1991, 104.

[32] See John Feinstein, *The Last Amateurs: Playing for Glory and Honor in Division I College Basketball* (Boston: Little, Brown, 2000), 14-20.

[33] See Craig Lambert, "The Greatest College Prank of All Time," *Harvard Magazine*, November-December 1990, 72.

[34] The postgame celebration was marred when a Harvard undergraduate was badly injured by a falling piece of goal post, eventually recovering $925,000 in a lawsuit against Yale and the city.

[35] "The Game Holds Its Appeal at 100," NYT, November 19, 1983.

[36] "Rituals and Reunions at 'The Game,'" NYT, November 21, 1983.

Chapter 12. *The Modern Game*

[1] "Giamatti's Challenge," PAW, January 26, 1981, 19.

[2] Tom Mathewson, "Do or Die for Columbia Football?" *Columbia College Today*, Fall 1987, 16.

[3] "Columbia Coach Furious After Rout," NYT, September 22, 1985.

[4] George Vecsey, "Jim Garrett: 4th-and-Long," NYT, September 24, 1985.

[5] "Columbia Reprimands Coach," NYT, September 24, 1985.

[6] Peter Alfano, "Lions Out of Their League," NYT, November 13, 1987.

[7] "On Campus, the Millennium," NYT, October 9, 1988.

[8] George Vecsey, "The Mess at Columbia," NYT, December 2, 1988.

[9] Mathewson, "Do or Die."

[10] "Eased Rules for Athletes Upset Many at Columbia," NYT, November 19, 1987.

[11] Clyde Haberman, "City's Image Plays Well at Baker Field," NYT, October 25, 1996.

[12] Noah Hutson-Ellenberg and Scott Judah, "Academics and Athletics Square Off," *Dartmouth Review*, March 10, 1999; "For Lions' Big Man, a Big Draft Day," NYT, April 15, 1997.

[13] N. Brooke Clark, "This Time the Replay Counted," SI, November 22, 1981, 62.

[14] Franz Lidz, "The Big Red's Bigger Bite," SI, September 28, 1987, 48.

[15] Goldstein, *Ivy League Autumns*, 209.

[16] Tim Layden, "Winning Ways," SI, August 28, 1995, 110.

[17] Eric A. Wong, "No Respect," *Cornell Daily Sun*, October 26, 1994.

[18] Elias was persuaded to choose Princeton thanks, in part, to the efforts of another Tiger football legend, cornerback Dean Cain, who set an NCAA record with twelve interceptions in 1987 and went on to greater fame playing Superman in the TV series *Lois and Clark*.

[19] Craig Lambert, "The Professionalization of Ivy League Sports," *Harvard Magazine*, September-October 1997, 36.

[20] Yale Department of Athletics, Annual Report 1996-1997, Statement of Revenues and Expenditures.

[21] "A Chair for the Coach," NYT, September 17, 1988.

[22] "Yale, Harvard Deny Access to Sportschannel Cameras," *Cornell Daily Sun*, September 17, 1992 [Football Supplement].

[23] Ibid.

[24] "New Building Sparks Field Realignment," *Harvard Crimson*, July 17, 1998.

[25] Jennifer Wulff, "Playing the Game," DAM, March 1998.

[26] SI, April 28, 1997.

[27] Address of Theodore Roosevelt at Harvard University, February 23, 1907, reprinted in Danzig, *Oh, How They Played the Game*, 150.

[28] See James L. Shulman and William G. Bowen, *The Game of Life: College Sports and Educational Values* (Princeton: Princeton University Press, 2001).

[29] "Ivy League Penalizes Brown over Recruiting," *Providence Journal*, August 2, 2000.

[30] William C. Rhoden, "Ivy League Steels for Another Post-Season Chill," NYT, November 3, 1995.

[31] Address at inauguration of Ernest Fox Nichols, October 14, 1909, Collected Papers of Woodrow Wilson.

[32] "Yuck Fale, And Other Observations," *Harvard Crimson*, November 15, 1998.

[33] "Yale's Got—All That Matters," YAM, June 1980, 23.

Personal and Institutional Papers
Brown
     Henry Wriston
     Brown Athletic Department
Columbia
     Nicholas Murray Butler
     Columbia Athletic Department
Cornell
     Livingston Farrand
     Edmund Ezra Day
     Deane Malott
     Cornell Athletic Department
Dartmouth
     Ernest Martin Hopkins
     John Dickey
     Dartmouth Athletic Department
Harvard
     Charles Eliot
     A. Lawrence Lowell
     James Bryant Conant
     William J. Bingham
     Harvard Athletic Association
Princeton
     Harold Dodds
     Princeton Athletic Department
University of Pennsylvania
     Harold Stassen
     University of Pennsylvania Athletic Department
Yale
     Arthur Twining Hadley
     James R. Angell
     Charles Seymour
     Yale Athletic Department

Books, Articles, and Manuscripts
Adams, Henry. *The Letters of Henry Adams.* Cambridge, Mass.: Belknap Press, 1988.
Admissions Policy of the Undergraduate Schools of the University of Pennsylvania
    [McGill Report], August 1, 1967.
The American Sporting Experience: A Historical Anthology of Sport in America.
    Steven A. Reiss, ed. Champaign, Ill.: Leisure Press, 1984.
Angell, Roger. "Just a Personal Thing." *New Yorker,* December 15, 1962, 156.

Ashe, Arthur. *A Hard Road to Glory: A History of the African-American Athlete.*
    New York: Warner Books, 1988.
Azoy, A. C. M. "Desire Under the (New Haven) Elms, 1873." Princeton-Yale football
    program, November 12, 1938, 15.
Baker, L. H. *Football Facts and Figures.* New York: Rinehart, 1945.
——. *The History of Yale Football*, 1947, unpublished, Yale Athletic Department.
Baltzell, E. Digby. *Philadelphia Gentlemen: The Making of a National Upper Class.*
    Glencoe, Ill.: Free Press, 1958.
"Barry Wood: Harvard's Football Meteor." *Literary Digest*, November 14, 1931.
Beale, Morris A. *The History of Football at Harvard, 1874-1948.* Washington, D.C.:
    Columbia, 1948.
Benezet, Louis P. *Three Years of Football at Dartmouth.* 1904.
Bergin, Thomas G. *The Game: The Harvard-Yale Football Rivalry, 1875-1983.*
    New Haven: Yale University Press, 1984.
"The Berkeley Athletic Club." *The Wheel*, October 5, 1888.
Bertagna, Joe. *Crimson in Triumph: A Pictorial History of Harvard Athletics,*
    1852-1985. Lexington, Mass.: S. Greene Press, 1986.
"The Big Scrimmage Over College Football." *Literary Digest*, November 9, 1929, 58.
Big-Time Football at Harvard, 1905: The Diary of Coach Bill Reid. Ronald Smith, ed.
    Urbana: University of Illinois Press, 1994.
Biographical Dictionary of American Sports. David L. Porter, ed. New York:
    Greenwood Press, 1987.
Biographical Dictionary of American Sports, 1992-1995. Supplement for Baseball,
    Football, Basketball, and Other Sports, David L. Porter, ed. Westport, Conn.:
    Greenwood Press, 1995.
Birmingham, Stephan. *The Right People: The Social Establishment in America.*
    Boston: Little, Brown, 1958.
Bishop, Morris. *A History of Cornell.* Ithaca, N.Y.: Cornell University Press, 1962.
Blaik, Earl H. *The Red Blaik Story.* New Rochelle, N.Y.: Arlington, House, 1974.
Blanchard, John Adams, ed., *The H Book of Harvard Athletics, 1852-1922.*
    Cambridge: Harvard Varsity Club, 1923.
Boyle, Robert H. "The Harvards and the Yales." SI, December 17, 1962, 21.
Brady, John T. *The Heisman, Symbol of Excellence.* New York: Atheneum, 1984.
Brands, H. W. *TR: The Last Romantic.* New York: Basic Books, 1997.
Bronson, Walter C. *The History of Brown University, 1764-1914.* Providence, R.I.:
    Brown University, 1914.
Broun, Heywood, and George Britt. *Christians Only: A Study in Prejudice.*
    New York: Vanguard Press, 1931.
Brown, Rollo Warren. *Dean Briggs.* New York: Harper & Bros., 1926.
Bruccoli, Matthew J. *Some Sort of Epic Grandeur: The Life of F. Scott Fitzgerald.*
    New York: Harcourt Brace Jovanovich, 1987.
Bryce, James, *The American Commonwealth.* Indianapolis: Liberty Fund, 1995.
Burrows, Edwin G., and Mike Wallace. *Gotham: A History of New York City*
    to 1898. New York: Oxford University Press, 1999.
Butterworth, Frank. "Honesty in Football." *Outing*, November 1904, 141.

Camp, Walter. "Intercollegiate Foot-Ball In America." *St. Nicholas*, January 1890, 242.

Caro, Robert A. *The Power Broker: Robert Moses and the Fall of New York.* New York: Vintage, 1975.

Carroll, John M. *Fritz Pollard: Pioneer in Racial Advancement.* Urbana: University of Illinois Press, 1992.

Charters, Ann. *Kerouac.* London: Andre Deutsch, 1974.

Chernow, Ron. *Titan: The Life of John D. Rockefeller, Sr.* New York: Random House, 1998.

Clark, N. Brooke. "This Time the Replay Counted." SI, November 22, 1981, 62.

Clark, Tom. *Jack Kerouac.* New York: Harcourt Brace, 1984.

Cohane, Tim. *The Yale Football Story.* New York: Putnam, 1951.

——. "The Penn Is Mightier Than the Ivy." *Look*, November 20, 1951, 70.

——. *Greatest College Football Coaches of the Twenties and Thirties.* New Rochelle, N.Y.: Arlington House, 1973.

Coon, Horace. *Columbia, Colossus on the Hudson.* New York: E. P. Dutton, 1947.

Cozza, Carm. *True Blue: The Carm Cozza Story.* New Haven: Yale University Press, 1999.

Daley, Arthur. "The Fabulous Herman Hickman." *NYT Magazine*, October 28, 1951.

Danzig, Allison. *The History of American Football: Its Great Teams, Players and Coaches.* Englewood Cliffs, N.J.: Prentice-Hall, 1956.

——. *Oh, How They Played the Game.* New York: Macmillan, 1971.

Davis, Kenneth S. *A Prophet in His Own Country: The Triumphs and Defeats of Adlai E. Stevenson.* Garden City, N.Y.: Doubleday, 1957.

Davis, Parke H. *Football, The American Intercollegiate Game.* New York: Charles Scribner's Sons, 1911.

Davis, Richard Harding. "Richard Carr's Baby." *St. Nicholas*, November 1886, 50.

——. "The Thanksgiving Game." *Harper's Weekly*, December 9, 1893, 1170.

Deford, Frank. "B.D." SI, September 5, 1988, 120.

Deming, Clarence. "Athletics in College Life." *Outlook*, July 1, 1905, 570-71.

Dunn, Jay. *The Tigers of Princeton: Old Nassau Football.* Huntsville, Ala.: Strode, 1977.

Dunnavant, Keith. *The Forty-Year Seduction: How Television Manipulated College Football's Development from Sport to Big Business.* Newnan, Ga.: Sovolox Publishing, 1997.

Durick, William G. "The Gentlemen's Race: An Examination of the 1869 Harvard-Oxford Boat Race." *Journal of Sport History*, Spring 1988, 41.

Dutton, Jacqueline. "The Legendary Sid Luckman '39." *Columbia College Today*, Fall 1990, 24.

Edwards, William. *Football Days.* New York: Moffat Yard, 1916.

"Effects of Football Reform at Columbia." *American Review of Reviews*, December 1909, 730.

Eisenhammer, Fred, and Eric B. Sondheimer. *College Football's Memorable Games, 1913 Through 1990.* Jefferson, N.C.: McFarland, 1992.

Feinstein, John. *The Last Amateurs: Playing for Glory and Honor in Division I College Basketball.* Boston: Little, Brown, 2000.

Fimrite, Ron. "Hobey Baker: A Flame That Burned Too Brightly." SI, March 18, 1991, 78.

"Football Poll Results." *Pennsylvania Gazette*, April 1953, 6.

"The Football-Schedule Survey." *Pennsylvania Gazette*, December 1951, 15.

Frank, Stanley. "He Doesn't Have to Win." SEP, November 16, 1946, 18.

Gifford, Barry, and Lawrence Lee. *Jack's Book: An Oral Biography of Jack Kerouac.* New York: St. Martin's Press, 1978.

Gilfoyle, Timothy J. *City of Eros: New York City, Prostitution, and the Commercialization of Sex, 1790-1920.* New York: W. W. Norton, 1992.

Goldberg, David L. "What Price Victory? What Price Honor? Pennsylvania and the Formation of the Ivy League, 1950-1952." *Pennsylvania Magazine of History and Biography*, April 1988, 227.

Goldstein, Richard. *Ivy League Autumns.* New York: St. Martin's Press, 1996.

Gorn, Elliot J., and Warren Goldstein. *A Brief History of American Sports.* New York: Hill & Wang, 1993.

Greene, Samuel Mitchell. "Intercollegiate Athletics at Pennsylvania: Corruption and Penitence." Senior thesis, University of Pennsylvania, 1993.

Hall, Robert A. "Cornell Goes to the Movies." SEP, October 26, 1940, 18.

Harris, Reed. *King Football: The Vulgarization of the American College.* New York: Vanguard Press, 1932.

"The Harvard-Oregon Football Game in Pasadena." *Literary Digest*, January 17, 1920, 114.

Haughton, Percy. *Football and How to Watch It.* Boston: Marshall Jones, 1922.

Heffelfinger, W. W. "Nobody Put Me on My Back." SEP, October 15, 1938, 14.

——. *This Was Football.* New York: A. S. Barnes, 1954.

Heymann, C. David. *RFK: A Candid Biography of Robert F. Kennedy.* New York: Dutton, 1998.

Higgs, Robert J. *God in the Stadium: Sports and Religion in America.* Lexington: University of Kentucky Press, 1995.

A History of Columbia College on Morningside. New York: Columbia University Press, 1954.

Hoffer, Richard. "A Real Birthday Bash." SI, October 21, 1991, 104.

Holbrook, Stewart H. "Frank Merriwell at Yale Again—And Again and Again." *American Heritage*, July 1961, 24.

Holland, Jerome. *Black Opportunity.* New York: Weybright & Talley, 1969.

Hubbard, Wynant Davis. "Dirty Football: A Former Harvard Player Tells Why His University Broke Relations with Princeton." *Liberty*, January 29, 1927, 38.

Hutson-Ellenberg, Noah, and Scott Judah. "Academics and Athletics Square Off." *Dartmouth Review*, March 10, 1999.

"Is The Ivy League Still the Best?" *Newsweek*, November 23, 1964, 65.

"Jerry Ford Out; Penn Seeks a 'New Personality.'" *Pennsylvania Gazette*, April 1967, 33.

Johnson, Owen. *Stover at Yale.* New Haven, Conn.: Yale Bookstore, 1997.

Jones, Howard. *How to Coach and Play Football.* Iowa City: Clio Press, 1923.

Kabaservice, Geoffrey. "Yale and the Creation of the Ivy League." Unpublished manuscript, August 1998.

Kahn, E. J., Jr. *Harvard Through Change and Through Storm.* New York: W. W. Norton, 1969.

Kahn, Roger. *The Battle for Morningside Heights*. New York: William Morrow, 1970.

Kane, Robert J. *Good Sports: 123 Years of Cornell Athletics*. Ithaca, N.Y.: Cornell University, 1992.

Kelley, Larry. "Everybody There Saw Kelley." SEP, October 23, 1937, 14.

Layden, Tim. "Winning Ways." SI, August 28, 1995, 110.

Leitch, Alexander. *A Princeton Companion*. Princeton, N.J.: Princeton University Press, 1978.

Lester, Robin. *Stagg's University: The Rise, Decline, and Fall of Big-Time Football at Chicago*. Urbana: University of Illinois Press, 1995.

Lidz, Franz. "The Big Red's Bigger Bite." SI, September 28, 1987, 48.

Lindholm, Karl. "William Clarence Matthews." *The National Pastime*, Society for American Baseball Research, June 1997, 67.

Longstreth, Thacher. *Main Line WASP*. New York: W. W. Norton, 1990.

Ludington, H. J. "Football Report for 1914-1915." Cornell University archives. Privately printed.

Manchester, William. *The Glory and the Dream*. Boston: Little, Brown, 1973.

Marshall, H. T. *What the Football Season of 1925 Taught Us About Business Administration*, American Management Association, 1926, Dartmouth College archives.

Mathewson, Tom. "Do or Die for Columbia Football?" *Columbia College Today*, Fall 1987.

McCallum, John. *Ivy League Football Since 1872*. New York: Stein & Day, 1977.

McKenzie, R. Tait. "Physical Education at the University of Pennsylvania—from 1904 to 1931—and the Gates Plan." *Research Quarterly*, May 1932, 19.

Mendenhall, Thomas C. *The Harvard-Yale Boat Race, 1852-1924*. Mystic, Conn.: Mystic Seaport Museum, 1993.

The Mind and Faith of Justice Holmes. New York: Little, Brown, 1943.

Mitchell, Martha. *Encyclopedia Brunonia*. Providence, R.I.: Brown University Library, 1993.

Montgomery, Cliff. "Football's Biggest Upset." *Coronet*, January 1955, 46.

Montville, Leigh. "Penn and Needles." SI, November 15, 1993, 44.

Morell, Parker. *Diamond Jim: The Life and Times of Diamond Jim Brady*. New York: Simon & Schuster, 1934.

Mullin, Anne. "The Compleat Spectator." *Harvard Football News*, October 19, 1963, 9.

"Multiflexing Its Muscles." SI, October 20, 1980, 59.

Murrin, John M. *Rites of Domination: Princeton, the Big Three, and the Rise of Intercollegiate Athletics*. Princeton 250th Anniversary Lecture, November 1996.

Needham, Henry Beech. "The College Athlete (Part I)." *McClure's Magazine*, June 1905, 118.

Nelson, David M. *The Anatomy of a Game*. Newark: University of Delaware Press, 1994.

Nobile, Philip. "Forty-two Seconds over Cambridge." *Esquire*, October 1975, 196.

Olderman, Murray. "Ivy League Revolutionary." SEP, November 8, 1958, 31.

Oren, Dan A. *Joining the Club: A History of Jews at Yale*. New Haven: Yale University Press, 1985.

Oriard, Michael. *Dreaming of Heroes: American Sports Fiction, 1868-1980.*
    Chicago: Nelson-Hall, 1982.
——. *Sporting with the Gods: The Rhetoric of Play and Game in American Culture.*
    New York: Cambridge University Press, 1991.
——. *Reading Football: How the Popular Press Created an American Spectacle.*
    Chapel Hill: University of North Carolina Press, 1993.
Our Cornell. Raymond Floyd Hughes, ed. Ithaca, N.Y.: Cayuga Press, 1939.
Papers Relating to the Game of Football, February 16, 1915, Columbia University.
Paterno, Joe. *Paterno: By the Book.* New York: Random House, 1989.
Patton, Howard, and W. T. Field. *Eight O'Clock Chapel.* Boston: Houghton Mifflin,
    1927.
Paulson, Jon. "Man of Action." *Harvard Football News,* November 2, 1968, 53.
Pender, Horace G., and Raymond M. McPartlin. *Athletics at Dartmouth.* Hanover,
    N.H.: Dartmouth College Athletic Council, 1923.
"Pennsy's Bitter Dose and Reducing Diet for Stadium Fever." *Literary Digest,*
    February 21, 1931.
Perry, Lawrence. "The Football Brahmins Make Peace." *Scribner's Magazine,*
    November 1934, 291.
Peterson, Robert. *Pigskin: The Early Years of Professional Football.* New York:
    Oxford University Press, 1997.
Pierson, George Wilson. *Yale College: An Educational History, 1871-1921.*
    New Haven: Yale University Press, 1952.
——. *A Yale Book of Numbers: Historical Statistics of the College and University
    1701-1976.* New Haven: Yale University, 1983.
Powel, Harford, Jr. *Walter Camp, The Father of American Football: An Authorized
    Biography.* Boston: Little, Brown, 1926.
"A Princeton Classic—Revisited After Half a Century." Privately printed, undated.
    Princeton Athletic Department.
"Princeton Proves Good Football Is Possible Without 'Overemphasis.'" SEP,
    January 5, 1952, 10.
Putnam, Pat. "Unbeatens Met, and What Happened Beats All." SI, December 2,
    1968, 75.
Rader, Benjamin G. *American Sports: From the Age of Folk Games to the Age of
    Televised Sports.* Engelwood Cliffs, N.J.: Prentice-Hall, 1996.
Reed, Elizabeth Abigail. "Pride, Prestige and Profit: Early Collegiate Football in
    America." M.A. diss., University of Pennsylvania, 1987.
Reed, Herbert. "Harvard, Gridiron Deceiver." *Harper's Weekly,* November 27,
    1915, 520.
——. "Harvard—Football Phoenix." *Outlook,* December 12, 1928, 1326.
Reiss, Steven A. "Sport and the Redefinition of American Middle-Class Masculinity,
    1840-1900." Reprinted in *Major Problems in American Sports History.* 1997.
"Remington and the Eli Eleven." *American Heritage,* October-November 1981, 98.
*A Report by the Special Committee On Athletic Policy of the American Council On
    Education.* New York: American Council on Education, 1951.

Report of the Committee on the Regulation of Athletic Sports, Harvard College, October 1925.

Report of the President of Harvard College and Reports of Departments.

Report upon Athletics, Harvard College, 1888.

Riordan, Leo. "The Football Blues Hit Penn." SEP, November 7, 1953, 25.

Roosevelt, Theodore. *The Letters of Theodore Roosevelt*. Elting E. Morison, ed. Cambridge, Mass.: Harvard University Press, 1952.

Rosenstone, Robert A. *Romantic Revolutionary*. New York: Alfred A. Knopf, 1975.

Rottenberg, Dan. *Fight On, Pennsylvania: A Century of Red and Blue Football*. Philadelphia: University of Pennsylvania Press, 1985.

Rudolph, Frederick. *The American College and University*. Athens: University of Georgia Press, 1990.

Samuels, Peggy, and Harold Samuels. *Frederic Remington*. Garden City, N.Y.: Doubleday, 1982.

Sanuelsen, Rube. *The Rose Bowl Game*. Garden City, N.Y.: Doubleday, 1951.

Savage, Howard J. *American College Athletics*. New York: Carnegie Foundation for the Advancement of Teaching, 1929.

Sayre, Joel. "Pigskin at Penn: A Real-Life Drama." SI, January 28, 1957, 56.

The Second H Book of Harvard Athletics. Geoffrey H. Movius, ed. Cambridge, Mass.: Harvard Varsity Club, 1964.

Shribman, David. *One Hundred Years of Dartmouth Football*. Hanover, N.H.: Dartmouth College Board of Trustees, 1980.

Shulman, James L. and William G. Bowen. *The Game of Life: College Sports and Educational Values*. Princeton: Princeton University Press, 2001.

Slosson, Edwin E. *Great American Universities*. New York: Macmillan, 1910.

Smith, Andrew F. *Souper Tomatoes*. New Brunswick, N.J.: Rutgers University Press, 2000.

Smith, Page. *The Rise of Industrial America*. New York: McGraw-Hill, 1984.

Smith, Richard Norton. *The Harvard Century: The Making of a University to a Nation*. New York: Simon & Schuster, 1986.

Smith, Ronald A. "Harvard and Columbia and a Reconsideration of the 1905-06 Football Crisis." *Journal of Sport History*, Winter 1981, 7.

——. *Sports and Freedom: The Rise of Big-Time College Athletics*. New York: Oxford University Press, 1988.

Sperber, Murray. *Onward to Victory: The Crises That Shaped College Sports*. New York: Henry Holt, 1998.

Stagg, Amos Alonzo. *Touchdown!* New York: Longmans, Green, 1927.

Stein, Gertrude. *Everybody's Autobiography*. New York: Random House, 1937.

"Still Ivied Autumn?" *Newsweek*, October 15, 1956, 75.

Stuart, Donald C., Jr. "When Eleven Were Twelve." *Princeton Athletic News*, November 21, 1936, 13.

Synnott, Marcia. "A Social History of Admissions Policies at Harvard, Yale, and Princeton, 1900-1930." Ph.D. diss. University of Massachusetts, 1974.

——. "The 'Big Three' and the Harvard-Princeton Football Break, 1926-1934." *Journal of Sport History*, Summer 1976, 188.

——. *The Half-Opened Door: Discrimination and Admissions at Harvard, Yale, and Princeton, 1900-1970*. Westport, Conn.: Greenwood Press, 1979.

Telander, Rick. "A Wildcat Strike Hits Princeton." SI, October 6, 1986, 53.

Thelin, John R. *The Cultivation of Ivy*. Cambridge, Mass.: Schenkman, 1976.

Townsend, Kim. *Manhood at Harvard: William James and Others*. New York: W. W. Norton, 1996.

A Treasury of Damon Runyon. New York: Modern Library, 1958.

Twombley, Henry Bancroft. *Personal Reminiscences of a Yale Football Player in the Early 'Eighties*. New Haven: Yale University Press, 1940.

Umphlett, Wiley Lee. *Creating the Big Game: John W. Heisman and the Invention of American Football*. Westport, Conn.: Greenwood Press, 1992.

Valenzi, Kathleen D., and Michael W. Hopps. *Champion of Sport: The Life of Walter Camp, 1859-1925*. Charlottesville, Va.: Howell Press, 1990.

Veysey, Laurence R. *The Emergence of the American University*. Chicago: University of Chicago Press, 1965.

Wallace, Francis. *Knute Rockne*. Garden City, N.Y.: Doubleday, 1960.

Watterson, John Sayle. *College Football: History. Spectacle. Controversy*. Baltimore: Johns Hopkins University Press, 2000.

Welch, Lewis Sheldon, and Walter Camp. *Yale, Her Campus, Class-Rooms and Athletics*. Boston: L. C. Page, 1899.

Weller, Jac. *History of Princeton Football, 1916-1942*. Privately printed, 1984.

Wertenbaker, Thomas J. *Princeton, 1746-1896*. Princeton: Princeton University Press, 1946.

Weyand, Alexander M. *The Saga of American Football*. New York: Macmillan, 1955.

Whitney, Caspar. "The Sports-Man's View Point." *Outing*, January 1903, 498-510.

Widmayer, Charles E. *Hopkins of Dartmouth*. Hanover, N.H.: University Press of New England, 1977.

Wilson, Woodrow. *The Papers of Woodrow Wilson*. Arthur S. Link, ed., 69 vols., Princeton, N.J.: Princeton University Press, 1966-94.

Woodward, Stanley. "Is Penn Too Tough for the Ivy League?" *Sport*, November 1951, 36.

Works Progress Administration. *Connecticut: A Guide to Its Roads, Lore, and People*. Boston: Houghton Mifflin, 1938.

Worthington, Del. *The Dartmouth Football Seasons of 1924 and 1925*. Scrapbooks. Dartmouth College archives.

Wright, Alfred. "Who Loves Harvard?" SI, November 4, 1963, 14.

Wynne, John. "The Preservation of Amateur Ideals." Senior thesis, Princeton University, 1998.

Yeomans, Henry Aaron. *Abbott Lawrence Lowell, 1856-1943*. Cambridge, Mass.: Harvard University Press, 1948.

Zang, David William. "Winning and Losing in the Vietnam Era: Redefining Athletic Excellence at the University of Pennsylvania." Ph.D. diss., University of Pennsylvania, 1986.

Metropolitan Newspapers

Boston Globe
Boston Herald
New York Times
New York Herald
New York Herald-Tribune
New York World
Philadelphia Inquirer
Providence Journal

Student Newspapers

Brown Daily Herald
Columbia Spectator
Cornell Daily Sun
The Dartmouth
Harvard Crimson
Daily Princetonian
Daily Pennsylvanian
Yale Daily News

Alumni Magazines

Brown Alumni Magazine
Columbia Alumni Magazine
Cornell Alumni Magazine
Dartmouth Alumni Magazine
Harvard Alumni Bulletin
Harvard Magazine
Pennsylvania Gazette
Nassau Literary Magazine (Princeton)
Princeton Alumni Weekly
Yale Alumni Weekly
Yale Alumni Monthly

ACKNOWLEDGMENTS

In researching this book, I have become something of an expert on the relative merits of Ivy League libraries. Although they differ in the extent of their holdings, one thing they share is a uniformly helpful staff of archivists and librarians who took an interest in an outsider's project. I would especially like to thank Martha Mitchell (Brown), Rhea Pliakas (Columbia), Elaine Engst (Cornell), Anne Ostendarp (Dartmouth), Marty Hackett (Penn), Ben Primer (Princeton), Judith Schiff (Yale), and the staff of the Harvard Manuscripts and Archives Collection at the Nathan Pusey Library. Geoff Zonder, the Yale athletic department's resident historian, answered my questions and made available the fabulous Baker Books, the most valuable unpublished resource on Bulldog football, while also permitting me to sit for a moment on the famous Yale fence, upon which all Eli captains have their official pictures taken.

The Ivy League office has also been unfailingly helpful, especially Jeff Orleans, the current executive director; Jim Litvak, his predecessor; and Chuck Yrigoyen, the league's associate director.

Two Princeton All-Americans—Stas Maliszewski, now president of the Princeton Football Association, and Thacher Longstreth, who is easily the greatest living repository of Tiger football lore—have been generous with their time and support. Dan Rottenberg wrote the book (literally) on Penn football, while Professor David Zang's dissertation on the Quakers' travails during the 1960s is an under-appreciated resource. Geoffrey Kabaservice shared his insightful manuscript on Yale's role in the creation of the Ivy League. Thanks, too, to the Carnegie Foundation for the Advancement of Teaching for loaning me a copy of their storied Bulletin Number 23.

I am grateful to Eric Halpern, director of the University of Pennsylvania Press, for conceiving this book and asking me to write it. Noreen O'Connor and Bruce Franklin were meticulous but gentle editors.

Randolph Slaughter provided an inspirational place in which to edit this manuscript. Rich Gorelick, who broadcast Princeton's stirring upset of Yale in 1981, gave enthusiastic comments.

Peter DeCoursey, a Yale fan without peer, encouraged this project throughout and never needs to be asked twice to attend an Ivy League game. To paraphrase baseball historian Bill James, if I am going to pay tribute to my friends, I don't want to begin in the middle of the list.

Thanks beyond words, finally, to Rebecca, Frances, and Taylor, who made it all possible.